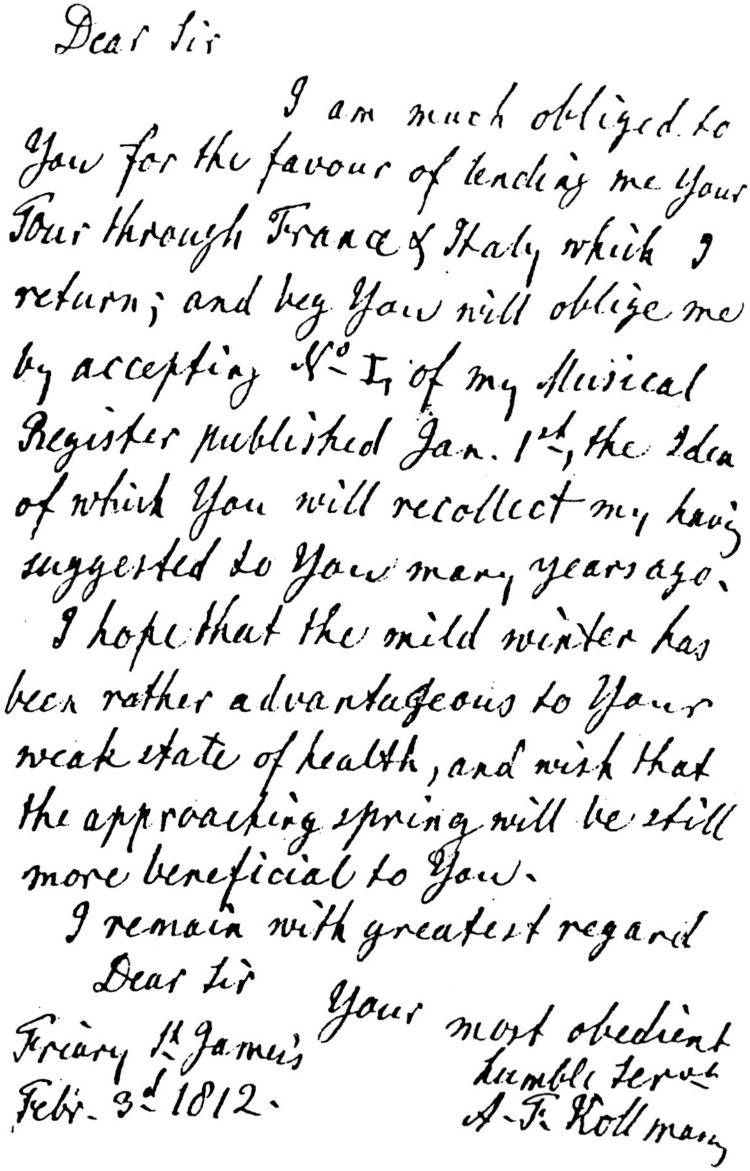

Dear Sir

I am much obliged to You for the favour of lending me Your Tour through France & Italy which I return; and beg You will oblige me by accepting No. I, of my Musical Register published Jan. 1st, the Idea of which You will recollect my having suggested to You many years ago.

I hope that the mild winter has been rather advantageous to Your weak state of health, and wish that the approaching spring will be still more beneficial to You.

I remain with greatest regard

Dear Sir

Your most obedient humble Servt

A. F. Kollmann

Friary St. James's

Febr. 3d 1812.

A. F. C. Kollmann's 3 February 1812 letter to Charles Burney, presenting the first number of The Quarterly Musical Register (by permission of the Bibliothèque Royale de Belgique)

A. F. C. KOLLMANN'S *QUARTERLY MUSICAL REGISTER*

A. F. C. KOLLMANN'S *QUARTERLY MUSICAL REGISTER* (1812)

An annotated edition
with an introduction to his life and works

MICHAEL KASSLER

Routledge
Taylor & Francis Group
LONDON AND NEW YORK

First published 2008 by Ashgate Publishing Limited

Published 2018 by Routledge
2 Park Square, Milton Park, Abingdon, Oxon OX14 4RN
52 Vanderbilt Avenue, New York, NY 10017, USA

Routledge is an imprint of the Taylor & Francis Group, an informa business

British Library Cataloguing in Publication Data

A. F. C. Kollmann's Quarterly musical register (1812): an
annotated edition with an introduction to his life and works
1. Kollmann, Augustus Frederic Christopher, 1756-1829 -
Criticism and interpretation 2. Kollmann, Augustus Frederic
Christopher, 1756-1829 3. Quarterly musical register
I. Kassler, Michael, 1941- II. Quarterly musical register
780.9'2

Library of Congress Cataloging-in-Publication Data

A. F. C. Kollmann's Quarterly musical register (1812): an annotated edition
with an introduction to his life and works / by Michael Kassler.
p. cm.
Includes bibliographical references and index.
1. Kollmann, Augustus Frederic Christopher, 1756-1829.-Criticism and
interpretation. 2. Music theory-England-History. 3. Musicology-England-History.
I. Kassler, Michael, 1941- II. Kollmann, Augustus Frederic Christopher, 1756-
1829. Quarterly musical register.

ML423.K75A3 2009
780.5-dc22 2008014277

Typeset in Monotype Bulmer by Computer Music Company, Sydney, Australia.

ISBN 13: 978-0-7546-6064-4 (pbk)
ISBN 13: 978-0-7546-6064-4 (hbk)

CONTENTS

ILLUSTRATIONS

MUSIC EXAMPLES

PREFACE

Augustus Frederic Christopher Kollmann (1756–1829) was one of the most profound music theorists of his time. He developed a theory of tonality—the 'musical language' in which Bach, Beethoven and their contemporaries composed—which (he said) was so complete that every note in their compositions could be explained by the theory's rules. Like the better-known theory of tonality proposed by Heinrich Schenker a century later, it began with simple musical structures from which more complex music could be generated by applying specified procedures.

Kollmann was born near Hannover in the duchy of Braunschweig-Lüneburg, a country that from 1714 was in 'personal union' with Great Britain. He came to London in 1782 to serve as organist and schoolmaster of the German Chapel in St James's Palace, and stayed there for the rest of his life. He played a leading role in linking German and English musical cultures and is particularly remembered today for his pioneering efforts to introduce J. S. Bach's music to England.

In addition to writing theoretical treatises—notably *A New Theory of Musical Harmony* (1st edition, 1806; 2nd edition, 1823) and *An Essay on Practical Musical Composition* (1st edition, 1799; 2nd edition, 1812)—Kollmann endeavoured to communicate knowledge of music to readers who had little prior awareness of its history or theory. *The Quarterly Musical Register*, a journal 'written and collected' by him, exemplifies this effort.

Intended (as he wrote in his Introduction to the journal) 'to promote a more *general*, and more *certain* acquaintance, with all that is *useful*, and *interesting*, in the study and practice of music, than can be obtained from the Treatises, Magazines, and other sources of public information hitherto known', *The Quarterly Musical Register* lasted for only two numbers, published in January and April 1812. It now is extremely scarce: just eight copies of the first number, and six of the second, are extant; and only two libraries have the wrappers that were issued with each number.

The Quarterly Musical Register nonetheless is important, not least because it can be regarded as England's first musicological journal. In addition to Kollmann's informative description of his own theoretical works, it includes historical accounts of the state of music in Britain and Germany with regard to knowledge, composition, performance and inventions, the first published English translation of portions of Johann Nicolaus Forkel's biography of Bach, remarks on organs and musical temperament, Kollmann's extraordinarily detailed review of John Wall Callcott's *A Musical Grammar*, an article (not by Kollmann) on the development of music in Bath, and much more.

The facsimile of *The Quarterly Musical Register* in this book has been made from three copies. The letterpress text and music examples are reproduced from the Manchester Central Library copy (Henry Watson Music Library, R780.5 Qd73), except for page 4 of the music examples which is incorrectly sewn in that copy and has been supplied from the Boston Public Library copy (**M.393.10). The wrappers, which are lacking in both the Manchester and Boston copies, have been scanned from the Staatsbibliothek zu Berlin copy (Musikabteilung, Mus. B. 4610). I am grateful to each of these libraries for permitting images of their copies to be printed in this book. The text pages of *The Quarterly Musical Register* are reproduced here at approximately their original size, but the journal's music examples which were issued as foldout sheets have been reduced in size and are printed here in 'landscape' orientation. Asterisks have been imposed in the outer margin of the facsimile to mark the beginnings of passages annotated in section II.5 below.

This book has three parts. It begins with an introduction to Kollmann's life and his works other than *The Quarterly Musical Register*, including the accomplishments of his children George and Joanna, who succeeded him as organist of the German Chapel in that order. The second part comprises the facsimile of *The Quarterly Musical Register*, preceded by comments about its production and followed by notes to its text. The third part includes a transcript of Kollmann's *c*1823 autobiography, listings of his and his son's literary, musical and artistic works, and summaries of the surviving correspondence of the Kollmann family.

My investigation of Kollmann's activities and writings has taken many years. I thank the American Philosophical Society, the John S. Guggenheim Memorial Foundation and the former Basser Department of Computer Science, University of Sydney, for supporting my research at various times, and the numerous archivists, librarians and scholars who retrieved information for me. The National Library of Australia and the State Library of New South Wales deserve special recognition for making distant documents and databases accessible.

Rachel Lynch, my editor at Ashgate, encouraged me to combine an edition of *The Quarterly Musical Register* with an introduction to Kollmann's life and works, and cheerfully found solutions to problems that arose during the preparation of this book. Kirsten Weissenberg led the book through its production process and Elizabeth Teague proofread its text. I am especially indebted to my wife, Jamie, who has shared with me her knowledge of British musical writings in the Georgian era and very much more.

Michael Kassler
Northbridge, NSW, Australia
September 2008

ABBREVIATIONS AND CONVENTIONS

The following acronyms name members of the Kollmann family:

AFCK	Augustus Frederic Christopher Kollmann (1756–1829)
GCK	Georg Christoph Kollmann (1758–1827, AFCK's brother)
CCK	Christina Catherina Kollmann (1745–1823, AFCK's wife)
JSK	Joanna Sophie Kollmann (1786–1849, AFCK's daughter)
GAK	George Augustus Kollmann (1789–1845, AFCK's son)

The name 'Kollmann' without a forename refers to AFCK himself, and 'Joanna' and 'George' without a surname identify Kollmann's children.

QMR stands for *The Quarterly Musical Register*, and *QMR1* and *QMR2* for its first and second numbers respectively. Page numbers in *The Quarterly Musical Register* are denoted by italic numerals.

The following abbreviations designate other works by AFCK. Their full titles are given in section III.2 below.

2nd PGTB	*A Second Practical Guide to Thorough-Bass*, 1807
EMH	*An Essay on Musical Harmony*, 1796
EMH^{Am}	*An Essay on Musical Harmony*, American edition, 1817
EPMC^{1}	*An Essay on Practical Musical Composition*, 1799
EPMC^{2}	*An Essay on Practical Musical Composition*, 2nd edition, 1812
NTh^{1}	*A New Theory of Musical Harmony*, 1806
NTh^{2}	*A New Theory of Musical Harmony*, 2nd edition, 1823
PGTB	*A Practical Guide to Thorough-Bass*, 1801
TAF^{1}	*Twelve Analyzed Fugues*, 1809–1810
TAF^{2}	*Twelve Analyzed Fugues*, 2nd edition, 1822

The following abbreviations also are used:

BL	British Library, London
BL Add Ms	British Library Additional Manuscript
Bodleian	Bodleian Library, University of Oxford

EBA	Michael Kassler (ed.), *The English Bach Awakening: Knowledge of J. S. Bach and his Music in England, 1750–1830*, Aldershot, 2004
fn	footnote
LSW	Philip Olleson (ed.), *The Letters of Samuel Wesley: Professional and Social Correspondence, 1797–1837*, Oxford, 2001
ms	manuscript
pmk	postmark
RCM	Royal College of Music, London
SOMIB	Jamie Croy Kassler, *The Science of Music in Britain, 1714–1830, A Catalogue of Writings, Lectures and Inventions*, New York, 1979
SWSB	Michael Kassler and Philip Olleson, *Samuel Wesley (1766–1837): A Source Book*, Aldershot, 2001
wmk	watermark

'BWV', followed by numerals, refers to a composition by J. S. Bach so numbered in the thematic catalogue of his works prepared by Wolfgang Schmieder.[1] Particular movements of a composition by Bach are designated using the format: BWV number/movement number.

Dates are presented in day/month/year format, i.e., the day precedes the month. The symbols '<' and '>' at the left of a date stand for 'before' and 'after', respectively.

A letter is specified by using the format: Sender→Addressee, Date of the letter. All known letters by or to Kollmann or his children are summarised in the Calendar of Correspondence in section III.4 below.

For a person of German origin I have generally used the name by which he or she was known in England when the Kollmann family lived there.

---

[1] Wolfgang Schmieder, *Thematisch-systematisches Verzeichnis der musikalischen Werke von Johann Sebastian Bach*, Leipzig, 1950.

~ I ~

INTRODUCTION TO KOLLMANN'S LIFE AND WORKS

1. Kollmann in Germany (1756–1782)

Augustus Frederic Christopher Kollmann was born at Engelbostel, a village near Hannover, on 21 March 1756.[1] His maternal grandfather, Johann Hennig Hachmeister, lived there from 1705, when he was appointed organist and schoolmaster at the village's Evangelical-Lutheran Martin church. In 1754 he was succeeded in both posts by Kollmann's father, Christoph Johann Heinrich Kollmann, who in December of that year married Hachmeister's daughter Sophia Margarethe, a few weeks after her father's death. Six months later a second Hachmeister-Kollmann wedding was celebrated when Sophia Margarethe's brother, Carl Christoph Hachmeister Sr, organist of the Heiligen-Geist church in Hamburg from 1748 and a published composer,[2] married Helena Christina Kollmann, Christoph Johann Heinrich Kollmann's sister. *Figure 1* on page 4 shows part of the Kollmann–Hachmeister family tree.

Little documentation of A. F. C. Kollmann's early years has survived. He said in his *c*1823 autobiography, printed in section III.1 below, that he was 'intended for a similar station in life' as his father. He must have met the future composer Johann Christian Firnhaber when they were infants, as Firnhaber's father, who was organist and schoolmaster at the neighbouring town of Langenhagen, was Kollmann's godfather.[3] Kollmann and his brother Georg Christoph, born in February 1758, most likely attended their father's school. As

---

[1] Engelbostel administratively is now part of Langenhagen in the greater Hannover region. Hannover airport is nearby.

[2] Hachmeister's *Clavirübung* was published in Hamburg in 1753 or 1754, according to Friedrich Wilhelm Marpurg's review of it in his *Historisch-kritische Beyträge*, v 1 no. 1, Berlin, 1754, p 51–55 at p 52.

[3] I am grateful to Rev. Herbert Brünjes, late pastor at Engelbostel, for transcribing Kollmann's baptismal record from the Verzeichnis der Getauften der evang.-luth. Kirchengemeinde Engelbostel, Jhg. 1756, p 77. For Firnhaber's family and career see Eberhard Firnhaber, 'Ein vergessener Musiker. Zum 250. Geburtstag von Johann Christian Firnhaber (1753–1828)', *Hannoversche Geschichtsblätter* neue folge v 57/58 (2003–2004) p 261–265, and his 'Johann Christian Firnhaber (1753–1828)', *Musikgeschichte in Mittel- und Osteuropa; Mitteilungen der internationalen Arbeitsgemeinschaft an der Universität Leipzig* v 9, Leipzig, 2004, p 72–94.

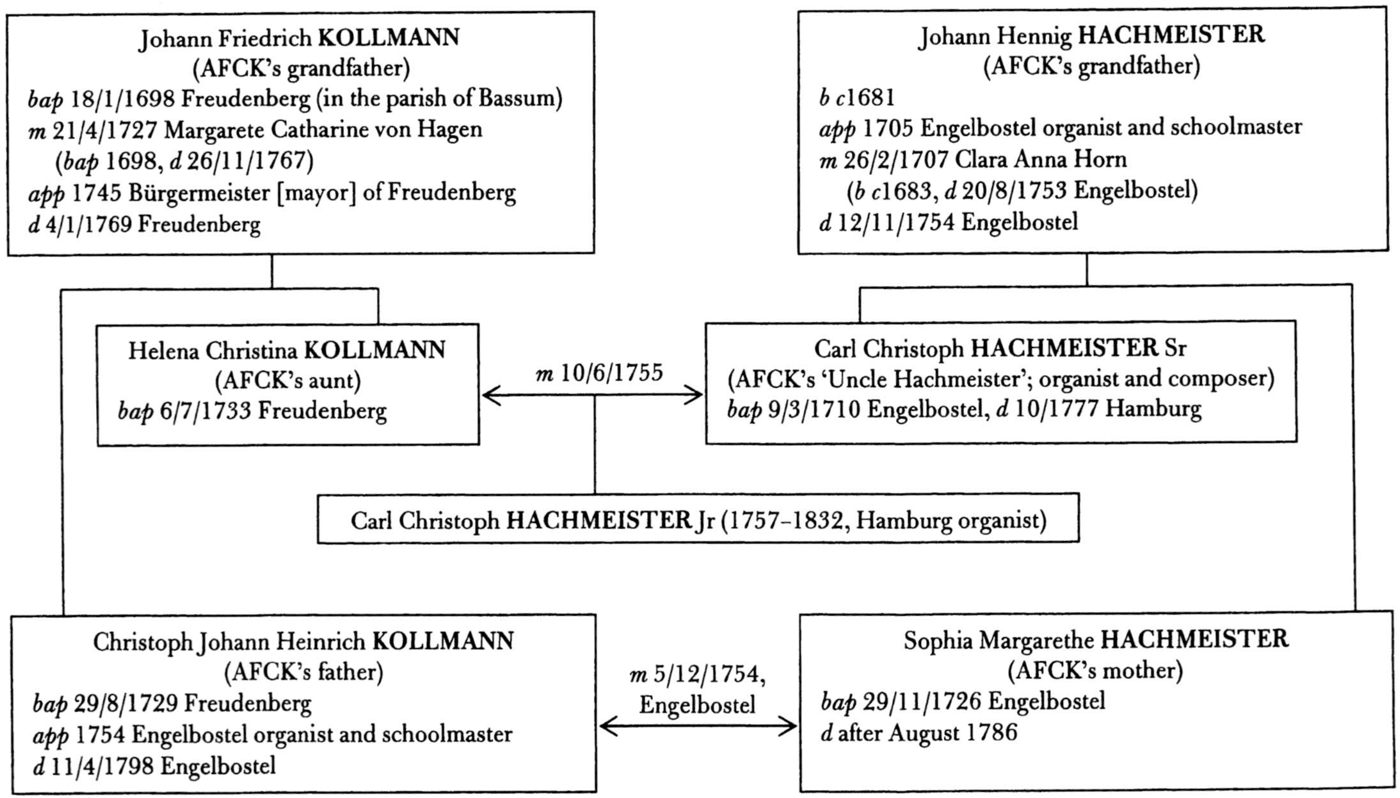

Figure 1. Kollmann and Hachmeister family connections

their father and maternal grandfather were organists, it is not surprising that both brothers learned to play the organ and earned their livings, when adults, primarily as church organists.

After learning Latin in Engelbostel from 'the son of the pastor'[4] Kollmann entered—at the age of fourteen—the Hannover Lyceum in the second class,[5] presumably after his confirmation in the Martin church.[6] He studied there for two years, from about 1770 to 1772. During the directorship of Ludwig Wilhelm Ballhorn, from 1759 to 1774, pupils were divided into five classes of scholars, of whom about twenty were *Sekundaner*, i.e., in the second class.[7] The ages of pupils in a class varied widely: the first class had pupils between thirteen and twenty-three years old. According to a later director, the class in which a child would be placed seems mainly to have been up to his parents.[8] In 1761 the *Sekundaner* received about thirty hours of instruction a week, of which eighteen were devoted to Latin and five to Greek. They also were taught world history, theology, geography and catechism.[9]

---

[4] According to Kollmann's autobiography. Jobst Christoph Salefeld was pastor at Engelbostel from 1751 until his death in July 1768; he was followed in 1769 by Johann Hartwig Kleberg, who died in November 1770. See Philipp Meyer (ed.), *Die Pastoren des Landeskirchen Hannovers und Schaumberg-Lippes seit der Reformation*, v 1, Göttingen, 1941, p 267.

[5] In his autobiography Kollmann called this school 'the Gymnasium at Hannover'. The name 'Gymnasium' was frequently used in the second half of the eighteenth century to describe the Lyceum, which had originated in the Middle Ages (see Franz Bertram, *Geschichte des Ratsgymnasiums (vormals Lyceum) zu Hannover*, Hannover, 1915, p 1–25 and p 436). I thank Dr Bettina Heckmann, author of *Die Entwicklung des hannoverschen Lyzeums zum neuzeitlichen humanistischen Gymnasium*, Hamburg, 2001, for the information that in 1770 the Lyceum was the only school in Hannover that could be considered a gymnasium.

[6] The *Catalogus Confirmatorum* of the Martin church records Georg Christoph Kollmann's confirmation in 1772, the year in which this catalogue begins. Earlier records of Engelbostel confirmations have not survived.

[7] Bertram, p 263. In 1774 the school's total student enrolment was about 170 (*ibid.*, p 264).

[8] Georg Friedrich Grotefend, *Geschichte des Lyceums der Königlichen Residenz-Stadt Hannover während des Zeitraums von 1733 bis 1833...*, Hannover, 1833, p 32, quoted in Bertram, p 264. Grotefend became director of the Lyceum in 1821.

[9] Bertram, p 257.

Remarkably, Karl Philipp Moritz, who was six months younger than Kollmann and who later became a renowned writer, appears to have entered the second class of the Lyceum at Easter 1771, and therefore to have been Kollmann's classmate for a time.[10] Although Moritz's book *Anton Reiser: ein psychologischer Roman* ostensibly recounts the experiences of a fictional 'Anton Reiser', studies have established that the experiences recounted in the novel coincide with Moritz's own activities, and that other persons mentioned in this book, such as the Lyceum director Ballhorn, appear there under their real names.[11] Moreover, in the preface to the second part of the book (Berlin, 1786) where the experiences of 'Reiser' at the Hannover Lyceum are described, Moritz noted that, although he had called this book a psychological novel, its account of a person's life was as true and faithful as could be written, down to the smallest nuances.[12]

The account in *Anton Reiser* of the Lyceum's second class in 1771 thus seems likely to describe events in which Moritz and Kollmann participated.[13] According to this story, the class had two

---

[10] No list of pupils in the second class at the Lyceum at this time seems to have survived. Hugo Eybisch, who investigated Moritz's studies there, concluded that 'bei dem Fehlen der Urkunden und Quellen ist es nicht viel mehr als eine wahrscheinliche Vermutung, daß Karl Philipp Ostern 1771 in die Sekunda aufgenommen wurde' [considering the lack of documents and sources it is not much more than a probable assumption that Karl Philipp was admitted to the second class at Easter 1771] (Eybisch, *Anton Reiser; Untersuchungen zur Lebensgeschichte von K. Ph. Moritz und zur Kritik seiner Autobiographie*, Leipzig, 1909, p 25).

[11] See Oskar Ulrich, 'Karl Philipp Moritz in Hannover: ein Beitrag zur Kritik des "Anton Reiser"', *Euphorion* v 5 (1898) p 87–106 and p 290–309, and Eybisch, *op. cit.*

[12] 'eine so wahre und getreue Darstellung eines Menschenlebens bis auf seine kleinsten Nüancen ist, als es vielleicht nur irgendeine geben kann'. In the preface to the first volume (Berlin, 1785), Moritz wrote 'Dieser psychologische Roman könnte auch allenfalls eine Biographie genannt werden, weil die Beobachtungen größtenteils aus dem wirklichen Leben genommen sind' [this psychological novel could have been called a biography, because its observations in large part are taken from real life]. Both prefaces are reprinted in the 1959 edition of *Anton Reiser* (Leipzig, Insel Verlag), p [7] and p 107.

[13] Information in this and the next paragraph comes from Moritz, *Anton Reiser* ... [with *Nachwort* by Hugo Eybisch], Leipzig, Insel Verlag, [1914] p 143ff; for an English translation see Moritz, *Anton Reiser* ... translated by Ritchie Robertson,

instructors: the *Konrektor* of the Lyceum, called 'Pastor Grupen' in the book and described as a very young man, and the *Kantor*, whom Moritz does not name, but portrays as an older and somewhat hypochondriacal teacher.[14] Lessons were taught from 7 to 10 a.m. and from 1 to 4 p.m. Grupen taught theology, history, the writing of Latin, and the New Testament in Greek; Winter, the *Kantor*, taught catechism, geography and Latin grammar. The history lessons followed the 'Synopsis of Universal History' by the Danish writer Ludvig Holberg,[15] and geography was taught according to the method of Johann Hübner.[16] The remaining class time was devoted to learning Latin, including its prosody and declamation, as pupils were graded only according to their abilities in that language.

'Anton Reiser', i.e., Moritz, and presumably Kollmann, had another classmate who subsequently became famous as an actor and author: August Wilhelm Iffland, who was three years younger than the other two.[17] In 1772 Moritz and Iffland moved to the first class of the

---

London, 1997, p 107ff. However, some of Robertson's translation may be misleading: for instance, he translates Moritz's 'die zweite Klasse'—the second class—as 'the fifth form', which connotes a class of pupils of nearly the same age who generally remain in that class for only one year. Kollmann's autobiography suggests that he spent two years in the Lyceum's second class, but no inference can be drawn that he failed to progress satisfactorily in his first year and was held back. Moritz, who was about fifteen years old when he entered the Lyceum, remarks in *Anton Reiser* that the second class included young people who were already rather grown up ('schon ziemlich erwachsene junge Leute'); some were eighteen years old.

[14] The first class was taught by the director (Ballhorn) and the rector, Rev. Johann Christoph Greve; the second class by the Konrektor and the Kantor (Bertram, p 257). In 1770, when Kollmann entered the second class, Rev. Johann Friedrich Gottfried Grupen, Konrektor of the Lyceum from 1765 to 1776, was twenty-seven years old, and Johann Christian Winter, Kantor of the Lyceum from 1762 to 1790, was fifty-two (*ibid.*, p 526–527).

[15] Holberg's *Synopsis historiæ universalis* was first published in Copenhagen in 1733.

[16] Hübner's *Kurtze Fragen aus der neuen and alten Geographie*, first published in 1693, went through many editions.

[17] In his memoir *Über meine theatralische Laufbahn*, first published in Leipzig in 1798, Iffland briefly mentions his enrolment in the second class (p 34 in the Leipzig 1915 edition of the memoir; see also p 42–43, and his discussion of his friendship with 'Anton Reiser' on p 47–48). While in the second class Iffland and Moritz both

Lyceum, and Kollmann left. He spent the next five years 'partly with his parents', presumably in Engelbostel.[18]

About 1777 he returned to Hannover to study music with Johann Christoph Böttner, organist of the Marktkirche, and in 1779 Kollmann was admitted to the Königliches Schullehrer-Seminarium in Hannover. Founded in 1751, it was Europe's first training college for schoolteachers.[19] Its resources were substantially increased in 1762 when King George III, in his capacity as electoral prince of Hannover, allocated a large bequest to it.[20]

Kollmann's admission to the college presumably was recommended by Böttner, who taught vocal and instrumental music there from 1755 until his death in 1800.[21] When Kollmann arrived the college had about thirty students, divided into three classes, and the course generally took three years to complete.[22] Instruction in religion, morality, history, law and justice was given by two 'inspectors'; in addition, three specialist teachers taught music (Böttner), mathematics and writing.[23] Associated with the college was a free school for children

---

participated in private lessons in German declamation and composition given by the Konrektor between 10 and 11 a.m.

[18] According to his autobiography. I am grateful to Doris Seemann and Peter Boison for searching Engelbostel church records and advising that the confirmation of Kollmann's brother Georg in 1772 appears to be the last record there of the Kollmann family. In the register entry for the August 1786 baptism of Kollmann's daughter Joanna Sophie at the German Chapel in London, Kollmann's mother (who was not present) is described as being from Engelbostel. Her date of death is not known. A 12 April 1798 letter (Niedersächsisches Landesarchiv, Hannover, Hann. 83c no. 13) from Christoph Wilhelm Erdmann, pastor at Engelbostel from 1790 to 1818, to the Hannover consistory, records that Kollmann's father died on 11 April 1798.

[19] Kenneth L. Ellis, 'The administrative connections between Britain and Hanover', *Journal of the Society of Archivists* v 3 no. 10 (October 1969) p 546–566 at p 555.

[20] J[ohann] C[hristoph] Salfeld, *Geschichte des Königlichen Schullehrer-Seminarii und dessen Freyschule zu Hannover*, Hannover, 1800, p 55–57.

[21] Salfeld, p 112. In 1792, eleven years after Kollmann had left, Böttner taught there for six hours a week (see Hermann Müller, *Leben und Streben in Seminar zu Hannover während der Jahre 1790–94*, Hannover, 1877, p 27–28).

[22] Salfeld, p 111, 116–118 and 334–335.

[23] *Königl. Groß-Britannisch und Chur-Fürst. Braunschweig-Lüneburgischer Staats-Kalender auf das Jahr Christi 1780 ...*, Lauenberg, 1780, p 159; Salfeld, p 112–113.

from poor families, where college students could gain teaching experience.[24]

Music was a significant part of the course, as many students expected after graduation to lead a choir and to play the organ in church services. Because the college had no organ, Böttner took his students to the Marktkirche, where they practised on its organ and learned about organ construction and registration.[25] Each student room, in which three students lived, had a bookcase, desk and clavier (a keyboard instrument such as a clavichord or harpsichord); the college also had a large clavier with a pedal.[26] While studying there Kollmann 'constantly heard' and 'assisted' Böttner on the Marktkirche organ and 'entirely officiated' for him for six weeks when he was ill. At the Schullehrer-Seminarium Kollmann also learned 'that methodical, and systematical manner of teaching, which has been very advantageous to him, not only for school instruction, but also in teaching music, and particularly in writing his musical treatises'.[27]

Following his college studies Kollmann was appointed organist and schoolmaster of the parish of Kloster Lüne, near Lüneburg, and began work there on 10 December 1781, after passing tests of his organ-playing and singing abilities.[28] The parish superintendent, Rev. Johann Christoph Greve, might have known him in Hannover.[29] The focus of this parish was its convent ['Kloster'], which was founded by Benedictines in 1172 but became a Protestant 'adliges Damenstift' [home for elderly noble ladies] in 1711. The parish church adjoined the convent and had an early baroque organ which Kollmann played.[30]

---

[24] Salfeld, p 91–93.

[25] *ibid.*, p 174–176.

[26] *ibid.*, p 117 and p 175.

[27] According to Kollmann's autobiography.

[28] Manuscript entry in the Kirchenbuch der ev.-luth. Kirchengemeinde Lüne, p 71. I am grateful to pastor H. H. Ahlrichs for a copy of this entry.

[29] Greve was rector of the Hannover Lyceum from 1765 to 1771 (Bertram, *op. cit.*, p 526; see note 14 above), where Kollmann studied from about 1770.

[30] See Urs Boeck, 'Die Orgel von Kloster Lüne: zu Geschichte und Restaurierung', *Niedersächsisches Denkmalspflege 7—Niedersächsisches Jahrbuch für Landesgeschichte*

He stayed at Kloster Lüne for only six months, leaving about Johannis-Tag (24 June) 1782 because he had been selected to become organist and schoolmaster of the Royal German Chapel in London. Greve recorded that Kollmann's departure pained everyone in the parish because he combined all didactic talents and had the best moral character.[31] Before setting out for London, probably in August, he presumably said goodbye to his parents and to his brother, who had accepted a post at the village of Allermöhe near Hamburg.[32] There is no evidence that Kollmann saw any of them again.

2. The Personal Union of Great Britain and Hannover

The country in which Kollmann spent the first twenty-six years of his life was the duchy of Braunschweig-Lüneburg.[33] As its duke also was the electoral prince of Hannover, it commonly has been called the electorate of Hannover.[34]

Throughout Kollmann's lifetime this country was in 'personal union' with Great Britain—i.e., they shared the same sovereign. The union began for the following reason. King William III of England had no children, and the only child of his successor, Queen Anne, died in 1700. To ensure that England would continue to be ruled by Protestants, the English Parliament passed the *Act of Settlement*

v 43 (1972) p 153–160. This organ was rebuilt between 1968 and 1970. Since 1995 much of the Kloster Lüne building has been used as a textile museum, but a small Protestant convent accommodating up to twelve women continues to function there.

[31] 'so schmerzlich auch uns allen sein Verlust fiel, weil alle didaktischen Talente in ihm vereingt waren und durch den besten moralischen Charakter noch erhöht wurden' (Kirchenbuch der ev.-luth. Kirchengemeinde Lüne, p 71). Greve was superintendent of Kloster Lüne and pastor of the Kirche St Nikolai in Lüneburg from 1781 to 1790 (Philipp Meyer (ed.), *Die Pastoren des Landeskirchen Hannovers und Schaumberg-Lippes seit der Reformation*, v 2, Göttingen, 1942, p 99).

[32] Georg Christoph Kollmann was organist, schoolteacher and chapel-keeper [Küster] at Allermöhe from February 1778 to November 1789.

[33] In English 'Braunschweig' often is translated as 'Brunswick'.

[34] The term 'electoral prince' ['Churfürst'; in modern German 'Kurfürst'] signified that the prince had a vote in the election of the Holy Roman emperor.

1700,[35] which provided that Sophia, dowager electress of Hannover, would be next in succession to the throne, followed by 'the heirs of her body, being Protestants'.[36] As she died in June 1714, two months before Queen Anne's decease, the British throne accordingly passed to Sophia's eldest son Georg Ludwig, elector of Hannover, who became King George I of Great Britain while continuing his responsibilities as duke of Braunschweig-Lüneburg.[37] Britain and Hannover continued to have the same monarchs until 1837—the personal union ending because British law allowed a woman (Queen Victoria) to reign but Hannoverian law did not.[38]

Although the link with Hannover appears to have been of comparatively little concern in England,[39] the government of Hannover, although never part of the British empire, included 'Großbritannisch' in

---

[35] 12 & 13 William III c. 2.

[36] Sophia today is particularly remembered for her support of and extensive correspondence with the philosopher Leibniz, who was employed by the Hannover court from 1676 to his death in 1716.

[37] The Kingdom of Great Britain was created in 1707 by the union of England and Scotland, which established a single parliament at Westminster with representatives from both countries in the House of Lords and House of Commons.

[38] Accordingly, Ernest Augustus, Duke of Cumberland became King Ernst August I of Hannover in 1837, Hannover having become a kingdom at the Congress of Vienna in October 1814.

[39] 'Throughout the period of the [personal] Union, 1714-1837, the attitude of the British political nation towards the Electorate was largely determined by ignorance and prejudice' (Ellis, 'The administrative connections between Britain and Hanover', see note 19 above, p 548). Philip Konigs, *The Hanoverian Kings and their Homeland: A Study of the Personal Union, 1714-1837*, Lewes, Sussex, 1993, states (p 65) that 'the people of Britain were not interested in Hanover', adding that 'the pages of the *Gentlemen's* [sic] *Magazine* and the *Annual Register*, publications widely read at the time, provide proof of this indifference, for they contain a considerable amount of information about the most diverse topics, such as the Indians of Patagonia, but practically nothing about Britons' fellow subjects in Hanover'. Brendan Simms, 'Introduction. Hanover: the missing dimension', in Brendan Simms and Torsten Riotte (eds), *The Hanoverian Dimension in British History, 1714-1837*, Cambridge, 2007, p 1-9, confirms (p 1) that 'the importance, and sometimes the centrality, of the Hanoverian context to British history is still not fully recognised'. Torsten Riotte, *Hannover in der britischen Politik (1792-1815)*, Münster, 2005, describes in detail how the connection with Hannover influenced British politics during this period.

the titles of its officials.[40] This word frequently appeared in the duchy's official and quasi-official publications,[41] as well as in books by local authors—such as Johann Nicolaus Forkel of the duchy's University of Göttingen—that were dedicated to duchy officials.[42] Coins featuring busts of George II and George III that circulated in the electorate while Kollmann lived there gave the monarchs' British as well as their Hannoverian titles.[43] Therefore, when Kollmann left for London, he could have felt that he was travelling to another part of the same realm.

Although George III—who succeeded his grandfather George II as Duke of Braunschweig-Lüneburg, King of Great Britain and King of Ireland in October 1760—never visited Hannover,[44] he was actively involved with the electorate's welfare[45] and in 1786 sent his three youngest sons to study at the University of Göttingen.[46] George III's

---

[40] Adolphus William Ward, *Great Britain & Hanover: some aspects of the personal union*, Oxford, 1899, p 2. From 1714 until the French occupation of Hannover in 1803, members of the Hannoverian privy council, who administered government policy, were styled 'Königlich Großbritannische zur Kurfürstlich Braunschweig-Lüneburgischen Regierung verordnete Geheime Räte' [Royal Great British privy council for the electoral duchy of Braunschweig-Lüneburg] (Uriel Dann, *Hanover and Great Britain 1740–1760*, Leicester, 1991, p 7).

[41] Such as the calendar cited in note 23 above.

[42] Forkel's dedication of his *Allgemeine Geschichte der Musik* (Leipzig, v 1, 1788) to the duchy's privy council reads 'Den Hochgebohrnen Königl. Großbritannischen, zur Churfürstl. Braunschweig-Lüneburgischen Landesregierung Hochverordneten Herren Geheimen Räthen'. Forkel, with whom Kollmann later would correspond, had been appointed director of music at the university in 1779. The University of Göttingen was founded by King George II in 1734.

[43] See R. B. Smith, *The Anglo-Hanoverian Coinage*, Newcastle upon Tyne, 1970.

[44] George III also never visited Ireland, Scotland, Wales or the north of England.

[45] See, for example, T. C. W. Blanning, '"That horrid electorate" or "Ma patrie germanique"? George III, Hanover, and the Fürstenbund of 1785', *The Historical Journal* v 20 no. 2 (June 1977) p 311–344, and, more generally, Konigs, *op. cit.*, p 125–128.

[46] They were Ernest Augustus (later Duke of Cumberland and King of Hannover), Augustus Frederick (later Duke of Sussex) and Adolphus (later Duke of Cambridge). Both Ernest Augustus and Augustus Frederick attended Forkel's 'academic concerts' at the university. When they left, in 1791, Forkel published his twenty-four variations on 'God save the King' as a departure gift to them. The British Library's copy of this

links with the duchy's government were maintained by the *Deutsche Kanzlei* [German Chancery] in London, which was established at the start of the personal union and continued until the union's dissolution. The Chancery's office, located in St James's Palace, was directed by a member of the duchy's *Geheimer Rat* [privy council] and was staffed by Hannoverians.[47] The director, who lived in London, was called the Hannoverian minister, although his duties differed from those of an ambassador of a foreign country.[48]

Kollmann wrote in his autobiography that George III had commanded 'that a person should be sent by the Hannoverian Government, to fill the place of Organist and Schoolmaster at the Royal German Chapel' at St James's Palace, and that he, Kollmann, had been 'called away' from Kloster Lüne in fulfilment of this command. A command from George III to the Hannoverian government presumably would have been transmitted via the German Chancery,[49] but no reference has been found in its extant records to Kollmann or to the German Chapel.[50] These records were removed from London to Hannover after the end of the personal union and by 1840 more than half of them apparently were destroyed.[51]

---

work was owned by Kollmann's cousin Carl Christoph Hachmeister Jr (see note 159 below), but no evidence has been found that Kollmann had a copy of it.

[47] The origins of the German Chancery at the beginning of the personal union are described in Rudolf Grieser, 'Die Deutsche Kanzlei in London, ihre Entstehung und Anfänge', *Blätter für Deutsche Landesgeschichte* n.s. v 89 (1952) p 153–168.

[48] The closeness and peculiarity of the relationship is further indicated by the circumstance that Britain sent no diplomatic or consular representatives to the duchy during the time of the personal union (Dann, p 10).

[49] According to Ellis, *op. cit.*, p 557, 'after 1730 the [Hannoverian] Minister became the sole channel of business between Britain and Hanover. The Minister ... had complete control of the German Chancery ... consisting of one or more Privy Chancery Secretaries with about a dozen officials seconded from Hanover. ... Throughout the period of the Union, the German Chancery served as the link between Britain and Hanover.'

[50] Now in the Niedersächsisches Landesarchiv, Hauptstaatsarchiv Hannover, file Hann. 92. I am grateful to Dr Sven Mahmens for this information.

[51] Ward, *op. cit.*, p 59.

The Hannoverian government's involvement with Kollmann's appointment suggests that the king's command for a schoolmaster and organist was forwarded to the consistory—the department responsible for the ecclesiastical and educational affairs of the duchy's established Evangelical-Lutheran church. The consistory oversaw the Schullehrer-Seminarium[52] and may have asked for the college's recommendation. This hypothesis is strengthened by the circumstance that two chaplains subsequently appointed to the German Chapel—Georg Joachim Hieronymus Röhrs in 1788 and Johann Hartmann Wilhelm Kuper in 1802—also came from the Hannover Schullehrer-Seminarium.[53]

3. The German Chapel at St James's Palace

The Royal German Chapel at St James's Palace was founded 'about the year 1700' by Queen Anne and her consort Prince George of Denmark and Norway, who was born at Copenhagen and had been raised in the Lutheran church.[54] Chapel services, conducted in German, were held initially in a palace room adjacent to the Great Court.[55] They were restricted at first to members of the royal family and household, but became available to a wider German-speaking community after the 1714 coronation of the Duke of Braunschweig-Lüneburg as King George I of Britain, which led numerous Germans to come to London

---

[52] 'Das Seminarium ist von seinem ersten Anfange an unter den Oberaufsicht des Königlichen Consistorii gestanden' (Salfeld, *op. cit.*, p 96).

[53] Salfeld, p 105 and p 112.

[54] See John Southerden Burn, *The History of the French, Walloon, Dutch, and other foreign Protestant refugees settled in England...*, London, 1846, p 235–237, who got much of his information about the German Chapel from Kuper, then its sole chaplain. The early years of the German Chapel are described in Daniel L. Brunner, *Halle Pietists in England: Anthony William Boehm and the Society for Promoting Christian Knowledge*, Göttingen, 1993, p 49–58.

[55] According to the 1729 ground floor plan of St James's Palace drawn by the architect Henry Flitcroft, of which a 1930 copy by Arthur Bolton is reproduced in *The Royal Palaces of Winchester, Whitehall, Kensington, and St James's...*, *Wren Society* v 7, Oxford, 1930, p 244. The Great Court now is called the 'Colour Court'.

Figure 2. Engraving by Charles Wild and Daniel Havell of the German Chapel, St James's Palace, in 1816, showing the organ that Kollmann played (from W. H. Pyne, The History of the Royal Residences…, London, 1819; by permission of Thomas Fisher Rare Book Library, University of Toronto)

Figure 3. Engraving of part of a picture designed by Kollmann, in which J. S. Bach appears as the central German composer (Allgemeine musikalische Zeitung, Leipzig, 1799; by permission of the Bach-Archiv, Leipzig)

to serve or to supply the court or to represent Hannoverian interests in England.[56]

Four Protestant services, each in a different language, were celebrated in St James's Palace at this time. King William III, a Dutch aristocrat born at The Hague, had founded a Dutch Chapel in the palace in 1689, soon after he and his wife, Queen Mary II, were crowned joint sovereigns of Britain.[57] In 1700 he granted to the Dutch Chapel and to a newly formed French Chapel the shared use of a vacant building known as the 'Queen's Chapel', which then was physically attached to the palace.[58] English-language services took place in the Chapel Royal, which relocated to a different part of the palace in 1702.

The Queen's Chapel building, designed by Inigo Jones, was constructed between 1623 and 1625 as a Roman Catholic chapel for Henrietta Maria, queen consort of King Charles I.[59] A cloistered friary adjoining the building housed Capuchin Franciscan friars from 1630. Additions made between 1682 and 1684 included an altar carved by Grinling Gibbons. The building served as a Catholic chapel for several subsequent queens, the last being Mary of Modena, consort of King James II.[60] Its use as a Catholic chapel ended in 1689, and in 1699 the organ that had been erected in the chapel in the 1660s was removed

---

[56] See J[ulius] Rieger, 'The British crown and the German churches in England', in Franz Hildebrandt (ed.), *'And other Pastors of thy Flock': a German tribute to the Bishop of Chichester*, Cambridge, 1942, p 101–123 at p 104; and J[ulius] Rieger, 'Der Bilderbogen, 27. Die Gemeinde der deutschen Hofkapelle (I)', *Der Londoner Bote* no. 40 (April 1952), p 52–53. I am grateful to the Institut für Auslandsbeziehungen, Stuttgart, for supplying a copy of the latter article.

[57] Burn, *op. cit.*, p 222. King William was William III in England and Ireland and William II in Scotland. His coronation led several Dutch-speaking courtiers to follow him to London.

[58] Burn, p 156–157; H[oward] M. Colvin (ed.), *The History of the King's Works*, v 5, London, 1976, p 253. In 1700 King William was the sole sovereign, as Queen Mary had died.

[59] For the history of the building, from which information in this paragraph is derived, see Colvin, *op. cit.*, v 4 part 2, 1982, p 248–249, and v 5, 1976, p 244–254 and the unpaginated plates at the end of that volume; Philip Sassoon, 'A royal chapel', *The Times*, 28 October 1938 p 15–16 and p 18; and Simon Bradley, 'The Queen's Chapel in the twentieth century', *Architectural History* v 44 (2001) p 293–302.

[60] In Scotland he was King James VI.

and presented to St Anne's, Soho. For the following eighty years, when the French and Dutch Chapels held services in the building, no organ was installed there.[61]

Kollmann's appointment to the German Chapel in 1782 was directly related to a decision in 1781 to move its services to the Queen's Chapel building and to transfer the French and Dutch services to the palace room previously used by the German Chapel.[62] The new, larger German Chapel premises were consecrated on 26 August 1781 by Rev. Henry Otto Schrader, the first of the two chaplains serving the German Chapel at that time.[63] This exchange of premises presumably reflected the increase in the number of German speakers and the decrease in the number of Dutch and French speakers in and around the palace during the reign of King George III.

---

[61] See Donald Burrows, *Handel and the English Chapel Royal*, Oxford, 2005, p 517.

[62] This decision was approved by Robert Lowth, Bishop of London, on 1 May 1781 (Burn, *op. cit.*, p 158–159). In a 17 May 1781 letter to Francis-Seymour Conway, 1st Marquess of Hertford, then Lord Chamberlain (National Archives, WORK 6/19 p 354), Henry Otto Schrader and Johann Frederick Mithoff, the first and second chaplains of the German Chapel, noted that approval to exchange premises had been 'granted by His Majesty [George III] and agreed to by both congregations'.

[63] Entry by Schrader in the German Chapel 'Kirchenbuch' for 26 August 1781. Baptisms, marriages and other events at the German Chapel between 1712 and August 1836 were recorded in a two-volume 'Kirchenbuch der königlichen deutschen Hofcapelle in St James's'. Only five entries were made from 1712 to 1716; in 1717 seven events were noted. In 1836 King William IV appointed commissioners to inquire into existing registers of baptisms, marriages, etc. in England and Wales not belonging to the Church of England (see *Report of the Commissioners appointed to inquire into ... Registers or Records ... other than parochial Registers*, House of Commons Parliamentary Paper no. 148, London, 1838, p 7 and Appendix Schedule A p 2). As a consequence of this inquiry many such 'non-parochial' registers, including the German Chapel Kirchenbuch, were deposited in the General Register Office which had been established in 1836. These registers subsequently were transferred to the National Archives, where the German Chapel Kirchenbuch now is stored at RG 4/4568–4569. Before it was deposited Rev. Johann Hartmann Wilhelm Kuper, the chaplain at that time, copied its entries into another volume of the same name, into which he and his successors added records of events at the German Chapel up to 1913. In the second Kirchenbuch Kuper also noted some pre-1837 Chapel events that were not mentioned in the original register. When the German Chapel congregation removed to the Deutsche Evangelische Christuskirche, Montpelier Place, Kensington, in 1904, this second Kirchenbuch was transferred to the care of that church.

Queen Charlotte, who was born in Germany and learned English only after her marriage to George III in 1761,[64] took a personal interest in the new premises. She gave the German Chapel an organ, which it had not had before, and also a large, 2.7 × 2.12 metre oil-on-canvas altar painting by Johann Heinrich Ramberg, entitled *Christus im Gebet auf dem Ölberg* [Christ in prayer at Gethsemane, at the foot of the Mount of Olives, Jerusalem].[65] Ramberg's painting and the pipes of this organ can be seen in the 1816 engraving, by Charles Wild and Daniel Havell, of the interior of the German Chapel. Their engraving is reproduced in *Figure* 2 facing page 14.[66]

Very little is known about this organ, which Kollmann played for more than forty years. Its construction presumably had been ordered before he left Kloster Lüne about Johannis-Tag (24 June) 1782, as the register entry describing his departure states that he was called to the German Chapel to become its organist and schoolmaster. In 1798 Rev. Johann Gottlieb Burckhardt, minister of St Mary's Church in the Savoy, another German church in London, described the organ as small ['eine kleine Orgel'].[67] It remained in the chapel until 1832, when it was replaced.[68]

Ramberg was born at Hannover in 1763 and was admired at an early age for his art: in 1777 Georg Christoph Lichtenberg, professor of physics at the University of Göttingen and posthumously famous as a

---

[64] Olwen Hedley, *Queen Charlotte*, London, 1975, p 28 and p 62. Edgar Sheppard's statement (*Memorials of St James's Palace*, London, 1894, v 2 p 78) that George III and Charlotte were married 'in the German Chapel Royal' at St James's Palace is incorrect: their marriage took place in the palace's Chapel Royal (Hedley, p 44). As noted in the next footnote, some other details of Sheppard's account of the German Chapel (v 2 p 245–260) also are inaccurate.

[65] Burn, *op. cit.*, p 236. Sheppard mistakenly wrote (v 2 p 249) that the donor of the organ and altar painting was 'Queen Caroline', and other scholars have repeated this error.

[66] This engraving was published on 1 August 1816 and reprinted in volume 3 of W[illiam] H[enry] Pyne, *The History of the Royal Residences of Windsor Castle, St James's Palace, Carlton House...*, London, 1819.

[67] Burckhardt, Johann Gottlieb, *Kirchen-Geschichten der deutschen Gemeinden in London...*, Tübingen, 1798, p 73.

[68] Thomas Baucott Mash→GAK, 6/12/1832. See page 147 below.

writer, called him a young Raphael.[69] To further his artistic education his father, an officer in the Hannoverian government, applied in December 1780 to the German Chancery in London, forwarding examples of his son's work and inquiring about opportunities for study there. The application came to George III's attention, and money was granted for Ramberg to travel to London.

In contrast to Kollmann's first years in London, Ramberg's visit is well documented. He arrived on 25 April 1781 and went immediately to see Johann Friedrich Mithoff, second chaplain of the German Chapel, who invited him to a meal and found him a place to stay.[70] The following morning Mithoff introduced Ramberg to General Heinrich Wilhelm von Freytag, field marshal of the Hannoverian army who had various assignments in London between 1764 and 1783, and also to Johann Friedrich Karl von Alvensleben, the director of the German Chancery. King George learned that Ramberg had arrived and on 27 April granted him a further stipend.[71]

The next day Ramberg heard from Henry Otto Schrader that the queen desired him to bring Ramberg to the court that evening, so that the king could see his drawings and paintings.[72] He was then presented to the king and queen, and was introduced to the king's historical painter Benjamin West,[73] with all of whom he stayed in close

---

[69] Information about Ramberg's London activities is taken principally from A[lexander] Conze, 'Aus Joh. Heinr. Ramberg's Nachlasse', *Preußische Jahrbücher* v 26 no. 1 (1870) p 83–103 (particularly p 87–96), and Alheidis von Rohr, *Johann Heinrich Ramberg, 1763 – Hannover – 1840, Maler für König und Volk*, Hannover, 1998 [exhibition catalogue], p 16–23.

[70] Ramberg→Johann Daniel Ramberg (his father), undated but written near the end of April 1781, printed in [Ferdinand] Stuttmann (ed.), *Johann Heinrich Ramberg Briefe*, Hannover, 1940, p 9–12.

[71] Franziska Forster-Hahn, *Johann Heinrich Ramberg als Karikaturist und Satiriker*, Sonderdruck aus *Hannoversche Geschichtsblätter*, neue folge v 17 (1963) p 155 note 8.

[72] Ramberg→Johann Daniel Ramberg, 1 May 1781, printed in Foster-Hahn, p 155–156 note 10.

[73] *ibid.*

association during his seven years in London.[74] Ramberg's altar painting for the German Chapel was commissioned with the king's approval before 8 April 1788[75] and presumably was presented to the Chapel before Ramberg left England on 15 August 1788.[76]

As the *Act of Settlement 1700* provided that 'whosoever shall hereafter come to the possession of this Crown, shall join in communion with the Church of England, as by law established', King George III, Queen Charlotte and other members of the British royal family did not attend German Chapel services. When they attended services at St James's Palace they took communion in the Chapel Royal.[77] However, some of their German relations did worship in the German Chapel when visiting London.[78] Its liturgy appears to have

---

[74] A detail from an engraving by Pietro Antonio Martini of Ramberg's drawing, 'Portraits of their Majesty's and the Royal Family viewing the Exibition [sic] of the Royal Academy, 1788', is featured as the frontispiece in Jane Roberts (ed.), *George III & Queen Charlotte: Patronage, Collecting and Court Taste*, published in 2004 by Royal Collection Enterprises Ltd, St James's Palace. This engraving incorrectly named the artist as 'P. Ramberg', and this misidentification was repeated in that book.

[75] See Ramberg→Johann Daniel Ramberg, 8 April 1788, printed in Stuttmann, *op. cit.*, p 37–38.

[76] I thank Leonora Clark of the Royal Collection for advising that this painting (Royal Collection Inventory No. 406798) was removed to Hampton Court Palace in 1955 and is now in storage there.

[77] Regarding the German Chapel, Burckhardt wrote (*op. cit.*, p 71): 'Man macht sich aber eine falsche Vorstellung, wenn man sich einbildet, daß die Königliche Familie diese Capelle besuche. Der König muß mit seiner Familie, den Parlementsacten zufolge, der hohen Kirche von England zugethan seyn, und hat daher auf dem Schlosse seine eigne Englische Hofcapelle, worinn Er auch das Abendmahl empfängt' [But one would have a false idea if one thought that the royal family attends this chapel. In accordance with acts of Parliament the king and his family must be attached to the High Church of England, and accordingly he has his own English court chapel in the palace, where he receives communion].

[78] In the words of Gebh[ard] Friedr[ich] Aug[ust] Wendeborn, *Der Zustand des Staats, der Religion, der Gelehrsamkeit und der Kunst in Großbritannien gegen das Ende des achtzehnten Jahrhunderts*, v 3, Berlin, 1785, p 421: 'Wenn etwa Verwandte der königlichen Familie, aus Deutschland, sich in England befinden; so wohnen sie wol, zu Zeiten, dem Gottesdienste in der deutschen Capelle bei'. Wendeborn, who was pastor of the St Johannis Kirche in Ludgate Hill, London, from 1770 to 1792, excluded the section on the ecclesiastical situation of foreigners in London, from

included parts of the Book of Common Prayer in German translation, together with other content.[79]

When the Chapel Royal was closed for repairs or for other reasons, its services were transferred to the German Chapel building. The royal family attended some of these services, which of course were conducted in English by persons other than the German Chapel chaplains, and would have seen Ramberg's altar painting then and heard the Chapel organ.[80] It is not known whether Kollmann played the organ on any of those occasions.

In September 1782, when Kollmann began work at the German Chapel, Schrader and Mithoff were his superiors. As Ramberg's experience indicates, both of them were well connected with the royal family. Schrader was engaged to teach German to the royal princesses[81]

---

which the above quotation is taken, from his translation of this book, published as *A View of England towards the Close of the Eighteenth Century*, London, 1791.

[79] The prayer book published in London in 1757 for use in the German Chapel is entitled: *Ein Gebet-Büchlein: Theils aus der Englischen Liturgie, theils aus andern geistreichen Gebet-Büchern zusammengetragen; und zum Gebrauch der Königlichen Deutschen Lutherischen Hof-Capelle zu St. James eingerichtet* [A little prayer book, compiled partly from the English liturgy and partly from other spirit-filled prayer books, arranged for use in the Royal German Lutheran Court Chapel at St James's].

[80] E.g., *The Times*, 23 February 1795, p 2, reported that 'yesterday being the first Sunday in Lent, their majesties and the three elder princesses came from Buckingham House to St James's Palace, and being joined by their attendants they went in State to the German Chapel, where they attended Divine Service; the Sermon was preached by the Right Rev. the Lord Bishop of Durham' [Shute Barrington]. At this time the Chapel Royal was 'undergoing a thorough change' in preparation for the 8 April 1795 wedding of George, Prince of Wales, and Caroline, Duchess of Braunschweig-Wolfenbüttel (*The Times*, 5 January 1795, p 3).

[81] On the title-page of his published sermons *Einige Predigten*, London, 1779, Schrader is identified as 'Hofprediger zu St. James's und Lehrer der deutschen Sprache bey Ihren Königl. Hoheiten den Prinzeßinnen von Großbritannien'. Flora Fraser, *Princesses: the six daughters of George III*, New York, 2005, suggests (p 58) that Princess Charlotte (the Princess Royal) and Princess Augusta studied German with him in 1778. According to Kollmann's probable former classmate Karl Philipp Moritz, who dined with Schrader in London in June 1782, Schrader instructed the young princes and princesses in religion (Moritz, *Journeys of a German in England*, translated by Reginald Nettel, London, 1983, p 71). As the *Act of Settlement* obliged the royal family to be in communion with the Church of England, Moritz's statement seems likely to be in error, perhaps as a consequence of Schrader saying that he was

soon after his 1776 appointment to the German Chapel and apparently undertook additional duties for Queen Charlotte. His father-in-law, the naturalist Johann Reinhold Forster,[82] in a 1782 letter to his colleague Thomas Pennant, described Schrader as 'one of the German Chaplains at St James, Librarian to the Queen, Teacher of the Princesses & Secretary to Her Majesty for her German Correspondence; & a man of excellent character'.[83] From July 1791 he also served as the chaplain of the Dutch Chapel in St James's Palace. Fanny Burney 'frequently heard' Queen Charlotte speak of Mithoff 'with praise' and recorded times when Schrader and Mithoff dined with the queen.[84]

Architectural changes to the Queen's Chapel building were made in 1781 to provide an apartment for the organist and schoolmaster who—it was planned—would be appointed to the German Chapel after its relocation.[85] As the chaplains and other staff of the German Chapel lived away from the palace, it seems likely that the duties of the new appointee were intended from the outset to include some caretaking of the premises. The Kollmann family occupied this apartment up to 1849. Its address, 'Friary, St James's Palace', recalled the Roman Catholic friary that had operated nearby.

---

instructing members of the royal family, and Moritz assuming that any instruction by Schrader was religious instruction.

[82] Schrader married Virginia Viktoria Forster in August 1781 (see Michael E. Hoare, *The Tactless Philosopher: Johann Reinhold Forster*, Melbourne, 1976, p 196).

[83] Forster→Pennant, 3 July 1782, Peabody Essex Museum, Salem, Massachusetts, USA, in collection MH-100. Forster added that letters or parcels for him should be sent to Schrader, who would 'find means to convey them' safely to the University of Halle, in which Forster was professor of natural history and mineralogy. (The naturalist Johann George Adam Forster, usually called 'George Forster', was his son.)

[84] [Charlotte Barrett] (ed.), *Diary and Letters of Madame d'Arblay*, v 3, *1786 & 1787*, London, 1842, p 151-154 and p 195.

[85] David Baldwin, *The Chapel Royal, Ancient & Modern*, London, 1990, notes (p 144) that 'in 1781 the ceiling in the royal closet was partitioned for the organist's quarters, hence the marks on the Inigo Jones chimney-piece'.

4. Kollmann's Work for the German Chapel

On 17 September 1782, sixteen days after his arrival in London, Kollmann was 'sworn and admitted into the place and office' of porter of the German Chapel by Rev. Anselm Bayly, subdean of the Chapel Royal, by virtue of a warrant from Robert Lowth, the Bishop of London and dean of the Chapel Royal.[86] On 9 April 1784, having quitted the office of porter, Kollmann was sworn by Bayly into the higher-paying position of chapel-keeper of the German Chapel.[87] Kollmann remained in that post to the end of his life and was succeeded as chapel-keeper first by his son and then by his daughter. The staff of the German Chapel during the time of the Kollmanns' employment there are shown in *Figure 4* on pages 24–25.

The offices of porter and chapel-keeper that Kollmann held do not coincide with the professions of organist and schoolmaster that he was brought from Germany to practise. Presumably it was administratively more convenient for him to fill and to be paid in accordance with existing posts than to create a new one for him.

The remuneration of German Chapel staff came from more than one source and was the subject of several representations by its chaplains. When the Chapel was established, revenue from certain property was allocated for its perpetual maintenance and the salaries of its staff, but this property was sold during the reign of George II and salaries and allowances subsequently were paid from the 'civil list' of expenditures associated with the royal household.[88] In 1816

---

[86] New cheque book of the Chapel Royal (manuscript, Chapel Royal archive), p 100, transcribed in Andrew Ashbee and John Harley (eds), *The Cheque Books of the Chapel Royal*, Aldershot, 2000, v 1 p 278. Since 1748 the Bishop of London has also been dean of the Chapel Royal. Bayly, in addition to his ecclesiastical work, wrote books on music, language and other subjects.

[87] *ibid.*

[88] See Wendeborn, *Der Zustand...*, *op. cit.*, p 419–420, and Burn, *op. cit.*, p 235. In 1813 Christian Hermann Giese and Johann Hartmann Wilhelm Kuper, then the first and second chaplains of the German Chapel, were paid annual salaries of £270 and £245 respectively, partly from the Lord Steward's Department and partly from a separate Vaudois Churches list (Giese and Kuper→The Prince Regent, 4 October 1813, BL Add Ms 38254 f 278–279). Twenty-one receipts for salary payments from

Kollmann's annual salary as chapel-keeper was £60 plus £10 from the Lord Chamberlain's office, from which £3 was allocated to the chapel's cleaner. After deductions, his net salary was about £54/12/–. He also had, free of charge, the 'use of the apartments at the Chapel, with the coals granted for them' and, until a recent retrenchment, had perquisites of candles, table linen and wine.[89] Apparently he received no additional payment for his duties as organist. Kollmann characterised his salary as 'small' and informed the Bishop of London in 1817 that elimination of these perquisites, which he valued at £25 per year, was 'a very grievous loss' to him.[90] The Lord Steward Department's account books for 1820 show that he received in that year a salary of £48 for services as chapel-keeper and a further £6/6/– compensation as a 'chapel royal servant'.[91]

Almost nothing is known about the German Chapel school of which Kollmann was master. He wrote in his autobiography that it took up 'part of four days every week', leaving him 'sufficient time for attending to musical pursuits'. He was not the first master: John Augustus Walter, Kollmann's predecessor as porter of the German Chapel, who died before Kollmann took up the post,[92] served as schoolmaster from at least 1772.[93] Earlier information about the school has not been found. Burckhardt briefly mentioned it in his 1798 book:

---

the Vaudois Churches list to German Chapel staff holding the office of chaplain, reader and porter between 1792 and 1818 are extant in National Archives E 404/598. None of these records a payment to Kollmann, who during that time held the post of chapel-keeper and clerk, and it is not known whether he was ever paid from this list.

[89] See Kollmann memorandum, 11/12/1816, enclosed with Kuper→William Howley (Bishop of London), 12/12/1816, in section III.4 below.

[90] Kollmann→William Howley, 24/1/1817.

[91] National Archives, LS 2/46, accounts of salaries for the year 1820. Kuper, then sole chaplain of the German Chapel, received a salary of £296 that year from the Lord Steward's Department but had to pay for his housing. It is not known whether Kollmann received remuneration that year from any other government-administered funds.

[92] New cheque book of the Chapel Royal, p 100 (see note 86 above).

[93] In the entry for the 30 September 1772 baptism of his son Wilhelm Friedrich, Walter is described as 'Porter und Schulmeister der hiesigen Hofkapelle' [porter and schoolmaster of this court chapel] (Kirchenbuch entry, see note 63 above).

First Chaplain	*Second Chaplain*	*Reader*	*Chapel-Keeper*	*Porter*	*Cleaner*
Henry Otto Schrader *first sermon* 10/1776 *consecrated the relocated German chapel* 26/8/1781 *d* 31/5/1802	Johann Friedrich Mithoff *b* 1747 *first sermon* 27/7/1777 *m 2nd* 6/12/1786 Miss Bosenberg *last sermon* 15/6/1788 *d* 1795, Clausthal	Frederick William Pasche 1751–1792 *d* 11/7/1792	Nicholas Daniel Kanmacher *b c*1703 *app* 27/2/1751 *d* 17/2/1784	John Augustus Walter *also Schoolmaster* *d* <17/9/1782	Sarah Walter
				A. F. C. Kollmann *app* 17/9/1782 *quitted c*21/2/1784	
			A. F. C. Kollmann *app* 9/4/1784 *d* 19/4/1829	Charles Heydinger *app* 28/2/1784 *d* 19/8/1801	
	Georg Joachim Hieronymus Röhrs *app* 7/1788 *first sermon* 3/8/1788 *last sermon* 6/8/1797 *left* for Gifhorn *d* 1802	C. Werner 1792?–1795 [after Werner the post of *Reader* filled successively by Röhrs, Giese and Kuper]			

First Chaplain	*Second Chaplain*	*Chapel-Keeper/Clerk/Organist*	*Porter*	*Cleaner*
	Christian Hermann Giese *first sermon* 17/12/1797 *promoted* <29/11/1802		John Conrad Köhler *b c*1746 *app* 8/2/1802 *d* 23/8/1813	
Christian Hermann Giese *app* 22/1/1803 *d* 13/1/1819	Johann Hartmann Wilhelm Kuper *b c*1772 *first sermon* 7/11/1802 [post abolished >13/1/1819]			
Sole Chaplain Johann Hartmann Wilhelm Kuper *app* >13/1/1819 *d* 27/11/1861			John Conrad Köhler *app c*9/1813 *d* 22/10/1855	Henrietta Veinberg 'necessary woman' in 1820
		George Augustus Kollmann *app* 25/5/1829 *d* 19/3/1845		Alice Nankerville in 1831 (see p 140 below)
		Joanna Sophie Kollmann *app* 13/5/1845 *d* 14/5/1849		Mary Haughton *app* ? *resigned* <1850
		Frederic Weber *b* 5/11/1819, Würtemberg *app* 25/5/1849 *d* 16/2/1909		Mary Maugham *app* 28/1/1850 *d* <11/3/1868

Figure 4. Staff of the German Chapel, St James's Palace, 1780–1850

> Bei der Capelle ist eine Deutsche Armenschule, wo die Prediger abwechselnd jede Woche eine Cathecisation halten. Der jezike Schulmeister ist Herr Kollmann, welcher als ein geschikter Musikus zugelich Organist der Capelle ist.[94] [At the Chapel is a free German school where the chaplains, alternating each week, give religious instruction in catechism form. The current schoolmaster is Mr Kollmann, who, being a capable musician, also is the Chapel's organist.]

As far as is known, only one student at this school left a record of his time there, and unfortunately this record is short. In his revised edition of William Thomas Lowndes's *The Bibliographer's Manual of English Literature*, the publisher Henry George Bohn appended the following paragraph to his article on 'Kolmann' [sic]:

> This talented man was *Kapell-meister* to George III. at St. James's Palace, and there, by the desire of the King, superintended the German and musical education of twelve boys, sons of Germans, of whom the present publisher, Henry G. Bohn, was one, Griesbach the composer another. They were under the religious direction of the late Dr Kuper, the amiable and learned tutor of the lamented Princess Charlotte.[95]

Bohn's father, John Henry Martin Bohn, was born at Weinheim, Germany and came to London in 1790, where he worked first as a bookbinder and later as a bookseller.[96]

'Griesbach the composer' almost certainly refers to John Henry Griesbach (1798–1895), whose father Henry was one of five Griesbach brothers who came from Hannover to England between 1778 and 1788 to play in Queen Charlotte's private band of musicians.[97] The brothers

---

[94] Burckhardt, *op. cit.*, p 86–87.

[95] London, v 3 part 5 (1860) p 1290. In fact, Kuper was alive in 1860.

[96] See 'Bookbinding', *The Art Journal* n.s. (1881) p 196 (which gives information from Henry G. Bohn about his father), and Anthony Lister, 'Henry George Bohn (1796–1884): Bookseller, Publisher and Controversialist', *Antiquarian Book Monthly Review* v 15 no. 2 (February 1988) p 54–61.

[97] Amongst the Griesbachs only John Henry achieved distinction as a composer. However, in his 30 October 1823 autobiographical letter (Glasgow University Library ms Euing R.d. 86/86) to John Davis Sainsbury, proprietor of the *Dictionary of Musicians* published in the following year, John Henry Griesbach mentions neither the German Chapel nor Kollmann.

were nephews of the musician and astronomer Sir William Herschel, who had come to England from Hannover in 1757.[98]

In answer to a query, Bohn wrote a further note about the German Chapel:

> As I received my early German education in the Lutheran Chapel in St. James's Palace—in the royal pew, a capacious room in the gallery—and had an opportunity of surveying the chapel every day for about two years, I ought to know something about it, but I confess that I know very little. ... The Hanoverian *Gesangbuch* was always used there,[99] and I well remember the stentorian German chants, in which I had to join. ... I have said something on this subject in my edition of Lowndes, article "Kolman" [sic]....[100]

Bohn's description of German Chapel scholars as 'boys' suggests that they generally were under fourteen years old, the age at which many youths began apprenticeship. The school's religious instruction presumably prepared these boys for confirmation, which in Lutheran churches commonly took place at age fourteen. It is plausible, therefore, that Kollmann taught Bohn and Griesbach about the year 1810. As the registers of the German Chapel have no entries for the Bohn or Griesbach families, attendance at the school appears to have been available to sons of Germans who belonged to congregations other than the German Chapel.

In the absence of further documentation, little can be said about Kollmann's work as schoolmaster, which occupied a considerable portion of his time for about thirty-five years. In his autobiography he recorded that the school was discontinued after Queen Charlotte's 1817 death, suggesting that its operation up to then had benefited from her personal interest.[101] Its curriculum appears to have differed

[98] See the memoirs of George Ludolph Jacob Griesbach, another of the five Griesbach brothers, edited by F. Anne M. R. Jarvis in *The Community of German Migrant Musicians in London c1750–c1850*, master's thesis, University of Cambridge, August 2003, v 2. I am grateful to Anne Jarvis for giving me a copy of this thesis.

[99] Presumably the *Hannoverisches Kirchen-Gesang-Buch*, of which the 25th edition was published in Hannover in 1794 and the 34th edition in 1803.

[100] *Notes and Queries* 3rd ser. v 9 (20 January 1866) p 69.

[101] Queen Charlotte's interest in German education in London is also shown by her patronage from 1812 of the German and English school associated with St George's

substantially from that of the school at St Mary's German church in the Savoy, whose scholars were taught in German in the morning and in English in the afternoon, and where the subjects of instruction included geography and history.[102]

Although Kollmann wrote most of his published works in English and stayed in London for more than half his life—there is no record that he ever left England—he always regarded himself as German and not as an Englishman.[103] Living in the palace of Hannover's sovereign where the German Chancery had its office, and working at a royal chapel where services and conversations were conducted in German, reinforced Kollmann's connection with the country of his birth.[104] It may even have encouraged him to bring German musical achievements to the attention of the English public.

5. Marriage (1783)

On 26 October 1783, just over a year after his arrival in London, Kollmann and Christina Catherina Ruel were married at St Luke's,

Lutheran Church, Little Alie Street, Whitechapel, which was founded in 1805. See Julius Rieger, 'The British crown and the German Churches in England', *op. cit.*, p 118, and *Jubiläums-Bericht der deutschen und englischen St. Georg's-Schule*, London, 1905, p 21 (copy in Local History and Archives Library, London Borough of Tower Hamlets).

[102] *Grundris einer Schul-Ordnung, bey der Deutschen Evangelischen St. Marien-Gemeinde, in der Savoy, in London*, London, 1782. This booklet was printed by Charles Heydinger, who succeeded Kollmann as porter of the German Chapel in 1784 when Kollmann was promoted to the post of chapel-keeper. Heydinger's association with Kollmann is discussed below.

[103] See, for instance, Kollmann→John Bernard Logier, 26 January 1822.

[104] It is relevant to note that Hannoverian ministers in London had musical interests and presumably discussed them with Kollmann. The posthumous sale of von Alvensleben's effects in July 1795 included 'a clear toned double key'd Harpsichord by [Jacob] Kirkman, a Piano-forte by [Christopher] Ganer ... and ... a quantity of Music' (advertisement, *The Times*, 22 July 1795, p 4). In his capacity as a member of the Hannover *Geheimer Rat* [privy council], von Alvensleben was the second dedicatee mentioned in Forkel's *Allgemeine Geschichte der Musik* (see note 42 above) and presumably owned a copy of it. Kollmann's dedication of a composition to von Alvensleben's successor, Baron von Lenthe, is noted below.

Chelsea. He was twenty-seven and she was thirty-eight. Christina was born in Heilbronn, Germany, where her father, Godfrey Ruel (born Gottfried Rühl),[105] was a senator in the government of that free imperial city.[106] The Ruel family apparently believed that they were related to Martin Luther; however, their descent was not direct.[107]

The first member of Christina's family to migrate to London was her older sister Johanna, who came with her husband, Charles Frederick Hempel, in 1770.[108] Christina, her parents, and her brother James followed two years later, settling in Chelsea, where Godfrey Ruel and Hempel established near Cheyne Row the variously styled firm of Ruel & Hempel, which made crucibles—pots for melting metals—and other pottery.[109]

---

[105] The Rühl family changed the spelling of their surname to 'Ruel' in England. For genealogical information about the family I am greatly indebted to the late Lt Col. William John Godfrey Ruel.

[106] A free city was responsible directly to the Holy Roman Emperor, in contrast to a city like Hannover that was represented to the Emperor via its electoral prince (King George III at the time of the Kollmanns' marriage).

[107] An obituary of Kollmann's son ('The late George Augustus Kollmann', *Dramatic and Musical Review* v 4 no. 158 (5 April 1845) p 174–175) reported that 'the maiden name of his mother was Ruhel [sic]; she was descended, we are informed, from one of the most ancient families of Germany, and reckoned amongst her progenitors the celebrated Reformer, Martin Luther'. Rev. Robert C[harles] Jenkins, grandson of Christina Kollmann's sister Johanna Hempel née Ruel, wrote in his *Some Account of the Family of Wezener or Wiesener, of the Town of Lauban, in the Margraviate of Upper Lusatia*, [London], privately printed (copy at BL 9903.c.27), 1865, p 24–25, that 'the family of Ruehl was originally of Wittenberg, and numbered among its earlier members ... Dr Johann Rül or Rühl, who married a sister of Luther, and accompanied the great reformer in his interviews at Augsburg with Cardinal Cajetan'. I thank Friedel Damm of the Lutheridenvereinigung e. V. for the information that Dr Johannes Rühl actually married a sister of Margarethe Luther, the second wife of Martin Luther's brother Jakob. Rühl subsequently became a friend of Martin Luther and his family: see, for instance, Theodore G. Tappert (ed.), *Luther: Letters of Spiritual Counsel* v 18, London, 1955, p 37–38.

[108] Hempel had been in London earlier, and was naturalised in 1765 by Act of Parliament (5 George III, c. 58). I am grateful to Jacob M. Price for the information that he worked as a tobacco merchant in 1768–1769, but became bankrupt.

[109] Ruel's name appears in the rate books for King's Road in September 1772 (Reginald Blunt, *The wonderful Village*, London, 1918, p 166). Ruel & Hempel received support from the Royal Society for the Encouragement of Arts, Manufactures

It is not known how Kollmann and Christina met, but it seems likely that on 8 October 1782—a month after he was sworn as porter—both were at the German Chapel when Mithoff baptised the Hempels' daughter Johanna Regina. A further Ruel family baptism took place there on 23 February 1783.[110]

On 21 October 1783 Kollmann appeared before Andrew Coltée Ducarel, the librarian at Lambeth Palace and a noted antiquary,[111] seeking a licence to marry Christina at her parish church, St Luke's, Chelsea.[112] They were married there five days later by Rev. Richard Sandilands, in the presence of Charles Frederick Hempel and Christina's brother James Ruel.[113] Kollmann's connection with the Ruel and Hempel families is charted in *Figure 5*.

No letters by or to Christina are known to be extant, but the achievements of her sister Johanna indicate that the Ruel daughters were educated. Johanna was one of the first women to receive an English patent (subsequently numbered 1778),[114] which was granted on 16 October 1790 for a new method of manufacturing basins to filter

---

and Commerce (see Gottfried Ruel and Charles Frederick Hempel→Samuel More, 15/3/1773, Royal Society of Arts letter PR MC/105/10/586, and the Society's *Transactions* v 2, London, 1784, p 109 and v 4, London, 1786, p 117–118). The company's premises adjoined those of Wedgwood & Bentley, and their crucibles were regarded as 'the finest in the country' (Reginald Blunt (ed.), *The Cheyne Book of Chelsea China and Pottery*, London, 1924 (republished 1973), p 80).

[110] On that day Mithoff baptised John Godfrey Ruel, son of Christina's brother James Ruel (whose full name was John James Godfrey Ruel) and his wife Sarah née James.

[111] See Robin Myers, 'Dr Andrew Coltée Ducarel, Lambeth Librarian, Civilian, and Keeper of the Public Records', *The Library* 6th ser. v 21 no. 3 (September 1999) p 199–222.

[112] Kollmann's allegation and bond for his marriage are in the Lambeth Palace Library.

[113] St Luke's, Chelsea, marriage register, London Metropolitan Archives P74/LUK/200 p 84 entry no. 249. Kollmann's name is entered in this register as 'Hollman'.

[114] According to M[oses] N[elson] Baker, *The Quest for Pure Water*, New York, 1948, p 67, Johanna Hempel is the first known manufacturer of household water filters in England and 'the only woman inventor and manufacturer of filters whose name has been found in the annals of filtration'. Deborah Jaffé, *Ingenious Women*, Thrupp, Gloucestershire, 2003, lists (p 169–170) five female recipients of English patents before 1790, but as her chronological list omits Johanna it must be incomplete.

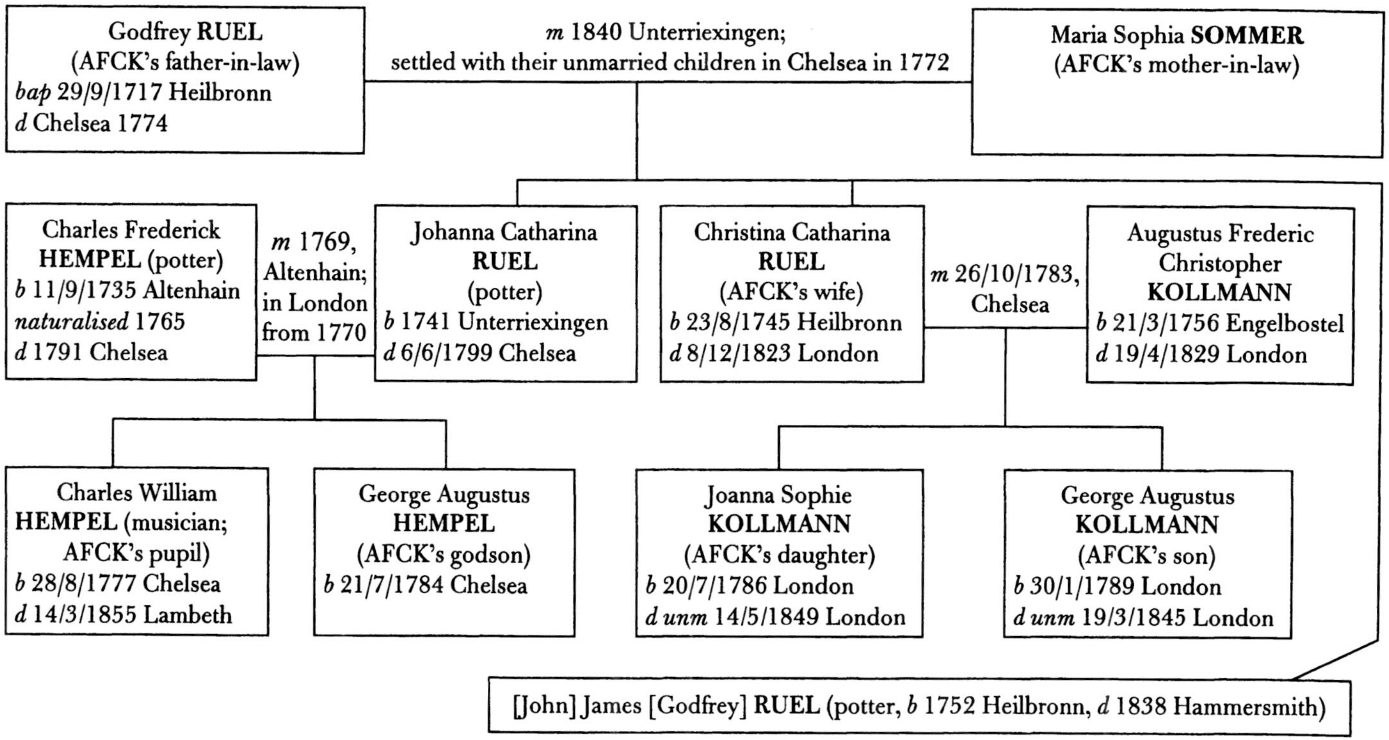

Figure 5. Kollmann, Ruel and Hempel family connections

water and other liquids. After her husband's death in 1791, she took over his business and received Queen Charlotte's patronage.[115] In 1796 Sir Benjamin Thompson, Count Rumford, engaged her to design a fireplace 'upon a principle entirely new'.[116] She was declared a bankrupt in 1797 and the assignees sold the firm's stock at auction.[117] In her will dated 5 June 1799 she named Kollmann and Rev. Weeden Butler joint executors of her estate, and Kollmann was granted administration of it on 7 June.[118] However, on 12 June, he and Butler 'retracted and renounced the probate and the execution' of her will in favour of her eldest son, Charles William Hempel.

As Charles William had shown 'very early indications of musical talent', his parents placed him under Kollmann's tuition, and at the age of eight—in 1785 or 1786—he performed during a German Chapel service.[119] He decided to pursue a musical career after working with his younger brother, John Frederick Hempel, in a pottery partnership.[120]

---

[115] A 24 June 1793 bill from the firm to Philip Yorke, 3rd Earl of Hardwicke (BL Add Ms 35663 f 193) includes the following printed text: 'Bought of Johanna Hempel, Manufacturer of Earthen Ware to Her Majesty, (and Widow of the late C. F. Hempel), At her Manufactory of Queen's Kitchen Ware or Fire-proof Earthen Sauce & Stewpans, Patent Dish, Plate & Coach Warmers, &c. Black Lead Melting Pots, Crucibles, Brown Stone Ware, &c. &c.'; accompanying this bill is Johanna Hempel's 8 July 1773 letter to Yorke. See also Thomas Faulkner, *An Historical and topographical Description of Chelsea and its Environs*, Chelsea, 1829, v 1 p 261.

[116] Rumford, *Essays, political, economical, and philosophical*, London, 3rd ed. v 1, 1797, p 354.

[117] *London Gazette* no. 13982 (21 February 1797) p 181. The auction was advertised in *The Times*, 13 September 1797 p 4, and 22 September 1797 p 4.

[118] The court copy of this will and of the grants of its probate is in the London Metropolitan Archives, Consistory Court of London, June 1799, X19/21. Because she wrote her will on 5 June and it was first administered on 7 June she presumably died on 6 June.

[119] Charles William Hempel→Proprietors of the Biographical Dictionary of Musicians, 2 February 1824, Glasgow University Library ms Euing R.d. 86/99, printed in altered form as Hempel's biography in *A Dictionary of Musicians, from the Earliest Ages to the Present Time...*, London, printed for Sainsbury & Co., 1824.

[120] The partnership was dissolved on 18 July 1800 (*London Gazette* no. 15280, 29 July 1800, p 881). In May 1804 Charles William was elected organist of St Mary's, Truro. See Michael Kassler, 'Hempel, Charles William', *New Grove Dictionary of Music and Musicians*, 2nd ed., London, 2001, v 7 p 365.

At the baptism of their brother George Augustus Hempel in the German Chapel on 20 August 1784, Kollmann was named a godfather.[121] From the time of his marriage to Johanna Hempel's death the Kollmanns and the Hempels clearly were close friends.

Kollmann and Christina had two children: Joanna Sophie, born 20 July 1786, of whom Johanna Hempel was a godmother, and George Augustus, born 30 January 1789, when Christina was forty-three years old. They were baptised at the German Chapel by Mithoff and Schrader respectively,[122] and their achievements are recounted below.

6. First Publication

Aside from his father, the only music instructor that Kollmann is known to have had was Böttner, whose pedagogy was focused upon giving pupils sufficient knowledge and practice to play the organ in church.[123] Kollmann's first publication—*Sechs geistliche Lieder* [*Six Hymns*]—resembles his teacher's music. Four of its six texts were taken, without

---

[121] In 1806 George Augustus Hempel was nominated a cadet on the Bengal establishment of the East India Company (BL Oriental and India Office Collections, cadet register IOR/L/MIL/9/258 and cadet papers IOR/L/MIL/9/115/422–423). Information about his subsequent career has not been found.

[122] Mithoff spelt Joanna's name 'Johanne Sophie' in the German Chapel register entry of her baptism but in surviving correspondence she signed her name 'Joanna S. Kollmann', with no 'h' in her first name. Curiously, Rev. David Walter Morgan, Confessor of His Majesty's Household, entered a notice of Joanna's birth and baptism in a Chapel Royal register labelled 'Register of Baptisms in His Majesty's Household', National Archives PRO 30/19/1 p 142 = f 71r. No entry was made in that register for George Kollmann, and as other entries in that book seem generally to record events at the Chapel Royal the reason for Joanna's entry in this register is not known.

[123] Böttner said this in the preface, dated 10 March 1787, to his first publication, *Choral-Vorspiele* [preludes to hymns], Hannover, 1787 (copy in Bibliothèque Royale de Belgique, Fétis 2091). He added that he had published this collection primarily for his pupils, of whom he had taught more than a hundred of varying skill during his many years at the Schullehrer-Seminarium. Böttner's only other publication was a hymnbook containing melodies with figured basses for use with the Hannover or the Lüneburg *Gesang-Buch* (*Johann Christoph Böttners ... Choralbuch zum Hannöverschen und Lüneburgschen Kirchen-Gesangbuche*, Hannover, 1800; a revised edition, by Heinrich Wegener, appeared posthumously in Hannover in 1817).

acknowledgement, from Christian Fürchtegott Gellert's *Geistliche Oden und Lieder*, first published in Leipzig in 1757.[124]

Sechs geistliche Lieder was printed by Johann Gottlob Immanuel Breitkopf in Leipzig. As Breitkopf did not publish this work, Kollmann presumably retained its copyright and paid him to print it. The year 1784 has been suggested as the work's publication date because the typography is similar to that used by Breitkopf to print C. P. E. Bach's edition of J. S. Bach's *Vierstimmige Choralgesänge* in four volumes between 1784 and 1787, and the vignette on the title-page of *Sechs geistliches Lieder* is the same as that printed in the first of those volumes but differs from the vignettes that Breitkopf used in the later volumes.[125] As Kollmann is described on the title-page as 'Organist an der Königlichen deutschen Hofcapelle zu St. James', the work must have been printed after September 1782, when his duties at the German Chapel began. He subsequently gave this work the opus number 1, so it almost certainly appeared before his opus 2 was published in July 1788.

Kollmann dedicated *Sechs geistliche Lieder* to Queen Charlotte, presumably in appreciation of her gift of the German Chapel organ which had led to his appointment there. It is not clear why he chose to have the work printed in Germany, as the hymns presumably were composed to be sung in London during German Chapel services, and a large sale of copies in Leipzig, where Kollmann was unknown, hardly could be expected, especially as established German composers had previously set Gellert's hymns to music.[126] The only copy of the work known to be extant in England is at the British Library, which acquired it by donation on 12 February 1949 and has no record of its donor.[127]

---

[124] The source of the first two texts set by Kollmann has not been determined.

[125] I am very grateful to Hans-Joachim Schulze for this dating reason and for the information that Breitkopf does not appear to have advertised *Sechs geistliche Lieder* in contemporary Leipzig newspapers.

[126] In particular, by Carl Philipp Emmanuel Bach, whose *Herrn Professor Gellerts Geistliche Oden und Lieder mit Melodien* was first published in Berlin in 1758. Curiously, the fifth edition of this work was published by Breitkopf in Leipzig in 1784, the year when it has been suggested Breitkopf printed Kollmann's setting.

[127] I thank Serena Kelly for this information.

Charles Heydinger, who succeeded Kollmann as porter of the German Chapel in February 1784 and thereafter saw him frequently, perhaps even daily, is a plausible link between Kollmann and Breitkopf. Between 1766 and 1796 Heydinger printed and sold German-language books in London, and for some time was the only person doing this.[128] He attended the Leipzig book fairs from 1770 to 1773[129] and probably met Breitkopf there, who then printed books as well as music. A further link between Heydinger and the Kollmanns occurred at a German Chapel baptism on 28 July 1788, when Heydinger was named godfather and Christina Kollmann godmother of William Ward.[130]

Only one review of *Sechs geistliche Lieder* is known. It appeared in 1792, eight years after the work's proposed publication date, in the *Allgemeine deutsche Bibliothek* under the signature 'Wk.', a pseudonym of the music theorist and composer Daniel Gottlob Türk, director of music in the University of Halle.[131] Türk found the work worthy of praise,[132] but criticised Kollmann's decision to present each hymn twice (first in four parts, secondly as a soprano part with figured bass) and said that particular passages were awkward, hard for congregations to sing, or too reminiscent of well known church melodies.

---

[128] According to Graham Jefcoate, 'German printing and bookselling in eighteenth-century London', *Archiv für Geschichte des Buchwesens* v 57 (2003) p 147–248 at p 211–228 *passim*. This article includes a bibliography of German-language books printed in London at that time. Heydinger's last known German-language publication was a sermon by Georg Joachim Heironymus Röhrs, who became second chaplain of the German Chapel in London in 1788, following Mithoff's return to Germany.

[129] See Graham Jefcoate, 'Heydinger, Carl', *Oxford Dictionary of National Biography*, Oxford, 2004, v 26 p 945–946; and *ibid.*, 'Charles Heydinger: a German bookseller in eighteenth-century London, 1766–1784', in Werner Huber (ed.), *The Corvey Library and Anglo-German Cultural Exchanges, 1770–1837*, Munich, 2004, p 35–53. I thank Graham Jefcoate for verifying that Heydinger's signature for a payment on 2 December 1792 from the Vaudois Churches list (see note 88 above) matches that in Heydinger→Albrecht von Haller, 2 March 1773 (Bürgerbibliothek Bern, N Haller).

[130] William's parents were Charles Ward of the sixth regiment of dragoon guards and his wife Eleonora. It is not known how the Kollmanns met the Wards nor what subsequent contact they had with them.

[131] G[ustav] Parthey, *Die Mitarbeiter an Friedrich Nicolai's Allgemeiner deutscher Bibliothek nach ihren Namen und Zeichen...*, Berlin, 1842, p 28–29 and p 71.

[132] 'Uebrigens machen diese Choräle dem Verfasser alle Ehre.'

7. Kollmann and the New Musical Fund

In May and June 1784, under the patronage of King George III, five musical performances in commemoration of Handel were held at Westminster Abbey and the Pantheon theatre, Oxford Street. Kollmann attended some of these concerts.[133] The event yielded £12736/12/–, of which nearly half was disbursed to the Fund for the Support of Decayed Musicians and their Families. This charity was soon afterwards given royal 'patronage and protection' and renamed the Royal Society of Musicians.[134]

There was some dissatisfaction with that Society. From 1742, it had required members to live in London for 'part of the year',[135] thereby, as Edward Miller deplored in a pamphlet, excluding musicians who resided entirely in the country.[136] The music seller George Smart was grieved because the Society rejected his membership application, apparently because he had differences with some of its directors.[137] Smart read Miller's pamphlet and they, with others, decided to start the New Musical Fund, which was formally established on 16 April 1786. The Royal Society of Musicians responded by expelling any member who joined the new Fund and by requiring prospective members to declare that they did not belong to it.[138]

---

[133] See *QMR p 16–17.*

[134] Charles Burney, *An Account of the Musical Performances in Westminster-Abbey, and the Pantheon ... in commemoration of Handel*, London, 1785, p 113 and p 122–123. See also Pippa Drummond, 'The Royal Society of Musicians in the eighteenth Century', in Betty Matthews (ed.), *The Royal Society of Musicians of Great Britain, List of Members 1738–1984*, London, 1985, p 191–216.

[135] Drummond, p 214. The charity had been established in 1738.

[136] Edward Miller, *Letters in behalf of Professors of Music, residing in the Country...*, London, 1784 (copy in Rowe Music Library, King's College, Cambridge, shelfmark Mn. 14.23).

[137] According to [Charles Dibdin], *The Musical Tour of Mr Dibdin...*, Sheffield, 1788, p 167–168, the Society resolved to exclude Smart forever by interpreting the statement in his application that he had a wife and four children as an attempt to gain membership 'by surreptitious means' because he had failed to record that his wife was then pregnant.

[138] Drummond, p 214.

Although documentation of the early years of the New Musical Fund has not been preserved, Kollmann apparently was a foundation member. The programme of the 6 March 1794 benefit concert for the Fund lists him as a member of its Court of Assistants,[139] and Article IV of the Fund's rules specified 'that the members of the committees for the years 1786, 1787, and 1788, shall be constituted a Court of Assistants for Life'.[140]

Kollmann served the New Musical Fund for the rest of his life. Together with other members including Smart and Miller, he signed the Fund's 30 April 1789 address to George III, expressing joy at the king's recovery from a dangerous indisposition.[141] In 1805 he was on the Fund's management committee and during the 1820s he was a trustee, sharing with other trustees the responsibility for ensuring that the charity's money was properly invested. Kollmann's commitment was time-consuming: Article XVI of the rules required the Court of Assistants to meet on the third Sunday of every month, and other duties included visiting sick members. However, it brought him into contact with many leading musicians. In the 20 April 1795 benefit concert for the Fund a symphony by Haydn was conducted by the composer,[142] and Kollmann almost certainly met him then.[143] As noted below,

---

[139] This is the earliest extant programme. Sir George Smart, the founder's son, who conducted the Fund's benefit concerts from 1815, collected the programmes of 1794, 1805 and 1815 to 1841 (the final concert). This collection is now at BL c.61.g.20.

[140] The rules were revised several times. A copy of the 1807 *Articles of the New Musical Fund* is in the John Rylands University Library of Manchester, shelfmark Deansgate Reference/15525.3. The regulations current in 1821, which list Kollmann as a trustee, are given in 'The New Musical Fund', *Quarterly Musical Magazine and Review* v 3 no. 11 (1821) p 328–335.

[141] This address is in the National Archives, HO 55/20/29. For detailed discussion of George's illness of 1788–1789 see Ida Macalpine and Richard Hunter, *George III and the Mad-Business*, London, 1969, p 1–107.

[142] Advertised in *The Times*, 14 April 1795 p 1. See also H. C. Robbins Landon, *Haydn in England 1791–1795*, London, 1976, p 303–304.

[143] Although no documentation of their meeting has been found, Kollmann's nephew and pupil Charles William Hempel, after returning from the continent in 1794, had 'the honor of being introduced to the immortal Haydn, whose works with those of Mozart I have always regarded as models of perfection' (Charles William Hempel→ Proprietors of the New Biographical Dictionary of Musicians, 2/2/1824, Glasgow

Kollmann's children made their débuts at Fund concerts, and the friendship of the Kollmann and Kendrick families arose because Joseph Kendrick also was a founder of the Fund, a member of its Court of Assistants for Life and, at least from 1825, a trustee.[144]

When Kollmann published his opus 2, 'Four Sonatas', on 5 July 1788, he extended his association with George Smart by selecting the latter's 'music warehouse' as the principal seller of this work.[145] As shown by entries at Stationers' Hall that identify him as proprietor of particular works and by the 'control signature' or monogram that he wrote in ink on the title-pages of those works, Kollmann retained the copyright of most of his publications. He therefore paid the 'up front' costs of engraving, printing and advertising these publications and received the income from their sale, less a commission to booksellers or music sellers like Smart for selling copies at their shops.

Two engravers produced the plates from which 'Four Sonatas' was printed. The title-page plate, engraved by Samuel John Neele, features a vignette that includes the first section of a minuet by Kollmann. He seems to have been particularly proud of this minuet, as he republished it in 1796 in *An Essay on Musical Harmony* and again, with musical variations, on plates 4–5 of *The Quarterly Musical Register*. Curiously, it has no thematic connection with the opus 2 sonatas.

The minuet, entitled 'Menuetto cancrino diaton: chrom: enharm:', appears to have been Kollmann's first 'theoretico-practical' work—a category he defined in his autobiography as 'compositions with theoretical explanations'. 'Cancrino' signifies that the second (and last) section of the minuet is obtained by playing the first section

---

University Library ms Euing R.d. 86/99, published with alterations and deletions in *A Dictionary of Musicians*, London, printed for Sainsbury & Co., 1824, v 1 p 359–360). Both Kollmann and Hempel subscribed to Haydn's *The Creation*, which appeared in March 1800 (see H. C. Robbins Landon, *Haydn: The Years of 'The Creation' 1796–1800*, London, 1977, p 626–627).

[144] Kendrick's death notice (*The Gentleman's Magazine* n.s. v 1 (January 1834) p 116) called him 'one of the founders of the New Musical Fund'.

[145] The work was entered at Stationers' Hall on this day, which can be taken to be its publication date. See Michael Kassler (ed.), *Music Entries at Stationers' Hall, 1710–1818*, Aldershot, 2004, p xxi and p 111.

backwards. As it is not generally true that a composition that makes musical sense also will make sense when played backwards, Kollmann presumably put this minuet on his title-page to show that he had the knowledge to compose a piece that satisfies the rules of music in both forward and reverse directions. His endeavours to understand the rules of music and to make them explicit characterise his later theoretical accomplishments.

'Four Sonatas', whose music plates were engraved by J. [B.] Scherer, was reviewed very favourably in the August 1788 *Analytical Review*.[146] The reviewer's name was not stated, but Kollmann identified him in *The Quarterly Musical Register* as Thomas Busby.[147] Notwithstanding some criticism, Busby found 'frequent and conspicuous traits of genius' in the sonatas and was happy 'to praise and recommend them, as both fanciful and scientific, pleasing and improving'. However, the music today does not stand out from the common practice of its time, and Kollmann subsequently acknowledged that his theoretical works had greater importance than his compositions.

That someone besides a music engraver was engaged to produce the plates of 'Four Sonatas' suggests that Kollmann desired, and had the money to commission, a title-page that would attract attention.

8. Collaboration with Johann Wilhelm Häßler (1791–1792)

The composer, pianist and organist Johann Wilhelm Häßler lived in London from about October 1790 to June 1792[148] and came to know Kollmann during this time. Häßler was born at Erfurt in 1747 and

---

[146] v 1 p 486.

[147] *QMR p 5.*

[148] See Helga Brück, *Johann Wilhelm und Sophia Häßler, Eine Erfurter Musikerfamilie*, Erfurt, 2003, p 59–61. This book gives much information about Häßler's activities in Germany and Russia but has few details about his London experiences. Its list on p 113–114 of his compositions published there during his stay is incomplete and inaccurate.

studied music at an early age with his uncle Johann Christian Kittel, who had been a pupil of J. S. Bach from 1748 to 1750.[149] Because of this, Häßler referred to himself in his October 1786 autobiography as Bach's musical grandson ['musikalischer Enkel']. In that document he recorded meeting Bach's son Carl Philipp Emanuel Bach in Hamburg in 1771, to whom he played one of the '48'. Häßler also met Johann Nicolaus Forkel in Göttingen that year—a musical scholar, notably of Bach, with whom Kollmann later would have considerable correspondence.[150]

Häßler's host in London was William Kerr, Earl of Ancram and later 6th Marquess of Lothian in the Scottish peerage,[151] who had lodged with Häßler and his wife in Erfurt for about three months in 1787 and was a godfather to their fifth child.[152] The earl had invited Häßler to London and helped him to find pupils there. While in London Häßler performed on the organ at St Mary's German church in the Savoy and on the piano forte before King George III and Queen Charlotte, and saw one of his compositions conducted by Haydn.[153]

---

[149] *ibid.*, p 12–15.

[150] Häßler, 'Lebenslauf', in his 'Sechs leichte Sonaten fürs Clavier oder Piano-Forte', part two, Erfurt, 1787, p i–xii at p v (facsimile reprint in Willi Kahl (ed.), *Selbstbiographien deutscher Musiker des XVIII. Jahrhunderts*, Cologne, 1948, p 51–74 at p 59–60; English translation in Christopher Hogwood, '"The inconstant and original Johann Wilhelm Hässler"—his 1786 autobiography and a thematic catalogue of his keyboard works to 1790' in Bernard Brauchli *et al.* (eds), *De Clavicordio III; Proceedings of the III International Clavichord Symposium, Magnano ... 1997*, Magnano, Italy, 1998, p 151–220 at p 162–179). Häßler's 1771 meetings with Forkel and C. P. E. Bach are described on p 167 of Hogwood's translation.

[151] On the *c*1792 publication of his composition *Night Thoughts on a Church Yard* Häßler's address is given as 13 Lower Brook Street, Grosvenor Square. Correspondence of the Earl of Ancram (National Archives of Scotland, GD40/9/198 bundle 1) shows that this was the address of his London residence then.

[152] Brück, p 44–54. Carl Wilhelm Häßler was born on 15 January 1778 (*ibid.*, p 49–50). In the manuscript journal of his tour (National Archives of Scotland GD40/15/60/3), Lord Ancram wrote, regarding his time in Erfurt, 'I boarded at Häßler's, the famous musician, but gave up so much of my time to German that I had little opportunity to study music'. I thank Gemma Tougher for transcribing this entry.

[153] Brück, p 59–61; Hans-Joachim Schulze (ed.), *Dokumente zum Nachwirken Johann Sebastian Bachs 1750–1800, Bach-Dokumente* v 3, Kassel, 1972, p 506–507; Landon, *Haydn in England 1791–1795*, p 79, 116–117, 131, 147, 163 and 170.

The evidence of Häßler's collaboration with Kollmann is limited and curious. During Häßler's stay in London more than ten of his compositions were published by Robert Wornum.[154] Three were songs that Häßler composed to English texts: 'Going into the country', 'The tender mother' and 'Sophy'. In each of these the name 'Kollmann', enclosed in parentheses, was engraved below the verse texts or was added on copies in ink, implying that Kollmann had written or translated these verses for Häßler.[155]

A further link between Häßler and Kollmann can be discerned from the circumstance that Wornum was their principal publisher during Häßler's stay in London and gave publicity to each of them in publications of works by the other. The title-page of Kollmann's 'Six Sonatinas for the Piano Forte', opus 4, advertised, as just published, three compositions by Häßler. The title-page of Häßler's song 'To Myra'[156] announced, as just published, 'A Scotch Song. Compos'd by A. F. Kollmann'—almost certainly his 'Charming Sally. A Scotch song written by a lady'. His choice of a Scottish text and his dedications of two works published at this time—*An Introduction to the Art of Preluding*, opus 3, to Miss Craufurd, whose surname looks Scottish, and opus 4 to the twelve-year-old Flora Mure-Campbell, Countess of

[154] Wornum frequently asserted on title-pages that a work was entered at Stationers' Hall, but in fact he rarely entered his publications. Between 1790 and 1792 he made no entries. Because deposit libraries received free copies from Stationers' Hall only of works that were entered there, no copies of some of his publications are known to be extant. See Kassler, *Music Entries at Stationers' Hall*, *op. cit.*, p xvii–xviii.

[155] These songs were first published in a collection of Häßler's music entitled *Select Pieces for the Harpsichord or Piano-Forte, intermixed with Songs* and were re-published from the same plates in a collection entitled *Six Songs, for the Harpsichord or Piano-Forte.* At least two impressions of the first collection were made, as the name 'Kollmann' is absent under the verses of 'Going into the country' in the copy at Sveriges Radio Musikbiblioteket, Stockholm but present on copies at Cambridge University Library MRA340.75.16 and in a private UK collection. The name 'Kollmann' has not been engraved in any copy of 'Sophy' seen, but has been handwritten in ink in copies in Cambridge University Library and a private UK collection. Both these songs also appear to have been published separately (see Wornum, *A Catalogue of Music...*, London, wmk 1802, copy at BL 7896.h.40.(19)).

[156] Wornum issued this song separately and also as one of Häßler's *Six Songs, for the Harpsichord or Piano-Forte.* The words were by George Granville, 1st Baron Lansdowne.

Loudoun, who was Scottish—perhaps reflect a connection between Kollmann and the Earl of Ancram.[157]

It is conceivable that Kollmann had heard of J. S. Bach before coming to London, perhaps from his teacher Böttner, whom Kollmann later characterised as 'an able organist in J. S. Bach's style'.[158] However, no evidence of this has been found. A claim that Kollmann's uncle, Carl Christoph Hachmeister Sr, who died in 1777, owned a Bach manuscript can be disregarded, as the ownership signature 'C C Hachmeister' on that manuscript almost certainly is that of his son, Carl Christoph Hachmeister Jr, who might have acquired it after Kollmann had arrived in London.[159]

Regardless of any knowledge that Kollmann may have had of Bach before 1790, it seems probable that Häßler mentioned his 'musical grandfather' to Kollmann and played some of Bach's music to him in London, including several of the '48'. Contact with Häßler thus seems likely to have aroused Kollmann's interest in Bach, and to have

---

157 Charles Edward Horn later described the countess as 'a very delightful musician and singer'. See Michael Kassler (ed.), *Charles Edward Horn's Memoirs of his Father and Himself*, Aldershot and London, 2003, p 35–36.

158 Kollmann's autobiography. Bach's style of organ performance is described by Kollmann in *QMR p 33–35*. His statement that Böttner played in Bach's style does not imply that Böttner had heard Bach play or knew his style. Schulze, *op. cit.*, reports no mention of J. S. Bach in Hannover publications between 1752 and 1800.

159 This claim was made in Hans-Joachim Schulze, 'Die Bach-Überlieferung', *Beiträge zur Musikwissenschaft* v 17 no. 1 (1975) p 45–57 at p 55; *ibid.*, *Studien zur Bach-Überlieferung im 18. Jahrhundert*, Leipzig and Dresden, 1984, p 26; Ludwig Finscher, 'Bach in the eighteenth century', in Don O. Franklin (ed.), *Bach Studies*, Cambridge, 1989, p 281–296 at p 288; and in the Kritischer Bericht by Karl Heller and Hans-Joachim Schulze for this work (BWV 1061a) in the *Neue Bach Ausgabe* (Kassel, 1990, p 75). However, the ownership signature 'C C Hachmeister' on the manuscript—a cembalo part in the handwriting of both Bach and his wife Anna Magdalena Bach, now Staatsbibliothek zu Berlin Mus. ms. Bach St. 139, fascicle 1—is virtually identical to the ownership signature 'C C Hachmeister' on a copy of Johann Nicolas Forkel's *Vier und zwanzig Veränderungen fürs Clavichord oder Fortepiano auf das englische Volkslied: God save the King*, Göttingen, 1791, now British Library e.120.a.(4), which was published fourteen years after Hachmeister Sr's death. Because these signatures are so similar it seems plausible that Hachmeister Jr signed his name on both copies in the 1790s.

led him to order a manuscript copy of the '48' from Germany.[160] The '48' was not printed during Bach's lifetime, and in 1799 Kollmann would be first in the world to publish an entire prelude and fugue from it in his *An Essay on Practical Musical Composition*.

9. *An Introduction to the Art of Preluding* (1792)

An Introduction to the Art of Preluding and Extemporizing, a 20-page work with many music examples, was Kollmann's first book. He wrote it for 'players of different capacities' who were studying music with or without a master's assistance.

The book begins with a reference to the music/language analogy which influenced Kollmann's writings to the end of his career:

> The science of music very much resembles a Language, and a Person who can only play by Notes or Memory but not out of his own Fancy or Invention may be compared to one who can read a Language and repeat some Parts of it, but who cannot converse in it. One principal Object therefore in the Study of Music should be to obtain the Capacity of expressing voluntary Thoughts, either before and between other Pieces of regular Composition or without Regard to any musical Piece.[161]

Although Kollmann understood that natural languages such as German and English were distinct systems, governed by separate sets of rules, he seems to have thought that all musical compositions belonged to a single system—let us call it a 'musical language'—which could be explained by one set of rules, although compositions within that system could express particular national characteristics or stylistic features. At

---

[160] Yo Tomita suggested ('The dawn of the English Bach awakening manifested in sources of the "48"', *EBA* p 35-167 at p 116-121) that the manuscript of part 2 of the '48' (BWV 870-893) copied in Germany for Kollmann—now St Andrews University Library, Scotland, ms M24.B2.—was ordered from the Breitkopf firm in the 1790s. No manuscript of part 1 of the '48' (BWV 846-869) is extant that Kollmann is known to have owned.

[161] *An Introduction to the Art of Preluding*, p 2. Kollmann's English improved in later years, when he probably would have written 'music very much resembles a language' instead of 'the science of music very much resembles a language'.

this time very little was known in Europe about contemporary non-European music or about the music of ancient cultures, and Kollmann did not anticipate that someone such as Arnold Schoenberg would later create a new musical language and compose music in it.

It is remarkable that a basic tenet of Kollmann's subsequent theoretical writings—that 'all musical harmony arises from two chords', the triad and chord of the seventh[162]—does not appear in *An Introduction to the Art of Preluding*, which has a lesson on common chords (i.e., triads) but not on chords of the seventh. It seems plausible that when he wrote this book he had not yet read or appreciated the treatises of Johann Philipp Kirnberger, who held this tenet and whose concepts greatly affected Kollmann's later work.

An Introduction included six preludes that Kollmann composed to be played before particular compositions by Charles Burney, Muzio Clementi, Häßler, Haydn, Charles Frederick Horn and Nicolas-Joseph Hüllmandel.[163] Horn had come to London from Germany in 1782, the same year as Kollmann, and seven years later became music master to Queen Charlotte and the royal princesses.[164] As Kollmann and Horn both were German musicians in contact with the royal family, it seems likely that they had met by the early 1790s, although no documentation of their meeting has been found. Horn had subscribed for ten copies of the third part of Häßler's 'Sechs leichte Sonaten', which was published in Erfurt in 1788 and dedicated to Lord Ancram, and presumably met Häßler and some of his acquaintances in London.[165]

About this time Kollmann composed some military and patriotic music. 'A characteristic march' was performed by the Third Regiment

---

[162] *EMH*, p 22–24.

[163] Kollmann also included a postlude that he composed to one of his opus 2 sonatas.

[164] A chronology of Horn's activities is given in Michael Kassler, *Charles Edward Horn's Memoirs...*, *op. cit.*, p 111–119.

[165] A copy with the subscription list is in the British Library, shelfmark 437.a. Horn also subscribed to Häßler's 'Acht und vierzig kleine Orgelstücke' (Leipzig, 1789) and to the fourth part of his 'Sechs leichte Sonaten' (Erfurt, 1790). It seems likely that Horn and Häßler were in correspondence as early as 1787, as a short biography of Horn was published in the *Erfurtische Gelehrte Zeitung* on 19 July 1787, p 264. I am grateful to Helga Brück for information about this biography.

of Foot Guards, known as the Scots Guards, who also used the sixth of his *c*1792 sonatinas as a signal for their regiment to assemble. 'A new march composed for the Corps of Light Horse Volunteers of the Cities of London and Westminster', published in June 1795, was played by a military band 'before their Majesties at Windsor'.[166] The latter march was 'printed and sold' by Joseph Dale, who shortly afterwards helped Kollmann to bring out his first major theoretical work, *An Essay on Musical Harmony*, by buying half of the work's copyright.[167] Dale's investment presumably covered at least some of the up-front costs of typesetting and printing its 146 folio pages of text, and engraving and printing the forty plates of music examples appended to the text.[168]

10. *An Essay on Musical Harmony* (1796)

An Essay on Musical Harmony appeared in January 1796, and was dedicated to Charles Burney 'as a sincere mark of real esteem'. It is not known when or how Kollmann and Burney became acquainted—perhaps they met at a Handel Commemoration concert or through connections with the royal family.[169] The posthumous 1814 sale catalogue of Burney's library includes many of Kollmann's works, the earliest being *An Introduction to the Art of Preluding*.[170] Although only

---

[166] 'A new march', p 2.

[167] See Kassler, *Music Entries at Stationers' Hall, 1710–1818*, *op. cit.*, p 286. Most extant copies of *An Essay on Musical Harmony* have Kollmann's control signature on the title-page, but the copy in the University of Sydney library instead bears the control signature 'JD 07' written in ink, presumably indicating that this copy was the seventh in Joseph Dale's allocation of copies to sell. I am grateful to Claire Mera-Nelson for information about Dale's handwriting.

[168] The title-page of *An Essay on Musical Harmony* states that the work was 'printed and sold by' Dale, but as he was not a letterpress printer he must have contracted out at least this part of the *Essay*'s production.

[169] King George III and Queen Charlotte both knew Burney, whose daughter Frances was in service to the queen as second keeper of the robes from July 1786 to July 1791 (see Joyce Hemlow, *The History of Fanny Burney*, Oxford, 1958, p 196–222).

[170] *A Catalogue of the valuable and very fine Collection of Music, printed and ms., of the late Charles Burney, Mus.D. F. R. S. ... which will be sold at auction by Mr [John]*

three letters between the two have survived, it is clear that they stayed in contact up to the last years of Burney's life.[171]

Kollmann's goal as a theorist was to determine 'the rules by which great composers have been enabled to produce' music.[172] His concern, as noted above, was limited to music composed in the single 'musical language' that governed western European music from before Bach to beyond Beethoven: the musical language that, after Kollmann's lifetime, became known as 'tonality'. Kollmann's accomplishments are significant because the theory he ultimately developed explains the structure of tonality more fully than the concepts of his predecessors. *An Essay on Musical Harmony* was a step towards that development but was superseded in 1806 by the first edition of his *New Theory*.

In the Introduction to *An Essay on Musical Harmony* Kollmann cited three objections previously made to the quest to find rules that account for musical compositions: that rules cannot be given (because 'music depends on fancy only, and ... no person can be taught what to fancy'), that rules need not be given (because the greatest musical works have been produced 'before the rules were known on which they depend'), and that rules ought not to be given (because 'rules are a confinement to genius; and a temptation to persons without genius, to compose'). He then refuted each of these objections.

Even in an extemporaneously improvised 'free fancy', he said, some constraints are required, and these constraints can be expressed as rules.[173] For instance, to compose a fantasia it is necessary to establish a key and mode at the composition's beginning and also at its end, and a fantasia also must have some 'rhythmical order'.[174] He

---

White, London, 1814, copy at British Library S.C. 1076(1) (facsimile reproduction, Amsterdam, 1973), lot 898.

[171] For instance, Kollmann wrote in his 1799 *Essay on Practical Musical Composition* that 'I have been very happy to learn from Dr Burney, that he has collected them [dance tunes and national songs] from all parts of the world' (p 103). Burney subscribed to this *Essay*.

[172] *EMH*, p xv.

[173] *ibid.*, p 121.

[174] As an authority for this rule Kollmann referred his readers to Carl Philipp Emanuel Bach, *Versuch über die wahre Art das Clavier zu spielen, Zweyter Theil*, Berlin, 1762.

agreed 'that the compleatest and most sublime fugues and canons were composed before Marpurg published his treatise on fugues; and that the rules of a fundamental bass were observed by all good composers before Rameau explained them'.[175] However, although a composer of 'a regular piece' may have been 'not disposed to publish the plan he pursued', he must have formed, before he began writing, 'some theory of what he intended to write', and have prescribed to himself 'some rules by which the purposes of his theory might be answered'.[176]

Kollmann countered the third objection by remarking that a composer who is 'so intimately acquainted with every rule, that he can observe it almost habitually' will not be confined by these rules. Although 'a person without genius may learn the rules of composition, and consequently be tempted to compose, without producing anything fine', the fault in that case, he suggested, is due to the person and not to the rules.[177]

In *An Essay on Musical Harmony* and his subsequent theoretical works, Kollmann adopted the principle that

> all musical harmony arises from *two chords*, called the *fundamental concord* [or triad] and the *fundamental discord* [or chord of the seventh]; and from the different uses that can be made of them.... And all musical harmony, even the most complicated, is only regular, if it is reducible to the said *two chords*; the fundamental note of which is called the *fundamental bass*.
>
> These two chords and their inversions therefore, may be called *essential* chords, in distinction from those which I shall call *accidental* ones.[178]

He acknowledged that this principle was due to Johann Philipp Kirnberger, noting that chords hitherto

> have been explained after two different systems of harmony, viz: that of *Kirnberger*, which I have followed in the present Essay, and which therefore I

---

[175] Friedrich Wilhelm Marpurg, *Abhandlung von der Fuge...*, Berlin, 1753–1754 (on *QMR p 90* Kollmann described this as 'the most profound, and most masterly work of its kind, in the German language'); Jean-Philippe Rameau, *Traité de l'Harmonie...*, Paris, 1722.

[176] *EMH*, p xvii.

[177] *ibid.*, p xviii.

[178] *ibid.*, p 22.

may be allowed to call *my* system; and that of *Rameau*, which has been followed by *Marpurg*, and universally admired, till *Kirnberger's* system came to be known.[179]

Kollmann took his statement of this principle from a short treatise published under Kirnberger's name in Berlin and Königsberg in 1773 and entitled *Die wahren Grundsätze zum Gebrauch der Harmonie, darinn deutlich gezeiget wird, wie alle möglichen Accorde aus dem Dreyklang und dem wesentlichen Septimenaccord ... herzuleiten und zu erklären sind, als ein Zusatz zu der Kunst des reinen Satzes in der Musik, von Johann Philipp Kirnberger* [The true axioms for using harmony, in which it will be clearly shown how all possible chords can be derived from and explained by the triad and the essential chord of the seventh, as an adjunct to the *Kunst des reinen Satzes in der Musik*, by Johann Philipp Kirnberger].[180] *Die wahren Grundsätze* starts by rephrasing a portion of its title:

> Die ganze Harmonie besteht nur aus zween Grundaccorden, die der Ursprung aller andern Accorde sind, und auf denen sich alles, was nach dem reinen Satz gesetzt ist, zuruckführen läßt.... [All harmony comes only from two fundamental chords, which are the source of all other chords, and to which all regularly composed music can be reduced....][181]

'Der reine Satz' was an important concept for Kirnberger. He defined it as follows in a dictionary article that he wrote on 'Baß (musik)':

> Wenn der Tonsetzer die Folge der Baßtöne gut gewählt, und die Töne der obern Stimmen regelmäßig daraus hergeleitet hat, so ist sein Satz rein. [If a composer chooses a good succession of bass notes, from which the notes in

---

[179] *ibid.*, p 45.

[180] The first volume of Kirnberger's major work *Die Kunst des reinen Satzes in der Musik* had been published in Berlin in 1771. *Die wahren Grundsätze* did not say, and Kollmann clearly did not know, that it was written not by Kirnberger but by his former pupil, Johann Abraham Peter Schulz. See David Beach, 'Introduction to the translation' [of *Die wahren Grundsätze*], *Journal of Music Theory* v 23 no. 2 (fall 1979) p 163–166. Beach notes (p 164) that the treatise nevertheless gives 'a concise and accurate summary' of Kirnberger's harmonic theory.

[181] *Die wahren Grundsätze*, p [5].

the upper parts can be derived according to the rules, then his composition is regular.][182]

Kollmann's translation of 'der reine Satz' as 'regular musical composition' is superior to the recent translation 'strict musical composition',[183] because the latter is the usual English rendering of 'der strenge Satz', a different concept exemplified by student counterpoint exercises. A free fancy can be an instance of *der reine Satz* but not of *der strenge Satz*. Regularity remained an important concept for Kollmann: in his *New Theory*, a composition is deemed regular—or, as one might say today, is a grammatical utterance in the musical language 'tonality'—if it can be reduced by specified processes to a permissible sequence of fundamental bass notes.

The contents of *An Essay on Musical Harmony* are given in *The Quarterly Musical Register* on pages 41–43. Kollmann noted in that periodical that three of the *Essay*'s several reviews are 'ascribed' to Burney.[184] His authorship of the one in *The Monthly Review*—where he said that the *Essay* was 'a work of uncommon merit, and much more complete than any [other] treatise on harmony in our language'[185]—is confirmed by an annotation made by Ralph Griffiths, the journal's editor, in his copy.[186]

The review of Kollmann's *Essay* by Johann Nicolaus Forkel in the July 1798 *Göttingische Anzeigen von gelehrten Sachen* is the earliest

---

[182] Johann Georg Sulzer (ed.), *Allgemeine Theorie der schönen Künste*, part 1, Leipzig, 1771, p 125. As Kollmann noted (*QMR p 83*), 'the musical articles of the first part [of this dictionary] are known to have been written by Kirnberger'.

[183] By David W. Beach and Jurgen Thym in their translation of *Die Wahren Grundsätze* (*Journal of Music Theory* v 23 no. 2 (fall 1979) p 167–225) and in their partial translation of *Die Kunst des Reinen Satzes in der Musik* (*The Art of Strict Musical Composition*, New Haven, Connecticut, 1982). By translating both 'rein' and 'streng' as 'strict' they eliminated the distinction that Kirnberger had made by using two non-synonymous words.

[184] *QMR p 5.*

[185] *Monthly Review* n.s. v 21 (September 1796) p 27–30 at p 30.

[186] See Benjamin Christie Nangle, *The Monthly Review Second Series 1790–1815, Indexes of Contributors and Articles*, Oxford, 1955, p 151, and the note to *QMR p 4–6* on page 197 below.

known document connecting Kollmann and Forkel.[187] Forkel said that the *Essay* deserved to be reviewed in Germany

> because the author is a countryman of ours who knows very well the principal developments that Germans have made in the musical sciences and, to their honour, seeks to make these developments known abroad; and secondly, because his book contains, beyond fundamental lessons in essential harmonic theory, many remarks of an uncommonly finer sort than one ordinarily is accustomed to find in such instruction books.[188]

At the start of the *Essay* Kollmann asserted that 'the science of music' can be divided into '*just harmony*' and '*practical composition*'. He compared the first division 'to the *grammatical*' part and the second 'to the *practical* part of a language'.[189] In his review, Forkel commented that practical composition could be likened to rhetoric in language,[190] and Kollmann henceforth adopted that term, for instance, in the preface to *A New Theory*.

Forkel's review mentioned two other works by Kollmann: his 1792 *An Introduction to the Art of Preluding* and *The First Beginning on the Piano-Forte*, op. 5. The latter work was entered at Stationers' Hall on 10 December 1796, although Forkel mistakenly wrote that it

---

[187] *Göttingische Anzeigen von gelehrten Sachen* no. 115 (21 July 1798) p 1137–1142. This review was published anonymously, but a note in the marked copy of this journal in the Niedersächsische Staats- und Universitätsbibliothek, Göttingen, confirm's Forkel's authorship. I thank Dr Haenel of that library for this information.

[188] 'weil der Verfasser unser Landsmann ist, der die vorzügliche Fortschritte, welche die Deutschen in den musikalischen Wissenschaften gemacht haben, sehr gut kennt, und sie zur Ehre derselben auch im Auslande bekannt zu machen sucht; und zweytens, weil sein Werk ausser dem gründlichen Unterricht in eigentlichen Theorie der Harmonie, noch manche Bemerkung von ungleich feinerer Art enthält, als man sie gewöhnlich in solchen Lehrbüchen zu finden pflegt', *ibid.*, p 1137–1138.

[189] *EMH*, p xv.

[190] 'und die practische Composition als die Rhetorik ... angesehen werden kann', [Forkel], *op. cit.*, p 1138. Forkel outlined his concept of musical rhetoric in the introduction ['Einleitung'] to the first volume of his *Allgemeine Geschichte der Musik*, Leipzig, 1788 (see especially §68–69 and §72; see also Vincent Duckles, 'Johann Nicolaus Forkel: The Beginning of Music Historiography', *Eighteenth-Century Studies* v 1 no. 3 (spring 1968) p 277–290). The absence of the term 'rhetoric' in *An Essay on Musical Harmony* suggests that Kollmann's first encounter with Forkel's ideas on this subject occurred after that work was published.

had appeared before the *Essay*.[191] It seems likely that Kollmann had sent copies of these works to Forkel before he wrote this review.[192]

There is another reason to believe that Kollmann and Forkel were in correspondence at this time. A song by Kollmann, with a German-language text in imitation of the English song 'My friend and pitcher', was published by Johann Christian Dieterich in the Göttingen *Musenalmanach* for the year 1797. As ten songs by Forkel were included in this annual almanac between 1773 and 1800, of which two were set to texts by the yearbook's editor, Karl Reinhard,[193] it seems plausible that Kollmann's song appeared there at Forkel's recommendation.

No evidence has been found that they ever met.

11. Three Theoretico-Practical Works (1796–1798)

Between *An Essay on Musical Harmony* and the first edition of *An Essay on Practical Musical Composition* Kollmann published three theoretico-practical works.

The title-page of *The First Beginning on the Piano-Forte*, opus 5, announced that this work was 'calculated for the use of grown persons as well as well as of children who can reach no more than a 6th on the instrument' and was 'constructed so that any person of common capacity who never touched an instrument or knew a note before, may in the very 1st Lesson learn to play something by notes'. It appeared at the end of 1796, when Kollmann's daughter Joanna was ten years old and his son George was seven, and almost certainly reflects their

[191] [Forkel], *op. cit.*, p 1141–1142.

[192] The posthumous sale catalogue of Forkel's library (*Verzeichniß der von dem verstorbenen Doktor und Musikdirektor Forkel in Göttingen nachgelassenen Bücher und Musikalien...*, Göttingen, 1819, copy at BL Hirsch IV.1082) included Kollmann's *c*1792 'Six Sonatinas' (lot 714), his 1796 *The Shipwreck* (lot 716) and *The First Beginning on the Piano-Forte* (lot 725), and numerous later works, including both numbers of *The Quarterly Musical Register* (lots 1427–1428).

[193] I thank Axel Fischer for this information.

father's experience in teaching them to play the piano.[194] The Kollmanns presumably had a piano in their apartment, as George later became an accomplished pianist and a piano maker. It is not known whether Kollmann taught other piano pupils at this time.

In the Introduction to *The First Beginning* Kollmann asserted that his way of teaching differed from 'those methods hitherto known'. In his method beginners are taught a few notes at a time—the first lesson teaches just Middle C and the next higher E and G—and learn to play notes of constant length before notes of different lengths. An important precept was that 'nothing must be laid before the scholar without a sufficient explanation'.[195] Elementary music theory therefore was taught together with teaching how to play the piano.

The Shipwreck, op. 6, published in 1796, commemorated a tragic event that occurred ten years earlier, in which nearly 200 people lost their lives.[196] Kollmann listed in this publication the 'things expressed' by passages in his music; one thing (for instance) is 'Some endeavour to save themselves by swimming but meet with the same distress under the rock'. He dedicated this work to Baron Ernst Ludwig Julius von Lenthe, who came from Hannover in 1795 following von Alvensleben's death to direct the German Chancery in St James's Palace.

In March 1798 Kollmann published his 'Symphony for the piano-forte, a violin, and violoncello; with analytical explanations', opus 7—a work that he subsequently referred to as his 'analyzed symphony'. He had composed it some years earlier, as extracts from it are quoted in *An Essay on Musical Harmony*, where he said that 'perhaps I shall publish [it] with a short analysis'.[197] He decided to bring it out two years later 'as an introductory piece' to *An Essay on*

---

[194] In his 6 January 1811 letter of application to join the Royal Society of Musicians—summarised in section III.4 below—George Kollmann declared that he had 'studied and practised music professionally under my father from my infancy'.

[195] *The First Beginning*, p [1].

[196] Perhaps Kollmann chose this subject because Thomas Miller, the fifteen-year-old son of Kollmann's New Musical Fund colleague Edward Miller, died in this accident. See Frederick Fowler *et al.*, *Edward Miller, Organist of Doncaster, His Life and Times*, Doncaster, 1979, p 63.

[197] *EMH*, p 115 and plate 35 nos. 7–8.

Practical Musical Composition, then 'preparing for publication'.[198] The analyses in the *Analyzed Symphony* identify the symphony's 'subjects and imitations, the modulations, the counterpoint inversions, and the rhythmical order'. Kollmann hoped that this analytical information 'rendered it useful for the study of composition, without lessening its utility for the practice of playing'.[199]

The *Analyzed Symphony* was dedicated to Count John Maurice de Brühl, who had lived in London from 1764 as the ambassador of Saxony. In addition to his diplomatic work Brühl was an accomplished astronomer and violinist, and several other musical compositions were dedicated to him.[200]

Kollmann recognised that his *Analyzed Symphony* was not outstanding music, saying:

> And though I know, that in point of fancy, and humorous elaboration, the piece in question stands far behind the Symphonies of *Haydn*, and other great composers; yet I presume to think it calculated to exemplify *simple regularity*, and the various manners in which longer or shorter *subjects may be treated*. These I have found to be important objects for a young Composer; and I do not doubt that a person who is once perfect in them, will find it easy to proceed to more bold and fanciful pieces.[201]

12. *An Essay on Practical Musical Composition* (1799)

In February 1798 Kollmann issued printed proposals for publishing his second major theoretical treatise, *An Essay on Practical Musical Composition*, by subscription. The work must have been nearly finished then, as the proposals give the planned title and content of each of its

---

198 Preface to the *Analyzed Symphony*.

199 *ibid.*

200 They include Johann Samuel Schroeter's 'Six sonatas', op. 1, *c*1775; Clementi's 'Six sonatas', op. 13, published in 1785, and Haydn's canons on the Ten Commandments composed *c*1792. See Landon, *Haydn in England 1791–1795*, *op. cit.*, p 358. 'Six sonatas for the piano forte or harpsichord with a violin accompaniment', op. 1, by 'Count de Bruhl', published by J[ohn] Welcker (London, *c*1780), has been attributed to the ambassador.

201 *EPMC*^{1}, p xix.

twelve chapters, from which there was little deviation when the *Essay* appeared in June 1799. The proposals promised that the work would be printed 'in the same size and type, but on a better paper' than *An Essay on Musical Harmony*, and that subscribers would pay sixteen shillings upon delivery of a copy, five shillings less than non-subscribers. If sufficiently many persons notified an intention to subscribe, the work would be published with a printed list of their names before the end of 1798. Otherwise, it would be delayed until the number of subscribers covered 'the expence of the publication'.

The proposals announced that the work was dedicated to King George III by permission. Presumably he gave his permission not only because he and Kollmann probably had conversed but also because he was sufficiently interested in his work to have acquired a copy of *An Essay on Musical Harmony*.[202] At some time—it is not known when—Kollmann was granted a pension of £50 by the king.[203]

On 3 December 1798 Kollmann advertised that *An Essay on Practical Musical Composition* 'shortly will be published'.[204] He had 'taken pains to collect examples, from the best and partly scarce works, of some of the greatest composers', to which he had presumed to add '4 fugues and 8 canons, written by himself'. He had been 'honoured with the subscription of Her Majesty, and their Royal Highnesses the Princesses'. Proposals could be had from him and 'all music shops'.[205]

---

[202] *Bibliothecae Regiae Catalogus*, London, v 3, 1826, p 462. I thank Emma Digby for verifying that this copy, now BL 50.f.5, has George III's monogram stamped at the top of the spine and 'G.R. III' stamped in red on the verso of the title-page. The king's interest in music theory also is shown by his gift of Philipp Joseph Frick's *Treatise on Thorough Bass* (London, 1786) to George Ludolph Jacob Griesbach (see his memoirs transcribed in Anne Jarvis's thesis—cited in note 98 above—v 2 p 25), a violinist in Queen Charlotte's private band of musicians and an uncle of John Henry Griesbach whom Kollmann would later teach at the German Chapel school—see page 26 above.

[203] Kollmann's pension 'granted by His late Majesty' is listed in *Accounts relating to the Royal Establishments at Windsor*, House of Commons parliamentary paper no. 230, London, 1820, p 2.

[204] *The Times*, 3 December 1798, p 2. An earlier advertisement soliciting subscriptions had been placed in *The Times*, 12 July 1798, p 2.

[205] The sole surviving copy of the proposals (BL 1879.cc.13.(56.)) has, on its back, Kollmann's handwritten annotation that 'Her Majesty' and 'Their R.H. The Princesses' had subscribed. The printed list of subscribers to the *Essay* includes three

When the work was entered at Stationers' Hall on 21 June 1799 the subscribers collectively had ordered 127 copies, which would have yielded £101/12/- if each copy were paid for in full. Musicians on the subscription list included Burney (who allowed some of his previously unpublished canons to be transcribed by Kollmann and included in the *Essay*[206]), John Wall Callcott, Forkel, William Horsley, John Peter Salomon and George Smart's son George Thomas Smart (later Sir George). Several music sellers subscribed for copies, presumably to sell to their customers: Broderip & Wilkinson (six copies); Corri, Dussek & Co. (one); George Kauntze (three); Longman, Clementi & Co. (six); Thomas Preston (three); George Smart (three); and Robert Wornum (three). The Countess of Loudon, to whom Kollmann had dedicated his 'Six Sonatinas', subscribed for two copies, and Baron von Lenthe, the Hannoverian minister to whom Kollmann had dedicated *The Shipwreck*, ordered one.

Kollmann's cousin, the organist Carl Christoph Hachmeister Jr, subscribed from Billwerder near Hamburg—perhaps because his late father's 'Fuga von sechs Subjecten' [fugue of six subjects], first printed in Hamburg *c*1760, was republished on plates 21–23 in the *Essay*. Three Hempels subscribed,[207] as did three Kollmanns: Kollmann's brother Georg Christoph, who had left Allermöhe to take up an appointment in November 1789 as organist of the St Katharinen church in Hamburg;[208] C. Kollmann of Hameln, who has not been positively

of the six royal princesses: Augusta, Elizabeth and Mary. Caroline, Princess of Wales, Frederick, Duke of York, and his wife Frederica, Duchess of York, also subscribed, as did Princess Sophia Matilda of Gloucester, a niece of George III.

[206] *EPMC*^{1}, p 69.

[207] They are listed as 'Mr Hempel' (probably Kollmann's pupil Charles William Hempel), 'Mr J. Hempel' (probably his younger brother John Frederick Hempel), and 'Miss Hempel' (presumably one of their sisters). The 'Miss Greenhead' who subscribed seems likely to have been Maria Greenhead, who was baptised at St Luke's, Chelsea, in 1784 and married John Frederick Hempel in 1802. I am grateful to Len Greenhead for information about the Greenhead family.

[208] I am grateful to Dr Schmidt of the Staatsarchiv Hamburg for information about George Christoph Kollmann's appointment. He held this post for thirty-eight years, until his death in 1827. See Julius Faulwasser, *Die St Katharinen-Kirche in Hamburg*, Hamburg, 1896, p 82, which describes him as a very good organ player ['ein sehr guter Spieler'].

identified;[209] and J. Kollmann, cantor and schoolmaster in the Garnisongemeinde, Lüneburg. The relationship of the latter two Kollmanns to A. F. C. Kollmann is not known. Curiously, Friedrich Kuhlau, who later became a well known composer, had lived in Lüneburg for a few years from about 1793, when he was seven, and apparently was a pupil of J. Kollmann at that time.[210]

The contents of *An Essay on Practical Musical Composition* are summarised in *The Quarterly Musical Register* on pages 105–112. Today the work is recalled chiefly for Kollmann's announcement of his plan to publish an 'analysed edition' of J. S. Bach's '48' (discussed in the next section) and for an early description of what later became known as 'sonata form'.[211]

Burney again reviewed Kollmann's work extensively and very favourably:

> We think that the author's promises, however great, have been well performed. ... We do not recollect to have seen a book (at least in our own language) which goes so deeply and methodically into the subject of composition, as the performance before us.... Mr Kollmann is a perfect master of his subject....[212]

---

[209] I thank Jonas Eberhardt of the Stadtarchiv Hameln for the information that a Konrad Kollmann, whose first name alternatively could have been spelt with a 'C', is known to have lived in Hameln in 1798, but his profession has not been ascertained.

[210] Kuhlau's father, Johann Carl Kuhlau, played the oboe in an army band that was stationed at Lüneburg for a few years, which would account for his son's attending the Garnisonschule [garrison school], where J. Kollmann taught from 1792 to 1814 (see Gustav Fock, 'Die Musik am Michaelis-Kloster in Lüneburg', typescript in Stadtarchiv Lüneburg, p 45–46). In a *c*1802 letter to his brother Johann Andreas (printed in Gorm Busk (ed.), *Kuhlau Breve*, Copenhagen, 1990, p 32–33), Friedrich Kuhlau wrote a poem which mentioned [J.] Kollmann. I am indebted to Dr Busk for information about the Kuhlau family and for advising that the word 'Kollmann' is not found in any other of Friedrich Kuhlau's extant letters. No evidence has been found that Kuhlau was aware of A. F. C. Kollmann or his works, or that J. Kollmann was in Lüneburg when Kollmann was at Kloster Lüne in 1781–1782.

[211] The latter feature led Pierro Weiss and Richard Taruskin to include an extract from the *Essay* in their *Music in the Western World: A History in Documents*, New York, 1984, p 316–319.

[212] [Charles Burney], review of *An Essay on Practical Musical Composition*, *Monthly Review* n.s. v 31 (February 1800) p 127–131. Burney's authorship of this review is confirmed by an annotation in the editor's copy: see note 186 above.

Burney added that as 'the ingenious author is a foreigner, we should not be too severe on his language'. However, he said that Kollmann's subtitle 'according to the nature of that science' should have read 'according to the nature of that art'.[213] Although, as will appear, Kollmann was sensitive about his non-native English, he did not change the subtitle when he published his revised edition of *An Essay on Practical Musical Composition* in 1812, suggesting that he disagreed with this particular criticism.

13. The Proposed Edition of Bach's '48'

Kollmann's first known mention of J. S. Bach is in his 1796 *Essay on Musical Harmony*. The few references there to Bach, including short extracts from his F minor prelude in part 2 of the '48' (BWV 881/1), did not suggest that his music deserved extraordinary esteem. Within a few years, however, Kollmann came to regard Bach as the greatest German composer. Evidence of this is found in a picture that he appears to have designed and had engraved and printed in London. The main part of this picture, shaped like a sun, placed Bach's name in the centre, from which the names of thirty-one other German composers radiated outwards. Under the sun was an Italian owl which could not bear the light of German music. An Italian capon and German cock were on the side, posed as if they were about to fight.

No copies of this engraving have been found, but Kollmann must have sent one to Forkel, as he described it in the 30 October 1799 number of the Leipzig *Allgemeine musikalische Zeitung*.[214] To illustrate his comments the journal's publisher, Breitkopf & Härtel, had a second engraving made of just the sun portion of Kollmann's picture, which

[213] The *Critical Review* (2nd ser. v 28 (February 1800) p 219–220) similarly bestowed 'on the work no inconsiderable eulogium' but lamented that Kollmann 'had not applied to some intelligent English friend to naturalise the style'.

[214] v 2 no. 5, col. 103–104. The article is signed 'F—l', a code for 'Forkel' (see Martha Bruckner-Bigenwald, *Die Anfänge der Leipziger Allgemeinen Musikalischen Zeitung*, Freiburg, 1938, facsimile reprint Hilversum, 1965, p 92).

they inserted into Forkel's letterpress article in a separate impression.[215] This second engraving is reproduced in *Figure 3* facing page 15, and the composers named in it are identified in the index to this book.

Forkel said that Kollmann's engraving related to a dispute that Haydn had had in London with the Italian composer and violinist Felice Giardini, and added that Haydn is supposed to have seen it. As Forkel was uncertain whether Haydn had seen the engraving, and as his information about it almost certainly came from Kollmann, Haydn probably did not see it before he left London in August 1795. Because Forkel and Kollmann were in regular correspondence from that time, it seems likely that the engraving was printed in London shortly before Forkel's description of it was published. It is plausible that Kollmann enclosed a copy of the engraving when he sent Forkel his subscription copy of *An Essay on Practical Musical Composition*, as Forkel described the *Essay* in the *Allgemeine musikalische Zeitung* four weeks before that journal printed Kollmann's 'sun',[216] and Breitkopf & Härtel would have needed a little time to make their second engraving.

In *An Essay on Practical Musical Composition* Kollmann published two entire works by Bach: his E♭ major organ trio sonata (BWV 525), and a prelude and fugue from part 2 of the '48' (BWV 870). This was the first publication of these compositions anywhere, and a significant step in the English Bach awakening.[217] In this *Essay* Kollmann also quoted substantial portions of the *Musical Offering* (BWV 1079) as well as extracts from the *Art of Fugue* (BWV 1080), the *Chromatic Fantasy and Fugue* (BWV 903) and other works by Bach.

Regarding the '48', Kollmann said that

> *Sebastian Bach's* work, entitled *Wohl temperirtes, Clavier*, (well tempered Harpsichord, or Keyed Instrument in general,) consist[s] of twice twenty-four Preludes and Fugues, or two in every major and minor Key. Every

---

215 The plate marks made by the engraved plate during the second impression are clearly visible in the copy at BL P.P.1945.

216 F—l [i.e., Forkel], 'Ueber den Zustand der Musik in England', v 2 no. 1 (2 October 1799) col. 5-9 at col. 6-7.

217 For instance, Samuel Wesley saw Kollmann's publication of this trio sonata before deciding to edit, with Charles Frederick Horn, all six trio sonatas (BWV 525-530). See Wesley→Benjamin Jacobs, 17 October 1808; *LSW*, p 78-80, *SWSB*, p 243.

Prelude and Fugue may be considered as a Sonata of two Movements, each of which can be used as a piece by itself. This most ingenious, most learned, and yet practicable work, is so highly esteemed by all who can judge of it, that as it is grown scarce, I intend to offer it to the public analyzed.[218]

The comment about scarcity referred of course to manuscript copies of the '48', such as the one Kollmann had obtained from Germany.[219]

In the *Allgemeine musikalische Zeitung* article in which Forkel described the *Essay*, he reported that an English organist (i.e., Kollmann) was venturing to publish an engraved edition of the '48' with explanations—an undertaking that two music firms in Germany had attempted a few years earlier in vain.[220] Four weeks later, when describing the sun engraving, Forkel again mentioned Kollmann's plan.[221]

Kollmann's analysed edition of the '48' never appeared. Years later he said that the *Allgemeine musikalische Zeitung* announcement of it 'created so great an emulation' that the '48', 'which *had never been printed before*, appeared in print about a year after, at *three* different places, viz: at Zurich, Bonn, and Leipzig'. As 'numerous copies of the

[218] *EPMC*[1], p 97–98. Kollmann's description of the '48' as 'twice twenty-four Preludes and Fugues' was a translation of the German 'zweymal vier und zwanzig Vorspiele und Fugen' used in earlier descriptions of the '48', including Bach's obituary by C. P. E. Bach and others published in Lorenz Mizler's *Musikalische Bibliothek* v 4 no. 1 (Leipzig, 1754) and the biography of Bach in Ernst Ludwig Gerber's *Historisch-Biographisches Lexicon der Tonkünstler* (Leipzig, 1790). Both documents are reprinted in Hans-Joachim Schulze (ed.), *Dokumente zum Nachwirken Johann Sebastian Bachs 1750–1800*, *op. cit.*, p 80–93 at p 86, and p 466–471 at p 469.

[219] See note 160 above. Manuscripts of the '48' in England in the eighteenth and nineteenth centuries are discussed in Yo Tomita, 'The dawn of the English Bach awakening manifested in sources of the "48"', *EBA* p 35–167.

[220] '... dass ein englischer Organist wagen kann, Joh. Seb. Bachs wohltemperirtes Klavier mit Erläuterungen in Kupferstich herauszugeben, welches zwey Musikhandlungen im Vaterlande dieses grossen Komponisten noch vor wenig Jahren vergeblich versuchten', Forkel, 'Ueber den Zustand...', *op. cit.*, col. 6.

[221] 'Ein englischer Organist an der Königl. deutschen Kapelle (eben derseble, welcher jetzt Joh. Seb. Bachs wohltemperirtes Clavier herausgeben will)' [an English organist at the Royal German Chapel (the same one who now wants to bring out Bach's '48')], Forkel, in the article cited in note 214 above, col. 103.

three first editions were imported in England, it made Mr Kollmann relinquish his intended edition'.[222]

The Bach scholar Alfred Dürr has questioned whether this announcement could have been the 'sole reason for the sudden appearance, in rapid succession, of three editions' of the '48' by Nägeli (in Zürich), Simrock (in Paris and Bonn) and Hoffmeister & Kühnel (in Leipzig), and doubted whether these publishers could have obtained a manuscript of the '48' suitable for 'immediate publication' soon after this announcement.[223] However, Kollmann's statement is plausible.

The Simrock edition of the '48', based upon a manuscript 'corrected' by Christian Gottlob Neefe, who died in January 1798, was announced in Bonn in December 1800.[224] It seems likely—although documentary proof has not been found—that Nicolaus Simrock heard of Kollmann's plan from John Peter Salomon. Salomon was born and raised in Bonn and must have known Simrock there, because in 1797 Simrock said that he and Salomon were old friends.[225] The two are known to have been in correspondence in the late 1790s, although most of this has not survived.[226]

---

[222] *QMR p 30.* Kollmann gave substantially the same explanation in *EPMC*², p 62.

[223] Alfred Dürr, 'On the earliest manuscripts and prints of Bach's *Well-Tempered Clavier I* in England', in Paul Brainard and Ray Robinson (eds), *A Bach Tribute: Essays in Honor of William H. Scheide*, Kassel, 1993, p 121–134 at p 128–129.

[224] *Allgemeine musikalische Zeitung, Intelligenz-Blatt* no. 5 (February 1801 [misprinted '1800']) col. [17–18]. A list of journals in which Simrock's announcement was reported is given in Karen Lehmann, *Die Anfänge einer Bach-Gesamtausgabe 1801–1865*, Hildesheim, 2004, p 41 fn 31.

[225] 'Salomon und ich wir sind alte Freunde'. Simrock→Georg Christoph Grosheim, 18 September 1797, copied into the Simrock firm's copy-book for 1797. See Alfr[ed] Chr[istlieb] Kalischer, 'Ein Kopierbuch der Simrock'schen Musikhandlung in Bonn vom Jahre 1797', *Zeitschrift der internationalen Musikgesellschaft* v 4 no. 9 (1903) p 531–542 at p 535.

[226] Three letters from Simrock to Salomon are in the 1797 copy-book (Kalischer, p 538–540). See also Hubert Unverricht, 'Die Simrock-Drucke von Haydns Londoner Sinfonien', in Herbert Drux *et al.* (eds), *Karl Gustav Fellerer zum 60, Geburtstag..., Studien zur Musikgeschichte des Rheinlandes II, Beiträge zur rheinischen Musikgeschichte* v 52, Cologne, 1962, p 235–259, and Christopher Hogwood, 'In praise of arrangements: the "Symphony Quintettos"', in Otto Biba and David Wyn Jones (eds), *Studies in Music History presented to H. C. Robbins Landon on his*

Kollmann presumably met Salomon frequently in 1792–1793, as the composer Johann Christian Firnhaber, whose father was Kollmann's godfather, lived in Salomon's house then for seven months.[227] Salomon subsequently subscribed to *An Essay on Practical Musical Composition* and probably read it soon after it appeared in June 1799. If, in a letter to Simrock later that year, Salomon mentioned Kollmann's plan to publish the '48', Simrock would have had ample time, before announcing his edition in December 1800, to acquire (if he did not already own) Neefe's manuscript.[228]

The Hoffmeister & Kühnel edition of the '48' was issued serially as part of a projected complete edition of Bach's works, for which a call for subscribers was made in January 1801.[229] The publishers informed Forkel about their intended edition,[230] and he and Kollmann, who were

---

seventieth Birthday, London, 1996, p 82–104. Hogwood states (p 85) that 'Salomon negotiated almost simultaneous publication in Bonn with Simrock' of the arrangements of Haydn symphonies that Salomon made for five instruments, and that the Simrock edition of these arrangements was publicly announced in March 1799.

[227] J[ohann] Ch[ristian] Firnhaber, letter to the editor dated November 1825, *Der Freimüthige* v 22 no. 240 (3 December 1825) p 960. I am grateful to Dr Eberhard Firnhaber for a copy of the published letter.

[228] Georg Christoph Kollmann would have known of his brother's plan to publish the '48', if only from reading *An Essay on Practical Musical Composition*, to which he had subscribed. It seems plausible that he mentioned his brother's plan to Christian Friedrich Gottlieb Schwenke, who in 1789 had succeeded his teacher Carl Phillip Emanuel Bach as music director of Hamburg's five principal churches (including the St Katharinen church where George Christoph Kollmann was organist), as Schwenke owned several autograph manuscripts by J. S. Bach and was much interested in his music. (See Robert von Zahn, *Musikpflege in Hamburg um 1800*, Hamburg, 1991, p 177–192.) Schwenke prepared a revised edition of the '48' for Simrock about 1801 and is thought to have been in contact with him earlier (*ibid.*, p 180); if so, Schwenke also could have given Simrock information about Kollmann's plan.

[229] Reprinted in Lehmann, p 278–280. The plans of both Simrock and Hoffmeister & Kühnel to publish the '48' were reported in the *Allgemeine musikalische Zeitung* v 3 no. 19 (4 February 1801) col. 336.

[230] In his 4 May 1801 letter to Hoffmeister & Kühnel, Forkel apologised for not replying long since ['schon längst'] to the announcement of their edition. This letter is printed (also in English translation by Arthur Mendel) in George B. Stauffer (ed.), *The Forkel-Hoffmeister & Kühnel Correspondence*, New York, 1990, p 2–7.

in correspondence then,[231] presumably discussed it in letters no longer extant. After seeing its first number, published in April 1801,[232] Forkel complained to Hoffmeister & Kühnel about some practices of its (unidentified) editor. They subsequently dismissed him and appointed Forkel in his place, who began to edit the '48' for them about August 1801.[233]

The Nägeli edition also was announced early in 1801, and part 1 was printed by September that year. It is not known upon what sources this edition was based,[234] although in May 1798 Hans Georg Nägeli had expressed interest in acquiring a manuscript of the '48'.[235]

The Simrock edition appeared in two books, of which the first—containing the entire part 2 of the '48'—was published in Paris and Bonn about April 1801. (The reversed numbering of the parts in this edition apparently derived from Neefe's manuscript.) Broderip & Wilkinson, who had subscribed for six copies of *An Essay on Practical Musical Composition* and would have read there of Kollmann's intention to publish the '48', obtained a copy of Simrock's Book I and presumably decided to re-engrave and publish it in London before Kollmann could produce the edition he had announced. Apparently to test the English market for this music, they brought out initially just the first twelve preludes and fugues of part 2 (ending at BWV 881) as their Book I, which they advertised as 'just printed' in *The Times* on 14 June 1802. The Broderip & Wilkinson edition of BWV 870–881 therefore was on sale in London several months before Forkel's edition of BWV 877–881 was published by Hoffmeister & Kühnel in Vienna and Leipzig.[236]

---

[231] See Kollmann→John Wall Callcott, 21/2/1801.

[232] Lehmann, *op. cit.*, p 125–126.

[233] Forkel→Hoffmeister & Kühnel, 2 August 1801, published (also in English translation by Arthur Mendel) in Stauffer, p 6–9.

[234] Lehmann, p 42–43.

[235] Edgar Refardt, 'Briefe Hans Georg Nägelis an Breitkopf & Härtel', *Zeitschrift für Musikwissenschaft* v 13 (1931) p 384–400 at p 389.

[236] See Michael Kassler, 'Broderip, Wilkinson and the first English edition of the "48"', *The Musical Times* v 147 no. 1895 (summer 2006) p 67–76. The Hoffmeister & Kühnel edition of BWV 877–881 appeared in two instalments, of which the first

Kollmann's assertion that the *Allgemeine musikalische Zeitung* announcement of his plan hastened the appearance of the three continental editions therefore seems credible. Although there is no evidence that many printed copies of the '48' were sold in London at this time, Kollmann's abandonment of his proposed edition seems prudent in view of the competition from Broderip & Wilkinson and imported editions and the small English market at this time for music by J. S. Bach, whose name was just beginning to become known there.

Kollmann did produce an edition of a work by Bach—his *Chromatic Fantasy and Fugue* (BWV 903). Published by Thomas Preston about May 1806, it was the first edition of this work printed in England[237] and appeared almost simultaneously with Kollmann's *New Theory*. This was not just a coincidence, as *A New Theory* included 'an analysis of the harmony of the first movement' of the *Fantasia Chromatica*.[238] Because each publication referred to the other, purchasers of one were potential buyers of the other.

Kollmann explained his editorial 'additions' to Bach's music as follows:

> The present Fantasia being universally esteemed as the most sublime Piece of it's kind hitherto known, it would be unpardonable to make any real alteration. But I have found that Players in general are at a loss how to divide the plain Chords of the first Movement, intended for Harpeggios, because some of them consist of more Notes or parts than others, and a long series of Harpeggios becomes tiresome if it does not contain a proper variety of

---

was issued in September or October 1802 and the last in December 1802 (Lehmann, p 136–139).

[237] Although the theme of the fugue had been published earlier by Marpurg, Kirnberger and Kollmann (in his *Essay on Practical Musical Composition*), Kollmann's edition was the second publication of the entire BWV 903. It was preceded by Forkel's edition which Hoffmeister & Kühnel published in April/May 1802 (Lehmann, p 135). According to Uwe Wolf (ed.), *Johann Sebastian Bach Neue Ausgabe Sämtlicher Werke Serie V Band 9.2 Kritischer Bericht*, Kassel, 2000, p 116–177 at p 158, Kollmann's edition was based not upon Forkel's edition but upon a manuscript that is no longer extant.

[238] Kollmann's analysis is described in detail in Michael Kassler, 'Kollmann's proof of the regularity of Bach's *Chromatic Fantasy*', *EBA* p 211–249. The name *Fantasia Chromatica* on the title-page of Kollmann's edition referred to both movements of BWV 903. Today the first movement alone is known as the *Chromatic Fantasy*; the second movement is the following fugue.

> divisions. This difficulty I have endeavoured to remove, by dividing those Chords....
>
> And as the running passages of the same Movement have but the effect of a Solo for one hand, tho' in the original both hands are to come in alternately, as the letters D and S (right and left hand) shew, I have ventured to double them in the Octave and other Intervals, for the use of both hands at once....
>
> The said additions I have distinguished from the original by expressing the former in small Notes throughout, and the latter in large ones.

Kollmann's edition received only one contemporary review, by Thomas Busby in *The Monthly Magazine.*[239]

14. Meeting with Johann Anton André (1800)

Kollmann appears to have met the German music publisher and composer Johann Anton André in July 1800.[240] André had stopped in Göttingen on his way to London,[241] so it seems plausible that Forkel recommended that he meet Kollmann. Their meeting established a professional relationship which continued for at least fifteen years by correspondence, although none of this has survived.

Following the death of his father, Johann André, in June 1799, Johann Anton André became head of his family's music publishing firm at Offenbach am Main, near Frankfurt. Within a few months he made two important acquisitions, buying rights to the lithographic printing process invented by Alois Senefelder and hundreds of Mozart manuscripts from his widow, Constanze Mozart.[242]

---

239 v 22 part 2 no. 1 (1 August 1806) p 57.

240 The only documentary evidence relevant to their meeting is Kollmann→John Wall Callcott, 27/7/1800, where Kollmann mentions hearing André and Samuel Wesley play the organs at St Paul's Covent Garden and St Mary's German Lutheran church in the Savoy. The latter organ was one of the few in London at that time with pedals.

241 See August Hermann André, *Zur Geschichte der Familie André, Offenbach am Main. Offenbacher Geschichtsblätter* no. 11 (October 1962) p 22, quoting Johann Anton André's account of his early years, in possession of the André family.

242 Ute-Margrit André and Axel Beer, 'Zeittafel zur Geschichte des Hauses André', in Ute-Margrit André and Hans-Jörg André (eds), *225 Jahre Musikverlag Johann André*, Offenbach am Main, 1999, p 7–12 at p 7–8. See also Jürgen Eichenauer (ed.),

After André returned to Offenbach he inscribed to Kollmann copies of five Mozart piano concertos that he had edited from the recently acquired manuscripts and published as Mozart's opus 82.[243] The title-pages of these editions were amongst the first that André's firm printed by lithography, although the music pages were printed from engraved plates.[244] Later, André gave copies of other of his publications to Kollmann, including Philipp Karl Hoffmann's cadenzas and 'amplifications' to these Mozart concertos[245] and, presumably, the

---

Johann Anton André (1775–1842) und der Mozart-Nachlass: Ein Notenschatz in Offenbach am Main, Offenbach am Main, 2006.

[243] The autograph manuscripts of these concertos (K. 482, 488, 491, 503 and 595) were subsequently dispersed. See Wolfgang Rehm, *Mozarts Nachlass und die Andrés*, Offenbach am Main, 1999, p 60.

[244] These copies, now BL Hirsch IV 119a, 171a, 97a, 97b and 91a, bear the printed 'publisher numbers' 1415–1419 respectively. With the exception of Hirsch 97a (presumably an oversight, as this has annotations by Kollmann's daughter Joanna—see page 171 below), each is inscribed in ink 'Mr Kollmann from the Proprietor' (see Kathi Meyer and Paul Hirsch (eds), *Katalog der Musikbibliothek Paul Hirsch* v 4, Cambridge, 1947, p 44 and p 53). According to Gertraut Haberkamp, *Die Erstdrucke der Werke von Wolfgang Amadeus Mozart, Bibliographie, Textband*, Tutzing, 1986, p 245–339 *passim*, all these editions were first published after July 1800. The term 'publisher number' (a translation of 'Verlagsnummer' in Britta Constapel, *Der Musikverlag Johann André in Offenbach am Main, Studien zur Verlagstätigkeit von Johann Anton André und Verzeichnis der Musikalien von 1800 bis 1840*, Tutzing, 1998) better describes André's publications than 'plate number', as he reused the same number when a work was re-engraved or reissued in a different format. For instance, BL Hirsch IV 97 and BL Hirsch IV 97b are *c*1800 André editions of the same Mozart piano concerto that both bear publisher number 1419. Hirsch IV 97 (uninscribed) is in 'portrait' format with an engraved title-page; Hirsch IV 97b (inscribed to Kollmann) is in 'landscape' format with a lithographed title-page. Haberkamp states (p 251–253) that Hirsch IV 97b was printed after Hirsch IV 97.

[245] These copies, inscribed by André to Kollmann, are now BL e.282.m./9 and BL e.57.w/4, and bear publisher numbers 1572 and 1658 respectively. Constapel, *op. cit.*, p 132 and p 136, suggests that they were published about September 1800 and in 1803 respectively. Both copies formerly were owned by A. Hyatt King: see his edition, *Hoffmann Cadenzas to Mozart's Piano Concertos and Elaborations of their slow Movements*, London, 1959, p 4–5. André had travelled with Hoffmann, whom he characterised as an excellent pianist ('des vortrefflichen Klavierspielers Hoffmann'), on his autumn 1799 European tour during which he contracted to purchase Mozart's manuscripts (August Hermann André, *op. cit.*, p 22).

1805 thematic catalogue of Mozart compositions which Kollmann cited and quoted from on page 104 of *The Quarterly Musical Register*.[246]

While in London André seems likely to have asked Kollmann to get biographies of English musicians for a revised edition of a dictionary of musicians that Ernst Ludwig Gerber was preparing.[247] Gerber had written to André in September 1799 soliciting information for a new edition of his *Lexicon der Tonkünstler*, and they apparently met about that time.[248] However, by January 1803 Kollmann had 'collected but very little' for Gerber's work.[249]

On 20 June 1801 Senefelder obtained an English patent (subsequently numbered 2518) for his 'new method and process of performing the various branches of the art of printing'. On 10 August 1801 he sold these patent rights to his lithographic process to André. To exploit these rights, André established a branch of his firm in London that year under the direction of his elder brother Philippe Henri. It was equipped with a lithographic press that apparently was used only to print drawings until 1805, when Philippe André returned to Germany and was succeeded by Georg Jacob Vollweiler, who had taught Johann Anton André musical composition in 1792–1793.[250]

---

[246] Lot 323* [sic] in the posthumously published *Catalogue of a valuable Collection of Music, including an important Selection from the Library of the eminent Theorist A. F. C. Kollman* [sic] ..., auctioned by Puttick & Simpson in London on 30 January 1877, was a box containing 'upwards of 30' volumes of 'original editions' of 'pianoforte music and pianoforte with accompaniments'. According to the printed description of this lot (p 13), 'Many [were] presented to Kollmann, by Andrè [sic]'. This auction is discussed in section I.30 below.

[247] Kollmann was in frequent correspondence with John Wall Callcott from 1798, but first mentions Gerber's lexicon to him in Kollmann→Callcott, 26 July 1800, immediately after describing André's organ performances in London. The first edition of Gerber's *Historisch-biographisches Lexicon der Tonkünstler*, published in Leipzig between 1790 and 1792, continued, with additions, the *Musicalisches Lexicon* edited by Johann Gottfried Walther (Leipzig, 1732).

[248] See [Klaus Hortschansky], *Die Andrés: Familie und Verlag*, exhibition catalogue, Offenbach, 1974, p 26.

[249] Kollmann→Callcott, 14/1/1803. In particular, Callcott had not supplied his own biography.

[250] Information in this paragraph is taken chiefly from Felix H. Man, 'Lithography in England (1801–1810)', in Carl Zigrosser (ed.), *Prints*, New York, 1962, p 97–130;

Vollweiler managed the firm's London branch until August 1807, eventually renaming it the 'polyautographic office'. In addition to drawings, he printed 'from stone' (i.e., lithographically) at least seven individually published pieces of music. One was a waltz by Johann Anton André, another was a march from Mozart's opera *La Clemenza di Tito*, which received its first London performance on 27 March 1806, and it is curious that four of the remaining works were composed or owned by musicians in London with close German connections.[251] It seems clear that Vollweiler met Kollmann in London, probably at the suggestion of Johann Anton André, as he conveyed Vollweiler's regards to Kollmann after Vollweiler had returned to Germany.[252]

15. THE FIRST *PRACTICAL GUIDE TO THOROUGH-BASS* (1801)

Kollmann realised that his treatises were too long, complex and expensive for readers who wished to learn only enough theory to be able to accompany singers or violinists on a keyboard instrument. To reach this much larger market, he published *A Practical Guide to Thorough-Bass* in February 1801. Whereas *An Essay on Musical Harmony* sold for £1/1/- and *An Essay on Practical Musical Composition* cost £1/11/6, *A Practical Guide* could be had for 10/6. It was dedicated to the Hon. George Pomeroy, an amateur musician who

---

Michael Twyman, *Lithography 1800–1850*, London, 1970; and Twyman, *Early Lithographed Music*, London, 1996. Vollweiler incorrectly is named 'Johann Georg Vollweiler' in the music encyclopædia *Die Musik in Geschichte und Gegenwart* and in Britta Constapel, *Der Musikverlag Johann André in Offenbach am Main*, *op. cit.* I am grateful to Axel Beer for the information that he uniformly signed his name 'G. J. Vollweiler' in each of his twenty-four letters preserved in the André firm archive in Offenbach.

[251] They were Nina d'Aubigny von Engelbrunner (German-born composer and writer), Charles Edward Horn (son of Charles Frederick Horn, who was born in Germany), Charles Saust (German-born flautist and composer) and Frederick Schirmer. Schirmer managed the German Theatre in London in 1805–1806 and was the proprietor of 'The favourite song in the celebrated opera *Die drei Freier*' composed by Matthias von Holst, which Vollweiler printed and Schirmer entered at Stationers' Hall on 30 January 1806.

[252] See Johann Anton André→GCK, 22/8/1809.

had subscribed to *An Essay on Practical Musical Composition* along with his brother, Rev. John Pomeroy of Dublin.[253]

In the preface Kollmann said that *A Practical Guide* 'differs from all others on Thorough-Bass published in this Country' in two ways. It explains harmony according to Kirnberger's system, which 'reduces all regular Harmony ... to seven essential chords'.[254] It also gives rules 'according to which the different Thorough-Basses of any other Author may be understood'.[255] Kollmann added that

> two musical Authors recently revived the most confused and obsolete Systems, without even so much attention to the Public, as to mention, whether they are acquainted with the described System [which Kollmann had presented in *An Essay on Musical Harmony*], or have a single argument to oppose it. One of these Authors, I am sorry to add, has taken great parts of his 'General Treatise', from my *Essay on Harmony*, without doing me the justice of acknowledging it, as is usual. But it appears he did not perfectly comprehend what he borrowed, as he has most faithfully transcribed a Term, and a whole Period, which ought to have been mentioned in a Table of Errata to the quoted Essay.[256]

The two musical authors were Matthew Peter King, whose *A General Treatise on Music* is dated 1 January 1800 on its dedication page, and William Shield, whose *An Introduction to Harmony* was published in June 1800.[257] Shield is not known to have responded to Kollmann's criticism but King reacted strongly, issuing a new edition of his book that replied to Kollmann's charge in an 'Advertisement' dated 8 April 1801:

---

253 For George Pomeroy, who subscribed to the Royal Institution music lectures in 1801, see Jamie Croy Kassler, 'The Royal Institution music lectures, 1800–1831: a preliminary study', *Research Chronicle* [Royal Musical Association] no. 19 (1983–1985) p 1–30 at p 27. Samuel Wesley later called him 'a most conceited pretender to musical criticism' (Wesley→Benjamin Jacobs, 28 September 1809?; *LSW*, p 122–123, *SWSB*, p 266–267).

254 i.e., the fundamental concord (triad) and its two inversions, plus the fundamental discord (chord of the seventh) and its three inversions.

255 *PGTB*, p [v]–vi.

256 *ibid.*, p vi. Kollmann consistently used 'period' as a synonym of 'sentence'.

257 Shield's book was advertised as published 'this day' in *The Times*, 16 June 1800, p 2.

> Established principles ... which have never yet ceased to be followed, and which will still be the doctrine of the greatest Masters, after his [Kollmann's] cobweb system is consign'd to oblivion, are absurdly and ignorantly called *obsolete*; and that which has never been *disused* is with equal correctness said to be revived. And how could he [Kollmann] vainly expect [Kirnberger's system, introduced in *An Essay on Musical Harmony*] ... to be noticed, which, according to himself, was not adopted or known in this country.... [The books by King and Shield] dared to follow the doctrines of the highest authorities in Europe, which have been uninterruptedly adopted in this country by every National and Foreign writer to the present day, Mr Kollmann alone excepted....

Kollmann's claim that King took 'great parts of his "General Treatise" from my Essay on Harmony' and 'did not perfectly comprehend what he borrowed' was, according to King, a 'malicious and unfounded assertion':

> When a charge of this nature, if true, could have been so easily substantiated by quotation, Why did he not do it? He could not. And from his own premises it is extremely improbable that a Work, which he presumes to call a *revival* of an *obsolete* system, could contain 'great parts' of his, which is avowedly founded on opposite principles.
>
> As to Mr Kollmann's *term* and *whole period*, I am utterly unconscious of what he may allude to; or whether the *great parts* are not at last dwindled into the *small* compass of this *term* and *period*, I do not sufficiently understand the phraseology to determine.[258]

Kollmann accepted King's challenge and later that year published *A. F. C. Kollmann's Vindication of a Passage in his Practical Guide to Thorough-Bass, against an Advertisement of Mr M. P. King.*[259] To 'convince the Reader, that at least one whole chapter of Mr King's work, (being no less than four pages in folio,) is entirely taken from my work', Kollmann reprinted King's Chapter XXIX 'Of suspension, anticipation, and transition' next to passages and music examples from Chapter VII of *An Essay on Musical Harmony*.[260] This demonstrated that King's chapter was a paraphrase of what Kollmann had written.

---

[258] King, *A General Treatise on Music*, new ed., London, 1801, p v–vi.

[259] This publication, which consists of 7+[1] folio pages, appeared after 2 May 1801, as noted in section III.2 below.

[260] *Vindication*, p 2–6.

Kollmann added that the term that 'ought to have been mentioned in a Table of Errata' is 'transition'.[261] In *An Essay on Musical Harmony* he wrote that a transition arises 'when in passing from one interval to another, some intermediate notes are introduced, which do not belong to the fundamental harmony'.[262] In an anonymous review of that book, Burney remarked that 'the author uses the word *transition* in a different manner from English musical writers; who generally make it synonymous with *modulation*, or passing from one key to another'.[263] Kollmann heeded this comment when writing *A Practical Guide to Thorough-Bass* where, in place of 'transition', he used the terms 'transient notes' and 'transient chords'. In *Vindication* he cited this criticism by 'a respectable reviewer' and asserted that King 'as an Englishman ... would not have adopted a Term for which I as a foreigner had been publickly censured, had he clearly comprehended what he borrowed'.[264]

The 'Period'—today one would say 'sentence'—in *An Essay on Musical Harmony* that Kollmann now realised was erroneous concerned 'anticipations'. He had written in that *Essay*:

> Anticipations are, when *one* or *more* notes of a *succeeding chord* are introduced in the *preceding one* to which they do not belong. Their nature is the same as that of suspensions: for they always appear on the *accented* part of the *bar* or *note*, and are resolved on the *unaccented* part of the same fundamental bass.[265]

King paraphrased this as follows on page 52 of *A General Treatise on Music*:

---

[261] *Vindication*, p 6.

[262] *EMH*, p 12.

[263] [Charles Burney], review of *An Essay on Musical Harmony*, *Monthly Review* n.s. v 21 (September 1796) p 27–30 at p 29. Burney also wrote (p 28) that 'a table of *Errata* to the text of this useful work is much wanting'. For Burney's authorship of this review see page 49 above and *QMR p 118*, where Kollmann asserts his belief that Burney was the reviewer.

[264] *Vindication*, p 6. Kollmann's description of the reviewer as 'respectable' suggests that he knew the reviewer's identity when he wrote *Vindication*.

[265] *EMH*, p 49.

> 1. A chord is anticipated, when one or more parts of a succeeding chord, are introduced on the bass of the one preceding.
> 2. Anticipations take place on the accented part of a bar, and their resolutions on the unaccented part of the same.

In *Vindication* Kollmann pointed out that the second sentence quoted above from his *Essay on Musical Harmony* was wrong, although the error had 'escaped me by oversight' at time of writing.[266] He added that 'nothing can therefore be more striking' than that King 'did not find the whole to be wrong', even though, in his paraphrase as sentence no. 2 in the above quotation from his treatise, he had 'ventured to alter a few words in this period' and 'consequently gave it some consideration'.[267]

Kollmann's failure to realise this error when writing *An Essay on Musical Harmony* shows that his concept of musical rhythm was then at an early stage of development. He revised his thoughts on this subject several times and published his most mature concept of rhythm in the second edition of *A New Theory* in 1823.[268]

16. Changes at the German Chapel

The death of Henry Otto Schrader in May 1802 necessitated changes at the German Chapel. Christian Hermann Giese, who had replaced Röhrs as second chaplain in 1791, was promoted to succeed Schrader, vacating the post of second chaplain. As might have happened with the selection of Kollmann and Röhrs, the Hannover Schullehrer-Seminarium may have been asked to suggest a candidate, as the post

---

[266] He should have said that anticipations take place on an unaccented part of a bar, and are resolved on an accented part.

[267] *Vindication*, p 6.

[268] King did not respond publicly to Kollmann's *Vindication*. When a 'new edition' of King's *A General Treatise on Music* was reprinted *c*1812 (copy at BL H.2878.(2.)) the only textual changes made were to efface the years on the plates, so that the date on the dedication page now read 'January 1,' instead of 'January 1, 1800', and the date on the 'Advertisement' against Kollmann now read 'April 8th' instead of 'April 8th 1801. ~' [sic].

was filled by Rev. Johann Hartmann Wilhelm Kuper, who had been teaching there for a few years.[269] Prince Adolphus Frederick, at that time a lieutenant general in Hannover, also could have recommended him, as the two had known each other for five years before Kuper arrived in England in late 1802.[270]

Kuper served the German Chapel for more than fifty years, becoming its sole chaplain after Giese's January 1819 death. His major literary achievement was a new German translation of the Book of Common Prayer, published by Samuel Bagster in 1820.[271] This translation presumably was used in German Chapel services after then, along with parts of the Lutheran liturgy.

At 2 a.m. on 21 January 1809 a fire broke out at St James's Palace, destroying part of the building. However, the 'German Chapel, situated immediately adjoining the conflagration, was not injured, from the durability of its construction, and it was found extremely useful as a place of deposit of such property as was saved from the flames'.[272] In 1880 George Grove wrote that Kollmann—whom he described as 'a person of much energy'—'in 1809 during a large fire in the palace is said to have saved the chapel by standing in the doorway and

---

[269] Salfeld, *Geschichte des Königlichen Schullehrer-Seminarii*, *op. cit.*, p 111–112. Kuper spelt his surname 'Küper' in German but dropped the umlaut when writing in English, and was known in England as William Kuper. One of his sons, Sir Augustus Leopold Kuper, became a distinguished admiral in the British navy; Kuper Island in British Columbia is named after him.

[270] Adolphus Frederick, the youngest son of King George III and Queen Charlotte, became Duke of Cambridge in 1801. In 1804 he supported the applications of Giese and Kuper for a salary increase, saying that he knew them both to be 'men of unimpeachable character' (Adolphus Frederick→William Pitt, 16 September 1804, National Archives PRO 30/70/4/237). In 1841 both he and Kuper said that they had known each other for forty-five years, including forty years in London (Kuper→ Adolphus Frederick, 27 September 1841, BL Add Ms 43051 f 46–47, and Adolphus Frederick→George Hamilton-Gordon, 4th Earl of Aberdeen, 1 October 1841, *ibid.*, f 44–45).

[271] *Das allgemeine Gebetbuch, oder, die Agende der vereinigten Kirche von England und Irland, nebst den Psaltern Davids, neu übersetzt von Dr J. H. W. Küper*, London, [1820]. This translation was reprinted several times in England and Germany (see David N. Griffiths, *The Bibliography of the Book of Common Prayer, 1549–1999*, London, 2002, p 500–501).

[272] *The Times*, 23 January 1809, p 3.

preventing the firemen from entering it to destroy it'.[273] No confirmation of this story has been found.

Kuper continued the previously established close association between German Chapel chaplains and the royal family.[274] He was German master to the Princess Charlotte from at least 1809 to 1813[275] and interpreted for the Prussian field marshal Gebhard Leberecht von Blücher during his official visit to London in 1814 that followed his victory over Napoléon I.[276]

William, Duke of Clarence—another son of King George III and Queen Charlotte—appointed Kuper as a domestic chaplain on 24 July 1818, eleven days after the duke married Princess Adelaide of Saxe-Meiningen.[277] The Clarences then removed to Hannover but returned to England in August 1819 so that any future heirs to the throne that they might produce would be born on English soil. Upon their return

---

[273] 'G.', i.e., George Grove, 'Kollmann, August Friedrich Karl' [sic], in George Grove (ed.), *A Dictionary of Music and Musicians...*, London, v 2 (1880) p 68. Grove's files relating to his dictionary articles apparently have not been preserved.

[274] In 1852, on the occasion of his fiftieth anniversary as chaplain of the German Chapel, Kuper received congratulations from Queen Victoria and King George V of Hannover, 'testifying their kind interest for one who, during so many years, has proved himself a most devoted and attached servant to their august family' (*The Times*, 5 November 1852, p 6). After Kuper's death, the queen's private secretary wrote to Admiral Kuper to convey her and Prince Albert's sadness at 'the death of your excellent and universally respected father' (Charles Beaumont Phipps→ Augustus Leopold Kuper, 29 November 1861, in Devon Record Office, Kuper family papers, deposit 6232).

[275] A 1 October 1809 diary entry by Sylvester Douglas (printed in Francis Bickley (ed.), *The Diaries of Sylvester Douglas (Lord Glenbervie)*, London, 1928, v 2 p 20), states that Kuper, Princess Charlotte's 'German master' (whose name is misspelled 'Küppler'), had made representations to Queen Charlotte regarding the princess's education. The *Autobiography of Miss [Ellis] Cornelia Knight, lady companion to the Princess Charlotte of Wales*, London, 1861, v 1 p 231, refers to Kuper as Princess Charlotte's German preceptor in 1813.

[276] Robert Isaac Wilberforce and Samuel Wilberforce, *The Life of William Wilberforce*, London, 1838, v 4 p 198.

[277] *London Gazette* no. 17382 (25 July 1818) p 1338. The Clarences' marriage, at Kew Palace, was a double wedding with his brother Edward, Duke of Kent, and Princess Victoria of Leiningen.

Kuper became chaplain to the duchess.[278] When the duke and duchess became King William IV and Queen Adelaide in 1830, she appointed Kuper her chaplain in ordinary.[279]

About 1803 Kollmann's relation George Frederick Kollmann came to England, bringing to Windsor Castle six large chandeliers and elaborately decorated silver plate from Herrenhausen Palace, the royal family's residence in Hannover, in order to protect these treasures from the French occupiers of that city.[280] He had gone into service at Herrenhausen Palace as a footman ['Hoflakai'] in 1790, and nine years later was put in charge of the palace silver ['Silberdiener'].[281] On 14 July 1795 he married Sophia Junck at the Martin church in Engelbostel.[282] As she came from Clausthal he must have had a close connection with the Engelbostel branch of the Kollmann family, but his place on their family tree has not been discovered.

On 20 March 1809 George Frederick—who was then a widower—married Louisa Davis at St George the Martyr, Southwark. Both were of that parish, according to the church register.[283] By August 1812 they had removed to Windsor, where their daughter Ellen

---

[278] In the *Royal Kalendar* for 1820 (London, 1820) Kuper's place in the Duke's household is described (p 130) as 'Domestic Chaplain, and Chaplain to the Duchess'.

[279] The Clarences' children did not survive infancy, and Princess Victoria, daughter of the Duke and Duchess of Kent, succeeded William IV to the British throne in 1837.

[280] This information was recorded by Sir George Smart in his 31 October 1825 diary entry of his tour in Germany (BL Add Ms 41774 f 56^r, transcribed inexactly in H. Bertram Cox and C. L. E. Cox, *Leaves from the Journals of Sir George Smart*, London, 1907, p 207). Sir George met George Frederick Kollmann that day at Herrenhausen Palace, of which he had been appointed keeper ['Schloßverwalter'] in 1820. Sir George described him as a 'fat, jolly ... pleasant fellow' who was 'related to those [Kollmanns] in London'; besides his palace duties, he 'gives lessons in music'. See also *The King's Silver: George III's Service in Hanover and England*, brochure published by Waddeson, The Rothschild Collection, Waddeson Manor, Buckinghamshire, 2003. Herrenhausen Palace was destroyed by an air raid in 1943.

[281] I am grateful to the secretariat of HRH the Prince of Hannover for information about George Frederick Kollmann's service to the royal family.

[282] I thank Peter Boison of the Martin church for information about this marriage.

[283] A copy of this register is in the Family History Library of the Church of Jesus Christ of Latter-day Saints, Salt Lake City. The church's International Genealogical Index mistakenly records the groom's surname as 'Hollmann'.

Augusta Johannah was baptised at Old Windsor church on 29 August.[284] He apparently worked at Cumberland Lodge, as the £20 annual pension that Queen Charlotte granted to Louisa Kollmann described her as 'wife of the Hanoverian silver scullery man at the Great Lodge'.[285] The extent of his contact with A. F. C. Kollmann during the more than fifteen years when they both lived in England is not known.

17. Public Performances by Kollmann's Children (1804–1806)

Kollmann's son George made his début at the New Musical Fund concert on 15 March 1804, playing a piano concerto that his father had composed for the occasion. He was fifteen years old. The concert was held at the King's Theatre, Haymarket, and the orchestra, led by François Cramer, consisted of 300 performers.[286] The concerto received at least one further hearing in London that year, as the title-page of its published piano forte part, entered at Stationers' Hall on 31 December 1804, mentions a performance at the 'Nobility's Concerts'. Kollmann said in his autobiography that he regarded this concerto as his principal practical composition. In contrast to works that he termed 'theoretico-practical', it was not written specifically to illuminate aspects of his theory.

On 4 April 1805 George played a 'Concerto piano-forte'—perhaps his father's concerto—in the Hanover Square rooms at a benefit concert for Mr Binger, a violinist.[287] And on 29 April, at a

[284] Copy in the Family History Library. The surname on the register of baptisms mistakenly has been written 'Hollmann', and the International Genealogical Index repeats this mistake.

[285] *Accounts relating to the Royal Establishment at Windsor*, House of Commons paper no. 230, 3 July 1820, p 4. It is not known when this pension started. It continued to be paid at least until 1837, as it is listed in *Return of Pensions now payable...*, House of Commons paper no. 351, 1 May 1838, p 2.

[286] Advertisements, *The Morning Post*, 14 March 1804, p 1, and *The Times*, 15 March 1804, p 1; title-page of the printed piano forte part of Kollmann's concerto.

[287] Advertisement, *The Times*, 27 March 1805, p 1; repeated 30 March 1805, p 1, and 4 April 1805, p 1. Mr Binger perhaps was the musician George Binger who was active

benefit for the oboist Frederick Griesbach, one of the five Griesbach brothers who had come to England from Hannover to join Queen Charlotte's private band,[288] George played a 'new concerto piano-forte' by Beethoven at Hyde's Rooms, Tottenham Street, with an orchestra again led by François Cramer.[289] As far as is known, this was the first public performance of a Beethoven piano concerto in England; the next such performance occurred fifteen years later.[290] Because the Beethoven concerto was advertised as 'new' it has been suggested that George played concerto no. 3, op. 37, which was first published in Vienna in 1804.[291] However, as no Beethoven piano concerto had previously been performed in London, each of the first three concertos—the remaining two were composed later—might have been described as 'new'. Thirty-three years later George played Beethoven's first piano concerto in London, but it is conceivable that by then he had mastered more than one Beethoven concerto.[292]

George's next performance was in the Great Room of the King's Theatre, Haymarket, where on 5 June 1805 he played a 'grand sonata' by the Austrian composer and pianist Joseph Woelfl, who had arrived in London the previous month.[293] This concert was held for the benefit of William Lee, who had charge of the box office of the Opera House and the Concerts of Antient Music. As François Cramer, who directed those Concerts, regularly led the orchestra at benefit concerts for Lee, it

---

in Plymouth, Devon in the years 1810–1814 (Plymouth and West Devon Record Office, ref. 219/1 and ref. 1/703/1816).

[288] See page 26 above.

[289] Advertisement, *The Times*, 27 April 1805, p 1; repeated 29 April 1805, p 1.

[290] See Therese Ellsworth, 'The piano concertos of Mozart and Beethoven: early performances in nineteenth-century London', in Jeremy Dibble and Bennett Zon (eds), *Nineteenth-Century British Music Studies*, Aldershot, 2002, p 169–181 at p 170–171 and p 178. George Kollmann's performance preceded the first London performance of a Mozart piano concerto by more than a year.

[291] *ibid.*, p 178.

[292] *The Musical World* (v 9 no. 122 (= n.s. v 2 no. 28), 12 July 1838, p 178) reported that George performed Beethoven's 'concerto in C major' on 5 July 1838.

[293] Advertisement, *The Times*, 4 June 1805, p 1. An advertisement in *The Times*, 23 May 1805, p 1, stated that Woelfl 'is just arrived in England'.

seems likely that George's participation in this concert was at Cramer's invitation.

The soprano Rosemond Mountain sang in the March 1804 and June 1805 concerts in which George played. She must have been impressed with his skill as she and her husband, the violinist John Mountain, invited him to join them on an Irish tour in August 1805. On 24 August she presented in Cork 'an entire nouvelle species of entertainment, in three acts, called *The Lyric Novelist, or, A Summer's Ramble*'.[294] Written by the Irish dramatist Andrew Cherry, with music by various composers, it was 'recited and sung' by Mrs Mountain, who was accompanied on the violin by her husband and on the piano by 'Master Kollman', billed as 'from the Nobility's Concerts, in Hanover-Square, London'. At the beginning of the entertainment's second act George played his father's piano concerto without an accompanying orchestra. Two evenings later these three musicians presented a different programme in Cork,[295] which they repeated in Waterford on 29 and 30 August.[296] For reasons not known, George apparently stopped playing in public after then until 1838, when he returned to the stage to demonstrate the novel piano that he had designed.

Joanna Kollmann made her first public appearance on 13 March 1806, singing a 'scena' by Mozart at the New Musical Fund concert in the King's Theatre, Haymarket.[297] François Cramer again led the band, and Woelfl played his new piano concerto featuring an Andante movement called 'The calm'. On 30 May 1806 she sang at a benefit concert for Frederick Griesbach, in which Woelfl repeated his concerto.[298] She was in good company as a 'principal vocal performer' at the New Musical Fund concert on 17 March 1808, as the other

---

[294] Playbill, Shaw Theatre Collection, Harvard University, Cork playbills no. 34.

[295] It included the entertainments (also written by Cherry) *All for Fame, or, A Peep at the Times* and *Life's Masquerade, or, Fortune's Wheel in Motion.* Playbill, Shaw Theatre Collection, Harvard University, Cork playbills no. 35.

[296] *Waterford Mirror*, 28 August 1805.

[297] Advertisement, *The Times*, 11 March 1806, p 1; repeated (with slight change) 13 March 1806, p 1.

[298] Advertisement, *The Times*, 26 May 1806, p 1; repeated 29 May 1806, p 1.

singers included Elizabeth Billington (a late substitute for Angelica Catalani, who was indisposed), Giuseppe Naldi and John Braham.[299]

Joanna's last known vocal performance was in the 'grand musical festival' at the Pantheon Theatre on 24 June 1811.[300] This was a benefit, conducted by Joseph Kemp, for the relief of Portuguese sufferers from the Peninsular war. She again appeared with Braham, Catalani, Naldi and other leading singers.

18. Development and Publication of *A New Theory* (1803–1806)

In his autobiography Kollmann said that 'with regard to music' he had 'applied himself' in England 'principally to its theoretical department', and in this area his accomplishments were profound. About 1803 he realised that the theory he had presented in *An Essay on Musical Harmony* was unsatisfactory because it failed to provide an adequate explanation for most occurrences of notes in musical compositions. He therefore endeavoured to devise a 'new theory' whose rules, he believed, could account for every note in a regular composition. Although a detailed presentation of his new theory would exceed the scope of this book, its structure needs to be described in order to appreciate his achievement and to understand the basis upon which he criticised people who held other theories.

As mentioned, Kollmann thought that the system in which Europeans of his era composed music was like a language. This system, accordingly, could be divided into grammatical and rhetorical components. Although he never clarified the boundary between musical grammar and rhetoric, the former includes notes, scales, chords, measures and some larger structures such as periods and

---

[299] Advertisements, *The Times*, 25 February 1808, p 1; 14 March 1808, p 1; and 15 March 1808, p 1.

[300] Advertisement, *The Times*, 17 June 1811, p 2 (repeated 18 June, 20 June and 21 June, all on p 2) and 24 June 1811, p 2; news report, *The Times*, 19 June 1811, p 4. The advertisements in *The Times* referred to 'Mrs Kollman' (except the 24 June advertisement had 'Miss Kullman'), but Joanna was the only known singer in her family.

sections. The organisation of periods and sections into movements, the character of a composition (for instance, whether it is a march, waltz, fugue or sonata), and the choice of voices or instruments to perform it, belong to musical rhetoric.

Kollmann wrote in his 1806 *New Theory* that 'all the systems of harmony hitherto known, seem to be reducible to three different sorts': those 'which depend on the mere individual appearance of intervals and chords', those 'which depend partly on the mere appearance, and in other parts on the proofs of intervals and chords', and 'systems which depend entirely on proofs'.[301] A 'proof', in this context, is a step-by-step derivation of a comparatively complex musical structure from a simpler musical structure whose regularity cannot be doubted.

Jean-Philippe Rameau's theory of harmony was a system of the second sort. Because Rameau required that 'all harmony must be reducible to a regular fundamental bass, as the *proof* of it',[302] the initial stage in his system was his theory of fundamental bass, which gave rules to determine whether a sequence of notes is an acceptable fundamental bass. A second stage of his theory reduced each chord in a musical composition to a fundamental bass note (or, proceeding in the other direction, generated each chord in a composition from a fundamental bass note). In this stage, therefore, different inversions of a chord were reduced to (or were generated from) the same fundamental bass note.

However, in his second stage, Rameau endeavoured to reduce every chord to a fundamental bass note according to the chord's 'individual appearance', without regard to the context in which the chord occurred. This (Kollmann said) led Rameau 'into the mistake of considering some suspensions as a sort of essential chords'.[303] In particular, his theory, and those of followers such as Marpurg, included categories for chords of the ninth, chords of the eleventh and chords of the thirteenth, and treated each of these categories separately.[304]

---

[301] *NTh*^{1}, p [1]-3. Kollmann summarised this distinction in *QMR p 45–46*.

[302] *NTh*^{1}, p 2. Kollmann remarked that this requirement was 'perfectly true'.

[303] *NTh*^{1}, p 2.

[304] The categories mentioned are Rameau's 'chords by supposition'. See *QMR p 53–54*.

Kollmann's first treatises on the grammatical and rhetorical components of music were *An Essay on Musical Harmony* and *An Essay on Practical Musical Composition* respectively. As noted above, he based the former essay principally upon Schulz's presentation of Kirnberger's theory in *Die wahren Grundsätze*. Like Rameau's theory, Kirnberger's theory had a fundamental-bass stage and a second stage in which essential chords—the triad and chord of the seventh—were reduced to, or generated from, their fundamental bass notes. However, it incorporated a third stage to account for a number of accidental (non-essential) chords—in particular, suspensions (which arise 'when one or more notes of a preceding chord, are carried into a following one, to which they do not belong'),[305] anticipations (which arise 'when one or more notes of a succeeding chord are introduced in the preceding one to which they do not belong'),[306] and transitions (which arise 'when in passing from one chord to another, some intermediate notes are introduced, which do not belong to the fundamental harmony' and 'need not always be contained' in the preceding or following chord).[307]

Kollmann claimed that Kirnberger's theory explained harmony in a simpler and more satisfactory way than the theories of Rameau or Marpurg. Instead of requiring hundreds of individual rules to account for chords of the ninth, eleventh and thirteenth in each of their inversions, Kirnberger and Kollmann analysed each of these chords as arising from suspension of the preceding essential chord, from anticipation of the following essential chord, or from the introduction of 'transient' intermediate notes between those chords. The resulting system—which Kollmann said 'is not the least perplexing' to students or performers—had the additional advantage of drawing musicians' attention '*to* some essential chord' in a composition, unlike the Rameau/Marpurg system, which required 'every accidental chord to be considered and figured like an essential one', and therefore drew musicians' attention away from the composition's essential chords.[308]

[305] *EMH*, p 46.

[306] *ibid.*, p 49.

[307] *ibid.*, p 50.

[308] *ibid.*, p 45–46.

After finishing *An Essay on Musical Harmony* Kollmann continued to give 'unremitted consideration' to the subject, 'either for the purpose of explaining it to others, or for my own clearer conviction in doubtful cases'.[309] He came to realise that, although Kirnberger's system depended 'entirely on the proofs of a regular connection' of the intervals and chords in a composition, and indeed was 'the only system hitherto known' that did this (rather than explaining them according to their 'mere individual appearance'), Kirnberger had 'stopped too short' in the development of his theory. He had 'confined his systematical doctrine of chords, to that of the fundamental concord and discord, with their inversions, as *essential* chords; and to the mere *prepared suspensions* of them, as *accidental* chords'. Accordingly,

> all the unprepared suspensions, as well as the preparing and unpreparing interruptions, made *no real part* of his system. For he considered the latter suspensions, and all the interruptions, merely in a manner as clouds may be considered in astronomy, viz. as occasional occurrences, which must be tolerated when there, but which must be passed by as if they were not there at all.
>
> And consequently his system is still incomplete; and disposes of more than one half of the notes and combinations useful in music in too arbitrary a manner.[310]

Kollmann 'therefore made it my particular study, to find out a simple method, by which every note that is useful in music, might have *as positive a rule*, as it denotes a *positive sound*'.[311] A theory that had sufficient structure to account for every note in a regular musical composition is one that he termed 'complete'.

About January 1803 he issued a printed prospectus of a work to be called *Key to a complete and natural System of Musical Harmony*.[312]

---

[309] *NTh*^{1}, p 4.

[310] *ibid.*, p 3–4.

[311] *ibid.*, p 4.

[312] See the entry 'Key Prospectus' in section III.2 below. No copy of the prospectus has been located. Kollmann sent one to John Wall Callcott with his letter of 14 January 1803 and probably included it with copies of *An Essay on Musical Harmony* that he sold about this time, as two copies of this *Essay* 'with Key' were sold as lots 194–195 in the 12–13 January 1860 Puttick & Simpson auction of the library of

The title indicates that he had formed by that time at least the outline of a complete theory. Although his intention at first was to publish the *Key* as a 'mere addition' to his *Essay on Musical Harmony*, he found after further consideration that he 'could not unite the two works, without spoiling them both'. He decided therefore to write a new treatise—the *New Theory*—in order to present 'the important improvements, which the proposed system makes in almost every branch of the science'.[313]

The way in which Kollmann achieved completeness was to incorporate rhythmic information about chords into the rules that generate (or analyse) them.[314] Whereas he had written in *An Essay on Musical Harmony* that a suspension arises 'when one or more notes of a preceding chord, are carried into a following one, to which they do not belong', the corresponding passage in the 1806 *New Theory* states that 'a suspension arises, when a retarding syncopation, or a transient note, is introduced in the *accented* time of an essential note' (i.e., a note that is part of an essential chord).[315] *A New Theory* accordingly provided, apparently for the first time, rules that accounted not only for a chord's constituent notes but also for its place within a measure.[316]

Kollmann used the word 'measure' to refer to 'the division of a harmonious or melodious progression, into certain equal portions of time'. *A New Theory* allows three 'simple' measures, in which a bar of music consists of two, three or four equal times; and also 'compound' measures, in which a bar contains two or more simple measures. Each of the equal times in a measure 'may be divided in as many lesser times, as can be produced in it'.[317] The 'principal characteristic' of a simple measure is that 'the first time of the measure is *accented*, and the rest *unaccented*'. Thus a simple measure of four equal times, whose time-signature is **C** or a fraction with numerator 4, has an accentuation

---

William James Brown Jr. The auctioneer's copy of this sale catalogue is at BL S.-C. Puttick 64 (3).

313 *NTh*^{1}, preface.

314 The word 'chord' refers here to one or more notes attacked simultaneously.

315 *NTh*^{1}, p 33.

316 Although time and rhythm were treated in Chapters XI–XII of *An Essay on Musical Harmony*, that treatise did not connect time or rhythm with chord generation.

317 *NTh*^{1}, p 76.

pattern that Kollmann represented as '— ⌣ ⌣ ⌣'.[318] It is useful to say—although he did not use these terms—that a chord has a 'measure accent' if it begins at the start of a measure, and has a 'beat accent' if it begins at the start of one of the equal times in its measure.[319]

The definition of 'suspension' in the first edition of *A New Theory* therefore can be understood as illustrated in *Example 1* on page 84. Its top staff depicts a fundamental bass. The symbol '7' above the second and fourth notes signifies that they represent fundamental discords, whereas the notes which have no '7' represent fundamental concords. Kollmann gave explicit rules to decide whether a sequence of fundamental concords and discords is allowable as a fundamental bass.

The middle brace of staves in *Example 1* presents a sequence of essential chords (triads or chords of the seventh) whose roots are the fundamental-bass notes shown on the top staff. Some rhythmic information about each of these chords is indicated at this stage. The first, third and last chords have a measure accent, but the second and fourth chords do not, and each of these chords has a beat accent.

The music in the bottom brace of staves is generated from the music in the middle brace by a rule that enables suspensions to be introduced under specified conditions. Although theorists who treated the first chord in the second bar of the bottom brace 'according to its individual appearance' would have classified it as a chord of the ninth and would have generated it directly from a fundamental-bass note, Kirnberger and Kollmann derive it from the composition in the middle brace rather than immediately from a fundamental-bass note. Because suspensions in *A New Theory* are introduced 'in the accented time' of an essential note, D and A in bar 2 of the bottom brace are beat-accented and displace the C and B—which had occupied an entire beat in the preceding stage—to an unaccented time of their beat.

A fuller example of a derivation worked out according to the *New Theory*'s rules has been published elsewhere.[320]

---

[318] *NTh*[1], p 75–76.

[319] The use of the word 'beat' to mean one of the equal portions of time in a measure began after Kollmann's lifetime.

[320] Michael Kassler, 'Kollmann's proof of the regularity of Bach's *Chromatic Fantasy*', *EBA* p 211–249.

A fundamental bass

Essential chords generated from the fundamental bass above

Two suspensions introduced into bar 2 of the preceding composition (the first suspension is a syncopation; the second is a transient note)

Example 1. Three stages of a composition's generation, according to Kollmann's A New Theory

A premise of Kollmann's theory is that every octave includes only twelve tones. Enharmonic equivalents, such as C♯ and D♭ in the same octave, are not distinguished in his theory. This premise is plausible because much European music of his time was composed for keyed instruments such as a clavier, organ or piano that could sound only twelve pitches per octave and therefore required enharmonic equivalents to be played on the same key. Although the premise was controversial, Kollmann defended it by noting that

> the twelve semitones in an octave, and their replicates, called the diatonic chromatic scale, are of so wonderful a constitution that, when properly tuned, they form a *compound*, of *twelve* diatonic and chromatic scales of the same use, in *one*.
>
> This *compound* nature of our scale answers the following great purposes. First, that every one, of its twelve notes, can be made a *key note*, of an equally constituted, and equally useful, diatonic chromatic scale, as that of the gravest note. Secondly, that every one, of the seven notes, of a modern diatonic scale, can carry the *same natural chords*, and take the same harmonious and melodious *progressions*, as the key note.[321]

Based upon this premise Kollmann later criticised inventions of keyed instruments that could produce more than twelve pitches per octave.[322]

A New Theory exposed Kollmann's original concepts to the public, and he endeavoured to ensure that it would have a wide readership. Its dedication to the president and council of the Royal Society of London presumably was designed to bring his ideas to the attention of England's leading researchers.[323] Although the Society's council ordered that thanks be sent to Kollmann for his gift of a copy,[324] other evidence of the book's influence on the Society has not been found.[325]

---

[321] *QMR p 75.*

[322] See, for example, *QMR p 74–79* and *p 148–152.*

[323] Particularly in its earlier years, the Royal Society welcomed reports of new musical discoveries alongside reports of discoveries in other fields. See Leta Miller and Albert Cohen, *Music in the Royal Society of London 1660–1806*, Detroit, 1987.

[324] At its 5 June 1806 meeting chaired by the president, Sir Joseph Banks.

[325] Royal Society of London, Council Book entry for 5 June 1806. Kollmann's gift also was recorded in the *Philosophical Transactions of the Royal Society of London* v 96

It is plausible that Charles Burney—who had been elected a fellow of the Royal Society in 1773 and regarded *An Essay on Musical Harmony* as the best book on the subject in English[326]—suggested that Kollmann dedicate *A New Theory* to the Society. Kollmann seems likely to have known other fellows of the Society such as George Best, the secretary of the German Chancery; William Herschel, the Hannover-born uncle of the Griesbach brothers; and Thomas Young, who had studied music with Forkel at the University of Göttingen.[327]

A New Theory had an additional link with the Royal Society, as Kollmann engaged the Society's printer, William Bulmer, to set and to print its letterpress text. The thirty-six pages of engraved music examples which accompanied that text presumably were printed elsewhere, as his biographer found 'no evidence that Bulmer ever printed engraved plates'.[328] Bulmer's partner George Nicol, bookseller to King George III, had subscribed to *An Essay on Practical Musical Composition* and conceivably introduced Kollmann to Bulmer, whose premises in Cleveland Row were a short walk from St James's Palace.[329]

When the Royal Society appointed Bulmer on 22 December 1791 to print its *Philosophical Transactions*, his predecessor, John Nichols, was informed that 'the only reason for the change was a preference to the new mode of Printing, which no one but Mr Bulmer can execute'.[330] In 1795 Bulmer described this new mode as an endeavour 'to combine the various beauties of printing, type-founding, engraving, and paper-making ... with a view to ascertain the near

---

part 2 (1806) p 472. Kollmann's presentation copy of *A New Theory* is in the Royal Society library. It has no handwritten inscriptions or annotations.

[326] Burney→Mrs Chambers, 19/1/1798, summarised in section III.4 below.

[327] Young owned at least one of Kollmann's works. See Michael Kassler, 'The English translations of Forkel's *Life of Bach*', *EBA* p 169–209 at p 173–174.

[328] Peter Isaac, *William Bulmer: the fine Printer in Context, 1757–1830*, London, 1993, p 140.

[329] The partnership between Bulmer and Nicol 'carried on under the name and firm of William Bulmer and Company, at the Shakespeare Printing-Office, Cleveland Row, St James's', was dissolved on 31 December 1819 (*London Gazette* no. 17650 (11 November 1820) p 2118). Their partnership seems likely to have preceded the establishment of W. Bulmer & Co. in 1790 (see Isaac, p 25–26).

[330] Isaac, p 41.

approach to perfection which those arts have attained in this country'.[331] He noted that the types used to print that book had been executed by William Martin (from which the 'Monotype Bulmer' font used to print this book has been derived) and that the ornaments had been engraved on blocks of wood by his acquaintances 'Messrs Bewicks'.[332] Bulmer acquired sole access to Martin's typefaces,[333] although he also used other typefaces in his work.[334]

The skill of the Bulmer firm is evident in the title-page of the first edition of *A New Theory*, reproduced in *Figure 6* facing page 142. In addition to letterpress text this page includes a 'vignette' which, Kollmann said, showed 'the whole system' of his theory in a single music example.[335] Although at first glance the vignette looks as if it were printed from an engraved plate, no plate marks are visible on the title-page, whereas they are clearly present on each of the separately printed pages of musical examples.[336] Printing engraved plates, which have intaglio surfaces, required a different press from that used to print type, which has a relief surface. As Bulmer lacked a press to print engraved plates, he and Kollmann presumably wanted to avoid the cost and difficulties of sending out partly printed sheets to someone who did.

Bulmer (it is hypothesised) solved the problem of printing letterpress text and music simultaneously in the following way.[337] First, the music example was engraved outside his firm in the usual way. A print made from the engraved plate then was pressed onto a metal block, transferring ink onto its surface at the points where notes, staff

---

[331] W[illiam] B[ulmer], 'Advertisement', in *Poems by Goldsmith and Parnell*, London, 1795, p [v]–viii at p [v]–vi. W. Bulmer & Co. printed this work.

[332] *ibid.*, p vi–vii. 'Messrs Bewicks' were the wood engravers Thomas Bewick and his brother John.

[333] Isaac, p 35–37.

[334] *ibid.*, p 131.

[335] *NTh*[1], p 81. The musical content of this vignette is discussed below in a note to *QMR p 58*.

[336] I thank D. W. Krummel for examining the Newberry Library copy of *NTh*[1] and Michael Twyman for examining the British Library copy of *NTh*[1] and the copies of both editions in the library of Jamie and Michael Kassler.

[337] I am very grateful to Michael Twyman for proposing this hypothesis.

lines and other symbols in the music example had been engraved. Next, using those points as a guide, the block's surface was etched so that the areas covered by these points were in relief. Finally the block was positioned, with type above and below it, into a forme from which the whole title-page was printed in a single impression. This hypothesis accounts for the engraving-like appearance of the music in the vignette. After the title-page was printed, the metal block was saved by Bulmer or Kollmann and reused—although the surrounding letterpress text was entirely reset—in the 1823 second edition of *A New Theory* that was printed by Bulmer's successor, William Nicol (George's son).[338]

As far as is known, Bulmer's use of a metal block to print music which appears at first sight to have been punched by engraving tools is unique. Kollmann must have liked the result, as he re-engaged Bulmer to print the first number of *The Quarterly Musical Register*, whose title-page also combined letterpress text with music notation. However, as described below, Bulmer used a different technique to print that page.

In *A New Theory* Kollmann said that friends had advised him to insert all the music examples 'between the text', but that 'the number, and the length of some of them', prevented this.[339] Presumably he could afford the cost of preparing a metal block for the title-page vignette, but not the expense of making hundreds of such blocks.

The content of each chapter of *A New Theory* is summarised on pages 45–59 of *The Quarterly Musical Register*. By 1806 both Burney

---

[338] The use of the same block to print the vignette in *NTh*[1] and *NTh*[2] is shown by the fourth staff line in the lowest staff having the same brief deviation from straightness in copies from both editions. In the copy of *NTh*[2] in the library of Jamie and Michael Kassler the vignette's lowest staff line turns up at its end, indicating that it was printed from a metal block that somehow had become bent, rather than from a wooden block.

[339] *NTh*[1], preface, p [i]. In his review of *A Practical Guide to Thorough-Bass*, which was printed from engraved plates, John Wall Callcott was pleased that Kollmann had 'made considerable improvements in his mode of publication, by intermixing precept and example' (*British Critic* v 18 (October 1801) p 389–399 at p 389; his praise of this is reiterated on p 398). In Callcott's book *A Musical Grammar* (London, 1806), the music examples were printed together with the text by Buchanan Macmillan, who used music type to set these examples. No evidence has been found that Bulmer had such type. Besides his work done for Kollmann he printed one other treatise on music, Samuel Rootsey's *An Attempt to Simplify the Notation of Music*, London, 1811, which Kollmann briefly describes in *QMR p 27–28*. The only music notation in Rootsey's work was separately printed from an engraved plate of illustrations.

and Callcott had stopped writing music reviews, and the only contemporary independent criticism of *A New Theory* appears to have been published in *The Monthly Magazine*.[340] The reviewer, presumably Thomas Busby, found the treatise 'elaborate and erudite', comprising 'as far as it is at present known, the whole science of musical harmony', and commented that it was 'meant as an improvement or correction of a former publication on the same subject'. After outlining the content of the treatise he concluded that

> Those musical students who wish to fathom the depths of the science, and see the *rationale* of their practice, will derive much and rapid improvement from the perusal of this volume, and soon find themselves adequate to the ready comprehension of the most abstruse passages of the classical masters.[341]

19. Kollmann and *La Belle Assemblée* (1806–1807)

On 1 March 1806, the publisher John Bell, an experienced newspaper proprietor, printer and typefounder,[342] issued the first number (dated February 1806) of a monthly periodical 'addressed particularly to the ladies' entitled *La Belle Assemblée, or, Bell's Court and Fashionable Magazine*. 'Embellishments' provided with the first volume included needlework patterns and music that were printed from lithographic plates. The printing of these embellishments is attributed to Georg Jacob Vollweiler because he had 'the only lithographic press known to have been working in the country at the time'.[343]

---

[340] As noted below, the remarks about *A New Theory* published in the December 1806 number of *La Belle Assemblée* apparently were written by Kollmann himself.

[341] *Monthly Magazine* v 22 no. 2 (1 September 1806) p 170. This review was reprinted in Philadelphia, with minor alterations, in *The Literary Magazine, and American Register* v 6 no. 39 (December 1806) p 479.

[342] For a biographical account of Bell that emphasises his printing and publishing activities see Stanley Morison, *John Bell, 1745–1831*, Cambridge, 1930.

[343] According to Twyman, *Early Lithographed Music, op. cit.*, p 383–385, needlework patterns for *La Belle Assemblée* were printed from lithographed plates to 'the middle of 1807', but only a few music embellishments were so printed. Most music embellishments in that magazine were printed from engraved plates. A prospectus for a publication by Bell had been printed by Philippe André about 1803 (see Twyman,

Kollmann was associated with *La Belle Assemblée* for a year, starting with the November 1806 number published on 1 December 1806, whose title-page said that the month's embellishments would include 'two German Waltzs, by Dr. Kellmann, and Mr. Andre' [sic].[344] The last page of this number, however, said that 'An original Walz, by Dr. Kollmann, is composed and given in the present Number' and did not mention André.[345] The embellishment itself—a single foldout sheet of engraved music headed 'Original country dances, strathspey, and waltz. Composed (for the Year 1807.)'—contains a 32-bar composition by Kollmann entitled 'General Hutchinson's Waltz', but no waltz by André, implying that Bell had excluded it at the last minute.[346]

Vollweiler's participation in the initial production of *La Belle Assemblée*, and the circumstance that the first mention of Kollmann in that periodical incorrectly called him a doctor and linked him with André, suggest that Bell had not met Kollmann when the journal began publication and that Vollweiler may have introduced them.[347]

Lithography 1800–1850, *op. cit.*, p 42–43), who presumably told Vollweiler that Bell was a potential client. The first lithographed music in *La Belle Assemblée*—a song 'Only tell her that I love' by Domenico Corri—bears the publication date 1 March 1806. This was not Vollweiler's first lithographically printed music in England: see note 251 above.

[344] *La Belle Assemblée*, v 1 no. 10 (November 1806) p [503]. The misspelling 'Kellmann' apparently was noticed while the title-page was being printed, and the type changed to read 'Kollmann' before printing resumed. Copies of both states of the title-page are in the library of Jamie and Michael Kassler, Northbridge, NSW, Australia.

[345] *ibid.*, p 558. Advertisements in *The Times*, 29 November 1806, p 1, and *Bell's Weekly Messenger* no. 556 (30 November 1806) p 382, said that 'a German Waltz, by Dr. Kolman' [sic] would be included in this number and did not mention André.

[346] Curiously, Vollweiler printed and sold about this time a single lithographed sheet (in the library of Jamie and Michael Kassler) containing André's *The Offenbach Waltz*.

[347] The British Museum Department of Prints and Drawings possesses (shelfmark 190*.b.01 p 52) a lithographed portrait of John Bell, bearing the ink inscription 'Mr Bell Editor of the Weekly Messenger by G Arnold', evidently a reference to the painter George Arnald. T[homas] Fisher→'Mr [Sylvanus] Urban' [editor of *The Gentleman's Magazine*], printed in *The Gentleman's Magazine* v 78 = n.s. v 1 (March 1808) p 193–196, stated (p 196) that the lithographed portrait of Bell was 'executed' for Bell. The portrait is undated, and it is not known whether it was printed by Philippe André or by Vollweiler. I am grateful to Alison Wright of the British Museum for information about their copy of this portrait.

La Belle Assemblée announced in its September 1806 number that it would publish articles on music.[348] A two-part article 'On singing' followed immediately and concluded two months later. It was not signed and its content does not indicate that Kollmann was the author.[349] However, the following number, dated December 1806 and published on 1 January 1807, included an unsigned article 'On thorough-bass' that obviously was contributed by Kollmann, as it deals exclusively with his published and forthcoming works and praises his and his children's achievements lavishly:

> ... we feel a particular satisfaction in having it in our power to make our readers acquainted with a new method of learning Thorough-Bass, which removes all the former difficulties, and which has been published in a work this summer, entitled, 'A New Theory of Musical Harmony'.... Nothing can ... be more easy, even for ladies and amateurs, who do not wish to spend all their time in the study of one art or science, than to obtain a true knowledge of harmony and thorough-bass, according to the proposed new system by Mr. Kollmann. ...
>
> It is ... a great mistake of a certain author, that the new theory [of Kollmann] is a mere improvement of the first essay [his *Essay on Musical Harmony*].[350] For the system of the latter work is as distinctly different from that of the former one, as Newton's system is from any other....
>
> [His] pieces standing with the greatest credit [in the *Essay on Practical Musical Composition*] among the masterly productions of Handel, Sebastian, and Emanuel Bach, Clementi, &c. ... shew that our author can not only reason upon composition, but also exemplify the practice of it by his own works. And to these we may add his concerto, Op. VIII. as one of the most classical, as well as most brilliant pieces of its kind. ...
>
> Mr. Kollmann has two children, viz. a daughter, (Miss K.) who is a capital singer, and one of those few, who at present know how to form and cultivate a voice in a regular manner. ... His son, (Mr. George K.) is known as a first-rate player on the piano forte; to which we may add, that he is also a very perfect harmonist, having had no other musical instruction than that of his father. Of this distinguished musical family, we shall, no doubt, have frequent opportunities to take further notice in our succeeding Numbers.[351]

---

[348] *La Belle Assemblée* v 1 no. 8 (September 1806) p 433.

[349] Kollmann stated some of his views on singing on *QMR p 20–21*.

[350] Kollmann was responding to the reviewer of *A New Theory* in the 1 September 1806 *Monthly Magazine*. See page 89 above.

[351] *La Belle Assemblée* v 1 no. 11 (December 1806) p 600–602.

The next music article, 'On the art of playing the piano-forte', appeared in the numbers for January and February 1807. Although anonymous, it also can be attributed to Kollmann because of its attention to and admiration of his work:

> The importance of these questions is evident; and the first and only author who seems to have attended to them is Mr. Kollmann, whose distinguished merit in the higher branches of the science of music we have shewn in our last number. The valuable, though small work, he has published for that purpose, is entitled: 'The first beginning on the Piano-Forte, according to an improved method of teaching beginners.' ...
>
> The two greatest and most celebrated professors of the piano-forte now in this country, are Mr. J. B. Cramer, and Mr. Woelfl ... and the only junior one we venture to mention immediately after them, is Mr. George Kollman....[352]

This article was followed by a long essay in the numbers for June and August 1807 reviewing a booklet by Charles, 3rd Earl Stanhope, called *Principles of the Science of Tuning Instruments with fixed Tones.*[353] This time Kollmann was identified as the author. The essay begins:

> Though persons of rank and fashion (amongst whom *La Belle Assemblée* is particularly circulated), cannot be expected to apply themselves to the tuning of their piano-fortes or organs, they may be desirous to know whether their instruments are in tune, and according to what principles they can be tuned....

Kollmann then outlined his concept of 'the modern scale', upon which his theory of tonality is based. In contrast to 'a scale of nature', whose

---

[352] *La Belle Assemblée* v 2 no. 1 (January 1807) p 36–38 and v 2 no. 2 (February 1807) p 94–96. A further indication of Kollmann's authorship can be seen on p 38, where the names of two composers appear as 'Heibelt' and 'Herkel' because the typesetter misread Kollmann's 'St' as an 'H'. The manuscript of Kollmann's autobiography, in which he wrote 'St' on the second line, shows that his writing of this pair of letters could readily be misinterpreted as an 'H'. (This is less clear in his 1812 letter reproduced as the frontispiece of this book, where he used a superscript underscored 't' rather than a 't' of normal size when writing his address 'Friary St James's'.)

[353] London, 1806. Kollmann's essay was published in *La Belle Assemblée* v 2 no. 18 (June 1807) p 321–323 and v 3 no. 21 (August 1807) p 99–101.

sounds are obtained by dividing a vibrating string in the ratios 1:1, 1:2, 1:3, ..., 1:16, the modern scale has just twelve notes in each octave.[354]

> [T]he twelve notes of our chromatic octave ... are to be considered as a compound of twelve ... scales, each of which must be calculated for the same use in harmony and melody as all the others.[355]
>
> Our modern scale therefore cannot contain that strict perfection of every interval which it might have [had] as a simple scale of one key note; and its compound state requires that some of its intervals lose a little of their individual perfection, for the purpose of producing a greater perfection and agreement in the whole.[356] This distribution, by which some intervals are rendered a little sharper, and others a little flatter, than strictly perfect, is called the temperament of our scale; and its different sorts can be brought under the two general heads of an equal, or some unequal temperament.
>
> By an equal temperament, is understood that distribution which renders the distances between the twelve notes of our scale so much alike that the ear cannot find any difference between them. And an unequal[357] one [which Earl Stanhope proposed in his booklet] is that by which the same intervals are rendered more perfect in some keys than in others.

Although an octave consisting just of twelve notes does not have to be sounded in equal temperament, Kollmann increasingly preferred that temperament to alternatives. In the first edition of *A New Theory* he had said:

---

[354] Kollmann provided greater detail about this concept in *A New Theory*, where he wrote that 'all modern music arises from the *twelve semitones* of the Diatonic-chromatic scale, and their repetitions in the octave, above or below; in a similar manner, as the books written in a language, are composed of the letters of its alphabet' (*NTh*[1], p 4). He went on to suggest how the modern scale might have developed from the tetrachords used in ancient Greek music.

[355] i.e., disregarding octaves, the 'modern' chromatic scale starting on C uses the same twelve notes as the 'modern' chromatic scale starting on C♯ or on any other of the twelve notes. The 'great purposes' answered by this 'compound nature of our scale' are further discussed in *QMR p 75–76*.

[356] Kollmann was adapting Leibniz's assertion 'that an imperfection in the part may be required for a greater perfection in the whole' (Leibniz, *Theodicy: Essays on the goodness of God, the freedom of man and the origin of evil*, translated by E[veleen] M. Huggard, London, 1951 [*recte* 1952], p 378; first published as *Essais de théodicée...*, Amsterdam, 1710).

[357] *La Belle Assemblée* v 2 no. 18 (June 1807) p 322, has 'equal' here, but this obviously is a mistake.

> Of the described two sorts of temperament, an *equal*, or nearly equal one, is the best for any instrument that shall be played with others. But a good *unequal* one, is better for an organ or piano forte, that is to be played without any accompaniment; particularly when a great performer is to play extempore fantasias upon it.[358]

In the June 1807 *La Belle Assemblée* he wrote that 'if one of those temperaments [equal or unequal] was to be adopted universally and exclusively of the other, the equal one undoubtedly must have the preference'.[359] And in the second, 1823 edition of *A New Theory*, he changed the previously quoted paragraph to read:

> Of the described two sorts of temperament, the ... *equal* temperament, is by far the most desirable one. For without it, no general agreement can be produced between the instruments of an orchestra, and the human voice; and the custom of making a difference between G sharp and A flat, D sharp and E flat, &c. on bow instruments, is justly disapproved by the best modern writers.[360]

Stanhope had rejected equal temperament because it requires every interval other than the octave to lose the 'perfection' it has in the 'scale of nature'; therefore 'every thing is discord'.[361] Although particular unequal temperaments rendered 'some keys too bad to modulate into them without offending the ear extremely', he felt that 'every key' in the unequal temperament proposed in his booklet 'is made pleasing, and fit for transposition and modulation, and has also a *peculiar character* which belongs to it. Some keys are fitted for chearful music; some, for grave. Some, for martial; some, for pastoral.'[362]

---

[358] *NTh*[1], p 9.

[359] *La Belle Assemblée, loc. cit.* See also *QMR p 76*: 'it is indespensably necessary, to dispose of those twelve notes either at *equal*, or at such nearly equal distances, as may pass for equal'.

[360] *NTh*[2], p 8.

[361] Stanhope, *op. cit.*, p 10.

[362] *ibid.*, p 12. On 15 November 1804, shortly after formulating his temperament, Stanhope wrote to Rev. John North (copy in Stanhope of Chevening mss, Centre for Kentish Studies, Maidstone, in folder U1590/C91/9), saying 'I have discovered a new and most delightful mode of tuning Instruments'. To test his discovery he had a 'large piano' tuned according to his new temperament and compared its sound with that of

Kollmann replied 'that as it is difficult to find in this world any thing perfect in the strictest sense, we must admit as perfect enough those things in which no imperfection is very perceptible'. Moreover, Stanhope's temperament 'is too intricate, not only to be produced, but also to be preserved in any stringed instrument'. Indeed, 'without the strict exactness of those almost infinite ratios' by which it is specified, 'the Stanhope temperament is a mere pretence' that 'has never yet existed, and can never exist'.[363]

Kollmann recognised that, although an equal temperament 'may at first sight appear easy to tune, it is hardly possible by the ear alone to temper every fifth no more and no less than' the small amount mathematically required, 'and therefore we must be satisfied, with producing it as nearly as possible'.[364] He did not say that Stanhope's temperament also could be approximated. Nevertheless, Kollmann's support of equal temperament was upheld by the subsequent common practice of musicians.

He made one further contribution to *La Belle Assemblée*: 'An Original Waltz for the Year 1808' appeared as an embellishment to its December 1807 number.[365] It is not known why his association with this journal ended, but the experience he gained from writing articles and music for it undoubtedly prepared and encouraged him to launch *The Quarterly Musical Register* four years later. That journal, like *La Belle Assemblée*, was aimed at readers who had an interest in music but had not necessarily studied treatises on the subject.

'another piano, by the same Maker, in the same ... Room' that was 'tuned in Dr Hayden's [Joseph Haydn's] Method, of equal distribution of the Imperfections'—i.e., in equal temperament—which is 'the most approved of by Dr Burney, by Mr [Augustus] Meves, Solomon [John Peter Salomon], &c. Mrs L [the pianist Walburga Lackner, Stanhope's housekeeper] tried charming pieces composed by Mozart, Hayden, Hanka [Karl Hanke], Steibelt, Pleyel, by herself &c. in the 12 major, and in the 12 minor Keys. There was no Comparison. My Method was found to be superior in every Key. And, in some, so superior that it is delightful!'

363 *La Belle Assemblée* v 3 no. 21 (August 1807) p 100–101.

364 *NTh*[1], p 9.

365 The review of Kollmann's *Twelve Analyzed Fugues* published amongst the 'Critical sketches of recent music' in the February 1811 supplementary number of *La Belle Assemblée* presumably was not by him, as it is not entirely complimentary.

20. *A Second Practical Guide to Thorough-Bass* (1807–1808)

Because *A New Theory* superseded Kirnberger's system, *A Practical Guide to Thorough-Bass*, which was based upon that system, no longer presented Kollmann's current thoughts. In December 1806 he noted that a replacement was 'in the press, and ready for publication',[366] and *A Second Practical Guide to Thorough-Bass* appeared in March 1807. It was dedicated to 'Her Royal Highness Princess Sophia Matilda'—i.e., Princess Sophia Matilda of Gloucester, who had subscribed to *An Essay on Practical Musical Composition*.[367] Nothing is known about her contact with Kollmann or her interest in thorough bass.[368]

Some plates of musical examples from the first *Practical Guide* were reprinted in the second guide with minor alterations such as changes of page number, but most of the text pages, including the title-page and dedication page, were printed from newly engraved plates.

In the Preface to *A Second Practical Guide* Kollmann claimed that his *New Theory* removed

> all former difficulties in the study of harmony so effectually, that it makes the almost infinite number of harmonious and melodious varieties, useful in composition, depend on a FEW simple general rules, WITHOUT ONE EXCEPTION; and that it disposes of every adopted or yet unadopted chord contained in our modern scale, in as positive and simple manner, as every visited and unvisited spot on the globe of our earth is ascertained by the degrees of Longitude and Latitude.

---

[366] *La Belle Assemblée* v 1 no. 11 (December 1806) p 601. He added 'This, we presume to say, will deserve to be in the hands of every musical person'.

[367] Princess Sophia, daughter of King George III and Queen Charlotte, also had the second name Matilda but did not subscribe to Kollmann's *Essay* and is not known to have had any connection with him. As in the subscription list to that *Essay*, Kollmann incorrectly gave Princess Sophia Matilda—daughter of Prince William Henry, Duke of Gloucester and Edinburgh, and niece of George III—the title 'Her Royal Highness'. She was granted that title in 1816 but was 'Her Highness' before then.

[368] She must have studied music, as the composer and harpist Joseph Elouis styled himself in 1802 'Harp Master to Her Royal Highness, Princess Sophia of Gloucester', according to an advertisement in *Berrow's Worcester Journal*. The text has been posted on the Internet at archive.worcesternews.co.uk/2002/8/23/ but the day when the advertisement was printed has not been recorded.

> According to this system therefore, a musical Lady or Amateur may now, by a moderate application, obtain a perfect and satisfactory knowledge of harmony; when according to former systems it is impossible to obtain the same knowledge, almost in any time, and with the utmost perseverance.[369]

He added that 'the present work is calculated more for a familiar guide to the knowledge of chords, and their practical use to a figured bass, than for a complete treatise of all the mysteries of harmony'. Readers interested in the 'reasons of all which is but simply taught in this work' were referred to *A New Theory*.[370]

After *A New Theory* was typeset Kollmann changed his nomenclature for accidental notes (notes not part of an essential chord), replacing 'suspension' and 'interruption' with 'forenote' and 'afternote' respectively. The new terms—first published in *A Second Practical Guide*—emphasised the rhythmic essence and the symmetry of these concepts. Whereas he had written on page 33 of the 1806 *New Theory*:

> A suspension arises, when a retarding syncopation, or transient note, is introduced in the *accented* time of an essential note. For the accidental note which thus appears, *suspends*, or defers the beginning of the essential note....

in *A Second Practical Guide* he said, regarding the same concept:

> A forenote is an accidental note introduced in the ACCENTED time of an essential one. In melody it is called an Appoggiatura, and in harmony a Suspension. But in both cases it is nothing more than a grace before the essential note, in whose time it stands, and into which it must be resolved.[371]

And in the 1823 second edition of *A New Theory* he changed the penultimate quotation to read on page 29:

> A forenote arises, when a *retarding syncopation*, or a *transient* note, is introduced in the *accented* time of an essential chord, or note. And the accidental note which thus arises *suspends*, or defers, the beginning of the essential note....

---

[369] *2nd PGTB*, p vi. The content of this book is outlined in *QMR p 113–115*.

[370] *ibid.*

[371] *2nd PGTB*, p 15.

In contrast to the first *Practical Guide*, where accidental chords were categorised as arising by suspension, by anticipation, and by the introduction of passing notes, the second *Practical Guide* treated passing notes as either forenotes or afternotes. Following *A New Theory*, organ points now were introduced as a third category of accidental chord.[372] Because Kollmann removed a section of music examples for students to practise, the second *Guide* was much shorter than the first, comprising viii + 46 pages instead of viii + 68 pages.

In return for Johann Anton André's gifts of some of his firm's publications, Kollmann sent copies of *A New Theory* and *A Second Practical Guide to Thorough-Bass* to André, perhaps via Vollweiler. André was sufficiently impressed with both works to republish *A Second Practical Guide* in a bilingual edition and to take steps to translate *A New Theory* into German.[373]

The bilingual edition, entitled *A Practical Guide to Thorough Bass | Practische Anleitung zum Generalbaße*, in which the English text and a German translation appear side by side, was printed from words and music handwritten on stone[374] and appears to have been one of the first two music treatises ever lithographed.[375] It has an introductory

---

372 See *PGTB*, Chapter VIII 'Of accidental chords', p 20–23, and *2nd PGTB*, Chapter VI 'Of accidental chords', p 15–20.

373 André's effort to have *A New Theory* translated is recorded in 'Nachrichten. London', *Allgemeine musikalische Zeitung* v 17 no. 31 (2 August 1815) col. 521: 'Von den ersten [edition of *A New Theory*] hat Hr. André in Offenbach eine Uebersetzung veranstaltet'. The same report said that Kollmann himself would translate the second edition of *A New Theory* after he finished it ['der Verf. ... wird auch selbst eine deutsche Uebersetzung davon liefern']. No translation of either edition was published, and it is not known whether any translation was ever completed.

374 Although the English title of André's bilingual edition is that of Kollmann's first guide, its text is that of *A Second Practical Guide*. It is not known whether Kollmann made the German translation. A reviewer commented (*Allgemeine musikalische Zeitung* v 11 no. 25 (22 March 1809) col. 390–395) that a bilingual edition was unnecessary for German readers, as it would have been sufficient if just the German translation had been published.

375 Michael Twyman, *Early Lithographed Books*, London, 1990, reported (p 107) that 'the earliest lithographed [music] method books to be traced so far were published by André in Offenbach', namely, Jean-Louis Duport, *Essai sur le doigté du violoncelle*, plate no. 2599, and Muzio Clementi, *Méthode pour le piano forte*, plate no. 2738. Both these works also were published from bilingual (French and German) text that was

note by the editor ['Anzeige des Herausgebers'] dated Offenbach, May 1808, stating that Kollmann's works have been recognised in England for more than ten years as the pre-eminent ['vorzüglichsten'] works of their type, and that his theory upon which the *Guide* is based—i.e., *A New Theory*—deserves to be known in Germany because of its simplicity. Although the editor was not named in the publication, he can be identified as André himself, because 'the editor' inscribed a copy of this work to Ernst Ludwig Gerber on behalf of Kollmann, and this inscription is in André's handwriting.[376]

Notwithstanding his support of Kollmann in the first two decades of the nineteenth century, André did not mention him in his 1832 textbook on musical composition, and the doctrines presented in that book do not appear to have been influenced by Kollmann's *New Theory*.[377]

21. Theoretico-Practical Works Illustrating *A New Theory* (1809–1810)

In addition to writing *A Second Practical Guide* to demonstrate how his 'new theory' would benefit students of thorough bass, Kollmann composed music to illustrate, often in a humorous way, some of this theory's features.

---

handwritten side by side (*ibid.*, p 108–110); according to Twyman, *Early Lithographed Music*, London, 1996, p 299, both were products of 'direct lithography' written on stone in reverse (*ibid.*, p 502-503). Kollmann's treatise, which has plate no. 2601 (two more than Duport's), was lithographed by the same process and presumably was printed about the same time.

[376] The inscription reads 'Im Namen des Autors des schätzbahren Herrn Hoffsecretair Gerber in Sondershausen | von dessen Bruder | dem Herausgeber' [In the name of the author, to the esteemed court secretary Gerber in Sondershausen, from his brother, the editor]. I thank Ingrid Fuchs of the Gesellschaft der Musikfreunde, Vienna, where this copy and many other items from Gerber's library are held, for transcribing this inscription and identifying its handwriting as André's. His use of the word 'Bruder' indicates the closeness of their relationship at this time. In his treatise *Lehrbuch der Tonsetzkunst*, v 1, Offenbach, 1832, p 339, André referred to Gerber as his deceased friend ['meinen verstorbenen Freund'].

[377] André, *op. cit.* A second volume of this book was published posthumously in 1843.

Opus 9, entitled 'The melody of the hundredth psalm, with examples and directions for an hundred different harmonies in four parts', appeared in April 1809. It gave—according to the preface—'an additional proof of the completeness, and natural simplicity' of *A New Theory*. The work consists of twenty-eight harmonisations of the Old Hundredth psalm tune, into which chord inversions, the minor mode, and diatonic and chromatic forenotes and afternotes are progressively introduced. By further applying and intermixing these techniques according to *A New Theory*'s rules, one hundred or more harmonisations of this psalm tune can be produced.[378]

Example 2 shows the third phrase of the tune's twenty-eighth variant, which contains numerous diatonic and chromatic forenotes. Passages like this were considered quite dissonant by contemporaries. A critic claimed that 'from many of the specimens' in this work 'one might infer, that harmony and noise are synonymous'.[379]

'The melody of the hundredth psalm' was dedicated to 'the Honourable Miss Charlotte Onslow', i.e., to Georgiana Charlotte Onslow, a cousin of the French composer George Onslow.[380] No evidence has been found that Kollmann taught her. They might have met through royal family connections. For instance, on 18 August 1802, Charlotte Onslow and her mother Charlotte, Viscountess Cranley, dined at a table whose guests reportedly included Princess Sophia Matilda of Gloucester and two children of King George III—Princess Mary and Prince Ernest Augustus, Duke of Cumberland.[381] In 1809, when Charlotte Onslow received her copy of Kollmann's opus 9,

[378] In the Preface to 'The melody of the hundredth psalm' Kollmann wrote that 'giving all those varieties at full length, would deprive Students of the satisfaction and improvement, which they may derive from trying to produce them themselves'. Presumably his own pupils were given exercises such as this.

[379] *The Gentleman's Magazine* v 84 part 2 (August 1814) p 156. The identity of the music reviewer in *The Gentleman's Magazine* at this time, who sometimes used the pseudonym 'Zero', has not been discovered.

[380] Viviane Naux, *George Onslow: Gentleman Compositeur*, Clermont-Ferrand, 2003, p 393. George Onslow dedicated his 1806 'Grande Sonate' for the piano, op. 2, to 'Miss Charlotte Onslow' (*ibid.*, p 259), indicating their shared interest in music.

[381] Francis Bickley (ed.), *The Diaries of Sylvester Douglas (Lord Glenbervie)*, London, 1928, v 1 p 325. The diary mentions 'Lady Cranley' and 'Miss Onslow', but as

Example 2. Passage from Kollmann's 'The melody of the hundredth psalm'

her mother appears to have been a lady in waiting to George III's daughter Princess Amelia, at whose funeral in November 1810 she served as a 'supporter of the pall'.[382] Queen Charlotte was fond of Viscountess Cranley and gave her silver tea pots and plate.[383]

At the end of 1809 Kollmann published the first number in a series of 'analyzed fugues with double counterpoints', opus 10, with 'introductory explanations' of each fugue. The second and last numbers appeared in April and October 1810. With the final number he issued a preface to the entire set and a title-page that named the set *Twelve Analyzed Fugues*. Publishing this work in instalments of course helped his cash flow, as revenue from the sale of one set of fugues could be applied to the expenses of engraving and printing the next.

On the wrapper of the first number Kollmann said that the work was

---

Viscountess Cranley had only one daughter the reference almost certainly is to Kollmann's dedicatee.

[382] See William S. Childe-Pemberton, *The Romance of Princess Amelia, daughter of George III (1783-1810)*, London, 1910, p 229, 231 and 243. According to a contemporary account both 'Lady Cranley and Miss Onslow' were present when Princess Amelia died at Augusta Lodge, Windsor (*ibid.*, p 229). Viscountess Cranley became Countess Onslow in 1814.

[383] See C[olwyn] E[dward] Vulliamy, *The Onslow Family 1528–1847, with some Account of their Times*, London, 1953, p 215, who states that Queen Charlotte called the viscountess 'my dearest Crany'. The gift of silver is reported in a memorandum attached to Georgina Charlotte Onslow's will, court copy in National Archives, PROB 11/1757.

> calculated to elucidate, by pieces for practical use, the principles of the Fugue, and of Double Counterpoint, as taught in the Author's theoretical works; and to give the Lovers of Music a knowledge of pieces of that kind [i.e., fugues], without troubling them with the less entertaining study of treatises alone.

He appears to have contemplated this work for some time. In the 'introductory explanation' of the twelfth fugue, whose opening is given in *Example 3*, he said that he had composed its subject 'about twelve years ago', thus about 1798.[384] In *The Quarterly Musical Register* he reported that he had written *Twelve Analyzed Fugues* in place of the analysed edition of J. S. Bach's '48' that he had announced in 1799 but relinquished after continental editions of the '48' reached England.[385]

Kollmann planned to publish 'an analysis of Sebastian Bach's Preludes and Fugues'—i.e., of the '48'—in the third number of *The Quarterly Musical Register.*[386] Because that number never appeared, Kollmann's analyses and commentary in *Twelve Analyzed Fugues* suggest what he might have said about the '48'. As *Example 3* shows, he marked in the score each occurrence of a fugue subject and its answer. 'cp' identifies a 'counterpoint', which he defined as 'a subject calculated to accompany the principal one, and to be inverted with it'.[387] Augmentations and diminutions in the note-durations of fugue subjects also were pointed out.

Kollmann's analytical categories differed from those of contemporaries. For instance, the edition of the '48' by Samuel Wesley and Charles Frederick Horn (London, 1810—1813) included analyses of each fugue but did not distinguish subjects from answers.[388]

---

384 TAF^1, p xv.

385 *QMR p 30.* For the continental editions of the '48' see pages 59ff above.

386 *QMR wrapper 6.*

387 TAF^1, p v. In the second edition (TAF^2, p 5) Kollmann introduced the phrase 'counter subject' for this concept. See page 115 below.

388 See Yo Tomita, 'Samuel Wesley as analyst of Bach's fugues', *EBA* p 379–402 at p 385–388. Wesley apparently owned the copy of the first number of Kollmann's 'analyzed fugues', now RCM D1489/14, which was published before the first book of the Wesley/Horn edition of the '48' (see *EBA* p 334 fn 86). As Tomita comments (*EBA* p 388), 'the evidence suggests' that Wesley and Horn 'disagreed with Kollmann's method of analysis'.

KEY: S: subject
A: answer
cp: counterpoint [at the unison/octave]
cp2: counterpoint at the second
inter: intermediate passage

Example 3. The opening bars of Kollmann's twelfth 'analyzed fugue'

Kollmann knew that the chromatic complexity of the twelfth 'analyzed fugue' (for instance, bar 7 in *Example 3*), although 'regular' according to *A New Theory*'s rules, exceeded the common practice of his day. He explained that

> though I have introduced in this fugue nothing, which, when properly performed, can be offensive to an unprejudiced ear; the uncommon, and intricate combinations, which arise from its counterpoint in those intervals, where dissonant passing notes become accented, require, that the notes of the counterpoint part should be played in a smooth connection, and not as a series of heavy single notes.[389]

Twelve Analyzed Fugues received a rave review by Gottlieb Lewis Engelbach in *The Repository of Arts, Literature, Fashions...*, published by the German-born lithographic printer Rudolph Ackermann:

> Such of our readers as are acquainted with the excellent works of our author on every branch of harmonic science, will rejoice to find ... that the complicated theory of fugues has had the good fortune to be treated by a master so competent to the task, and so luminous in every subject he undertakes to illustrate. ... [T]he clearness, precision, and skill, which pervade every part of the work, the didactical as well as the experimental, do him the greatest credit, and no doubt will, in the eyes of every competent judge, give to this performance the stamp of classical merit.[390]

Kollmann's last publication before *The Quarterly Musical Register* was 'A rondo on the chord of the diminished seventh, shewing the immediate progression of that chord to all the twelve major and minor keys'. He had remarked in *A New Theory* that a diminished-seventh chord, such as {B, D, F, G♯}, was 'so equivocal' that it could progress immediately to the tonic chords of eight major or eight minor keys.[391] If the B is regarded as a forenote to B♭, the chord can progress directly to the tonic chords of E♭ major or E♭ minor. If the D in {B, D,

---

[389] *TAF*[1], p xvi; *TAF*[2], p 15.

[390] *The Repository of Arts, Literature, Fashions...* v 5 no. 25 (January 1811) p 46–47. Reviews in 'Ackermann's *Repository*' (as this journal was known) were anonymous, but Engelbach is identified as its music reviewer in W. P., 'Rudolph Ackermann', *Notes and Queries* 4th ser. v 4 no. 84 (7 August 1869) p 109–112 at p 112.

[391] *NTh*[1], p 55.

F, G♯} is a forenote to C♯, a major or minor F♯ chord can follow immediately. If F and G♯ are treated as forenotes, the same chord can resolve respectively to a tonic chord on A or on C. If the G♯ in the above chord is considered as an afternote to A, then this chord can be followed immediately by the E major or E minor tonic chord.

After *A New Theory* was published, Kollmann realised that a diminished-seventh chord also could proceed immediately to a tonic chord whose root is one of the former chord's four notes. Thus {B, D, F, G♯} could be followed by {B, D♯, F♯, F♯}, because D, F and G♯ can be considered forenotes to D♯, F♯ and F♯ respectively. Therefore a diminished-seventh chord could be followed immediately by a chord whose root is any one of the twelve notes. Kollmann considered this finding 'to be new' and composed his rondo to demonstrate this discovery.[392] *Example 4* shows a passage from the rondo in which {B, D, F, G♯} is followed immediately by four different chords.

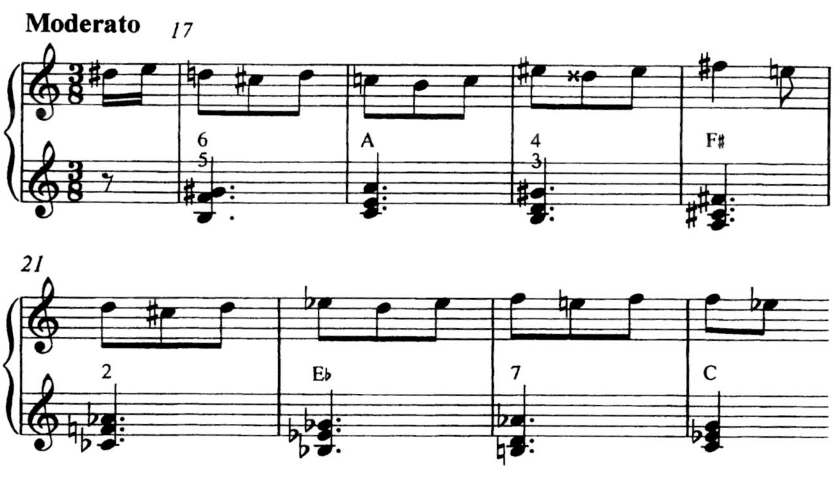

Example 4. Passage from Kollmann's 'rondo on the chord of the diminished seventh'

---

[392] *NTh*^{2}, p 50. Kollmann's rondo was followed by other composers' demonstrations of the curious functionality of the diminished-seventh chord. Joseph Major's *Specimens of Modulation, from the equivocal chord to 26 minor & major keys*, London, *c*1819, was one such work. However, in contrast to Kollmann, Major regarded enharmonically equivalent keys—e.g., B and C♭—as different keys.

22. George Kollmann's Published Compositions (1808–1812)

Three compositions by George Kollmann were published. Opus 1, 'Three grand sonatas for the piano forte', appeared about April 1808, and was dedicated to his father 'by his son and pupil'. George's variations on Handel's 'Harmonious Blacksmith' air, dedicated to the Misses Wyndham (not identified), came out in December 1808. Both works were warmly reviewed in *The Monthly Magazine*.[393]

Kollmann apparently sent copies of these works to his brother in Hamburg, who forwarded them to Johann Anton André, conceiving that he might like to publish them in Germany. André replied on 22 August 1809, praising George's music but saying that as the music trade now was almost at a standstill it was impossible for him to publish music by a composer who was not yet known in Germany.[394]

In January 1811 Frederick Griesbach recommended George for membership of the Royal Society of Musicians, noting that he had 'studied music under his father, teaches singing and the pianoforte' and 'plays the organ and violin'.[395] As required, George declared in his application that he was not a current nor a prospective member of the New Musical Fund. He was elected unanimously on 7 April, at the age of twenty-two, and went on to serve the Society in several capacities, becoming a governor in 1813 and in 1831 a member of its Court of Assistants.[396] His association with the Royal Society of Musicians gave him an opportunity to work independently of his father.

George's last published composition, 'Six waltzes for the piano forte', dedicated to Miss Douglass (not identified), was entered at Stationers' Hall on 19 August 1812. His decision to stop publishing

---

[393] The reviewer, presumably Thomas Busby, said of 'Three grand sonatas' (*Monthly Magazine* v 25 no. 5 (1 June 1808) p 447) that 'we cannot withhold from it our warmest commendation, or dismiss the article without giving the tribute of praise due to Mr Kollmann, senior, as the tutor of the composer'.

[394] Johann Anton André→GCK, 22/8/1809.

[395] See the entry for 6/1/1811 in section III.4 below.

[396] Minute books of the Royal Society of Musicians, in the Society's archives. I am grateful to Marjorie Gleed for showing me these records.

may have been affected by the financial loss that his father sustained from *The Quarterly Musical Register*. His unpublished compositions have not survived.

Perhaps George considered that his prospects were brighter in areas other than musical composition. In 1811 Charles Burney told Kollmann that he had heard of George's 'inquiries and attainments in other parts of knowledge' besides his 'miraculous power' of execution on keyed instruments.[397] These abilities would be manifested in George's subsequent career as an inventor.

23. Years after *The Quarterly Musical Register* (1812–1823)

When Kollmann launched *The Quarterly Musical Register* he presumably expected to publish it for many years. His decision to stop the journal after its April 1812 second number, because 'the sale of the work has not been a sufficient inducement to Mr Kollmann to continue it',[398] must have desolated him. Besides abandoning a channel through which he could communicate his theory to a readership beyond those who knew his books, and suffering the embarrassment of breaking his promise to produce a quarterly periodical,[399] he must have lost money on the venture.[400] Whether from lack of will or lack of money, after the

---

[397] Burney→Kollmann, 8/4/1811.

[398] According to the review of the *QMR* in *The Gentleman's Magazine* v 83 part 1 (April 1813) p 354–356.

[399] Besides the second number's announcement of articles that the third number would contain, the list of Kollmann's works on p [68] of the 1812 second edition of *An Essay on Practical Musical Composition* stated that *The Quarterly Musical Register* was 'to be continued' beyond the two numbers published when *EPMC*[2] was printed.

[400] No records of the *QMR*'s finances survive. The assumption that it was unprofitable is consistent with the circumstance that the second number had no paid advertisements, that Bulmer was not retained to print it (Collins presumably being a cheaper printer), and that only a few copies of the journal are extant. See section II.3 below. The *QMR* was not the only unprofitable English music journal in the early nineteenth century. According to Leanne Langley, 'The life and death of *The Harmonicon*: an analysis', *Research Chronicle* [Royal Musical Association] no. 22

second number of the journal and the second edition of *An Essay on Practical Musical Composition*, which appeared about July 1812, he published no new works for eight years.[401] As mentioned, George Kollmann stopped publishing his music entirely after August 1812.

In 1819 the Leipzig *Allgemeine musikalische Zeitung* reported that Kollmann had discontinued *The Quarterly Musical Register* after the second number because of poor health.[402] No confirmation of this statement has been found, and an 1815 *Allgemeine musikalische Zeitung* article, apparently based upon an interview with Kollmann, said of the periodical's cessation just that 'up to now, unfortunately, only two numbers have appeared'.[403]

The single contemporary review of *The Quarterly Musical Register* appeared in *The Gentleman's Magazine* and consisted mainly of extracts from the journal.[404] The reviewer regretted its closure, saying that 'it was highly in his [Kollmann's] power to communicate useful information to the musical publick, particularly in regard to the musical literature of his native country'. However, 'his Register has too much of the appearance of being principally designed to promote the sale of his other works'. The reviewer also remarked that it would have been better if Kollmann 'had withheld his numerous objections to Dr Callcott's Musical Grammar, till that admired composer had been in a state of health to reply, if the objections deserved notice'.

(1998) p 137–163 at p 148–151, that journal, published in London between 1823 and 1833, also was unprofitable.

[401] As noted in section III.2 below, new impressions of Kollmann's *Analyzed Symphony* and 'Melody of the 100th psalm' were printed *c*1815. In the 1809 first impression of the latter work the verso side of the title-page has a list of Kollmann's publications; in the *c*1815 impression that page is blank. I am grateful to Peter Ward Jones for information about these *c*1815 copies in the Bodleian library.

[402] 'Uebersicht des Zustandes der Musik in London (Fortsetzung...)', *Allgemeine musikalische Zeitung* v 21 no. 51 (22 December 1819) cols. 865–873 at col. 869; 'blos wegen Kränklichkeit des Verfassers mit dem zweyten Stücke hat aufhören müssen'.

[403] 'Nachrichten. London.', *Allgemeine musikalische Zeitung* v 17 no. 31 (2 August 1815) cols. 518–523 at cols. 519–520: 'bis jetzt leider nur noch 2 Hefte erschienen sind'. This report gives information about the second edition of *A New Theory* according to Kollmann's assurances—'seiner Versicherung nach' (col. 521; see note 408 below)—which presumably were given to the reporter by Kollmann himself.

[404] *The Gentleman's Magazine* v 83 part 1 (April 1813) p 334–336.

The second edition of *An Essay on Practical Musical Composition*, like the first, was published by subscription.[405] The subscribers' names are not known; presumably no list was printed. For the new edition the *Essay*'s letterpress text was reset, some music plates were corrected, and a new Plate 30 was engraved so that a different canon could be used as a music example.[406]

Little documentation of Kollmann's activities in the immediately following years has survived. He subscribed to the first season of the Philharmonic Society in 1813 and continued to subscribe for the rest of his life.[407] By August 1815, according to the *Allgemeine musikalische Zeitung* article about him, the first edition of *A New Theory* had nearly sold out and he had finished the manuscript of an improved second edition.[408]

In January 1817 he completed a bilingual oratorio entitled *The Praise of God* in English and *Das Lob Gottes* in German. Its biblical texts could be sung in either language. The work was dedicated to the Prince Regent, to whom Kollmann presented the manuscript copy that

---

[405] Kollmann advertised on *QMR1 wrapper 3* and on *QMR2 wrapper 7* that the first edition had been out of print for seven years and that the second would be 'put to press, as soon as one hundred copies are subscribed'.

[406] *EPMC*², p [v]. Corrections made to plate 52 for the new edition are listed in Yo Tomita, 'The dawn of the English Bach awakening manifested in sources of the "48"', *EBA* p 35–167 at p 115 fn 244. The engraver of plate 30 in the 1812 edition used a different time-signature c punch from his predecessor. It produced no hook at the top right of the c, whereas the c and ¢ time-signatures in plates engraved for the 1799 edition and (except for plate 30) reused in the 1812 edition have such hooks. Imogene Horsley did not realise that the music plates in the second edition differed from those in the first, as her facsimile edition of the *Essay* (New York, 1973) reprints the text of *EPMC*¹ together with the music plates of *EPMC*².

[407] Copies of the printed annual lists of subscribers are in BL K.6.d.3 (Sir George Smart's collection) and in BL RPS ms 318 (lacking lists for the years 1816 and 1818). Joanna Kollmann joined her father as a subscriber in 1815 and subscribed until 1842. George Kollmann subscribed in 1815 and became an associate of the Philharmonic Society in 1816, but appears not to have participated in Society activities after then.

[408] In 'Nachrichten. London.', *Allgemeine musikalische Zeitung* v 17 no. 31 (2 August 1815) cols. 518–523 at col. 521, the anonymous London correspondent wrote, regarding the *New Theory*, 'die erste Ausgabe dieses Werks ist beynahe vergriffen, und der Verf. hat das verbesserte Manuscript zu einer zweyten, seiner Versicherung nach, schon fertig'.

is now in the Royal Music Library.[409] No information has been found about the Prince Regent's interest in this oratorio or that it was ever performed. Kollmann intended to publish at least the English-language text of the oratorio, as an autograph copy of this survives with his handwritten statement 'Printed for the Author, Friary St James's Palace'.[410] However, that plan seems not to have been fulfilled, as no printed copies are known of any part of *The Praise of God.*

About this time Kollmann appears to have approached Bulmer to print a revised edition of *A New Theory.* Although the second edition was not published until February 1823, when it bore the imprint of Bulmer's successor William Nicol, its letterpress text and engraved music were printed on paper watermarked '1817'.[411] Nicol had worked in his father's bookselling business from about 1800 and joined Bulmer in 1820, when his firm was renamed 'W. Bulmer & W. Nicol'.[412] On 1 January 1822 Bulmer announced that he had 'retired from his profession, as a printer; and that Wm Nicol, the son of his late Partner, has succeeded to the whole establishment of the Shakespeare Printing-Office'.[413] It seems improbable that Kollmann first engaged this firm to print a second edition of *A New Theory* in 1822, and that Nicol then chose paper for the job that was five years old. It seems much more likely that Bulmer ordered paper in 1817 for a new edition of *A New Theory*, and perhaps printed some sheets of it, before Kollmann advised that he did not have enough money to proceed, and that production therefore had to pause.

Documents summarised in section III.4 below show that salaries of German Chapel staff were retrenched about this time. On 24 January 1817 Kollmann wrote in a letter to Rev. William Howley, the Bishop of London, that his reductions amounted to about £25 per annum, 'a very

[409] Shelfmark BL R.M. 21.g.1. The Royal Music Library was presented to the British Museum by Queen Elizabeth II in 1957 and is now in the British Library.

[410] It is included in Bodleian ms Tenbury 852.

[411] As noted in section III.2, only five copies of *NTh*[2] are known to be extant. The 1817 watermark is found in all copies in Australia and England listed there.

[412] Philip A. H. Brown, *London Publishers and Printers c1800–1870*, London, 1982, p 28 and p 138.

[413] *London Gazette* no. 17800 (19 March 1822) p 471.

grievous loss to me, considering my small salary, and the increasing disproportion of it to its original value'.[414] It is plausible that this loss of income caused Kollmann to abandon his plan to publish *The Praise of God* and to defer publishing the second edition of *A New Theory*. As recounted below, George Kollmann received a bequest of £180 in 1822 that may have enabled production of this edition to resume.[415]

On 6 May 1817 the musician Samuel Wesley, fearing arrest because he had failed to pay an annuity to his estranged wife Charlotte, jumped out of a window and soon afterwards was confined in a private lunatic asylum for nearly a year.[416] Without regular remittances from her husband, Charlotte Wesley and their three children, who lived with her, had insufficient income to subsist adequately. Kollmann learned of the family's difficulties and proposed a benefit concert to raise money for Samuel and to relieve Charlotte's 'exigencies', and made 'several necessary applications with success'.[417]

Kollmann apparently got in contact with his New Musical Fund colleagues about the proposed concert, as an advertisement headed 'Mr S. Wesley's benefit concert' was published in June 1818 by 'T. King, Secretary, Little Chapel-street, Soho'—almost certainly a misprint for James King, the secretary of the New Musical Fund, who lived at 15 Little Chapel Street.[418] This advertisement said that the committee managing Wesley's benefit concert, of which King was secretary, had decided to postpone it until the next year.[419] As the advertisement did not name the New Musical Fund, the committee organising the concert presumably had been set up separately. However, Sir George Smart,

---

[414] Kollmann→William Howley, 24 January 1817.

[415] See page 132ff below.

[416] See Michael Kassler, 'Samuel Wesley's "madness" of 1817–18', *History of Psychiatry* v 14 no. 4 (2003) p 459–474.

[417] Charles Wesley III [son of Samuel and Charlotte Wesley]→Sarah Wesley [sister of Samuel Wesley], 5 June 1817, Emory University, John Wesley Collection in box 6; *SWSB*, p 363–364.

[418] *The Times*, 16 June 1818, p 2.

[419] No evidence has been found that this benefit concert ever took place.

who conducted the Fund's concerts at that time, apparently had agreed to conduct this benefit performance.[420]

It seems likely that Kollmann heard about Charlotte Wesley's distress from Wilhelm Kuper. Charlotte and Kuper both lived in Pimlico, and her eldest son Charles Wesley III tutored Kuper's sons in English. Kuper was so impressed with Charles's teaching that he arranged for him to go to Cambridge.[421] As Charles was admitted to Christ's College, Cambridge on 20 April 1819 at the age of twenty-five,[422] his tutoring of Kuper's sons presumably had started at least two years before then.[423]

At the New Musical Fund concert on 16 April 1818 'Miss Buchwald (pupil of Mr Kollmann)' gave her 'first public performance', playing a 'Concerto for grand piano forte' by Dussek which, according to the programme, had never been performed previously. As she was a pianist it is conceivable that she was a pupil of George Kollmann, but

---

[420] In a manuscript called 'Events in the Life of George T. Smart from 1776 (the year of his birth) to 1830 inclusive', now BL Add Ms 41772, Smart wrote (f 36^v) '1818. I conducted 8 Professors Concerts including a Benefit Concert for Mr S. Wesley & his Family on June 17th—I gave £10—' and (f 37^r, regarding 1818 events) 'June 22 Present to Mr Wesley £10—'. These entries obviously were written some time after the events described, when Smart presumably had forgotten that the benefit concert for Wesley and his family scheduled for 17 June had been cancelled.

[421] According to a letter by John Henry Skelton, whose sister Eliza married Charles Wesley III in 1824, 'Charles Wesley is one of the first scholars of the age—he educated the Sons of Dr Kuper—and made them such fine scholars that in Return the Dr sent Mr Wesley to Cambridge' (Skelton→Arthur Wesley *later* Wellesley, Duke of Wellington, docketed as received 4 June 1831, University of Southampton Library, special collections ms WP1/1187/12). Kuper later recorded that his eldest son, Henry George Kuper (who had been baptised Georg Heinrich Kuper at the German Chapel), 'received a careful classical education by myself and his excellent English tutor, the Rev. Dr Wesley' (Kuper→Adolphus, Duke of Cambridge, 27 September 1841, BL Add Ms 43051 f 46–47).

[422] John Peile, *Biographical Register of Christ's College 1505–1905*, Cambridge, 1913, v 2 p 393. I thank Geoffrey T. Martin, honorary archivist of Christ's College, for information about Charles Wesley III's time there.

[423] Later, George Kollmann and Wilhelm Kuper each subscribed for two copies of Charles Wesley III's *A Guide to Syllogism, or, a Manual of Logic; comprehending an account of the manner of disputation now practised in the schools at Cambridge*, London, 1832.

this seems unlikely because Kollmann was active in the Fund whereas George participated in the rival Royal Society of Musicians. Louisa Eleanor Buchwald also composed music and was sufficiently interested in music theory to subscribe to the English translations of Johann Georg Albrechtsberger's *Methods of Harmony* (London, *c*1834) and Luigi Cherubini's *Course of Composition and Fugue* (London, 1837).[424]

Albrechtsberger's treatise was translated into English by Arnold Merrick, who also had studied with Kollmann.[425] The date of these studies is not known, but as Merrick's translation referred to the first editions of *An Essay on Practical Musical Composition* and *A New Theory* rather than the 1812 and 1823 second editions of these works, it is plausible that his lessons took place before 1812.[426] He had quoted from the former treatise in a letter printed in 1806, so perhaps his instruction had begun before then.[427]

In November 1820 Kollmann published *An Introduction to Extemporary Modulation*, opus 11, the last work to which he gave an opus number. In its preface he noted that the work was similar in some respects to his 1792 *An Introduction to the Art of Preluding*, which had been 'out of print these several years'. Although the former work was

---

[424] In his diary entry for 30 May 1821 (printed in [Charlotte Moscheles], *Recent Music and Musicians as described in the Diaries and Correspondence of Ignatz Moscheles*, New York, 1875, p 37), the composer and pianist Ignaz Moscheles called Louisa Buchwald 'a very clever pupil of [Friedrich Wilhelm] Kalkbrenner', a pianist and composer who lived in London from 1814 to 1823. Moscheles had heard her play that evening in a benefit concert for the visiting French flautist Jean-Louis Tulou. An advertisement for this concert (*The Times*, 30 May 1821, p 3) gives Tulou's address as 5 Charles Street, Grosvenor Square. This was the address of the grocer and tea dealer Joseph Buchwald, who therefore seems likely to have been Louisa's father. Moscheles subsequently dedicated his op. 54 'Introduction and Rondo for the Piano Forte' (London, [1822]) to her.

[425] In a footnote to this translation Merrick described (v 1 p 252) 'Mr Kollmann, sen.' as 'my late master in harmony'. Some biographical information about Merrick, but not about his musical interests, is given in Michael McGarvie, 'Arnold Merrick and the black box', in his *The Meyricks of Bush: the Story of a Pembrokeshire Family*, Glastonbury, 1988, p 134–137.

[426] Merrick's references to these treatises are in footnotes in v 1 of his translation, on p 252 and p 87 respectively.

[427] Merrick→Editor of the *Monthly Magazine*, 20 April 1806, published in v 21 no. 5 (1 June 1806) p 389.

'calculated, only for the junior part of the learners of music', opus 11 was not so limited. The inclusion of a separate lesson on chords of the seventh and their inversions reflected a development in Kollmann's theory after the earlier publication.

An Introduction to Extemporary Modulation was designed to enable readers 'to express some voluntary passages of their own choice, according to their own fancy; and not merely to modulate in some major and minor keys, but in all of them with equal facility, and perfection'. The work was meant to be useful to violinists and cellists as well as pianists and players on 'the new harp, with complete pedals', without requiring them to study harmony or thorough bass.[428] A few of the music examples in this work, such as those on the bottom of page 4, were taken from the earlier work and newly engraved.

Gottfried Lewis Engelbach's review of *An Introduction to Extemporary Modulation* again was very favourable:

> Mr Kollmann's works claim a foremost rank among the theoretical treatises on music published in this country. With some disadvantages as to style, they contain a systematical digest of musical science, the utility and excellence of which render them deserving of a much wider circulation than they have hitherto enjoyed. ... [W]e think it a duty we owe to our readers, to take this opportunity of calling their attention to the writings of our author, and to recommend the study of them as a sure means of attaining a solid knowledge of the science in all its branches. ... No work extant could better serve the purpose of a zealous master.[429]

In 1822 Kollmann wrote to the Royal Academy of Music, giving 'his opinions as to modes of teaching'. His letter was discussed at the Academy's committee meeting on 28 August, which ordered that a reply be sent to him. Presumably this reply included an offer to make him an Honorary Member of the Academy, as he declined that offer in a letter dated 29 August. None of this correspondence is preserved.[430]

---

[428] *Introduction to Extemporary Modulation*, p 1–3. The 'new harp' was Sebastian Erard's double-action pedal harp, whose utility was anticipated on *QMR p 159.*

[429] *The Repository of Arts, Literature, Fashions...* 2nd ser. v 11 no. 61 (1 January 1821) p 57–58. For Engelbach's authorship of this review see note 390 above.

[430] The correspondence is mentioned in the book of minutes of the Academy's committee meetings (Royal Academy of Music archives).

In late 1822 and early 1823 Kollmann published the second (and last) editions of his *Twelve Analyzed Fugues* and *A New Theory*, advertising that both works now were much improved.[431] For the new edition of *Twelve Analyzed Fugues* he revised the text of his 'introductory explanations', which was re-engraved. Here he introduced the term 'counter subject', apparently for the first time in the English language.[432]

Neither of these second editions is known to have been reviewed. The *Journal of Music and the Drama* promised that *A New Theory* was 'under review', adding that 'it is a work which requires attention of so profound a nature, that we cannot pledge ourselves to any *immediate* remarks'.[433] However, in the following month, before any comment had appeared, the journal folded.

Kollmann's connection of musical with linguistic rhythm was embraced by Rev. Richard Roe, a writer on language. In his 1823 book, *The Principles of Rhythm, both in Speech and Music...*, Roe wrote that

> *notes* are equivalent to syllables, *bars* or *measures* to feet, *periods* to lines, and *sections* to what I have called clauses. I cannot indeed say, that these denominations are the only ones in use among musicians; but, as some choice was necessary, I have adopted those of Mr Kollmann, whose views of musical rhythm are more consonant to my own than those, which I have found in any other writer.[434]

---

[431] *Journal of Music and the Drama* v 1 no. 2 (22 February 1823) p 31, where both works are said to have been 'just published'. *TAF*[2] has an imprint date of 1822, so seems likely to have been published late in that year. *NTh*[2] was advertised as published 'this day' in *The Times*, 7 February 1823, p 4, and—as explained in section III.2 below—its letterpress portion apparently was typeset before 15 January 1823.

[432] I am grateful to Margot Charlton of the Oxford English Dictionary for the information that no earlier occurrence of this phrase is in their records.

[433] *Journal of Music and the Drama* v 1 no. 3 (1 March 1823) p 47.

[434] Dublin, printed by R. Graisberry, 1823, p 164. The book was advertised for sale in London by Longman, Hurst, Rees, Orme, Brown & Green in *The Times*, 26 June 1824, p 7. Roe refers (p 219–220) to the *New Theory* but gives insufficient information to tell which edition he had. In the 30 January 1877 Puttick & Simpson auction of items from Kollmann's library—see section I.30 below—a copy of this book was sold (lot 83) to Rev. Sir Frederick Arthur Gore Ouseley, who presumably gave it to St Michael's College, Tenbury. However, the copy formerly in that college's

24. The American Edition of *An Essay on Musical Harmony* (1817)

The 'first American edition, with notes' of *An Essay on Musical Harmony* was published by Seward & Williams at Utica, New York early in 1817, 'under the patronage of the Oneida Musical Society'.[435] No evidence has been found that Kollmann knew of it. Although he never withdrew his 1796 *Essay* from sale,[436] its concepts were superseded in 1806 by *A New Theory*, and three years later he reprimanded Rev. Charles John Smyth for following the displaced doctrines, saying 'Why would you revive an old confuted system, as you possess the confutation of it?'[437] It seems clear that if Kollmann had been asked to authorise an American edition of the grammatical part of his music theory he would have insisted that *A New Theory* be published instead of the *Essay*. However, his consent was not required.[438]

Seward & Williams regarded their edition as the first 'regular treatise' on music published in the United States. In a 'literary notice' announcing their intention to publish the book, they said that

---

library—its present whereabouts are unknown—showed no overt evidence of having belonged to Kollmann. Jamie C. Kassler, 'Representing speech through musical notation', *Journal of Musicological Research* v 24 no. 3/4 (2005) p 227–239, describes efforts made about this time to explore and to exploit connections between musical rhythm and speech rhythm.

[435] Asahel Seward withdrew from his publishing partnership with William Williams early in 1817, when the business continued under Williams's name alone. See John Camp Williams, *An Oneida County Printer, William Williams, Printer, Publisher Editor, with a Bibliography of the Press at Utica ... 1803–1838*, New York, 1906, p 70 and p 73. According to the list of 1817 Utica imprints in *American Imprints Inventory No. 36, A Check List of Utica Imprints 1799–1830*, Chicago, 1942, p 61–67, Kollmann's *Essay* is the only 1817 publication in which Seward's name appears; the remainder were printed or published by Williams alone.

[436] The list of his works that he published on p [80] of the 1823 second edition of his *New Theory* noted that *An Essay on Musical Harmony* was available for purchase then.

[437] Kollmann→C. J. Smyth, 20/2/1809.

[438] Before 1891 United States copyright law did not protect foreign authors from piracy of their works by United States publishers. See Edward Cutler, *A Manual of Musical Copyright Law*, London, 1905, p 120–131.

> Callcott's excellent Grammar, has ... passed through one American edition.[439]—But that work, although it may serve as a valuable Text Book, for the already finished theorist occasionally to refer to, is, from its nature, too general and concise to subserve the purpose of one who has yet to become accomplished in the science. And a work explaining in a scientific and masterly manner, not only the ancient modes, but the progress and use of some of the most delicate and finished modern improvements, and which could be afforded at a price that would give it free and general circulation among the lovers of music, has long been a desideratum with those who wish to encourage, among our citizens the cultivation of a correct and polished taste for this elegant accomplishment. Perhaps no treatise has ever made its appearance, better adapted than Kollmann's 'Essay on Musical Harmony', to promote so desirable an object.[440]

Because Seward & Williams used different printing technology they could offer 'this work to the American public at a price much below the European Edition', from which they said their edition was 'printed verbatim'.[441] In particular, the music 'Examples, which were originally placed at the end of the volume, are for the greater convenience of the Student, and to prevent the expense of engraved plates, inserted typographically, in the body of the work.'[442]

---

[439] This edition (Boston, 1810) reprinted the second London edition of *A Musical Grammar*, about which Kollmann wrote critical remarks in *The Quarterly Musical Register*.

[440] *Patriot & Patrol*, Utica, 31 December 1816, p 3. The partners of Seward & Williams were two of the three proprietors of this weekly newspaper: see John Camp Williams, *op. cit.*, p 67. I am indebted to Mariam Touba of the New-York Historical Society for a copy of this notice and for advice that the statement (*ibid.*, p 73) that Kollmann's *Essay* was advertised in its 27 December 1816 number is incorrect, as the *Patriot & Patrol* was not issued on that day.

[441] A few copies of the London edition of the *Essay on Musical Harmony* had found their way to America before 1817. It is entered, for instance, in *A Catalogue of the Books, &c. belonging to the Library Company of Baltimore*, Baltimore, 1809, p 35.

[442] *ibid.* Subscribers paid \$2.50 = 10/- for the Utica edition (John Camp Williams, p 73), whereas the 1796 London edition sold for £1/1/-, more than twice that price. I am grateful to D. W. Krummel for the information that the music type used to print the Utica edition appears to have been of the same manufacture as that used in many other American publications at this time, and that this type probably was cast by the Philadelphia foundry Binny & Ronaldson.

Kollmann's *Essay* was reviewed by 'X.' in the *American Monthly Magazine and Critical Review*, published in New York City.[452] Describing the state of music theory in the United States, 'X.' said that

> our countrymen are not yet too far advanced in the theory of musical composition to derive benefit even from an elementary treatise; and will have only to regret that such a work has not earlier appeared.... To those who have had access to the works of the great German, Italian, and English harmonists, the indigenous productions ... will rarely fail to become tasteless, if not positively disgusting. They will feel the want of variety, of originality, and science in these productions. ... We trust that no one will hereafter venture to appear in the character of a musical writer till he can at least determine the fundamental note of a harmony, and figure a thorough bass.
>
> It is not till lately that even any work on musical composition has been accessible in this country. The Massachusetts Compiler ... is ... immethodical and defective ... and written in so obscure, not to say barbarous English, (the compiler was a German), that few ... have ever considered the principles it contains worth the labour of decyphering.[453] The Encyclopedia, published in Philadelphia in 1798, contains entire the treatise of d'Alembert ... but [it] is quite insufficient for the purposes of the contrapuntist.[454] To the foregoing we can now add, what is worth more than the rest, the Essay of Kollmann.

'X.' told his readers that *The Monthly Review* had called the *Essay* 'the most complete treatise of the kind in the English language'.[455] He proceeded to give 'nearly unqualified commendation to Mr Kollmann's views of practical harmony', but disagreed with Kollmann's concept that the scale should have only twelve 'chromatic degrees in the octave' and its consequence 'that the chord of the diminished 7th ... divides the octave into four equal minor 3ds'.

'X.' can be identified as Alexander Metcalf Fisher, who in 1817 had been elected adjunct professor of mathematics and natural

---

[452] v 2 no. 5 (March 1818) p 344–349.

[453] Hans Gram, Samuel Holyoke and Oliver Holden, *The Massachusetts Compiler of Theoretical and Practical Elements of Sacred Vocal Music*, Boston, 1795. Gram was from Denmark, not Germany.

[454] This encyclopaedia, which began publication in 1789, was 'amended' from the third edition of the *Encyclopædia Britannica* published in Edinburgh. See Robert D. Arner, *Dobson's Encyclopaedia: The Publisher, Text, and Publication of America's first Britannica, 1789–1803*, Philadelphia, 1991.

[455] See page 49 above. Presumably 'X.' did not know that Burney wrote that review.

philosophy at Yale College.[456] A month before his review appeared, the *American Monthly Magazine* had published, under the pseudonym 'X. of New-Haven', his solution to a mathematical problem posed in that journal.[457] Besides his repeated use of 'X.' in contributions to that periodical, Fisher's authorship is confirmed by a copy in his handwriting of the concluding paragraphs of the review.[458] Fisher read music fluently and was particularly interested in mathematical aspects of musical temperament.[459] His essay on temperament, published in 1818,[460] referred to the Utica edition of Kollmann's *Essay*,[461] and recommended a system of twenty pitches per octave.[462] After Fisher died at the age of twenty-seven in a shipwreck off the Irish coast in 1822, his acquaintance, the New Haven composer Daniel Read, wrote

---

[456] James L[uce] Kingsley, *An Eulogy on Alexander Metcalf Fisher, A.M....*, New-Haven, Connecticut, 1822, p 8. Yale College became Yale University in 1887.

[457] 'X. of New-Haven', 'Solution to the prize question of no. V vol. I', *American Monthly Magazine and Critical Review* v 2 no. 4 (February 1818) p 317–319. For this solution Fisher was awarded 'a set of the magazine for a year' (*ibid.*, p 319). Fisher's use of the signature 'X.' when writing for this magazine is disclosed in 'Reminiscences of Alexander Metcalf Fisher', *The New Englander* v 1 no. 4 (October 1843) p 457–469 at p 464–465. The anonymous author of these reminiscences, which describe Fisher's musical interests and accomplishments, is said (p 457) to have been his 'intimate friend and classmate'.

[458] In Beinecke Library, Yale University, ms Vault Fisher, Box 5, file 'music'. I am grateful to Kevin Repp for locating this manuscript and authenticating Fisher's handwriting. The manuscript clearly is part of Fisher's copy of his submission to the magazine, from which several small changes were made prior to publication.

[459] 'Reminiscences of Alexander Metcalf Fisher', p 463–464.

[460] Alex[ander] M[etcalf] Fisher, 'Essay on musical temperament', *American Journal of Science* v 1 (1818) no. 1 p 9–35 and no. 2 p 176–199. The first part of this essay was the first article published in this journal, commonly referred to as 'Silliman's journal' because it was conducted by Benjamin Silliman, Fisher's colleague at Yale College.

[461] *ibid.*, p 15.

[462] Fisher's essay evoked an extensive response from John Farey in London, who found it 'a rich treat': John Farey→Benjamin Silliman, 30 April 1819, printed as 'On different modes of expressing the magnitudes and relations of musical intervals...', *American Journal of Science* v 2 no. 1 p 65–81.

that 'the constellation of scientific musicians has lost one of its brightest stars'.[463]

The comparatively large number of surviving copies of the Utica edition listed in section III.2 below suggests that its print run exceeded that of any other work by Kollmann, and that the book was widely read in America. In 1902 the American music teacher and critic William Smythe Babcock Mathews praised Kollmann's *Essay* as 'a more satisfactory book for class use than a great many issued within the last twenty years'. He went on to say that 'the fact of so serious and comprehensive a text-book in print at a remote small city like Utica in the year 1817 is one of the most striking I have noticed'.[464]

25. Controversy with John Bernard Logier (1821–1824)

John Bernard Logier was born at Kassel, Germany in 1780 and grew up in Göttingen, where Forkel had appointed his father, a violinist, as leader of the orchestra.[465] Young Logier went to England in the 1790s and from there to Ireland, initially playing in a military band and later serving as church organist in Westport, County Mayo. While teaching his seven-year-old daughter to play the organ there 'he found a great obstacle from her intractability of hand' that stopped her retaining 'a proper position of the hands' while playing. As he recognised that

[463] Daniel Read→Rev. Samuel Merwin, 7 May 1829, quoted in Irving Lowens, 'Daniel Read's world: the letters of an early American composer', in his *Music and Musicians in early America*, New York, 1964, p 159–177 at p 175. In this letter Read said that he had studied writings by Kollmann, presumably the Utica edition of the *Essay*.

[464] W. S. B. M., 'A remarkable token of American progress in 1818 [sic]', *Music: an Illustrated Magazine* v 21 no. 5 (April 1902) p 419–420.

[465] Logier's autobiography—published with his approval by Sainsbury & Co. in *A Biographical Dictionary of Musicians*, London, 1824, v 2 p 78–82—gives his birth year as 1780. Some later sources say that he was born in 1777. The relevant baptismal register was destroyed in World War II (see Georg Pügner, *Johann Bernhard Logier Leben und Werk: ein Beitrag zur Entwicklung des musikalischen Gruppenunterrichtes*, doctoral dissertation, Karl-Marx-Universität, Leipzig, 1960, p 278). Information in this paragraph comes mainly from Logier's autobiography.

'execution on the piano forte' was 'purely mechanical', he 'considered that mechanical assistance might be afforded' to 'remove those difficulties which naturally present themselves to every beginner on that instrument'. This 'led him to the invention of the chiroplast', an apparatus in which the wrist, thumb and fingers of each hand are placed above five consecutive white keys and their intermediate black keys of a keyboard. He did not commercialise this invention immediately but proceeded to establish a business in Dublin that sold music and manufactured bugles and other military musical instruments.

Much of his subsequent commercial success and fame seems due to John Green, who was employed by Clementi & Co. from about 1811 to 1816 'to superintend their publications and to travel'.[466] On a visit to Dublin, Green met Logier and encouraged him to patent the chiroplast and to grant rights to Clementi & Co. to manufacture and sell the chiroplast and 'publications connected with it'.[467] Logier subsequently opened an academy in Dublin according to his 'new system of musical education', in which beginners were taught to position their wrists and fingers by using the chiroplast, and more advanced pupils were taught the principles of harmony and musical styles.[468] A feature of his system was that much elementary instruction took place not by individual

---

[466] John Green *c*1823 autobiography, Glasgow University Library, Special Collections, ms Euing R.d.86/85. Green prepared this for the Sainsbury & Co. dictionary, which published a much reduced extract from it. I thank David Rowland for the information that the wholesale sales register in the John Broadwood & Sons archive (Surrey History Centre, ref. 2185/JB/29/9/1) records orders to Mr Green at Clementi's shop between the years 1811 and 1816 inclusive.

[467] Logier's 'apparatus for facilitating the acquirement of proper execution on the piano forte' received an English patent on 28 April 1814, subsequently numbered 3806. On 19 August 1814 Muzio Clementi expressed his 'warmest approbation and recommendation' of the chiroplast in a letter to Logier (printed, with letters of recommendation from other noted musicians, in Logier's *An Explanation & Description of the Royal Patent Chiroplast or Hand-Director* published by Clementi & Co. *c*1814, p 22, and reprinted in other works by Logier). Clementi & Co. advertised that chiroplasts were ready for delivery in *La Belle Assemblée* v 10 no. 64 (December 1814), p 37 of the separately paginated *Bell's Monthly Compendium of Advertisements*. Logier's numerous publications about the chiroplast are described in *SOMIB* v 2 p 702–723.

[468] Logier, *A Syllabus of the 2d Examination of Mr Logier's Pupils, on his new System of Musical Education...*, Dublin, 1816.

tutoring but in classes where pupils played simultaneously. When Samuel Webbe Jr 'proposed to introduce' Logier's system in London,

> Mr Green, having retired from Clementi's unable to arrange a partnership, entered into an agreement with Mr Logier for the Patent of the Chiroplast and the Copyright of all the Works then published or afterwards to be published appertaining to his System. He [Green] arranged and managed the affair of Mr Logier's first Academy in Bedford Place [London] until the whole was in regular train when his [Green's] own Academy was opened in Soho Square.[469]

This business appears to have been very lucrative to Green, whose marketing skill helped to propagate Logier's system to such an extent that the Sainsbury & Co. dictionary reported in 1824:

> From Mr Green, of Soho-square, who is sole proprietor of the chiroplast, and publisher of Logier's works connected with his system, we have been able to ascertain, that there have been already published of the elementary works upwards of fifty thousand copies, and of the chiroplast nearly sixteen hundred have been sold. He further informs us, that about one hundred professors have paid Logier one hundred guineas each to be initiated in his method.[470]

The opening of 'Logierian' academies in London and the provinces caused an enormous row in the music profession, with numerous articles and pamphlets published for or against the new system. Early in 1818 a committee of twenty-nine 'professors in London' issued *An Exposition of the Musical System of Mr Logier; with Strictures on his Chiroplast*,[471] which found the apparatus 'useless' and 'injurious' (p 24–25), the attempt 'to teach piano forte playing to children in classes' absurd (p 25), and the musical examples printed in

---

[469] John Green *c*1823 autobiography, *op. cit.* According to Logier's advertisement (*The Times*, 11 November 1817, p 1), 'pupils of Mr Webbe ... have only received instruction on Mr Logier's plan from 3 weeks to 4 months', so Webbe probably began teaching according to this system in July 1817. 'Messrs Logier and Webbe's Academy' was advertised (*The Times*, 21 November 1817, p 1) 'to be opened early in December' at 20 Bedford Place, London.

[470] *A Biographical Dictionary of Musicians*, *op. cit.*, v 2 p 82.

[471] It must have appeared before Logier's advertisement in *The Times*, 21 April 1818, p 1, that his reply to this pamphlet would be published 'in less than a fortnight'.

Logier's *The First Companion to the Chiroplast* full of 'grammatical errors' such as 'consecutive fifths and octaves' (p 59).[472] The committee noted 'that an academical plan of teaching music'—i.e., teaching in classes rather than individually—'must be far more lucrative than any which has hitherto been practised' (p 68), and implied that professors of Logier's system were principally concerned with the income it promised to bring to them. *An Exposition* concluded by saying of his system that 'whatever is good in it is not new; and whatever is new in it is not good' (p 69). In his reply Logier relied primarily upon the favourable testimonials that Clementi, Frederick William Kalkbrenner and other prominent musicians had written about the system.[473] Kollmann took no public part in the 1818 controversy but may have been dismayed to find his former pupil John Henry Griesbach listed amongst the professors who had adopted Logier's system.[474]

German readers were alerted to the controversy by articles in the Leipzig *Allgemeine musikalische Zeitung* that year about the introduction of Logier's system in England.[475] The composer Louis

---

[472] Logier's publications had many editions and their titles and text often changed from one edition to the next. A highly commendatory review of Logier's *Companion* appeared in the *European Magazine* v 67 (March 1815) p 235–237. The reviewer presumably was Samuel Wesley, one of the dedicatees of the work, who had written on 1 September 1814 a testimonial for the chiroplast that Logier included in several of his publications. See Philip Olleson, 'Samuel Wesley and the *European Magazine*', *Notes* v 52 no. 4 (June 1996) p 1097–1111.

[473] Logier, *A Refutation of the Fallacies and Misrepresentations contained in a Pamphlet entitled 'An Exposition...'*, London, 1818. The dedication page is dated 4 May 1818.

[474] Logier, *A Refutation*, p 51, refers only to 'Mr Griesbach', but he almost certainly was John Henry Griesbach, who had begun piano lessons with Kalkbrenner before Queen Charlotte's death in November 1818 (John Henry Griesbach→Mr Sainsbury, 30 October 1823, Glasgow University Library special collections R.d. 86/86, printed with minor alterations in *A Biographical Dictionary of Musicians*, *op. cit.*, v 1 p 302).

[475] A brief notice in v 20 no. 37 (16 September 1818) col. 673 was followed by a substantial article about Logier's system: C[hristian] F[riedrich] M[ichaeli]s, 'Einige Nachricht über den Chiroplasten und die neue musikalische Unterweisung des Herrn Logier in England' [Some news of Mr Logier's chiroplast and his new musical instruction in England], v 20 no. 52 (30 December 1818) col. 893–900. In this report Michaelis, a Leipzig polymath, was descriptive rather than judgemental. For instance, he commented (col. 893) that *An Exposition* was written to place Logier and his cause

Spohr, who during his stay in London in 1820 visited Logier's academy several times, subsequently noticed the system very favourably in that journal.[476] He was especially impressed by the circumstance that

> with the very first lessons in pianoforte playing he [Logier] teaches his pupils harmony at the same time. How he does this, I do not know; and that is his secret, for which each of the teachers in England who give instruction on his system pay him one hundred guineas. The results of this method with his pupils are nevertheless wonderful; for children between the ages of seven and ten years solve the most difficult problems.[477]

Spohr concluded his comments by wishing very much that Logier's teaching method would become known in Germany.[478]

Apparently influenced by Spohr's remarks, the Royal Prussian Ministerium des Cultus—the government ministry responsible for religion and education in that country—asked Franz Stoepel to visit Logier's academy in London in 1821 and to report his observations. He attended the academy on 23 June, accompanied by the Prussian ambassador, Ignaz Moscheles and others, and was impressed by an examination of young female pupils there. Four days later Stoepel sent an extract of his report to the *Allgemeine musikalische Zeitung*, who printed it in their 8 August number.[479]

---

in an unfavourable light ['abgefasst, stellt Hrn. Logier und seine Sache in ein ungünstiges Licht'], without saying whether that placement was correct.

[476] 'Musikalische Notizen gesammelt von Louis Spohr während seines Aufenthalts in London vom Ende Februars bis Ende Juny 1820' [Musical memoranda collected by Louis Spohr during his stay in London from the end of February to the end of June 1820], *Allgemeine musikalische Zeitung* v 22 no. 31 (2 August 1820) col. 521–530 at col. 526–528. Much of the section about Logier was translated into English in *Louis Spohr's Autobiography*, London, 1865, v 2 p 98–100, but the parallel octaves in the third bar of the example on p 100 of this translation are a misprint not found in the original journal article.

[477] *Louis Spohr's Autobiography*, v 2 p 99, a translation of sentences in col. 527 of his *Allgemeine musikalische Zeitung* article.

[478] 'Es wäre sehr zu wünschen, dass Hrn. Logier's Lehrmethode auch in Deutschland bekannt würde!', Spohr, *Allgemeine musikalische Zeitung*, *op. cit.*, col. 528. This sentence was not translated in *Louis Spohr's Autobiography*.

[479] Fr[anz] Stoepel, 'Auszug aus einem Berichte an das königlich Preussische Ministerium des Cultus, das Logiersche Lehr- und Unterrichts-System in der Musik

This interest of the Prussian government induced Kollmann to submit an article to the *Allgemeine musikalische Zeitung*, which was published in three consecutive numbers of that journal in November 1821, followed by a sequel in March 1822.[480] In this article Kollmann said that he had previously not taken part in the controversy surrounding Logier's system because 'I was convinced the thing must fall of itself'.[481] However,

> as I learn that attempts are making to introduce it in Germany; I think it my duty to lay before the Public of my native country the following remarks, which, I hope, will be sufficient to prevent that not many may be captivated by that System, without sufficiently knowing it.[482]

Kollmann had learned of Stoepel's visit to London and his Prussian government support from Johann Buschmann, who had accompanied him to London:

> Mr Buschmann, inventor of the Terpodion, who was in London with that instrument about a year ago [in the first half of 1821], told me ... he had been so captivated by Spohr's description of a Logierian examination, given in the 'Allgemeine Mus. Zeitung,' No. 31, for 1820, that as he once met a Mr

betreffend' [Extract from a report to the Royal Prussian Ministerium des Cultus concerning the Logierian system of teaching music], *Allgemeine musikalische Zeitung* v 23 no. 32 (8 August 1821) col. 553–557. Stoepel proceeded to open music academies in Berlin and Potsdam that he said were based upon Logier's methods, but Logier claimed that Stoepel did not have the knowledge to do this correctly and in 1822 opened his own academy in Berlin (see J[ohn] B[ernard] Logier, *A Short Account of the Progress of J. B. Logier's System of Musical Education in Berlin, and its subsequent Introduction by Order of the Prussian Government into the public Seminaries, for its general Promulgation through the Prussian States...*, London, 1824, p 21–22; and 'Streit über die Logiersche Methode', *Allgemeine Schul-Zeitung* v 3 (1826) no. 27 col. 213–215).

[480] Kollmann, 'Bemerkungen über Hrn. J. B. Logier's sogenanntes "Neues System des Musikunterrichts" (New System of Musical Education)' and 'Nachtrag zu den Bemerkungen...'. Publication details, including an 1828 reprint of the first article, are given in section III.2 below. In 1824 Kollmann published his English translation of 'Bemerkungen' and 'Nachtrag zu Bemerkungen' as a pamphlet entitled *Remarks on what Mr J. B. Logier calls his New System of Musical Education*. The following extracts from and references to his remarks on Logier are taken from that translation.

[481] *Remarks on Logier*, p 1.

[482] *ibid.*, p 2.

> Stoepel, he mentioned it to him, observing, he might try to become acquainted with the undertaking, and perhaps make some use of it; that in consequence Mr S. had applied to the royal Prussian ministry of public education, for support to that purpose, which had been granted to him; and that he came over to England together with Mr Buschmann.[483]

Kollmann's article presented several criticisms of Logier and his system. The chiroplast, employed in the teaching of beginners, was unnecessary and could be harmful, because its finger guides were used

> only for the purpose of distributing the five fingers, over five keys in succession, so that neither of them can miss its respective key. But they only fit hands grown so much, that their fingers run in parallel lines with those of the partitions; and those very hands, whom they really fit, do not want them at all, because their fingers lie exactly over their respective keys, and cannot miss them. And for small hands, whose fingers do not cover five keys, those Finger Guides are not calculated, because the partitions of them run in lines parallel with those of the keys, and the fingers stretch in extended lines, like those of a fan: so that small fingers must press against the corners of the partitions, which can be hurtful to their small bones. To the smallest hands, which are the only ones that may at first miss a key, those Finger Guides are particularly detrimental, because, if the children shall stretch their fingers so far as into these partitions, they cannot sufficiently bend them, and are compelled to play with straight fingers, which is contrary to the rules of a proper use of them.[484]

Logier's method of teaching in classes also was wrong. 'Even the best method of instruction, generally speaking, is not applicable to all pupils in one and the same manner', and a 'very frequent playing of several together, can produce nothing more than a mechanical keeping of time, and a coarse and vulgar touch and expression'.[485]

Although the chiroplast was used only in the initial stages of a child's musical education, Logier's emphasis on it when promoting his system was of the sort 'generally considered as *quackery*'. He 'makes such an incessant use of the term Chiroplast, both in his works and his advertisements, and of the Chiroplast itself at his exhibitions [of his

---

[483] *ibid.*, p 47–48. For Buschmann's visit to London and a description of his new musical instrument see 'The Terpodion', *Quarterly Musical Magazine and Review* v 3 no. 11 (1821) p 321–322.

[484] *ibid.*, p 25.

[485] *ibid.*, p 19–20.

pupils], that it cannot but disgust any attentive observer'.[486] By endeavouring 'to render his Chiroplast so particularly noted', he seems to be drawing public attention away 'from the objectionable nature, and the universally evil tendency, of his system; and to dazzle with it [the chiroplast] for some time, the eyes of the unwary, as with something very curious, and very useful'.[487]

Further, Logier promoted his system by 'making it understood' that it 'contains a secret, for the communication of which he expects an hundred guineas, besides a bond of security for not divulging that secret'. This

> created in the credulous part of the Public, high expectations of such a secret; in consequence of which they gladly submitted numerous children, to be instructed according to the Logier system. And on the other hand, it animated teachers of music who could pay the required 100 guineas, to secure to themselves so valuable a secret, serving them to obtain a great increase in pupils.[488]

Kollmann perceived, from practices such as this, that Logier, 'in connection with as many associates as he can obtain, endeavours to monopolize all musical instruction'.[489] In branding, marketing and franchising this system Logier and John Green anticipated some business practices that became common in the twentieth century.

Remarkably, Kollmann claimed that Logier, in his *A Companion to the Royal Patent Chiroplast*, passed off as his own invention the 'fundamental principle' of instruction that Kollmann had introduced eighteen years earlier in *The First Beginning on the Piano-Forte*.[490] He presumably was referring to precepts in that work such as 'Rule 1. The

---

[486] *ibid.*, p 10; italics in the original. Kollmann cites as examples Logier's Chiroplast Hall in Dublin, his Chiroplast Club 'with a particular costume and emblematical buttons', and his calling his publications *Chiroplast Companion* and *Sequel to the Chiroplast Companion.*

[487] *Remarks on Logier*, p 10.

[488] *ibid.*, p 10–11.

[489] *ibid.*, p 5.

[490] 'He passes the fundamental principle of my system of instruction as his, and as a principal advantage of his system over all those known before', *ibid.*, p 12–13.

Scholar must not be troubled with more rules or explanations of things at a time, than are required for his immediate use',[491] and to its plan of introducing new concepts progressively. Kollmann's first lesson in that book, for instance, is composed of just three notes and two note durations.[492] Although the chiroplast constrained the lessons in which it was employed to five consecutive white keys in each hand and their intermediate black keys, Kollmann deprecated Logier's *Chiroplast Companion* for introducing in its first lesson ten keys (five in each hand), two clefs, and two different note durations, which is 'more than a young pupil can learn at once'.[493] Kollmann said that Logier must have been acquainted with *The First Beginning on the Piano-Forte*

> because that work has been in constant request since its publication, as I trust the first Music sellers in London, and many respectable Masters who make use of it, will be ready to testify: particularly also, because I know that he [Logier] has been acquainted with my theoretical works in which that work is mentioned; and that he could not have left it quite unattended to, because it particularly belonged to his intended department.[494]

Following the publication of Kollmann's *Bemerkungen*, Logier wrote to him on 22 January 1822, expressing surprise at his 'strictures' and inviting him to attend an examination of Logier's pupils. Kollmann declined the invitation in his 26 January reply, noting that he had said in *Bemerkungen* why such examinations were a flawed test of Logier's system: 'he knows always to collect at those exhibitions a great majority in his favour, so that the most reasonable objections must be rejected, and be received as mere envious malevolence'.[495] Kollmann added that he would publish a translation of their correspondence—which he did in *Nachtrag zu Bemerkungen*—and also an English translation of *Bemerkungen* together with their exchange of correspondence.

---

[491] *The First Beginning*, p [1].

[492] *ibid.*, p 15. See also page 51 above.

[493] *Remarks on Logier*, p 16–17.

[494] *ibid.*, p 16.

[495] *ibid.*, p 9. Kollmann's correspondence with Logier is summarised in section III.4 below.

Remarks on Logier, the promised English translation, appeared in two editions, both printed by William Nicol and published in April and May 1824 respectively. The second edition includes an additional preface that was motivated by Logier's issuing a pamphlet which responded to Kollmann's criticisms in the first edition only by saying that they were 'not deserving of an answer'.[496]

Remarks on Logier received two reviews. The *Monthly Critical Gazette* commended Kollmann 'for his acute investigation, and clear exposure of as fallacious and unfounded a project [Logier's system] as ever deluded the lovers of novelty'.[497] The *Philomathic Journal and Literary Review* expatiated upon the entire controversy with Logier and concurred with Kollmann's conclusions.[498] These conclusions, however, had no impact upon the family of Count Ernst Friedrich Herbert Münster, who had succeeded von Lenthe in 1805 as director of the German Chancery. In 1827 his wife took their four eldest children twice a week to a Logierian academy in London for music lessons.[499]

26. George Kollmann's Piano Patent (1825)

In the decade after George and Joanna stopped performing in public, little is known of their activities. The 1819 *Literary Pocket-Book*, compiled by Leigh Hunt, has separate entries for G. A. Kollman [sic] and G. Kollman Jun., both at Friary, St James's.[500] The former is said to

---

[496] Logier, *A Short Account of the Progress of J. B. Logier's System of Musical Education in Berlin*, *op. cit.*, p 20. This pamphlet was advertised as 'in the press' in *The Times*, 21 April 1824, p 3.

[497] *Monthly Critical Gazette* v 1 no. 1 (1 June 1824) p 47–48. I thank Peter Alexander for obtaining a photocopy of this review.

[498] *Philomathic Journal and Literary Review* v 2 part 2 (April 1825) p 433–450.

[499] Haase, Carl (ed.), *Das Leben des Grafen Münster (1766–1829), Aufzeichnungen seiner Gemahlin Gräfin Wilhelmine...*, Göttingen, 1985, p 102.

[500] *The Literary Pocket-Book; or, Companion for the Lover of Nature and Art*, London, 1819, p 177. Substantially the same information was reprinted in subsequent numbers of this annual (in the last, 1823, edition it appears on p 158), in *The Literary*

teach organ and theory (and therefore might be a mistake for Augustus); the latter to teach piano forte. It seems safe to conclude that George earned money by giving piano lessons, although none of his pupils at this time has been identified.

In a will dated 11 December 1818, the composer and pianist John Samuel Charles Possin named George one of his four executors and bequeathed £180 to each of them.[501] Possin was born at Berlin in 1753. He studied composition with Kirnberger's pupil Johann Abraham Peter Schulz and accumulated a significant collection of Carl Phillip Emanuel Bach's music.[502] From the 1790s he was in London where, according to his biography in the Sainsbury & Co. dictionary, he adapted for Salomon the twelve symphonies that Haydn had composed for him and 'added a thorough-bass accompaniment to them'.[503] As Kollmann and Possin had common interests, it is plausible that Salomon introduced them.[504]

Blue Book or Kalendar of Literature, Science, and Art for MDCCCXXX, London, 1829, p 132, and in *The Boarding School and London Masters Directory*, London, *c*1829, p 96. Copies of all these directories are in the British Library.

[501] Court copy at National Archives, PROB 11/1650. I am grateful to Anne Jarvis for bringing this will to my attention.

[502] See Ingolf Sellack, 'Possin, Johann Samuel Carl', *Die Musik in Geschichte und Gegenwart*, 2nd ed. Personenteil v 13, Kassel, 2005, col. 820; Christoph Henzel, 'Agricola und Andere, Berliner Komponisten im Notenarchiv der Sing-Akademie zu Berlin', in Günther Wagner (ed.), *Jahrbuch des Staatlichen Instituts für Musikforschung Preußischer Kulturbesitz, 2003*, Stuttgart, 2003, p 31–98 at p 57–60; and Darrell M. Berg, 'Sources of C. P. E. Bach's solo keyboard works in the Sing-Akademie archives', in Annette Richards (ed.), *C. P. E. Bach Studies*, Cambridge, 2006, p 67–83 at p 81–82. Wagner, p 87–95, lists all manuscripts copied by Possin that now are in the archives of the Sing-Akademie zu Berlin.

[503] 'Possin, John Samuel Charles', *A Biographical Dictionary of Musicians*, London, 1824, v 2 p 304. Information for this biography came from Possin's pupil, the flautist and composer Charles Saust, who was a close friend of Salomon and, like Johann Christian Firnhaber, lived for a time in Salomon's London house. See Saust→Joseph Berridge (a compiler of the Sainsbury dictionary), pmk 23 December 1823, Glasgow University Library, Special Collections, R.d. 88/171, and Alan Tyson, 'Salomon's will', *Beiträge zur rheinischen Musikgeschichte* v 3 (1965) p 43–45 at p 45. According to Saust's letter, Possin left him 'all his manuscript music, mostly vocal, and his journal, which He, (the journal) ordered me to burn after his death, [sic] and not to publish any of his music nor write anything about his life'. I am grateful to Armin Raab of the Joseph Haydn-Institut, Cologne, for suggesting that Possin was the

On 10 November 1821 the Prerogative Court of Canterbury granted administration of Possin's estate to George Kollmann and his co-executors.[505] It seems likely that the bequest from Possin enabled George to advance his ideas for a novel piano and to afford the £100 in fees required to patent his concept in England.[506] The administration of Possin's estate brought him into contact with another co-executor, William Gray Thwaites, who served as George's solicitor in his application to patent 'certain improvements in the mechanism and general construction of pianofortes', which received King George IV's consent on 26 February 1825.[507] As suggested above, this bequest also may have enabled George to advance money to his father to pay the remaining upfront costs of typesetting, engraving and printing the second edition of *A New Theory*.

The patent grant, valid for fourteen years, obliged George to enrol a written description of his invention in the High Court of

---

anonymous arranger of Haydn's London symphonies for piano 'with an accompaniment for a violin & violoncello ad libitum'. Salomon published this arrangement—catalogued as 'Coll.Sy.15b' in Anthony van Hoboken, *Joseph Haydn Thematisch-bibliographisches Werkverzeichnis* v 3, Mainz, 1978, p 29—under the title 'Haydn's celebrated symphonies', and entered the arrangements of symphonies 7–12 from this set at Stationers' Hall on 2 October 1797 (Kassler, *Music Entries at Stationers' Hall, 1710–1818*, *op. cit.*, p 345).

[504] The composer Augustus Meves is another conceivable link between Kollmann and Possin, as Meves studied counterpoint and composition with Possin before 1802 and Meves's father attended the German Chapel, at least occasionally. See William [Augustus] Meves and Augustus Meves [Jr] (eds), *The Authentic Historical Memoirs of Louis Charles, Prince-Royal, Dauphin of France ... who ... personated through supposititious means, Augustus Meves*, London, 1868, p 12 and p 14.

[505] A copy of the grant of administration follows the court copy of Possin's will (see note 501 above). George's co-executors were sworn four days earlier.

[506] Neil Davenport, *The United Kingdom Patent System: A brief History*, Homewell, Hampshire, 1979, p 15–18, details the eight stages involved in obtaining an English patent before 1852 and the fees payable at each stage. In the 1840s these fees totalled £94/17/-. If a patent agent were employed his charges would have been additional. An English patent such as George's was valid in England, Wales and the town of Berwick-upon-Tweed. Ireland and Scotland had separate patent systems at this time. Fees of £310 would have been required to obtain patent grants in 1829 that covered the entire United Kingdom (Davenport, p 57 and p 62).

[507] The original patent grant to George is preserved as BL Additional Charter 75474.

Chancery within two months. This document, including four pages of drawings and Thwaites's attestation of George's signature and seal, was deposited on 25 April 1825. Although English patents were not printed or numbered until the 1850s, their specifications and drawings could be read at the court's Rolls Office upon payment of a small fee,[508] and summaries of their content were published soon after enrolment, notably in William Newton's *London Journal of Arts and Sciences*, which featured 'reports of all new patents'.[509]

George's patent has been described as the first English patent for a down-striking piano action,[510] and the first novelty he claimed was 'a new and original manner of placing the whole mechanism of horizontal, grand and square pianofortes above instead of beneath the strings'. However, John Joseph Merlin had obtained an English patent for 'a new kind of compound harpsichord' in 1774: it could be played as an ordinary harpsichord but its performer also could cause down-striking hammers to hit its strings, thereby producing sounds like a piano forte. As Charles Burney apparently owned one of these instruments, it is plausible that Kollmann saw it.[511] Merlin's design therefore may have had some influence upon George's piano action.

---

[508] See JSK→Henry Brougham, 2/10/1843. George's patent was retrospectively numbered 5107, and *Kollmann's Specification* with its accompanying drawings was printed by Eyre and Spottiswoode in London in 1857.

[509] George's piano patent is summarised there in v 12 no. 72 (1826), p 139–141 and plate VIII. Newton complained that George's drawings were 'extremely rude' and that the descriptions he had given of them were 'far from intelligible'.

[510] Rosamond E. M. Harding, *The Piano-Forte: its history traced to the great exhibition of 1851*, Cambridge, 1933, p 263. However, she noted that 'George Pether of London had invented a down-striking action for a square pianoforte towards the end of the eighteenth century' (p 263). One earlier patent application for a down-striking action is known: it was granted to Johann Baptist Streicher in Austria in 1823, and pianos including this action were made in Vienna in 1825 by Nannette Streicher geb. Stein und Sohn, a partnership of Johann Baptist Streicher and his mother. See Martha Novak Clinkscale, *Makers of the Piano 1820–1860*, Oxford, 1999, p 365–366. I am grateful to Dr Clinkscale for this information.

[511] *John Joseph Merlin: the ingenious mechanick*, London, 1985, p 97. Merlin's patent subsequently was numbered 1081. According to Frances Palmer, 'Merlin and music', *loc. cit.*, p 85–96 at p 88, Burney 'surely' owned one of Merlin's compound harpsichords. She added, however, that 'conclusive evidence' of this 'is lacking'.

George's concept positioned the keyboard above the strings, allowing the piano's legs to be shorter than usual while retaining room for the player's knees. Other novelties were 'a new and original kind of hammers' (which he called 'counterbalancing hammers'), 'two new and original catches, which are to prevent the hammers from moving more than is intended', and 'a new and original way of placing the dampers'.[512] It seems likely that George spent time with piano makers to learn practical aspects of piano construction before he applied to patent his invention, but this has not been substantiated.

Thirteen years elapsed before pianos based upon George's patent were manufactured and sold. To accomplish this he had to establish his own business, as recounted below.

27. Kollmann's Last Years (1823–1829)

Christina Kollmann died on 8 December 1823, some months after her seventy-eighth birthday and a few weeks after her fortieth wedding anniversary.[513] None of her correspondence has survived, and all that is known about her has been told in this book. On 16 December, in a ceremony conducted by Rev. Carl Friedrich Adolph Steinkopff, pastor of St Mary's German Church in the Savoy, her remains were placed in vault no. 3 in a plot adjacent to that church.[514] Because the German

---

[512] See *Kollmann's Specification, op. cit.*, plan 1 fig. 1 and plan 2 fig. 1, and George's 1839 memorandum listing eight (in fact, seven) points that distinguish his pianos from others, reproduced in *Figure* 7 facing page 143.

[513] Her death was noticed in the *Asiatic Journal and Monthly Register* v 7 no. 97 (January 1824) p 112, which reported that she died 'at the Friary, St James's Palace' but gave her date of death incorrectly as 9 December 1823. This notice seems likely to have been copied from a newspaper announcement that has not been located.

[514] *Register-Buch derer Gestorbenen und Begrabenen beÿ der Deutschen Evangelischen Gemeinde in der Savoÿ in London seit dem Jahre 1781*, National Archives, RG 4/4630, f 63^{r}. An English translation of this register, covering deaths and burials between 1794 and 1840, is in National Archives RG 4/4631; Christina's burial is noted there on f 72^{v}. On 21 December 1823 £6 was paid to the church—presumably by Kollmann—for her burial (City of Westminster Archives Centre, Archives of St Mary's German Lutheran Church of the Savoy, account book 1810–1830, SMGLC/0090/4/5).

Chapel had no burial ground its congregation were laid to rest elsewhere. Six years later Kollmann was buried in the same vault.

The remains of Kollmann and his wife—and of their children, who were buried years afterwards in St Mary's vault no. 15—did not lie undisturbed. To make way for development, St Mary's congregation were removed to a new Lutheran church in 1877, and three years later the 'considerable human remains from the Lutheran burial ground in the Savoy' were transferred to the Great Northern London Cemetery.[515]

From October to December 1825 'Mr Kollmann' received £10/10/- 'for professional attendance' in the household of the Duchess of Kent, and in 1826 he was paid £16/16/- for the same reason, plus 11/- 'for music'.[516] The household account book does not give Mr Kollmann's Christian name, but probably he was George, because the duchess's bank account at Coutts & Co. shows payments of £8/8/- and £3/3/- to 'G A Kollman' on 31 January and 26 April 1827, and no payments to Augustus from that account are recorded.[517] George's engagement seems likely to have arisen from Kuper's and Kollmann's connections with the duchess and her household. It is not clear when these connections began.

In May 1818, Edward Augustus, Duke of Kent—a son of King George III and Queen Charlotte—married Victoria, widow of Emich Carl, Prince of Leiningen, at Coburg, Germany. She had two children from her first marriage: Prince Carl, born in 1804, and Princess Feodore, born in 1807. On 13 July 1818 the Kents had a second marriage ceremony at Kew Palace (a double wedding with the Duke of Clarence—the future King William IV—and the Princess of Saxe-Meiningen—the future Queen Adelaide), after which they returned to Germany to live in the Duchess of Kent's castle at Amorbach. Following Princess Charlotte's death in 1817 it was apparent that a child of the Kents might succeed to the British throne. So that their baby would be born in Britain, they removed to Kensington Palace in

---

[515] Robert Somerville, *The Savoy*, London, 1960, p 117–118. In 1993 the Great Northern London Cemetery was renamed 'New Southgate'.

[516] Royal Archives ms Add 057/B p 193 and ms Add 057/C p 49. I thank Allison Derrett for this information.

[517] I am grateful to Tracey Earl, archivist of Coutts & Co., for this information.

April 1819, when the duchess was close to giving birth. Princess Victoria, the future queen, was born there in the following month.

About this time Kuper began to instruct Princess Feodore, and the duke asked him to help find a governess for her.[518] After inquiries, Louise Lehzen was selected. Kollmann (and later Kuper) must have known her father, Rev. Joachim Friedrich Lehzen, because from 1775 until his death in 1800 he was pastor of the Marktkirche in Hannover,[519] where Kollmann had 'entirely officiated' as organist for six weeks while his teacher, Böttner, was ill.[520] She arrived from Hannover on 3 December 1819, and Kuper escorted her to Kensington Palace.[521] Five years later, when Feodore was seventeen, Louise Lehzen became Princess Victoria's governess and close companion.

After the Duke of Kent's death in January 1820 Kuper appears to have been close to the duchess and her children. The given names of his ninth child, Victor Carl Feodor Kuper, who was baptised at the German Chapel on 5 October 1820, matched those of the duchess's

---

[518] Louise Lehzen→Queen Victoria, 6 September 1867, Royal Archives VIC/Y 203/79. Princess Charlotte had arranged the first meeting of the Duke of Kent (her uncle) with Princess Victoria of Leiningen (who was a sister of Princess Charlotte's husband Prince Leopold), and Princess Charlotte subsequently urged them to marry (see Cecil Woodham-Smith, *Queen Victoria: Her Life and Times, 1819–1861*, London, 1972, v 1 [all published] p 13–15). As Kuper had tutored Princess Charlotte it is conceivable that she or Prince Leopold introduced him to the Duke of Kent.

[519] Alheidis von Rohr, 'Louise Lehzen: Queen Victorias hannoversche Gouvernante', *Hannoversche Geschichtsblätter* n.s. v 46 (1992) p 187–195 at p 187. Conceivably Kollmann or his father had met Joachim Lehzen earlier, as he was pastor at Langenhagen, the village next to Engelbostel, from 1766 to 1771 (see Philipp Meyer (ed.), *Die Pastoren des Landeskirchen Hannovers und Schaumberg-Lippes seit der Reformation*, v 2, Göttingen, 1942, p 47). From 1771 to 1775 he was pastor at Celle, where he comforted George III's sister Queen Caroline Mathilde of Denmark and Norway, who died there in exile. Before his Langenhagen appointment Lehzen had served in London, and after returning to the duchy of Braunschweig-Lüneburg he translated several English books into German.

[520] See Kollmann's *c*1823 autobiography.

[521] Louise Lehzen→Queen Victoria, 6 September 1867, *op. cit.* Lehzen's autobiographical account in this letter contradicts assertions in Michaela Blankart and Siegfried-H. Hirsch, *The Private Album of Queen Victoria's German Governess Baroness Lehzen*, Bamberg, 2001, p 14–15 and p 38–39, that Lehzen had worked for the Kents at Amorbach and had arrived with them in England in April 1819.

three children, and the child's godparents included Prince Carl and Princess Feodore. Up to 1827, when church services were instituted at Kensington Palace, the Duchess of Kent 'always frequented the German Chapel in St James's Palace',[522] usually with Princess Feodore, who was confirmed there by Kuper on 18 April 1824.[523] At Kensington Palace on 12 February 1828 he conducted the Lutheran ceremony in which Feodore was married to Prince Ernst of Hohenlohe-Langenburg.[524]

It is plausible, therefore, that the duchess—who would have heard Kollmann play the organ many times at the German Chapel—met George there. It is not obvious whether he taught Carl, Feodore, Princess Victoria or the duchess herself, but as Carl 'lived primarily in Germany' he seems unlikely to have been George's pupil.[525] Victoria probably also can be excluded because, in consideration of services rendered 'to Her Majesty during her education', £100 pensions were granted on 23 July 1840 to John Bernard Sale 'teacher of singing' and to Lucy Anderson 'teacher of music', and no such reward was given to George, nor is he known to have claimed to have taught the queen.[526]

Two pupils of Kollmann in the 1820s have been identified. The pianist, composer and teacher Maria Hinckesman described herself as a 'pupil of Madame Szymanowska and Mr Kollmann' on a manuscript dated 1825 of her song 'Wae is my heart'.[527] The first named teacher was the visiting Polish pianist Maria Szymanowska. The second must

---

[522] According to 'A Lady', *Anecdotes, Personal Traits, and Characteristic Sketches of Victoria the First*, London, 1840, p 92.

[523] *The Morning Chronicle*, 19 April 1824, p 3.

[524] *The Times*, 19 February 1828, p 4.

[525] Lynne Vallone, *Becoming Victoria*, New Haven, 2001, p 8–9. Although this book describes Princess Victoria's education in detail it does not discuss her musical education, except for such passing remarks as that in the early 1830s she and the Duchess spent 'time together in writing [i.e., copying] music and playing duets' (p 100).

[526] House of Commons, *A List of all Pensions granted between the 20th day of June 1840 and the 20th day of June 1841*, London, 1842, p [2].

[527] BL Add Ms 42882 f 394-397 on f 395^r. For details of her life and a list of her compositions see Michael Kassler, 'The remarkable story of Maria Hinckesman', *Musicology Australia* v 29 (2007) p 43–67.

have been Augustus, as in 1826 Maria Hinckesman advertised that she taught 'thorough bass, &c., on Mr Kollmann's approved system',[528] and she announced, after migrating to Sydney in 1842, that 'her academy is now opened upon Mr A. F. C. Kollmann's approved system, which combines tasteful and elegant execution with the theory'.[529] In London she was a leading exponent, both as performer and composer, of the sostenente piano patented by Isaac Henry Mott in 1817. It is plausible that Mott, who called Kollmann in 1824 his 'esteemed friend', recommended that she study with Kollmann.[530] In the 1830s she associated with George Kollmann and performed on his pianos in London.

Another pupil, Jonathan Robert Ogden, was introduced to Kollmann by Ignaz Moscheles:

> His [Ogden's] indulgent mother was proud of her son, and with a view to gratify his wish for the best musical instruction, she ... left Leeds with her children and took a house in London. Here Mr Ogden became a pupil of Moscheles, from whom he experienced great kindness but whom he never esteemed as a composer. Through the aid of Moscheles, Mr Ogden obtained the great privilege of studying the theory of music under Kollmann, 'Organist of H. M. German Chapel, St James's', an excellent master, whose system he always spoke of as superior to that of any other writer. Later in life, however, he maintained that Kollmann's system might be simplified.[531]

Ogden composed and adapted songs, but did not pursue a musical career.

---

[528] *The Harmonicon* v 4 part 1 no. 48 (December 1826) on p 1 of a sheet included with this number headed 'Advertisements. December, 1826'.

[529] *New South Wales Examiner*, 12 August 1842, p 2; this advertisement was repeated several times. In contrast to the awareness of Kollmann in America that followed publication of *An Essay on Musical Harmony* there in 1817, Maria Hinckesman's attempt to promote his methods in Australia in the 1840s does not appear to have had significant impact.

[530] Isaac Henry Robert Mott, *I. H. R. Mott's Advice and Instructions for Playing the Piano Forte, with Expression, and brilliant Execution*, London, 1824, p 55.

[531] [William Thornley], 'The late Jonathan Robert Ogden', *The Inquirer*, 22 April 1882, p 261–262. I am grateful to Rev. Kenneth Twinn of Dr Williams's Library, London, for a copy of this obituary, attributed to Thornley by Alexander Gordon in his *Dictionary of National Biography* article on Ogden (v 14 p 906).

During the 1820s, probably after Christina's death, Kollmann hired Alice Nankerville as a servant. She worked for him for three years, and George rehired her from July to October 1831 to clean the German Chapel. Although her work seemed satisfactory, she subsequently was indicted for stealing a pair of trousers and other property belonging to him and was sentenced to transportation for fourteen years.[532] She served her sentence in Hobart, Tasmania, where she married and had children, and in 1846 she received her 'free certificate'.[533]

On 31 August 1827 Kollmann's brother died at Hamburg.[534] No correspondence between the brothers is extant and the scope of their relationship after Kollmann came to London is not known.

On 10 October 1827 Kollmann joined the funeral procession of the violinist Carl Christoph Gottfried Kiesewetter to the Savoy Chapel, where his remains were buried in a vault.[535] Kiesewetter had been first violinist of the court orchestra in Hannover before he removed to London in 1821,[536] where he performed frequently at Philharmonic Society concerts.

Two letters from Kollmann to editors of journals were published in 1828. In April 1828 *The Harmonicon* printed an extract about the Old Hundredth psalm tune from *The Parochial History of Bremhill* by William Lisle Bowles, the vicar of that parish and an accomplished poet.[537] Based upon 'internal evidence' that the tune's musical accents

---

[532] Summary of the trial of Alice Nankerville, 5 January 1832, *Old Bailey Proceedings Online*, www.oldbaileyonline.org, trial ref. t18320105-39.

[533] Archives Office of Tasmania, CON 18/24 (a description of her) and CON 40/2 (a report of her conduct). I am grateful to Trudy Cowley for information about Alice Nankerville's life in Tasmania.

[534] Staatsarchiv Hamburg, Archiv der Hauptkirche St Katharinen, A XII a 11, p 62. I thank Dr Schmidt of the Staatsarchiv for this information.

[535] *The Times*, 11 October 1827, p 2. Christian Kramer, master of King George IV's private band of musicians, was a chief mourner. Other mourners included Thomas Attwood, François Cramer, Ignaz Moscheles and Sir George Smart.

[536] He is listed as 'Concertmeister' of the orchestra in the *Königlich Großbritannisch-Hannoverscher Staats-Kalendar auf das Jahr 1822*, Nienburg, 1822, p 90–91.

[537] This extract, in *The Harmonicon* v 6 (April 1828) p 76–78, was taken from William Lisle Bowles, *The Parochial History of Bremhill, in the County of Wilts.*, London, 1828, p 206–215.

coincided with the stress patterns of the English-language psalm text, Bowles concluded that the tune 'must have been composed originally to these words' and therefore was English in origin. He suggested that John Dowland had composed it.

The Harmonicon's June 1828 number contained two replies to Bowles. The first, written under the pseudonym ΚΛΗΠΚΟΣ, noted that Dowland had set English text with 'utter contempt for' its accent.[538] Kollmann wrote that he had seen the Old Hundredth psalm tune in a collection of German psalms 'printed for the use of the reformed church of Calvin, at a place in Switzerland, as early as the year 1530', before Dowland's birth in 1563. He added that the tune 'contains internal evidence ... of its being ... an alteration of an earlier composition', probably the German hymn 'Nun' lob' mein' seel' den Herren'.[539]

Bowles responded by reaffirming his belief in Dowland's authorship of the tune, saying that Kollmann's comments proved 'very little or nothing'.[540] However, subsequent scholarship has located a 1551 Geneva publication of the Old Hundredth tune and a 1530 Augsburg source of 'Nun' lob' mein' seel' den Herren' in which the first line of the tune is virtually identical to that of the Old Hundredth,[541] and has dismissed Bowles's attribution of the tune to Dowland.[542]

Kollmann's letter in the November 1828 *Gentleman's Magazine* was his only publication that was not about music.[543] He wrote it after

---

538 ΚΛΗΠΚΟΣ→Editor of *The Harmonicon*, 17 April 1828, *The Harmonicon* v 6 (June 1828) p 122–123. 'ΚΛΗΠΚΟΣ' is a Greek word for priest or clergyman. The editor of this journal was William Ayrton.

539 Kollmann→Editor of *The Harmonicon*, 5 May 1828, *The Harmonicon* v 6 (June 1828) p 123.

540 Bowles→Editor of *The Harmonicon*, 10 June 1828, *The Harmonicon* v 6 (October 1828) p 151–152.

541 I am indebted to Robin Leaver for this information.

542 See W[illiam] H[enry] Havergal, *A History of the Old Hundredth Psalm Tune, with Specimens*, New York, 1854, p 35–37. Havergal refers (p 32) to Kollmann's letter and reprints inaccurately (on p 66) one variant of this tune in his 'The melody of the 100th psalm'. Curiously, the use of the phrase 'internal evidence' by Bowles and Kollmann predates by many years the examples of this phrase in the Oxford English Dictionary.

543 Kollmann→'Mr [Sylvanus] Urban' [pseudonym of the editor of *The Gentleman's Magazine*], *The Gentleman's Magazine* v 98 part 2 (November 1828) p 412.

reading, in the August number of that journal, a report by John Herschel, son of Sir William Herschel and cousin of the five Griesbach brothers who had played in Queen Charlotte's private band of musicians.[544] In this report John Herschel described progress towards building a machine designed by Charles Babbage 'for calculating and printing mathematical tables'. That machine, now known as Babbage's 'difference engine no. 1', was never completed.

Kollmann said in his letter that he possessed two pamphlets on calculating machines: Babbage's *A Letter to Sir Humphry Davy, Bart, President of the Royal Society, ... on the application of Machinery to the Purpose of Calculating and Printing mathematical Tables* (London, 1822), and Phillip Engel Klipstein (ed.), *J. H. Müller's ... Beschreibung seiner neu erfunden Rechenmaschine ...* (Frankfurt and Mainz, 1786). Translating from the latter, Kollmann noted that Johann Helfrich Müller had built a calculating machine and had demonstrated it in Göttingen in 1784, thereby accomplishing a goal that Leibniz had unsuccessfully attempted. Kollmann 'presumed that the want of encouragement which it [Müller's machine] may have suffered from the long war and from numerous other causes, has made it escape' Babbage's and Herschel's attention.[545]

Kollmann's interest in calculating machinery seems likely to have been related to his quest to find rules that collectively account for every note in regular musical compositions. Ada Lady Lovelace made this

---

[544] Herschel's report, printed in *The Gentleman's Magazine* v 98 part 2 (August 1828) p 163, was extracted from John Herschel→editor of *The Times*, 13 August 1828, published in *The Times*, 19 August 1828, p 2.

[545] Michael Lindgren, *Glory and Failure: the difference engines of Johann Müller, Charles Babbage and Georg and Edvard Scheutz* (translated by Craig G. McKay), Linköping, Sweden, 1987, investigated (p 68–70) when Babbage and Herschel first read Klipstein's pamphlet and learned from it about the calculating machine that Müller demonstrated at Göttingen and about Müller's subsequent (unfulfilled) plan to build a difference engine. Although Lindgren did not determine when Babbage read this pamphlet, he concluded (p 246) that 'Babbage must have been aware of Müller's design, through Klipstein, at an early point in the history of the Difference Engine No. 1'. It is conceivable that Kollmann's letter alerted Herschel and Babbage to Klipstein's booklet, of which Kollmann had one of the few copies then in England. Lindgren was unaware of Kollmann's letter when he wrote his book (Michael Lindgren, personal communication).

A

NEW THEORY

OF

MUSICAL HARMONY,

ACCORDING TO A COMPLETE AND NATURAL

SYSTEM OF THAT SCIENCE.

BY

AUGUSTUS FREDERICK CHRISTOPHER KOLLMANN,

ORGANIST OF HIS MAJESTY'S GERMAN CHAPEL AT ST. JAMES'S.

page 81.

LONDON:

PRINTED BY W. BULMER AND CO. CLEVELAND ROW,
FOR THE AUTHOR, (FRIARY, ST. JAMES'S PALACE), AND TO BE HAD OF HIM,
AND ALL THE PRINCIPAL MUSICSELLERS AND BOOKSELLERS.

PRICE A GUINEA AND A HALF.

Entered at Stationers' Hall.

1806.

Figure 6. Title-page of Kollmann's A New Theory of Musical Harmony, London, 1806, containing the music example that exemplifies this system (by permission of Jamie and Michael Kassler, Northbridge, NSW, Australia)

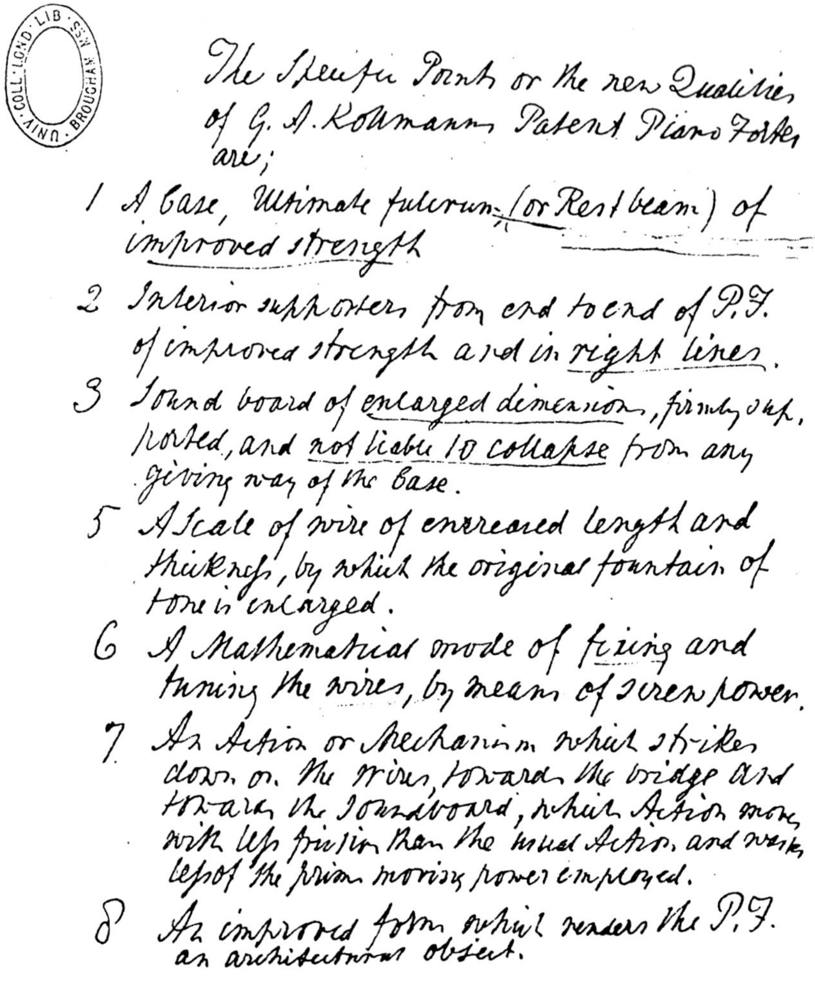

The Specific Points or the new Qualities of G. A. Kollmann's Patent Piano Fortes are;

1 A Case, Ultimate fulcrum (or Rest beam) of improved strength

2 Interior supporters from end to end of P.F. of improved strength and in right lines.

3 Sound board of enlarged dimension, firmly supported, and not liable to collapse from any giving way of the Case.

5 A Scale of wire of encreased length and thickness, by which the original fountain of tone is enlarged.

6 A Mathematical mode of fixing and tuning the wires, by means of screw power.

7 An Action or Mechanism which strikes down on the wires, towards the bridge and towards the soundboard, which Action moves with less friction than the usual Action, and wastes less of the prime moving power employed.

8 An improved form which renders the P.F. an architectural object.

Figure 7. 11 February 1839 memorandum to Lord Brougham from George Kollmann, listing qualities that distinguish his pianos from the competition (by permission of University College London Library Services, Special Collections)

link explicit in 1843 when she wrote of Babbage's 'analytical engine'—the forerunner of the modern computer which he began to design in 1834 but also never completed—that

> The operating mechanism [of the analytical engine] ... might act upon other things besides *number*, were objects found whose mutual fundamental relations could be expressed by those of the abstract science of operations.... Supposing, for instance, that the fundamental relations of pitched sounds in the science of harmony and of musical composition were susceptible of such expression ..., the engine might compose elaborate and scientific pieces of music of any degree of complexity or extent.[546]

Kollmann died suddenly on Easter Sunday afternoon, 19 April 1829, presumably a few hours after he had played the organ in a German Chapel service. He was seventy-three. In the Chapel register Kuper recorded that Kollmann was greatly esteemed and, throughout forty-six years of service, had carried out all his official duties with the greatest fidelity and skill, up to the day of his death.[547]

The funeral procession, on 27 April, started

> from his apartments at St James's Palace. It proceeded to the Savoy Chapel, attended by some of his oldest and most intimate friends; the service was read by the Rev. Dr [Frederick William] Blomberg, Clerk of the Closet to his Majesty, and concluded with one of Mr Kollmann's own hymns.[548]

Blomberg—who then also was prebendary of St Paul's Cathedral—had been adopted by Queen Charlotte in 1763, when he was two. He was raised as a companion to the Prince of Wales and his brother Prince

---

[546] L. F. [i.e., Federico Luigi] Menabrea, 'Sketch of the analytical engine invented by Charles Babbage', in Richard Taylor (ed.), *Scientific Memoirs* v 3 (London, 1843) p 666–731 at p 694. This comment appears in Note A, signed 'A. A. L.' (i.e., Augusta Ada King, Countess of Lovelace), to her translation of Menabrea's article.

[547] Kuper wrote: '1829† den 19te April, am Oster Sonntage Nachmittags verstarb plötzlich der sehr geachtete Chapel Keeper und Organist dieser Capelle, Hr August Friedrich Kollmann, 73 Jahre alt. Er hatte bis von seinen Todestag alle seine Amtsverrichtungen mit der grösster Treue und Geschicklichkeit, 46 Jahren hindurch geleitet' (entry in the first Kirchenbuch—see note 63 above—v 2 p 160–161). I am grateful to Torsten Riotte and Kirsten Weissenberg for their help in transcribing this passage.

[548] *The Morning Post*, 4 May 1829, p 3.

Frederick, later Duke of York,[549] and was 'distinguished for his taste and skill in music'.[550] He remained close to King George IV and later became chaplain to Queen Victoria.

The king was notified of Kollmann's death and named George Kollmann to succeed his father at the German Chapel.[551] George IV reportedly 'greatly admired' George's talents and 'retained him at Brighton for three weeks' in or about the year 1822, 'attending continually in the music-room [of the Royal Pavilion] during the time' of his performances.[552] By virtue of a warrant from Charles James Blomfield, Bishop of London, George was 'sworn and admitted into the Place and offices of Organist, Clerk and Chapel Keeper of His Majesty's German Lutheran Chapel St James's', where his duties began on 24 June 1829.[553] His appointment enabled George and Joanna to continue living in the home in which they had been raised.

Perhaps because Kollmann had no intimation that his life was about to end, he left no will. On 6 July 1829 the Prerogative Court of Canterbury granted the administration of his estate, whose value was estimated at £600, to George.[554]

---

549 See Olwen Hedley, *Queen Charlotte*, London, 1975, p 97 and note 22 on p 340, which dismisses the rumour that Blomberg, whose father had died, was a natural son of King George III.

550 Hill Wickham (ed.), *Journals and Correspondence of Thomas Sedgewick Whalley, D.D.*, London, 1863, v 2 p 450. The composer and organist Richard John Samuel Stevens recorded, in his 'Anecdotes, Occurrencies [sic], Extracts, Opinions, and Observations' (Cambridge University Library Ms Add 9111/2 p 116), that Blomberg was 'an excellent performer on the violin'.

551 Kuper, *loc. cit.*, wrote 'Zu seinem [Kollmann's] Nachfolger wurden sein einziger Sohn Hr Georg August Kollmann seiner Majestät ernannt'.

552 'The late George Augustus Kollmann', *Dramatic and Musical Review* v 4 no. 158 (5 April 1845) p 174–175 at p 174. No confirmation of George's performances at Brighton or of George IV's regard for him has been found.

553 New cheque book of the Chapel Royal (manuscript, Chapel Royal archive), p 101, transcribed in Andrew Ashbee and John Harley (eds), *The Cheque Books of the Chapel Royal*, Aldershot, 2000, v 1 p 279.

554 National Archives, PROB 6/205 f 219^{v}. The administration bond dated 2 July 1829, signed by George and two sureties (Thomas Catherall—then a burgess of the governing Court of Westminster—and John Robert Dickinson), is in the National Archives, PROB 46/782 1829 July Seat 4 Admons. In this bond George pledged to

Kollmann's autobiography, as printed in the 1824 Sainsbury & Co. *Dictionary of Musicians*, formed the basis of several of his obituaries.[555] Journals giving more information about him included *The London Literary Gazette*:

> We know we shall give pain to many of our readers when we acquaint them with the demise of Mr A. F. C. Kollman, [sic] Organist of his Majesty's German Chapel, at St James's Palace, which took place unexpectedly on the evening of Easter Sunday;—for no one could be more esteemed by all who knew him, through the course of a long life, than was this distinguished author. His memory, however, will live in his works, which may be designated as the Encyclopædia of Musical Science. Mr Kollman was the first person who published a treatise on the Rhetoric of Music; but the chief feature of his life was his New System of Musical Harmony.[556]

The Harmonicon said:

> The small number of laborious musical theorists and controversialists suffered a further diminution in May last, by the death of Augustus Frederick Charles Kollman, [sic] forty-six years organist of His Majesty's German chapel. ... In 1812 he commenced a *Quarterly Musical Register*, in octavo, the objects of which were, the promotion of musical literature, and a review of all new musical publications; but the work met with no encouragement, and only reached a second number. It must be confessed that its failure did not excite any surprise in those who understood the nature of such works. Mr K. also published some fugues, and other scientific compositions, for the organ or piano-forte. His reputation as a theorist stands high, and he left a private character without blemish. He is succeeded at the German Chapel by his son, an accomplished musician, a brilliant performer, and a well-informed man.[557]

The 1829 annual Royal Academy exhibition included a bust of Kollmann by his New Musical Fund colleague, Joseph Kendrick, which

---

forfeit £1200 if he did not provide an inventory of Kollmann's estate by 31 January 1830. This inventory does not appear to have been preserved.

555 For instance, the obituary in *The Annual Register ... of the year 1829* (London, 1830, p 233–234) mostly was copied from the Sainsbury & Co. *Dictionary*.

556 *The London Literary Gazette* no. 641 (2 May 1829) p 291.

557 'Extracts from the diary of a dilettante', entered under the date of 23 August 1829, in v 7 (October 1829) p 253. It is not known whether William Ayrton, editor of *The Harmonicon*, wrote the 'diary of a dilettante' that appeared in many numbers of this journal.

is the only likeness of Kollmann known to have been made.[558] This sculpture, presumably finished shortly before his death, was exhibited by the Society of British Artists in 1831, but its subsequent provenance and present location are not known.[559] The friendship of the Kollmann and Kendrick families is additionally demonstrated by the circumstance that Kendrick's daughter Emma Eleonora Kendrick painted a watercolour portrait of Joanna Kollmann, which the Society of British Artists exhibited in 1834.[560] The whereabouts of this portrait after then also have not been traced.

The musicality of the Kendrick family was particularly manifested in Emma's elder sister, the harpist Josephia Jane Mary Kendrick. She first performed in public at the New Musical Fund concert on 6 April 1815,[561] and on 27 February 1819 she was recommended as a female professional subscriber to the Philharmonic Society by the harpists Frederic Charles Meyer and Philip James Meyer Jr and the composer and organist Thomas Attwood.[562] Later, she gave harp lessons.[563] In 1822 she and Emma became life subscribers to the New Musical Fund, which continued to hold annual benefit concerts until its dissolution in 1842.

---

558 *The Exhibition of the Royal Academy. MDCCCXXIX. The sixty-first*, London, 1829, p 45, no. 1133 (copy at BL Ac.4643.R). It opened to the public on 4 May (*The Morning Post*, 4 May 1829, p 3). As noted on page 38 above, Kendrick's activities in the New Musical Fund paralleled those of Kollmann.

559 Jane Johnson (ed.), *Works exhibited at the Royal Society of British Artists, 1824–1893*, [Woodbridge, *c*1975], v 1 p 266–267, exhibit no. 888.

560 Jane Johnson, *op. cit.*, v 1 p 266, exhibit no. 588. The sitter is identified in the catalogue as 'Miss Kollmann', but Joanna is the only plausible candidate. Emma Kendrick was appointed miniature painter to King William IV in 1831, following the publication of her book *Conversations on the Art of Miniature Painting* (London, 1830). See Annette Peach, 'Kendrick, Emma Eleonora', *Oxford Dictionary of National Biography*, Oxford, 2004, v 31 p 216–217.

561 A copy of this programme is in BL c.61.g.20.

562 BL Royal Philharmonic Society ms. 315 f 172. She was subsequently admitted.

563 'Miss Kendrick', i.e., Josephia, is listed as 'professor of the harp' in *The Boarding School and London Masters Directory*, London, *c*1829, p 103. The only known copy of this book (BL Cup. 402.k.2) lacks the title-page.

28. Activities of Kollmann's Children (1829–1840)

George Kollmann's post at the German Chapel enabled him, as it had his father, to meet members of the royal family, visitors from Germany and Germans living in London. For instance, when Queen Adelaide attended divine service at the Chapel on 25 July 1830, she heard Kuper deliver the sermon and, presumably, George play the organ.[564] A report that this organ—which Queen Charlotte had given to the Chapel about the time of Kollmann's appointment—was unsatisfactory must have reached King William IV, as he decided to have it replaced in 1832 by an organ previously installed in Buckingham House, which has been attributed to John Snetzler.[565] The organ that Kollmann had played throughout his London years was then taken down and given by the king to the Royal Academy of Music.[566]

Before 1835 the piano maker John Charles Schwieso was engaged by George to make one or more prototypes of his patented piano,[567] but this aroused insufficient interest to justify manufacturing

---

[564] *The Times*, 26 July 1830, p 3. The queen was accompanied by Wilhelmine Münster, wife of Count Münster, director of the German Chancery.

[565] See Thomas Baucott Mash→GAK, 6/12/1832. The replacement organ has been rebuilt several times and remains in the Queen's Chapel today. It is described in Andrew Freeman, 'The organs of St James's Palace', *The Organ* v 4 no. 16 (April 1925) p 193–202 at p 201–202, and Gordon Paget, 'The rebuilt organ in Marlborough House Chapel', *The Organ* v 18 no. 71 (January 1939) p 170–174. (The building in which the German Chapel had been housed was called Marlborough House Chapel when Paget wrote.) Alan Barnes and Martin Renshaw, *The Life and Work of John Snetzler*, Aldershot, 1994, doubt (p 104) that Snetzler built this organ but speculate that he might have built the organ that Kollmann had played.

[566] Mash→GAK, *op. cit.*, said that the organ builder James Chapman Bishop would transfer the organ to the Royal Academy of Music. Its transfer is confirmed in the 27 December 1832 minutes of the Royal Academy of Music committee meeting (Royal Academy of Music archives) and in an 8 January 1833 letter to Bishop from his foreman, James Eagles, partly printed in Laurence Elvin, *Bishop and Son Organ Builders*, Swanpool, Lincoln, 1984, p 56. The Academy no longer has this organ, and no record has been found of it after 1833. I am grateful to Joan Harington, Katharine Hogg and Kathryn Adamson for information from the Academy's archives.

[567] According to GAK→Henry Brougham, 11/2/1839 (2). Schwieso was born in Hannover and came to London in 1808. I am grateful to Dr Joshua Schwieso for a copy of his ancestor's 1825 application for denization.

the pianos at that time. 'Professors of music ... would not come to look at my piano fortes', George recalled in 1839, and he felt 'that a great opposition was against me'.[568] Perhaps because of this he decided to apply his mechanical design skills to a different and potentially more lucrative field.

Although railway concepts have been traced back to the sixteenth century,[569] the first intercity passenger service in which locomotives operated trains to a timetable began in September 1830, between Liverpool and Manchester. This event excited enormous activity. In the next decade about £60,000,000 was invested in the British railway industry, yielding 'upwards of 1100 miles of railroad for the transit of passengers and merchandise',[570] and numerous schemes were proposed to improve the operations, economics and reliability of railways.

On 23 April 1836 King William IV granted George a patent for a method of 'preventing carriages running off the road, and for enabling the carriages passing along railroads so improved to move or pass along much sharper curves with safety than can be effected' by existing methods.[571] His system required that a specially designed third rail be laid between the usual two rails of a railway track. Besides wheels that ran on the outer rails, carriages needed to have horizontal guide wheels whose contact with the middle rail would 'prevent the carriage wheels running on other rails from being thrown off by any sudden jerk'.

To demonstrate his invention George had a ⅛-size steam locomotive and model railway built, which he exhibited three days a week at 6 Carlisle Street, Soho, in 1839. This prototype locomotive reportedly was 'beautifully manufactured at an expense of £300'.[572] As

---

[568] *ibid.*

[569] See R[obert] A[lexander] Peddie, *Railway Literature 1556–1830: A Handlist*, London, 1931.

[570] According to 'Railways of Great Britain' in *The British Almanac ... for the year of our Lord 1841*, London, [1840], p 60–97 at p 60. An accompanying table lists 135 British railway companies that had been sanctioned by Acts of Parliament up to 1840.

[571] The specifications of this patent, subsequently numbered 7069, were enrolled on 22 October 1836.

[572] 'Kollman's [sic] patent railway', *Mechanics' Magazine* v 30 no. 808 (2 February 1839) p 304; and 'Lond[on] Observer', 'An important discovery connected with

income from his German Chapel position and private teaching would have been insufficient to afford so large an outlay, he must have attracted other investment capital by 1838 to develop and promote this concept.[573]

In early 1839 George issued, and probably handed to visitors to his exhibition, a folio sheet entitled *Comparative Statement of the Imperfections of the Present System of Railways ... and of the Improvements offered in the new plan proposed by Mr G. Kollmann.* William Nicol was engaged to print it, no doubt because he had printed the letterpress part of the second edition of Kollmann's *A New Theory* and both editions of his *Remarks on Logier.*

Comparative Statement gave eleven reasons why George's scheme was superior to prior technology. The locomotive carriage and trains cannot 'run off from the rails', can 'run on any required curve', and can ascend and descend 'all acclivities that can ever be required ... with speed'. Carriages 'will be relieved of all the dead weight rendered necessary by the old system' and will be 'much less costly' to repair. Railway construction will be cheaper because fewer tunnels and embankments will be required. Finally, the 'new locomotive' can be 'easily applied to ordinary roads'. In this application the outer wheels of a carriage would travel on existing roads, so only one new rail would have to be built, and saddle horses could be used instead of steam to propel the carriages.

---

railroads', *American Railroad Journal, and Mechanics' Magazine* n.s. v 2 no. 5 (1 March 1839) p 130–131. The latter report noted that George's exhibition was attended by a 'vast assemblage' of the nobility, fellows of scientific institutions, patrons of the arts and sciences and other eminent persons. In GAK→Henry Brougham, 2/2/1839, George invited Brougham to see this exhibition.

[573] According to the 1835–1836 'Returns as to Establishments in the Lord Chamberlain's Department', National Archives LC 3/72 p 324–327, George received from that department in the year ended 31 December 1835 a 'fixed salary' of £10 as chapel-keeper, and £3 for 'cleaning the Chapel annually'. An additional £60 annual salary continued to be paid from another source to the clerk of the German Chapel ([Jasper Tomsett Judge], *Sketches of Her Majesty's Household*, London, 1848, p 73). George's salary appears to have been the same as his father had received in 1816 (see page 23 above). In 1846 Charles James Blomfield, Bishop of London, said that the salary paid to the German Chapel keeper and organist was insufficient to maintain a single person. See Blomfield→Mr Barker, 19/1/1846, in section III.4 below.

While developing his railway concepts George continued to pursue musical activities. In December 1836 Ferdinand Arnold Wortmann, a 'professor of the piano forte' from Krefeld, Germany, came to London to 'propagate' a new method of equal-temperament tuning that had been invented by Johann Heinrich Scheibler.[574] This 'mode of tuning organs' was applied to the open diapason of the German Chapel organ on 15 December, and George attested that it combined 'more equality and purity in all keys' than he and other competent judges had previously heard.[575] In the following year George joined a committee guided by its secretary, George Herbert Rodwell, to raise £50,000 of capital in £5 shares to establish a 'grand national opera in London', but the venture did not succeed.[576]

It is conjecturable that the financiers or friends who supported the construction of George's model locomotive and railway helped him to obtain funds to exploit his piano patent.[577] When granted in 1825 its fourteen-year term could be extended only by a private act of Parliament, which was neither easy nor cheap to secure.[578] The law changed on 10 September 1835 when *An Act to amend the Law touching Letters Patent for Inventions* received royal assent.[579] Proposed by Henry Lord Brougham, Lord Brougham's Act, as it

---

[574] See Ignaz Moscheles→Editor of *The Musical World*, 20 December 1836, in section III.4 below. Scheibler's method, which involved multiple tuning forks for pianos and tuning rings for organs, is described in *An Essay on the Theory and Practice of Tuning in General, and on Scheibler's Invention...*, London, 1853, p 33–64. Its reception in Germany is reported in Myles W. Jackson, *Harmonious Triads*, Cambridge, Massachusetts, 2006, chapter 6.

[575] George's testimonial was appended by Moscheles to his 20 December 1836 letter, printed in *The Musical World* v 4 no. 41 (23 December 1836) p 5–6.

[576] A copy of the prospectus dated 1837 and entitled 'National Opera' is at Bodleian Tenbury e.2(5a). The venture was advertised in *The Times*, 17 April 1837, p 2.

[577] JSK→Henry Brougham, 2/10/1843, states that 'in all probability money has been borrowed' to manufacture an invention. Although her statement is asserted hypothetically, it seems likely to reflect George's experience, i.e., that at least some of the money used to start manufacturing and marketing his pianos was lent to him.

[578] See H[arold] I[rvin] Dutton, *The Patent System and inventive Activity during the Industrial Revolution 1750–1852*, Manchester, 1984, p 48–51.

[579] 5&6 William IV c. 83.

subsequently became known, allowed the Judicial Committee of the Privy Council, which had been created largely as a result of his initiative two years earlier, to inquire into applications for prolongation of patents.[580] The act authorised the Committee to recommend whether a patent extension should be granted for up to seven years, and empowered the king to grant new letters patent for such a term. A condition of any extension was that the original patent had to have been 'prosecuted with effect' before its grant had expired.

Therefore George and his backers would have lost their investment in his 1825 patent if his pianos were not on the market by 1838. Their manufacture appears to have begun late in 1836, when George rented space as a piano maker at several Brompton premises,[581] and continued from about 1838 to 1841 at 67 St Martin's Lane.[582]

By April 1838 George also had a room at 21 Old Bond Street where his pianos could be seen and tried.[583] In a full-page advertisement headed 'New Invention', published in *The Musical World* on 26 April, he announced that 'four classes' of his 'new patent pianofortes' were for sale there.[584] Each class—horizontal grand, horizontal square, upright grand, and upright semigrand—came with a 6½-octave keyboard and could be had with a rosewood or a mahogany

---

[580] According to D[avid] B[erridge] Swinfen, 'Henry Brougham and the Judicial Committee of the Privy Council', *Law Quarterly Review* v 90 no. 349 (July 1974) p 396–411 at p 396, 'the creation of the Judicial Committee of the Privy Council [by the act 3&4 William IV c. 41] was, by common consent, Henry Brougham's most personal and durable achievement'. For further information about Brougham's parliamentary accomplishments see John E[ardley] Eardley-Wilmot, *Lord Brougham's Acts and Bills, from 1811 to the present Day...*, London, 1857.

[581] Documented in fire insurance policies of the Sun Fire Office dated 21 December 1836 and 1 February 1837 (Guildhall Library ms 11936/554 no. 1238924 and ms 11936/555 no. 1244665).

[582] He is listed as a piano forte maker there in several directories (see Rosamond E. M. Harding, *The Piano-Forte: its history traced to the Great Exhibition of 1851*, *op. cit.*, p 398). Presumably he rented space from the sole ratepayer Alexander Flint, a cabinet maker and spirit merchant (Westminster rate books, Westminster Archives Centre).

[583] The Westminster rate books show that these premises were then occupied by George Stanley, an auctioneer, particularly of art, who presumably let space to George.

[584] *The Musical World* no. 191 = n.s. no. 17, 26 April 1838, p [296].

case. This advertisement mentioned a feature not in his patent and therefore presumably a later development: that 'the entire plan of tuning is new, and rendered a mathematical operation, regulated with ease and certainty, by means of screw power'. In 1839 it was claimed that George's pianos 'could be carried to two or three concerts in succession, and would not require tuning, whereas an instrument on the old construction must be tuned after each concert'.[585]

One of the first purchasers of a Kollmann piano—and the only buyer of a Kollmann piano who has been identified—was General José Antonio Páez. He had declared Venezuela independent from Gran Colombia in 1830 and served as the country's president three times, although he was not president when the order for a Kollmann grand piano was placed.[586] This piano, which cost 150 guineas (£157/10/-) plus considerable delivery charges, was shipped to the port of La Guaira and carried by '40 men at two relief across the mountain' to Caracas in mid-October 1838.[587] In support of the claim that George's pianos 'stand in tune in a manner not attainable by any other mode of construction', an 1840 advertisement noted that the instrument sent to General Páez 'scarcely required tuning' when it arrived at Caracas, notwithstanding the warmth of the climate there.[588] The subsequent provenance of this piano has not been traced.

In addition to a promotional campaign which included twelve further advertisements in *The Musical World* in 1838 and at least one in *The Times*,[589] George organised three concerts at the Hanover Square

---

[585] Thomas Webster, *Reports and Notes of Cases on Letters Patents for Inventions*, London, v 1, 1844, p 565, reporting evidence given in February 1839 in favour of renewing George's piano patent.

[586] Páez and Barbarita Nieves, with whom he lived, both played piano and had other musical interests. See José Antonio Calcaño, *La Ciudad y sa Música (Crónica musical de Caracas)*, Caracas, 1958, p 242-246. The reason why Páez chose to buy one of George's pianos is not known.

[587] According to the British ambassador's diary entry for 18 October 1838 transcribed in Walter Dupouy (ed.), *Sir Robert Ker Porter's Caracas Diary 1825-1842*, Caracas, 1966, p 1010. I am very grateful to Carlos F. Duarte for this reference, in which George's surname is misspelled 'Kollerman'.

[588] *The Times*, 8 June 1840, p 2; repeated 9 June 1840, p 8.

[589] *The Times*, 1 August 1838, p 1.

Rooms that year to publicise his instruments. On 18 June he played before 'a numerous audience' a sonata of his own composition and (with others) a Beethoven 'concerto and grand trio'.[590] On 5 July he performed Beethoven's piano concerto no. 1 in C major and a Beethoven violin sonata with Henry Gamble Blagrove.[591] His concert on 18 December 'was honoured with a full and fashionable attendance'; and a reviewer remarked that his piano 'possesses a bell-like clearness of tone, with great depth, brilliancy, and power'.[592]

George's marketing extended beyond London. For the 'annual concert' of the singer Emily Woodyatt in Hereford, her birthplace, he played on 30 October 1838 'a concerto and fantasia on one of his improved pianofortes, which had been sent down expressly for the occasion'.[593] At this concert he 'circulated through the room' a printed description of his piano's features—presumably the prospectus that he had mentioned in his *Musical World* advertisements from May.

Following these efforts, which demonstrated that George's piano patent was being 'prosecuted with effect', his solicitor, William Harry Surman, lodged George's petition to the Judicial Committee on 29 November, praying that his piano patent be prolonged for seven years 'or such other term not exceeding seven years, as Her Majesty shall please'. Any opponents of the petition had to enter their caveats before 22 December.[594] On 24 December the matter was set to be heard on 10 January 1839, but it subsequently was deferred to 1 February.[595]

---

[590] This concert was reviewed in *The Times*, 19 June 1838, p 5, and in *The Musical World* no. 119 = n.s. no. 25 (21 June 1838) p 137.

[591] Reviewed in *The Musical World* no. 122 = n.s. no. 28 (12 July 1838) p 178.

[592] *The Aldine Magazine of Biography, Bibliography, Criticism, and the Arts* v 1 no. 4 (22 December 1838) p 63.

[593] *The Musical World* no. 138 = n.s. no. 44 (1 November 1838) p 138; *Hereford Times*, 3 November 1838, p 3; *Hereford Journal*, 7 November 1838, p 3. I am indebted to Jane Cox of the Hereford Library for locating the last two articles.

[594] Patent petition book of the Judicial Committee of the Privy Council, National Archives PCAP 5, f 5. Advertisements, *The Times*, 20 November 1838, p 2; repeated 22 November 1838, p 1. No opposition to George's petition has been found.

[595] Minute book of the Judicial Committee of the Privy Council, National Archives, PCAP 5, p 101 and p 103. Advertisement, *The Times*, 27 December 1838, p 1.

Although transcripts of the Committee's hearings between 1836 and 1908 regarding patent prolongation have not survived,[596] contemporary reports provide limited information about the hearing on 1 February.[597] The attorney general, Sir John Campbell, watched the case on behalf of the Crown and cross-examined witnesses regarding George's invention. Dr Andrew Ure, who had written extensively about manufacturing, told the Committee that George's 'invention was a most valuable one, and a complete reform in the manufacture of piano fortes'.[598] Testimony was presented, presumably by George, that 'the number of pianos sold by Mr Kollman [sic] was twenty-three, and hitherto he had been a great loser by his invention'.[599] Joanna, who assisted George in his piano business,[600] also was a witness.[601]

Sir John told the Committee that George's invention appeared to be meritorious and that the Crown would not oppose his petition, as 'from circumstances beyond his control' he 'had not obtained compensation' for it. The solicitor general, John Singleton Copley, Baron Lyndhurst, said 'we think this is a case for an extension of the patent for seven years', the maximum term allowed by Lord Brougham's Act.[602] The Committee so recommended, and Queen Victoria approved their recommendation on 4 February 1839.[603]

---

[596] I am grateful to J. K. Dixon of the Privy Council Office for advice that these transcripts were destroyed in 1940 as part of the war effort, in response to an urgent request for waste that could be used for pulping.

[597] Webster, *op. cit.*, p 564-565; William Carpmael, *Law Reports of Patent Cases* v 2, London, 1851, p 520.

[598] *Manchester Guardian*, 6 February 1839, p 4. Ure's *The Philosophy of Manufactures: or, An Exposition of the scientific, moral, and commercial economy of the factory system of Great Britain*, was published in London in 1835.

[599] Webster, p 565.

[600] See JSK→Mr F. Crouch, 29/5/1839 and JSK→Frances Braham, 23/1/1840.

[601] In JSK→Henry Brougham, 22/4/1845, Joanna hoped that Brougham would remember her 'examination before the Privy Council'.

[602] Carpmael, *loc. cit.*

[603] Report of the 4 February 1839 meeting at the Court at Buckingham Palace, 1839 register of the Privy Council, National Archives PC 2/221, p 15ff at p 55-56. The

Lord Brougham, who served on the Judicial Committee and took 'a keen interest in its day-to-day-workings',[604] participated in George's hearing.[605] They evidently had a conversation that day in which George mentioned his railway invention, as he wrote to Brougham on the next day, enclosing information about it—probably his *Comparative Statement*—and inviting him to see the model locomotive at 6 Carlisle Street.[606] On 11 February, after George returned to London from Wales, where he got a 'verbal promise' from the managers of Monmouthshire Ironworks 'that my Railway is to be used on a new short line' near Pontypool,[607] he gave two models of parts of his patented piano to Brougham, who had a collection of patent models.[608]

In a note acknowledging this gift Brougham asked whether George had connections with a piano manufacturer in Paris.[609] George replied, in his second letter to Brougham that day, that 'I have not any connexion in Paris relative to the manufacture of Piano Fortes whatever'.[610] Brougham's query may have arisen, George believed, because in 1825, when his piano patent was granted, Jean-Henri Pape was working in London (George thought for the piano maker William Stodart). Shortly afterwards Pape went to Paris and

> commenced making Piano Fortes according to my plan of striking downwards, but he made alterations in the means by which this object was effected, and used an arrangement of mechanism more complex than mine is.

---

patent that prolonged George's initial piano patent for seven years from 26 February 1839 subsequently was numbered 7979.

[604] Swinfen, 'Henry Brougham and the Judicial Committee of the Privy Council', *op. cit.*, p 406.

[605] Webster, *op. cit.*, p 564.

[606] GAK→Henry Brougham, 2/2/1839.

[607] I thank Robert Protheroe Jones of the National Waterfront Museum, Swansea, for advising that no railway track is known to have been built in south Wales according to George's concept.

[608] GAK→Henry Brougham, 11/2/1839 (1) is endorsed 'Mr Kollman [sic] with models'. The present location of Brougham's collection is unknown.

[609] Brougham's note is not extant; its content has been inferred from George's reply.

[610] GAK→Henry Brougham, 11/2/1839 (2).

Although Pape—who received a French patent for a down-striking piano action in 1826—did not duplicate George's pianos,

> I believe Pape has not imitated my plan of tuning, and has also left the structure of the Case nearly what it was heretofore by leaving the keys in the *Grand* P.F. as is usual *under* the strings, while he placed in imitation of my plan the hammers *over* the strings.

George nevertheless regarded Pape's pianos as 'a piracy of mine', 'modified for the worse'.[611] Joanna later suggested to Brougham how such a piracy could have been accomplished:

> All have free access for *one* shilling to this Office [the Rolls Office, where the specifications and drawings of George's piano patent were enrolled]. They can go every day; so that what a Man sees and cannot carry away in His Mind in *one day* He may attain on *repeated visits*.[612] Here foreigners can go, and thereby carry the invention abroad (There we know all work is cheaper than here in England) and produce it, and benefit by it, (and even introduce it *into England*, if the Patentee does not obtain an injunction to prevent it, this *again costs Money*) long before the inventor can in any way help himself here.[613]

'About the beginning of 1835', George continued, Pape sent some of his pianos from Paris to George's former contractor Schwieso, which he exhibited in Marlborough Street, but after 'a few months' they disagreed and their connection ended. Pape then returned to London where he 'gave some evening parties at Frith Street and many Professors of music who would not come to look at my P. Fortes, went to these Parties'.[614] George correctly thought that this apparent opposition 'would not succeed in defeating me', as Pape left England soon afterwards and the few of his pianos that had been brought to England were entrusted to a music seller 'to be disposed of'.

---

[611] *ibid.*

[612] The Rolls Office did not allow patents to be copied. See Stephen van Dulken, *British Patents of Invention, 1617–1977*, London, 1999, p 24.

[613] JSK→Henry Brougham, 2/10/1843. Pape was a 'foreigner', having been born at Sarstedt near Hannover.

[614] GAK→Henry Brougham, 11/2/1839 (2). A report of Pape's 25 June 1836 'soirée' at Frith Street and the advantages of his down-striking piano action appeared in *The Musical World* v 2 no. 16 (1 July 1836) p 39–40.

Although George appears not to have advertised his pianos after 1838, he continued to promote them vigorously in the first half of 1839. Following an initial concert in January, when he played a Beethoven cello sonata with Georg Hausmann at the Hanover Square Rooms,[615] he organised four further concerts 'for the express purpose of continuing the performance on the patent pianoforte invented by him'.[616] In the first concert of this series, on 15 April, George played 'an extemporaneous fantasia', and his quartet for piano, violin, horn and cello (presumed lost) was performed by George, Nicholas Mori, Giovanni Puzzi and Georg Hausmann respectively. George, Mori and Hausmann also played a Beethoven trio. *The Times*'s reviewer complimented the piano and reported that 'the room was crowded with company'.[617]

The second concert took place, exceptionally, at Willis's Rooms on 7 May. The Lord Mayor and Lady Mayoress attended, and the room was full.[618] At the third concert, on 27 May, George and his pupil, Miss Rippon, played a Mozart piano duet.[619] The final concert, on 19 June, in which they played a duet by Czerny,[620] had 'scarcely standing room for the auditors'.[621] *The Literary Gazette* recorded that 'these concerts are given by Mr Kollman in order to display the powers of his

[615] Reviewed in *The Musical World* no. 150 = n.s. no. 56 (24 January 1839) p 62. The concert was said to have been 'on Wednesday evening', presumably 16 January, as a report of an event on the evening of 23 January seems unlikely to have been published the next day.

[616] Advertisement, *The Times*, 10 April 1839 p 1; repeated 15 April 1839 p 1. The advertisement stated that 'tickets (10s.6d. each)' could 'be had at Mr Kollmann's pianoforte rooms, 21, Old Bond-street, and at all the principal music shops'.

[617] 'Mr Kollmann's concert', *The Times*, 17 April 1835, p 5.

[618] According to the review in *The Musical World* no. 165 = n.s. no. 71 (9 May 1839) p 26. At this time the Lord Mayor of London was Col. Samuel Wilson.

[619] *The Charter*, 2 June 1839, p 291. This was her first public performance.

[620] *The Era*, 23 June 1839, p 464. Its reviewer liked the performance but said that Czerny's duet was 'abominable'. No further information about Miss Rippon has been found.

[621] *The Times*, 20 June 1839, p. 5.

patent pianoforte, and if we may judge from the applause bestowed, his purpose has been fully answered'.[622]

George took part in two other concerts in 1839. In support of Maria Hinckesman, his father's former pupil, he conducted the band at her benefit concert on 19 April and played 'a grand fantasia on his newly invented patent pianoforte'. She also performed works by Hummel and Moscheles on George's piano.[623] On 4 July George played at the Melodists' Club meeting in Freemasons' Hall.[624]

Meanwhile he continued to advance, and to pursue opportunities to exploit, his railway invention. On 29 April the House of Commons Select Committee on Turnpike Trusts examined him regarding its applicability to travel on ordinary roads. He testified how this could be accomplished but admitted that it had not yet been done.[625] Also in 1839 'friends ... interested in the success of Mr Kollmann's invention' persuaded the architectural publisher John Weale to issue a pamphlet by an unnamed writer that described it very favourably.[626]

On 17 August 1839 George received his second patent relating to railways, locomotives and other carriages.[627] Its principal object was 'to improve the invention' specified in his 1836 railway patent by 'facilitating the ascent of the locomotive carriage up inclined planes'.

---

[622] *The Literary Gazette; and Journal of Belles Lettres, Arts, Sciences, &c.*, no. 1170 (22 June 1839) p 397.

[623] Advertisement, *The Times*, 13 April 1839, p 1.

[624] *The Times*, 6 July 1839, p 7. The notice says that George performed on a piano but does not say whether it was one of his pianos. The Melodists' Club had been founded in 1825 'for the promotion of melody and ballad composition'.

[625] *Minutes of Evidence taken before the Select Committee on Turnpike Trusts*, House of Commons Paper no. 295, 6 June 1839, p 17–19 and p 67. George's examination by the Committee was reprinted in *The Times*, 26 October 1839, p 7. This committee had been 'appointed for the purpose of ascertaining how far the formation of Railroads may affect the interest of Turnpike Trusts, and the Creditors of such Trusts' (p ii). (Turnpike trusts were established by Parliament to build privately owned toll roads.)

[626] *Some Observations of the present System of constructing Railways; with an account of the new metho[d] of construction invented by Mr Kollmann, Railway Papers* no. 1, London, 1839.

[627] This patent subsequently was numbered 8200.

A small number of other changes to his original design were described and illustrated in the patent specification.

About this time George was persuaded that the best way to attract the capital needed to promote his railway patents would be to establish a company for this purpose. Presumably he was promised a significant shareholding or remuneration in exchange for assigning his patents to the company. A company could issue shares to numerous investors, whereas the number of individuals who could hold rights in a patent was limited then to twelve.[628]

In November 1839 Messrs Martineau, Malton and Trollope, solicitors, gave notice that an application would be made in the next session of Parliament for an Act to authorise the assignment of George's shares to a company, and to enable it to make or use, or to grant licences for others to make or use, George's railway inventions and future improvements of them.[629] The area of this company's proposed activities embraced Great Britain, Ireland and the rest of Queen Victoria's dominions. George's petition for leave to bring in such a bill was presented to the House of Commons on 31 January 1840 and was referred to the Select Committee on Petitions for Private Bills.[630] To secure patent rights for George's railway concepts elsewhere, these solicitors applied on his behalf for *brevets d'invention* which were granted on 9 December 1839 in France and on 18 February 1840 in Belgium.[631]

---

[628] van Dulken, *British Patents of Invention*, *op. cit.*, p 63.

[629] *The Times*, 8 November 1839, p 2; repeated 12 November 1839, p 2, and 19 November 1839, p 2.

[630] *Journal of the House of Commons* v 95 (31 January 1840) p 48.

[631] According to p 8 of a copy of the 18 March 1845 'Deed of Settlement of Kollmann's Railway Locomotive and Carriage Improvement Company' (National Archives, C101/5339, henceforth referred to as 'Copy of Deed of Settlement'), the French *brevet* was granted to Edward Trollope, the solicitor at Martineau, Malton & Trollope who apparently acted for George at this time. See page 163 below.

29. Downfall of George and Joanna (1840–1849)

On 7 February 1840 George, describing himself as a 'piano-forte maker, dealer and chapman' of 67 Saint Martin's Lane, filed a declaration that he was 'in insolvent circumstances' and was 'unable to meet his engagements with his creditors'.[632] A fiat in bankruptcy was awarded against him on 14 February.[633] Joanna later told Henry Brougham that George's solicitors, Messrs Martineau, Malton and Trollope, 'made my brother a bankrupt.... They constituted themselves Petitioning Creditor, Solicitors and Assignee.'[634] Presumably they had sent him a bill for their services which he did not pay when due, and they then acted to render him a bankrupt.[635]

On 10 March George was required 'to surrender himself' and to disclose 'his estate and effects' to Joshua Evans, a commissioner of the Court of Bankruptcy.[636] The creditors—their number is not known—then had to prove their debts and to choose an assignee (they chose the accountant James Jones Dransfield of the British Iron Company) who would sell or manage George's assets for their benefit under the supervision of the court-appointed official assignee, Patrick Johnson.[637]

At the 10 March meeting a dispute arose. Joanna, who had worked for George's piano business and apparently had advanced funds to him, claimed that she was the 'chief creditor' of his business. Martineau, Malton & Trollope disagreed, maintaining that she and

---

[632] *London Gazette* no. 19821 (7 February 1840) p 254–255.

[633] *London Gazette* no. 19859 (26 May 1840) p 1282.

[634] JSK→Henry Brougham, 22/4/1845.

[635] The stages of bankruptcy proceedings at this time are outlined in Sheila Marriner, 'English bankruptcy records and statistics before 1850', *Economic History Review* v 33 no. 3 (August 1980) p 351–366. To be declared bankrupt in 1840 a trader had to owe at least £100 and to have committed an act of bankruptcy such as preventing or delaying collection of the amount owed (p 357).

[636] *London Gazette* no. 19830 (28 February 1840) p 463.

[637] Johnson's and Dransfield's appointments are noted in *An Act for forming a Company to be called 'Kollmann's Railway Locomotive and Carriage Improvement Company', and for enabling the said Company to purchase certain Letters Patent*, 3 & 4 Victoria c. 138, § I.

George had been partners, and that she was therefore personally responsible for his debts.[638] A further meeting was called for 10 April so that the creditors collectively could decide whether to submit this dispute to binding arbitration and could determine whether George's railway and piano patents and stock of pianos should be sold.[639]

Martineau, Malton & Trollope told Joanna that if she persisted in her claim they would sue her, which would stop George's affairs from being settled. As she had no money to defend a lawsuit she relinquished her claim. She later told Brougham that she was 'the most severe loser' from George's bankruptcy and had been 'defrauded by the Petitionary Creditor'—Martineau, Malton & Trollope—out of her 'just claim' and her 'power as chief creditor'. Besides 'suffering from this loss' she was 'left to pay responsibilities on the [bankruptcy] estate, which has inflicted a grievous hardship on me, and further rob'd me of my income'.[640] Joanna's income at this time, and the amount of money that she had advanced to George, are not known.

Before 8 June the assignees apparently ordered that George's unsold pianos be removed from 21 Old Bond Street to 27 Duke Street, Grosvenor Square, as an advertisement in *The Times* that day invited the public to inspect and buy them there.[641] Although the assignees may have allowed pianos under construction to be finished, they stopped the manufacture of new ones. It seems likely that the remaining stock of George's pianos and factory equipment was auctioned, as one of the reforms of the bankruptcy process that Joanna proposed to Brougham in 1843 was that a bankrupt's 'stock at first not to be sold by Auction but reserved and sold on demand, to be in trust towards paying

[638] JSK→Henry Brougham, 2/10/1843 and 22/3/1845.

[639] *London Gazette* no. 19837 (20 March 1840) p 710.

[640] JSK→Henry Brougham, 2/10/1843 and 22/4/1845.

[641] *The Times*, 8 June 1840, p 2; repeated 9 June 1840, p 8. The 'upright, semi-grand', 'quite new' Kollmann piano advertised in *The Times*, 14 May 1841, p 5, by the piano dealer Henry Ray Wilcocke at a discount price—'the maker's price 95 guineas: will be sold for 60'—conceivably was bought at the 27 Duke Street sale. These premises had been occupied earlier by the piano maker James Ball, who died in 1822, and by his son and successor Edward Ball, who died in 1836, but no record has been found that pianos were made or shown there between 1837 and 1839.

Creditors by instalments, and working the factory'.[642] The first dividend arising from the sale of George's assets was declared on 24 June, and dividends continued to be paid to creditors until May 1846.[643]

During this time George took part in one more concert, playing a fantasia and (with others) a Beethoven trio in a 'soirée musicale' at the Hanover Square Rooms on 3 April 1840.[644] This concert was given by the widow of the composer and singer Ernest Augustus Kellner, whom George had known for many years. When preparing an obituary of Kellner, the phrenologist Richard Cull spoke to George, who said that Kellner had called upon him 'when he received from abroad the first copy of the *Semiramide*' and 'without the slightest hesitation' had sung through one of its bass parts.[645] George and Kellner therefore were acquainted in 1823–1824, when Rossini's opera was first performed,[646] and perhaps earlier, as Kellner's father, a German-born violinist, was a member of Queen Charlotte's band of musicians and King George III had taken an interest in Kellner's early musical education.[647]

In 1841 Calkin & Budd, 'booksellers to Her Majesty', issued *A Catalogue of a Miscellaneous Collection of Music* for sale.[648] Lots 2190–2199 consisted of printed works by Kollmann, and the catalogue

---

[642] JSK→Henry Brougham, 2/10/1843. In this letter Joanna said that she had not received a reply to a letter (not preserved) that she had sent to Brougham 'in the spring of this year' regarding patent rights.

[643] *London Gazette* no. 19861 (2 June 1840) p 1329, and no. 20596 (21 April 1846) p 1462.

[644] *The Musical World* no. 212 = n.s. no. 119 (9 April 1840) p 230.

[645] Richard Cull, 'Case of precocious musical talent, being a notice of the late Ernest Augustus Kellner ... with some phrenological remarks on his head and character', *The Phrenological Journal, and Magazine of Moral Science* v 13 = n.s. v 3 (1840) p 146–155 at p 150. Kellner was a member of the London Phrenological Society and presumably had met Cull there.

[646] Its first performance was at Venice in February 1823. The first London performance was in July 1824.

[647] Cull, p 147. Curiously, the Kellner family also claimed descent from Martin Luther. See http://www.clewervillage.co.uk/churchyard.htm#_Toc483193981 .

[648] The collector William Euing's copy of this catalogue (Glasgow University Library, Special Collections, B.x.64) is dated August 1841.

noted that 'Kollmann's Works are all *very scarce*, and the above is presumed to be the largest collection ever offered for sale'.[649] It seems likely that George sold these copies to Calkin & Budd in order to raise money, or that they offered to sell these copies on his behalf. He and Joseph Calkin saw each other regularly, as both were members of the Court of Assistants of the Royal Society of Musicians.[650] In 1844 Calkin & Budd issued another catalogue with the same title, in which copies of 'nearly all' of Kollmann's publications were offered for sale.[651]

While the assignees were taking control of George's piano business the House of Commons was considering, and on 1 June 1840 passed, *A Bill for Forming a Company to be called* 'Kollmann*'s Railway Locomotive and Carriage Improvement Company'*.[652] This bill, which Martineau, Malton & Trollope had drafted, passed with only a few slight amendments,[653] and the Commons ordered that it be carried to the House of Lords for their concurrence.

On 15 June a committee of the House of Lords gave initial consideration to the bill. They were addressed by Edward Trollope—the solicitor concerned with this matter—who produced 'from the possession of the Patentee' the two original letters patent for George's railway concept and the subsequently enrolled specifications of these

[649] The catalogue also included Kollmann's edition of Bach's *Chromatic Fantasy* (lot 143) and George's 'Three grand sonatas for the piano forte' (lot 1115).

[650] George was appointed to the Court of Assistants in 1831 (Royal Society of Musicians minutes, 4 September 1831) and Calkin was a member from 1835 (see 'Calkin, Joseph', *A Biographical Dictionary of Actors, Actresses, Musicians...*, Carbondale, Illinois, v 3 (1975) p 33). Their appointments were for life. The other partner in Calkin & Budd, Elizabeth Budd, was Calkin's wife. George's shortage of money in 1842 is evidenced by his failure (recorded in the Society's minutes) to pay his subscription to the Royal Society of Musicians that year.

[651] Euing's copy of the 1844 catalogue (Glasgow University Library, Special Collections, B.x.65) shows that he purchased two lots of works by Kollmann from this catalogue which now are in the Glasgow University Library. Some Kollmann items in the 1841 Calkin & Budd catalogue were still for sale in their 1844 catalogue. The second portion of Calkin & Budd's stock, auctioned by Puttick & Simpson on 19–20 May 1852, included six lots of publications by Kollmann.

[652] *Journal of the House of Commons* v 95 (1 June 1840) p 387.

[653] The manuscript record is in House of Lords Record Office, Main Papers, 1 June 1840 (Kollman's [sic] Patent Bill), catalogue no. 596.

patents.[654] Then, according to the minutes of the meeting, 'the 3rd Paragraph of the Preamble [of the bill] is read, and the same witness [Trollope] produces an Office Copy of the Fiat in Bankruptcy, therein-mentioned, bearing date the 14th February 1840'.

However, the bill that the House of Commons passed on 1 June had not contained that third paragraph, which refers to the appointment of Johnson and Dransfield as assignees, nor did it mention George's bankruptcy. The new paragraph, which appears in the Act that received royal assent on 3 July 1840, therefore must have been inserted at the urging of Martineau, Malton & Trollope, after the House of Commons had passed the bill.[655]

In a further meeting of the Committee on 22 June, at which the civil engineer Joseph Gibbs 'proved the allegations' of the preamble (such as the claim that George's inventions 'will be of great public benefit and utility'),[656] the Committee ordered 'that the Bill be reported without amendment' to the Lords.[657] On the next day the Lords resolved to pass the bill,[658] and on 3 July the Clerk Assistant pronounced Queen Victoria's royal assent: 'La Reyne le veult'.[659]

---

[654] House of Lords Record Office, House of Lords Committee Book, 15 June 1840, p 277–279.

[655] *An Act for forming a Company to be called 'Kollmann's Railway Locomotive and Carriage Improvement Company'*, *op. cit.* Apparently at the same time, a clause was added to §3 that it shall be lawful for Johnson and Dransfield, as well as for George, to sell letters patent to the company. The bill that had been passed by the Commons did not mention either Johnson or Dransfield.

[656] House of Lords Record Office, House of Lords Committee Book, 22 June 1840, p 304. Gibbs designed several railway lines and had published the pamphlet *Some Observations relative to the Introduction of Railway Bills into Parliament*, London, *c*1836, which had called for committees of each House of Parliament 'to examine the merits of every proposed railway' (p 7).

[657] Presumably the Lords' standing orders allowed a bill to be 'reported without amendment' in circumstances such as this, even though its text had been changed. However, the standing orders then in force have not been examined to verify this hypothesis.

[658] *Journal of the House of Lords* v 72 (23 June 1840) p 424.

[659] *Journal of the House of Lords* v 72 (3 July 1840) p 459.

On 15 October 1841 it was announced that a certificate of conformity would be granted to George, stating that he had satisfied all requirements of the Court of Bankruptcy.[660] This allowed him to resume business activities without accounting to the assignees or the court. He later applied for Scottish and Irish patents on his railway concepts, which were granted on 4 October and 15 October 1844.[661]

In June 1844, almost four years after Parliament had enabled Kollmann's Railway Locomotive and Carriage Improvement Company to be created, 'a number of gentlemen met together' to form it and 'a provisional committee were elected'.[662] It seems clear that Wilhelm Kuper, who would have had many conversations with George about his bankruptcy and its aftermath, endeavoured to help him by encouraging family and friends to participate in the new company.

Kuper's son John George William Kuper was involved from the outset as deputy chairman of the provisional committee and subsequently was elected deputy chairman of the company's Board of Directors. Eventually he held thirty shares in the company, for which he paid £260.[663] His brother, Augustus Leopold Kuper of the Royal Navy (later Admiral Sir Augustus), also subscribed for thirty shares.[664]

Rev. John Merewether, from 1832 dean of Hereford, was another early director of the company and became chairman of its board. He and Wilhelm Kuper had been colleagues for several years. Adelaide, when Duchess of Clarence, had appointed Kuper her domestic chaplain in 1819 and named Merewether as another of her chaplains in 1824. In 1830, when she became queen, Kuper and Merewether

---

[660] *London Gazette* no. 20028 (15 October 1841) p 2557.

[661] Copy of Deed of Settlement, *op. cit.*, p 10–11. I thank Jennifer Duffy for advising that the original specification of George's Scottish patent is in the National Archives of Scotland, ref. C20/45/9.

[662] 'Beresford's case', in John P[eter] de Gex and John Smale, *Reports of Cases decided in the High Court of Chancery by the Right Hon. Sir J. L. Knight Bruce, Vice-Chancellor*, London, v 3, 1852, p 175–180 at p 175.

[663] 'Kuper's Assignees' case', in de Gex and Smale, *op. cit.*, p 113–116 at p 113. John George William Kuper, a wire rope manufacturer at Camberwell, used the name 'William Kuper'.

[664] Copy of Deed of Settlement, p 72–73.

became her two chaplains in ordinary.[665] Merewether's 'distant cousin' Henry Alworth Merewether, who was Queen Adelaide's solicitor general from 1832 and from 1842 town clerk of the Corporation of London, was named the company's standing counsel.

The company's prospectus sought capital of £10,000 in 500 shares of £20 each, for which an initial deposit of £2 per share was called.[666] This capital would be used to purchase 'patents already granted', to take out patents for George's system in other countries, and 'to exemplify' it by experiments. On 15 July 1844 Dransfield and Johnson, the assignees of George's bankruptcy estate, agreed to sell George's two English railway patents and the French and Belgian *brevets* to the company for £1500. The company also bought George's 'model engine and tender' for £120 from George Laurie, an attorney.[667]

In the prospectus the directors said they 'confidently expected' that revenue from licensing George's system to railway companies would 'render a very considerable return for the capital invested, and confer incalculable benefits on the public in general'. A special general meeting of the company on 12 December 1844 authorised directors to 'connect themselves' with railway companies that were interested in adopting George's system, and Merewether, John George William Kuper and other directors accordingly became promoters of the London and Worcester Railway Company.[668]

---

[665] Thomas Seccombe and Ellie Clewlow, 'Merewether, John', *Oxford Dictionary of National Biography*, Oxford, 2004, v 37 p 884-885; and *Royal Kalendar ... for the year 1831*, London, 1831, p 128. Merewether's appointment of Samuel Sebastian Wesley as organist of Hampton, Middlesex in 1831 and Hereford Cathedral in 1832 conceivably was influenced by the friendship of Charles Wesley III—Samuel Sebastian Wesley's half-brother—with Kuper (see page 112 above). In 1835 Samuel Sebastian Wesley married Merewether's sister Mary Anne. See Peter Horton, *Samuel Sebastian Wesley: a Life*, Oxford, 2004, p 29, p 35 and p 74.

[666] Sir Isambard Kingdom Brunel's copy of the prospectus—the only copy known—is in the National Archives, RAIL 1149/53. It bears no date but presumably was printed before 4 September 1844, as the company advertised on p 3 of *The Times* that day that prospectuses could be had at its offices.

[667] Copy of Deed of Settlement, *op. cit.*, p 9–10. It is not known how Laurie acquired the model engine and tender (i.e., wagon) that George had earlier exhibited.

[668] *ibid.*, p 16; sworn statement by William Goodenough Dunt, clerk to George Smith, solicitor, dated 13 July 1850 (National Archives, C101/5342 p 609) regarding a

On 31 January 1845 Kollmann's Railway Locomotive and Carriage Improvement Company was registered as a joint stock company.[669] On 17 March it obtained an exclusive licence from George Spencer to use the English patent he had been granted on 11 January 1845 to 'enable locomotives to draw barges and vessels along inland waterways'.[670] This patent specification referred to 'an arrangement of axle frame similar to that patented by Mr G. A. Kollmann', and the licence enabled the company to offer systems for travel not only on rails and ordinary roads but also for 'canal traction'.[671] Spencer and George must have made contact some time before this patent was granted, as a drawing by Spencer of George's locomotive engine, reproduced in *Figure 8* facing page 174, was published in December 1844.[672]

George's participation in the company was an important component of its prospectus, which proposed to vest his patents 'in trustees for the mutual benefit of the shareholders and the original inventor and patentee, with whom the Directors have entered into an arrangement, and thereby secured his very skilful and eminent services'. This arrangement, formalised in the Deed of Settlement dated 18 March 1845, stipulated that for the rest of his life, health permitting, he

---

'project for forming a line of railway from London to Worcester which was intended to adopt Kollmann's principle'; House of Commons, *A Return of all Joint Stock Companies provisionally registered...*, 25 July 1845, p 30. Although 'negotiations' were in progress in late 1844 to lay 'upwards of one hundred miles' of that railway line ('Railway Improvements. Kollmann's Invention', *Polytechnic Review and Magazine* n.s. v 1 no. 6 (December 1844) p 431–433 at p 432), no evidence has been found that work on this line ever commenced.

[669] House of Commons, *A Return 'of the Joint Stock Companies which have been registered...'*, 20 July 1846, p 22.

[670] Copy of Deed of Settlement, p 16–18. Spencer's patent subsequently was numbered 10458. P[eter] L[ester] Payne, *Rubber and Railways in the Nineteenth Century: a study of the Spencer papers*, Liverpool, 1961, remarked (p 2) that 'nothing came' of Spencer's patent.

[671] Advertisements, *The Times*, 21 July 1845, p 3, and 25 July 1845, p 2; the latter stated that the company's 'Directors have secured patents for a most important application of the system to canals'. Both advertisements were repeated several times in that month.

[672] As a foldout plate bound between p 432 and p 433 in 'Railway Improvements. Kollmann's Invention', *op. cit.*

would 'inspect and superintend the manufacturing of the apparatus and machinery' made by the company or under its licence. For each year that he did this he would receive an annuity equal to three-eighths of the company's profits for that year. After his death, if Joanna survived him, annuities in respect of his years of service to the company would be paid to her for as long as she lived.[673]

Any services that George may have provided to the company were limited by his spinal injury in 1844 and the subsequent kidney disease that caused his death at St James's Palace on 19 March 1845,[674] the day after the company executed the Deed of Settlement. As the company never produced anything or made a profit, George and Joanna never received any money from it.

George's death notice in the 29 March *Dramatic and Musical Review* described him as 'a highly esteemed subscriber and contributor to this Review'.[675] His contributions to that weekly have not been identified, but a letter to its editor written under the pseudonym 'A Lover of the Great Masters' might have been one. This letter, of which an extract was published in the *Review*'s 2 December 1843 number, asserted that Kollmann

> in his most important theoretical works, first gave examples from those of that great master [J. S. Bach], which works he first introduced to the late Mr Samuel Wesley, and from copies lent by Mr Kollman to that gentleman, the edition of Messrs Wesley and Horn was originally published.[676]

Although somewhat obscurely written—the editor conjectured that 'A Lover of the Great Masters' was Bach's 'countryman'—its text strikingly resembles a note that Joanna wrote on the flyleaf of the manuscript of part 2 of the '48' that had belonged to her father:

---

673 Copy of Deed of Settlement, *op. cit.*, p 18–19 and p 38–39.

674 According to the 27 March 1845 entry of his death at the General Register Office. His obituary, 'The late George Augustus Kollmann', *Dramatic and Musical Review* v 4 no. 158 (5 April 1845) p 174–175, said that 'he had lingered for more than a twelvemonth under a paralytic affection, occasioned by a spinal injury which he received from a violent fall'.

675 *Dramatic and Musical Review* v 4 no. 157 (29 March 1845) p 163.

676 *Dramatic and Musical Review* v 2 no. 88 (2 December 1843) p 581.

> This Copy of These Splendid Fugues and Preludes was the first Copy which came into England for the expres [sic] use of Aug Fred Christ Kollmann and transcribed in Germany by his desire. and from this Copy ~~and it was the Copy~~ which was lent to the late Mr Samuel Wesley and from which He (Mr S: Wesley and the late Mr Horn) Ed: the Publication of the 24 Preludes & Fugues by Seb Bach bearing Wesley & Horns Name.[677]

As this copy was still in George's and Joanna's possession in 1843 and presumably had not been seen by many other readers of the *Dramatic and Musical Review*, 'A Lover of the Great Masters' seems likely to have been a pseudonym that George or Joanna used on this occasion.

A week after his death notice the *Review* published an obituary of George for which Joanna probably supplied information.[678] It recorded that:

> Young George was educated at home, under the eye of his parents, and gave early indications of superior mental powers. ... we can remember the very warm eulogium passed on his playing, when he was but a boy, by the late Samuel Wesley.... The estimation in which that unfortunate genius held Mr Kollmann's matured powers, we have reason to know was very high.[679] ... [George] was trained up to his profession under the most skilful superintendence; the works of his father, Augustus Kollmann, being universally admitted to indicate the most profound acquaintance with the science of music.... The abilities of the youth were further cultivated by a constant attendance at the Ancient concerts, from the time when he attained his seventh year....[680]
>
> Mr Kollmann's powers as an extempore player were of no ordinary character; his grasp was gigantic, and ... his command over the instrument was absolute. ... His published works are ... such as to justify very high expectations of some grand symphonies and various other musical MSS.,

---

677 This manuscript is now St Andrews University ms M24.B2. For its history and the validity of Joanna's claim, see Yo Tomita, 'The dawn of the English Bach awakening manifested in sources of the "48"', *EBA* p 35–167 at p 112–122.

678 'The late George Augustus Kollmann', *op. cit.*

679 Confirmation that Samuel Wesley heard George play when he was a boy has not been found. The first extant document linking the two is a letter from Wesley tentatively dated 30 September 1809 (*LSW*, p 123–124; *SWSB*, p 267), in which he mentions telling Charles Burney that George was 'quite capable' of playing the keyboard part of J. S. Bach's violin sonatas.

680 Kollmann's name does not appear in the list of subscribers to the Concerts of Antient Music. Perhaps he received complimentary tickets.

> which we understand it is intended to bring out.[681] ... [He] was a gentleman whose virtues and attainments shed a lustre on the profession. With a vigorous understanding and a lively fancy, he combined a readiness and force of expression that exhibited the stores of his diversified reading in a manner the most instructive and agreeable.

The Times said of George that 'this highly talented man earned for himself by his extraordinary genius and scientific inventions a distinguished position in society, and has left a large circle of friends to deplore his loss'.[682]

One of the persons who apparently attended the June 1844 meeting to form Kollmann's Railway Locomotive and Carriage Improvement Company was Francis Marcus Beresford. He was appointed to the company's provisional committee and was elected a director before its prospectus was issued. On 30 July 1844 he was allotted five shares in the company and by June 1845 he had paid £40 in respect of them.[683] Beresford grew up in London, where he attended King's College School from 1833 to 1835.[684] After serving for several years in the North American militia, presumably in Canada, he managed a wharf in Newcastle upon Tyne *c*1843–1844[685] and about 1845 went into business as a wharfinger at Pickleherring Wharf, Southwark.[686] It is not known when or how he got to know George or

---

[681] These works were never published and their manuscripts are presumed lost.

[682] *The Times*, 24 March 1845, p 7.

[683] 'Beresford's case', *op. cit.*, p 175–176.

[684] F[rank] R. Miles, *King's College School: A register of pupils in the school under its first headmaster...*, London, 1974, p 28. Beresford's father, Rev. Gilbert Beresford, was rector of St Andrew's, Holborn, from 1819 to 1838.

[685] I thank Pamela Cunningham of Newcastle Libraries for the information that he is listed as a wharfinger and manager of the London Steam Packet office in *Williams' Commercial Directory of Newcastle-upon-Tyne* (Newcastle, 1844). He was still living in Newcastle when he was allotted five shares of the company in July 1844 ('Beresford's Case', *loc. cit.*).

[686] He was at this Southwark address by March 1846 (JSK→[Hugh] William Ruel, 16/3/1846) and is listed there in *The June Edition of the Post Office London Directory, 1846*. In a short profile entitled 'Statesmen. No. 222. Mr Marcus Beresford, M.P.', *Vanity Fair* v 15 (13 May 1876) p 283, 'Jehu Junior' (pseudonym of the magazine's editor, Thomas Gibson Bowles) said that when Beresford was elected MP for

his railway concepts, or whether he considered that they might have application on wharves, but the two must have become friends as (according to Joanna) Beresford was George's 'executor' and endeavoured to put his affairs in order after his death.[687]

George's friendship with Beresford also is suggested by the latter's withdrawal from the railway company soon after George's death,[688] and by evidence that several items from Kollmann's library that had passed to George and Joanna, including Kollmann's manuscript copy of part 2 of the '48', apparently were transferred to Beresford in 1845. Joanna wrote 'F. M. Beresford 1845' on the first page of the '48' manuscript,[689] on the first page of the second bassoon part of the André edition of Mozart's piano concerto K. 482 (whose piano part had earlier been inscribed 'Mr Kollmann from the

---

Southwark in 1870 he 'had conducted a thriving business in the borough of Southwark' for 'seven and twenty years'. Bowles's profile was accompanied (p 282) by a caricature of Beresford by the artist 'Spy' (pseudonym of Sir Leslie Ward). It was entitled 'Southwark' and is reproduced as *Figure 9* facing page 175.

[687] JSK→[Hugh] William Ruel, 16/3/1846. Joanna's description of Beresford as her dear brother's 'executor' presumably did not imply that George had written a will that gave Beresford this duty, as no will by George nor record of administration of his estate has been found. George would have been involved in discussions leading to the Deed of Settlement executed on 18 March 1845 and probably did not anticipate that he would die the next day.

[688] Beresford was required to sign the company's Deed of Settlement by 18 April 1845. He did not do this, and his name, which had been listed as a director in the company's advertisements in 1844 (e.g., *The Railway Times* v 7 no. 33 (17 August 1844) p 931, repeated multiple times; *The Times*, 25 September 1844, p 3), does not appear in the company's list of directors advertised in *The Times*, 28 July 1845, p 3. The company resolved on 19 August 1845 that if he did not sign this deed by 25 August his shares would be forfeited. He did not sign it, and on 29 August his shares were forfeited and his £40 investment was lost (see 'Beresford's case', *op. cit.*, p 176–178). Beresford's acquiescence in this loss suggests that he had no confidence in the company's ability to prosper without George's participation.

[689] This title-page of this manuscript, showing Joanna's inscription, is reproduced in *EBA Figure 1.7* (between p 234 and p 235). Joanna's handwriting of Beresford's name (in which the initial of his middle name resembles a 'U') is quite unlike Beresford's *c*1844 autograph in the signature book for Kollmann's Railway and Carriage Improvement Company's bank account with Cocks, Biddulph & Co. (Barclays Group Archives, Manchester, ref. 230/57). I thank Jessie Campbell and Maria Sienkiewicz for information about this signature book. The bank's customer account ledgers for this time have not survived.

Proprietor'),[690] and on the first pages of all parts except the piano part of the André edition of Mozart's piano concerto K. 491.[691]

As no other indication has been found that Beresford collected rare music or had musical interests, it seems plausible that Joanna gave these items to him as compensation for his work in administering George's estate. The Kollmann/Beresford manuscript of part 2 of the '48' subsequently was auctioned as lot 58 in the 30 January 1877 Puttick & Simpson sale of items from Kollmann's library, and the Mozart editions that passed to Beresford also may have been sold in lot 323* [sic] of that sale, which the catalogue described as including 'upwards of' thirty volumes of music, of which 'many were presented to Kollmann, by André'.[692] However, Beresford's name was not put onto every item from Kollmann's library sold at that auction. For instance, the manuscript of Kollmann's *The Praise of God* sold as lot 53 in that auction bears no inscription to Beresford.[693]

It seems likely that Joanna occasionally had substituted for George as organist of the German Chapel, and that Kuper admired her playing and recommended that she succeed George. By virtue of a warrant from Charles James Blomfield, Bishop of London, she was 'sworn and admitted into the Place and offices of Organist, Clerk and Chapel Keeper of His Majesty's German Lutheran Chapel St James's', where her duties began on Lady Day (25 March) 1845, less than a week after George's death.[694] She did not enjoy a peaceful tenure.

Between December 1844 and June 1846 Blomfield received letters from three people seeking his help to recover money that they claimed was owed by Joanna. One was from George Smith, presumably the man of that name who was solicitor to Kollmann's Railway

---

690 Now BL Hirsch IV 91a. See page 65 above.

691 Now BL Hirsch IV 97a. The piano part has no inscription to Kollmann from the proprietor, presumably an oversight by André or his representative.

692 See section I.30 below.

693 This manuscript was purchased by Sir Frederick Arthur Gore Ouseley at this sale. It is now Bodleian ms Tenbury 852–853.

694 New cheque book of the Chapel Royal (manuscript, Chapel Royal archive), p 101, transcribed in Andrew Ashbee and John Harley (eds), *The Cheque Books of the Chapel Royal*, Aldershot, 2000, v 1 p 279–280.

Locomotive and Carriage Improvement Company.[695] If the company had acquired a promissory note signed by Joanna to repay debts arising from her participation in George's piano business, it might have instructed Smith to try to collect this money.[696] Blomfield stressed in his replies that Joanna had got 'into great difficulties' through 'no fault of her own', that she would pay her debts if she could, but was unable to pay now because her income consisted only of a small salary from the German Chapel 'and the little that she earns by teaching'.[697]

Creditors continued to pursue her and, on her own petition, her 'estate and effects' were vested by the Court for Relief of Insolvent Debtors in its Provisional Assignee on 5 September 1846.[698] By then she had spent time in several prisons, as she was described as:

> Joanna Sophia Kollmann, formerly of the German Chapel Royal, Saint James's, Middlesex, then a Prisoner for Debt in the custody of the Sheriff of Middlesex, then occasionally of Brewer-street, Pimlico, then a Prisoner for Debt in the Queen's Prison, Surrey, then of Brewer-street, Pimlico aforesaid, then of the Debtors' Prison for London and Middlesex, then again of Brewer-street, Pimlico aforesaid, then occasionally of No. 25 or 27, Upper Albany-street, Regent's-park, Middlesex, then of the German Chapel Royal aforesaid, then occasionally of the Priory-road, Wandsworth, and for a short time of Brixton, both in Surrey, then of the German Chapel Royal aforesaid, and late of the German Chapel aforesaid, Teacher of Music, Organist and Chapel Keeper of the aforesaid Chapel, and occasionally Buying and Selling Piano Fortes.[699]

---

[695] See Blomfield→George Smith, 6/6/1845; Blomfield→Mr Barker, 19/1/1846; and Blomfield→Samuel Frederick Langham, 18/6/1846; all summarised in section III.4 below. Langham was a solicitor who specialised in bankruptcy matters. The letters to Blomfield from these correspondents have not been preserved.

[696] In JSK→Henry Brougham, 22/4/1845, Joanna wrote that her name 'stood as security' on some documents connected with George's business.

[697] The 1841 census listed George Kollmann as an organist and Joanna as a 'professor of music'.

[698] *London Gaxette* no. 20639 (8 September 1846) p 3241; *The Jurist* v 10 no. 505 (12 September 1846) p 350. On 10 October 1846 the court appointed two assignees of her estate and effects, of whom one was William Gray Thwaites, who had been George's solicitor when he applied for his 1825 piano patent (*London Gazette* no. 20649 (13 October 1846) p 3618).

[699] *London Gazette* no. 20640 (11 September 1846) p 3284.

Joanna died suddenly on 14 May 1849 at St James's Palace. She

> was transacting business in the Lord Chamberlain's office when she was struck by epilepsy, and, notwithstanding the medical gentlemen connected with the palace were in attendance upon her, she remained perfectly insensible for several hours, and died on Monday evening [14 May].[700]

An inquest held before Frederick John Manning, coroner of the queen's household, on 17 May, returned a unanimous verdict of 'natural death',[701] and her funeral service took place at the Savoy Chapel on 21 May.[702] All Kollmann family possessions that remained in their German Chapel apartment apparently were removed soon afterwards, as Frederic Weber was sworn (by virtue of a warrant from Blomfield) as Joanna's successor on 25 May, and his duties, which gave him the perquisite of the Chapel apartment, commenced on 1 July.[703] Perhaps at this time Beresford acquired some additional items from Kollmann's library that subsequently were auctioned by Puttick & Simpson on 30 January 1877.[704]

Weber, who was born at Würtemberg, Germany, arrived in England in 1841 and was appointed organist of the Hamburger Lutherische Kirche in London in 1845.[705] Kuper's daughter Charlotte Augusta had married the pastor of that church, Adolphus Walbaum, two years earlier, so it is plausible that Walbaum recommended Weber to Kuper as a suitable replacement for Joanna.[706] Weber composed music and wrote on musical subjects, but does not appear to have

[700] *The Times*, 19 May 1849, p 7.

[701] *ibid.*

[702] Charles Godfrey Ruel→'Dear Sir', 18/5/1849, in section III.4 below.

[703] New cheque book of the Chapel Royal (manuscript, Chapel Royal archive), p 102, transcribed in Andrew Ashbee and John Harley (eds), *The Cheque Books of the Chapel Royal*, *op. cit.*, v 1 p 280.

[704] See note 692 above. Evidence to confirm this conjecture has not been found.

[705] For Weber see James Love, *Scottish Church Music: its Composers and Sources*, Edinburgh, 1891, p 297, and the obituary 'Mr Frederic Weber', *The Musical Times* v 50 no. 793 (1 March 1909) p 175.

[706] Walbaum later succeeded Kuper as sole chaplain of the German Chapel.

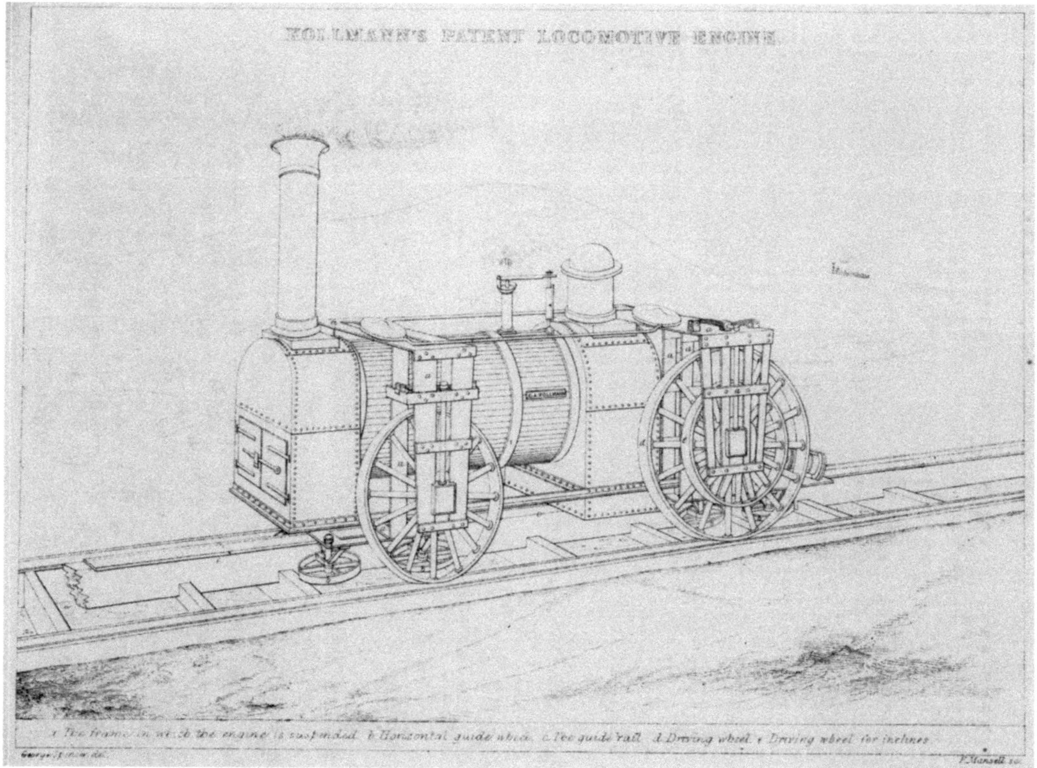

Figure 8. George Spencer's drawing of George Kollmann's locomotive engine (Polytechnic Review and Magazine of Science, Literature, and the Fine Arts, London, 1844; by permission of the Library Company of Philadelphia)

Figure 9. Caricature by 'Spy' (Sir Leslie Ward) of Col. Francis Marcus Beresford, MP, who received part of Kollmann's library in 1845 (Vanity Fair, London, 1876; by permission of Jamie and Michael Kassler, Northbridge, NSW, Australia)

known Kollmann's publications or to have been influenced by them. He remained organist of the German Chapel until 1901, when King Edward VII terminated the German services in St James's Palace.[707]

Kollmann's Railway Locomotive and Carriage Improvement Company persisted for ten more years. In 1845 it arranged to have the model locomotive that George had earlier shown at Carlisle Street exhibited 'every day and evening' at the Royal Adelaide Gallery in the Strand.[708] Additional publicity for his system also was secured.[709]

By the end of July the company's directors had

> resolved, at the recommendation of several eminent engineers, to construct a full-sized locomotive engine and carriage, and lay down as near to the metropolis as convenient a short but sufficiently extensive line of railway, with such curves and gradients as have hitherto been deemed insurmountable.[710]

To achieve this goal the directors increased the share capital of the company by £50,000, and the public were invited to apply for 5000 new £10 shares by August 1845.[711] The response to this offering is not known, but it was made during a time that later became known as the 'railway mania', when railway shares were at their height. In October 1845 there was 'panic in the share-market' as investors rushed to sell their speculative holdings in railway companies.[712] No full-size

[707] The German Chapel congregation subsequently removed to the Deutsche Evangelische Christuskirche, Montpelier Place, Kensington, which was consecrated in 1904. See John Greenacombe (ed.), *Knightsbridge* (*Survey of London* v 45), London, 2000, p 124–126.

[708] Royal Adelaide Gallery advertisement, *The Times*, 19 July 1845, p 1; repeated 25 July 1845, p 1, and 1 August 1845, p 1. 'Kollmann's locomotive engine' continued to be displayed there in January 1846 (advertisement, *The Times*, 10 January 1846, p 1; repeated 14 January 1846, p 1, and 19 January 1846, p 1).

[709] See, for instance, 'Kollman's [sic] new locomotive railway apparatus', *The Pictorial Times*, 22 November 1845, p 324–325, which has several illustrations of the system.

[710] Advertisement, *The Times*, 25 July 1845, p 2; repeated several times.

[711] Advertisement, *The Times*, 22 August 1845, p 2; repeated 23 August 1845, p 10, and 26 August 1845, p 9.

[712] See 'Epoch the first. The railway mania and its effects' in D[avid] Morier Evans, *The Commercial Crisis 1847–1848...*, London, 1848, p 1–52 at p 18–19.

locomotive based upon George's designs was ever built, and a petition to wind up the company was presented to the Lord High Chancellor on 29 December 1848.[713]

During the winding-up process it was discovered that:

> Considerable sums had been paid for the patents, and brevets of invention were granted for the Continent. Two years passed [from the establishment of the company in 1845], in the course of which nothing was done beyond the spending by the provisional committee of 4,000*l.* of the deposit, besides borrowing other moneys. The official manager now reports, that there are no assets, but claims to the extent of 2,000*l.*[714]

To liquidate these debts Sir Richard Torin Kindersley, master of the High Court of Chancery, required shareholders to pay £12 per share by the end of August 1849,[715] an additional £12 in 1850,[716] and a further £9 by 17 April 1851.[717] A meeting was set for 25 January 1853 to consider how the patents held by the company might be disposed.[718]

In March the auctioneers Fuller & Horsey advertised that George's and George Spencer's patents and George's model locomotive would be sold in the following month.[719] The patents did not find a buyer then, and in March 1855 a barrister's opinion was obtained that no sale of them was likely to succeed, particularly as they had never been worked.[720] The model locomotive may have been sold,

---

[713] *London Gazette* no. 20933 (5 January 1849) p 35.

[714] *The Times*, 15 August 1849, p 8.

[715] A printed copy of Kindersley's order, signed by the accountant William Goodchap, who was appointed official manager of the company by Kindersley on 17 February 1849 (advertisement, *The Times*, 2 March 1829, p 2), is in National Archives C101/5342 p 45.

[716] *The Times*, 16 May 1850, p 8.

[717] *The Times*, 31 March 1851, p 2.

[718] *London Gazette* no. 21453 (18 January 1853) p 148–149.

[719] Advertisement, *The Times*, 9 March 1853, p 16; repeated 14 March 1853, p 16, and 28 March 1853, p 12.

[720] The 6 March 1855 report to William Goodchap from the barrister William Eldridge, with Goodchap's concurring comment, is in National Archives C101/5342 p 847–849.

as a statement of assets and liabilities when the company was wound up in 1855 includes a liability of £25/3/- to Fuller & Horsey for 'sale of models'.[721] Its subsequent provenance is not known.

30. The Sale of Kollmann's Library (1877)

On 30 January 1877 'an important selection from the library of the eminent theorist A. F. C. Kollman' [sic] was auctioned in London by Puttick & Simpson along with other properties relating to music.[722] Items from Kollmann's library started to be sold in lot 53 and ended with lot 323*—an addendum catalogued between lots 323 and 324—but did not constitute all the intermediate lots.

The auctioneer's copy of the sale catalogue, now British Library S.-C. Puttick 177(10), is annotated with buyers' names, prices fetched and identifications of people who consigned items to the sale. The initials 'REL' written next to lots 53 and 323* in this copy indicate that the items in this auction from Kollmann's library had been consigned to Puttick & Simpson by the music seller Robert Edward Lonsdale.[723] He was present at the auction and bought back a number of items for which the bidding presumably did not reach his reserve price.

For instance, lot 57 in this sale, described in the catalogue as:

> BACH (J. S.) DIE KUNST DER FUGE, a splendid MS. with 6 pages of Introduction dated 1752, signed Marpurg
>
> The important MS. from which the Work was published.

---

[721] National Archives C101/5342 p 852-853.

[722] The printed sale catalogue also includes items auctioned on 31 January 1877, but none of these appears to have belonged to Kollmann.

[723] Lonsdale, son of the music seller Christopher Lonsdale, apparently was in charge of his father's business by 1863, when he had possession of the correspondence that Beethoven had exchanged with Christopher Lonsdale and his predecessor, Robert Birchall. See Friedrich Chrysander, 'Beethoven's Verbindung mit Birchall und Stumpff in London', *Jahrbücher für musikalische Wissenschaft* v 1 (1863) p 429–452 at p 429.

was bought back by Lonsdale for 9/6. It was consigned to Puttick & Simpson later that year for sale as lot 74 in their 22 August 1877 auction, where it was catalogued as:

> MARPURG'S ORIGINAL MS. COPY, for the Engraver, of BACH'S ART OF FUGUE, with 6 pages of Introduction, dated 1752, signed "Marpurg." Fine Folio MS. of 111 pp. from Kollman's [sic] library.[724]

It is not known when or how Kollmann had acquired this manuscript, and its subsequent whereabouts have not been traced.

The later provenance of lot 89 in the sale, catalogued as:

> Müthel, Duetto für 2 Claviere, 2 Flügel, oder 2 Fortepiano, VERY RARE *Riga*, 1771

can be traced. Lonsdale bought it back at the 30 January 1877 sale for 2/–. He returned it to Puttick & Simpson for sale on 27 July 1877, when it again failed to find a buyer, and he bought it back then for 1/–.[725] It next appeared in the 22 August 1877 Puttick & Simpson sale, where J. Harvey purchased it for 1/–.[726] Thomas William Taphouse bought it for 1/– in the sale of Harvey's collection, where it was described as being uncut and bearing the 'autograph of John Fred^{k} Hempel', Christina Kollmann's nephew.[727] At Taphouse's sale this item was bought for 6/– by Louis Thompson Rowe,[728] and it subsequently passed to the Rowe Music Library in King's College, Cambridge.[729]

---

[724] BL S.-C. Puttick 181(13). At this auction it was sold for 4/6 to a buyer identified as 'Money', presumably indicating a cash sale rather than a sale to someone surnamed 'Money'.

[725] BL S.-C. Puttick 181(5), lot 386.

[726] BL S.-C. Puttick 181(13).

[727] Lot 311 of the 6 July 1885 Sotheby sale, BL S.-C. Sotheby 892(3). John Frederick Hempel probably was 'Mr J. Hempel' who had subscribed to Kollmann's *An Essay on Practical Musical Composition*. His musical activities and interests are otherwise unknown.

[728] Lot 602 of the 3–4 July 1909 Sotheby sale, BL S.-C. Sotheby 1289(1).

[729] Shelfmark 33.30 RES. I am grateful to Margaret Cranmer for showing me this score.

Apart from Hempel's ownership inscription the copy is very clean and shows no overt evidence that it ever belonged to Kollmann.[730]

As mentioned, the 30 January 1877 sale included items from Kollmann's library that had passed to Francis Marcus Beresford in 1845: lot 58 (the manuscript of part 2 of Bach's '48') and presumably some of lot 323* (a collection of 'upwards of 30' volumes of 'original editions', 'many presented to Kollmann, by André'). It is not clear whether Lonsdale owned the items from Kollmann's library when he consigned them to auction or was selling them at auction on behalf of others.

Rev. Sir Frederick Arthur Gore Ouseley successfully bid for two items from Kollmann's library. One was a volume containing five of Kollmann's printed works; the other was the manuscript of his oratorio *The Praise of God* that he had given to his son George. Ouseley bought both items for the library of St Michael's College, Tenbury, which he had founded in 1856. They are now in the Tenbury collection in the Bodleian Library, Oxford.

Henry George Bohn was eager to acquire one of his former master's publications. He bid up to 25/- for a copy of the second edition of *An Essay on Practical Musical Composition*, which he got for 10/6, and advised Puttick & Simpson before the sale that he would pay up to 25/- for the autograph manuscript of the full score of Kollmann's piano concerto (lot 79) if his bid for that *Essay* failed.[731] At the auction the manuscript of Kollmann's piano concerto was bought by the Sheffield antiquary William Thomas Freemantle. His extensive collection subsequently was dispersed to several repositories, but efforts to locate this score have been unsuccessful.

---

[730] Kollmann conceivably might have been interested to own it because Müthel had been a pupil of J. S. Bach, but the copy could have reached Hempel by another route. The harpist Philip James Meyer Sr, who settled in London in 1784 and associated with the German community there (he was buried, like Kollmann, in St Mary's German Church in the Savoy), had studied with Müthel and might have met the Hempel family through the Kollmanns. Joanna Kollmann subscribed to Meyer's *A Collection of Hymns and Psalms arranged for the Harp & Piano Forte*, London, *c*1815.

[731] According to the auctioneer's copy of the sale catalogue.

Besides numerous printed and manuscript compositions by Bach, the sale catalogue shows that Kollmann owned works by Graun, Handel, Haydn, Mozart and other masters. However, the auction did not include all the books and music that Kollmann had possessed. Books with his ownership inscription not in that sale catalogue include a copy of Kirnberger's *Die Kunst des reinen Satzes in der Musik* (which in 1877 apparently was owned by the musicologist Carl Engel)[732] and a copy of Türk's *Klavierschule* (which belonged to the collector William Euing before his 1874 death).[733] Although lot 62 in the January 1877 sale catalogue was a 'splendid contemporary ms.' of C. P. E. Bach's 'Sechs Sonaten fürs Clavier' dated 'Berlin, 1760',[734] Kollmann also owned a manuscript copy of C. P. E. Bach's 'Clavirsonaten' published in Leipzig in 1776. This manuscript, not in the 1877 sale catalogue, is now in the University of California, Berkeley.[735]

Several works to which Kollmann subscribed—Maria Barthélemon's 1795 'Three Hymns and Three Anthems', Charles Hague's 'The Ode as performed in the Senate-House at Cambridge on the 29th of June 1811', and Charles William Hempel's undated *c*1820 'Sacred Melodies, adapted to the Psalms of David'—are absent from the 1877 sale catalogue. Many of Kollmann's own publications, including *The Quarterly Musical Register*, also are not listed. It is conceivable that Lonsdale acquired Kollmann's library some years before the 1877

---

[732] It appeared as lot 171 in the 17 July 1881 Puttick & Simpson auction of part of Engel's library (BL S.-C. Puttick 203(5)) and was bought at that sale by Reeves (probably the music seller William Dobson Reeves) for 5/-. Its subsequent provenance and present location are not known.

[733] *The Euing Musical Library: Catalogue of the Musical Library of the late Wm Euing, Esq.*, Glasgow, 1878, p 123. The copy of Türk's *Klavierschule* previously owned by Kollmann was acquired as part of the Euing music collection by Glasgow University Library, where it is now Sp. Coll. U.e.13. Kollmann had lent this book to John Wall Callcott in 1799 (see Kollmann→Callcott, 8/1/1799).

[734] Lonsdale bought this back for 4/-. It reappeared as lot 39 in the 27 July 1877 Puttick & Simpson sale (BL S.-C. Puttick 181(5)), where 'Rob^{n}' (probably the music seller William Robinson) purchased it for 1/-. Its subsequent whereabouts have not been traced.

[735] Music Library ms 807. The route through which this manuscript passed from Kollmann to Berkeley is not known. It was written by two different hands on paper watermarked 'J. Kool' which was manufactured by Jan Kool in Holland.

auction, and that Engel, Euing and others bought items from it before Lonsdale consigned some or all of the residue to Puttick & Simpson.

The auction catalogue correctly noted that the goods offered for sale were 'a selection' from Kollmann's library. In particular, publications that he owned in subject areas other than music (such as hymn texts or works on calculating machinery) do not appear in this catalogue. Presumably Lonsdale had no interest in handling them.

Two items that belonged to Kollmann's library, according to the sale catalogue, were published in 1830, after his death. They were the first editions anywhere of Bach's *St Matthew Passion*: a full score (lot 60 in the sale) and a piano reduction (by Adolph Bernhard Marx, lot 66).[736] Both editions were published by Adolf Martin Schlesinger in Berlin, following the work's celebrated 'revival' there—its first complete performance after Bach's lifetime—by Felix Mendelssohn-Bartholdy in March 1829. It seems more likely that Kollmann ordered copies of these editions than George or Joanna, who are not known to have been especially interested in Bach's music.

Kollmann almost certainly would have been aware of Mendelssohn's performance of the *St Matthew Passion*, either from German reports or from Charles Klingemann, a close friend of the Mendelssohn family who was appointed in 1827 to the German Chancery in St James's Palace.[737] Fanny Mendelssohn-Bartholdy, Felix's sister, wrote to Klingemann on 14 April 1828 and again on 27 December 1828 about Schlesinger's plan to publish the *St Matthew Passion*,[738] and Schlesinger publicly announced his plan in October

---

736 'Rob^{n}' bought lots 60 and 66 for 6/- and 1/- respectively.

737 Klingemann's appointment as a 'Canzlist' [chancery officer] in the German Chancery in London is listed in the *Staats- und Adress-Kalender für das Königreich Hannover auf das Jahr 1828*, Hannover, 1828, p 29, but not in the 1827 calendar.

738 See Martin Geck, *Die Wiederentdeckung der Matthäuspassion im 19. Jahrhundert*, Regensburg, 1967, p 23–24. I am grateful to Regina Back for the information that in Klingemann's extant correspondence from 1827 to 1829 there is little mention about his work for the German Chancery and no mention at all of Kollmann. At least in later years Klingemann attended the German Chapel, as between 1848 and 1854 three of his children were baptised there by Wilhelm Kuper.

1828.[739] It is plausible therefore that Kollmann ordered copies of both editions that were delivered after his death to his son.[740]

[739] 'Auffoderung', *Berliner allgemeine musikalische Zeitung* v 5 no. 44 (29 October 1828) p 421. Schlesinger was the publisher of this journal.

[740] In the printed subscription lists that accompanied the two Schlesinger editions the only Londoners named are the music sellers T. Boosey & Co. and R. Cocks & Co. Each subscribed for three copies of the full score; Boosey & Co. subscribed also for three copies of the piano reduction. Kollmann therefore could have ordered both editions from Boosey & Co.

~ II ~

THE QUARTERLY MUSICAL REGISTER

1. The Purpose of *The Quarterly Musical Register*

The Quarterly Musical Register endeavoured to disseminate information about music that theorists and historians of the subject had acquired. Although Kollmann did not assume that his readers were learned in the history or theory of music, it can be regarded as England's first musicological journal.[1] The following two examples show its difference from other contemporary English periodicals.

Kollmann's treatises that preceded *The Quarterly Musical Register* received numerous reviews, but none of these was in an English periodical concerned principally with music, as no such serial existed then that noticed the latest books about music. The English journals that reviewed Kollmann's treatises—*The Analytical Review*, *The British Critic*, *The Critical Review*, *The Monthly Magazine* and *The Monthly Review*—covered a variety of topics, of which new musical publications were just one. By contrast, the bilingual edition of his second *Practical Guide to Thorough-Bass* was reviewed in the *Allgemeine musikalische Zeitung*, a Leipzig weekly devoted to the field of music.

The *New Musical Magazine, Review and Register*, published monthly in London between 1809 and 1810, was concerned solely with music. More than one hundred compositions, including the first set of Kollmann's *Twelve Analyzed Fugues*, were reviewed in its thirteen numbers. However, its purview apparently did not extend to reviewing books or pamphlets about music.[2]

---

[1] The phrase 'musicological journal' is anachronistic, as the word 'musicology' was first used in the twentieth century, and musicological journals now usually are written only for specialists. It is relevant to note that Kollmann's correspondent Forkel has been considered the founder of musicology: see Wolf Franck, 'Musicology and its founder, Johann Nicolaus Forkel (1749–1818)', *The Musical Quarterly* v 35 no. 4 (October 1949) p 588–601. Music periodicals published in Britain during the Georgian era are described in *SOMIB* v 2 p 1227–1241. In assessing *The Quarterly Musical Register*'s priority the 1811 *Grand Musical Magazine* has not been taken into account, as no numbers of it are extant. On *QMR p 3–6* Kollmann listed earlier periodicals known to him that had published articles about music.

[2] Exceptionally, in v 1 no. 11 (January 1810) p 186, this journal recommended, and promised in a future number to 'enlarge on the advantages' of, John Marsh's *A Short*

Although Kollmann wrote most of *The Quarterly Musical Register* and described his books and concepts in it, a recent portrayal of it as a journal 'of self-promotion' is inaccurate because its content was not focused primarily upon him.[3] 'A retrospect of the state of music in Great Britain since the year 1789', for instance, is a historical survey of events that occurred after the last two volumes of Burney's *A General History of Music* were published.[4] Kollmann did not write all of this survey: its section on cathedral music was contributed by 'a learned gentleman' who presumably knew more about this subject than Kollmann did.[5] Another correspondent wrote a major article 'on the origin, progress, and present state of music in Bath'.[6] No evidence has been found that Kollmann ever visited that city or investigated its musical accomplishments.

Kollmann believed that his treatises belonged to a distinct class from 'those of all the other theoretical authors, which depend more or less, either on the system of Rameau, or on a still more ancient system',[7] and felt obliged to point out the features of his new theory in his journal. However, he promised to make 'no other remarks' on his own treatises 'than any author may with propriety make on his own works', leaving 'the right of judging of their merit, in regard to doctrines, as well [as] to plan, and execution, to the discerning reader'.[8]

Introduction to the Theory of Music..., Chichester, 1809. However, no further comment on Marsh's work appeared in this journal.

[3] L[eanne] L[angley], 'Musical press', in Iain McCalman (ed.), *An Oxford Companion to the Romantic Age*, Oxford, 1999, p 615.

[4] *QMR p 6–28.*

[5] *QMR p 10–11.*

[6] *QMR p 131–143.* Neither contributor has been identified.

[7] *QMR p 8.* See also *QMR p 40.*

[8] *QMR p 41.*

2. The First Number (1 January 1812)

As its title-page stated, *The Quarterly Musical Register* was 'published for the editor' by the booksellers Becket & Porter. This statement indicates that the up-front costs of preparing, printing and promoting the periodical were paid by Kollmann, in expectation that revenue from advertising and sales would exceed these expenses and yield a profit. Buyers paid 3/– per copy to Becket & Porter who, after deducting their sales commission, would have credited the balance to Kollmann. The charge for advertising in the journal is not known.

By 1812 Kollmann was experienced with this way of publishing and he clearly preferred it. After sharing the copyright, and the costs and income, of *An Essay on Musical Harmony* with the music seller Joseph Dale,[9] all of Kollmann's works individually printed in England, except his 1803 'A hymn with various harmonies' and his 1806 edition of Bach's *Chromatic Fantasy*, were published 'for the author'. Although most prior music journals had been issued in Germany—'the former principal seat of musical learning, and musical art'—Kollmann observed that the 'general study, and cultivation' of music in England had increased significantly in the past twenty years.[10] He must have been confident that investment in his journal would provide a satisfactory return.

His choice of Becket & Porter, booksellers and stationers to the Prince Regent and other members of the royal family, was appropriate. The firm, which Thomas Becket had started under his own name in 1760, were the principal sellers of the prominent literary journal *The Monthly Review* and therefore had considerable experience in marketing periodicals in London and the provinces.[11] Their shop, at 81 Pall Mall, offered the additional advantage of being a short walk from the German Chapel.

---

[9] See page 45 above.

[10] *QMR p 1–2.*

[11] A short account of Becket's initial years in business is given in Henry R. Plomer *et al.*, *A Dictionary of the Printers and Booksellers who were at work in England, Scotland and Ireland from 1726 to 1775*, Oxford, 1932, p 20–21.

On 24 June 1809 Becket—then in his late eighties—sold his business to John Porter and authorised him to trade as 'Becket & Porter', provided that Becket was indemnified against claims that might arise because his name was retained in the name of the firm.[12] After the sale he apparently continued to advise the firm, as Porter testified on 17 December 1813, when he authenticated the handwriting in Becket's will, that Becket had been 'in partnership with him for several years before and down to the time of his death'.[13]

It is plausible that William Bulmer recommended Becket & Porter to Kollmann. By the end of 1811 Bulmer's company had printed more than twenty books for Becket or Becket & Porter, and Bulmer's premises in Cleveland Row were close to Becket & Porter's shop.[14] The circumstance that Bulmer and his partner George Nicol joined Porter to provide the indemnity that Becket required when he sold his business indicates that Bulmer was a friend of both Becket and Porter.[15]

Kollmann clearly was pleased with Bulmer & Co.'s work on *A New Theory*, as he returned to them to print the letterpress portion of the first number of *The Quarterly Musical Register*. His desire to have a music example surrounded by letterpress text on the first page of the journal's wrapper would have been a particular reason to go back to Bulmer, whose uncommon skill in doing this had been demonstrated on the title-page of *A New Theory*. In contrast to that title-page, for

---

[12] The indenture for this sale is not known to be extant but is described in and said to be 'of even [i.e., the same] date' as the surviving bond of indemnity to Becket dated 24 June 1809. I am grateful to Barry McKay for sending me a photocopy of this bond, which is now in a private collection.

[13] The court copy of Becket's will and of Porter's authentication of Becket's handwriting is at National Archives PROB 11/1550.

[14] Peter Isaac, *William Bulmer: the fine printer in context*, London, 1993, p 97. One other work printed by W. Bulmer & Co. for sale by Becket & Porter concerned music. Entitled *Short Instructions for tuning a Piano-Forte* and written under the pseudonym 'Musicus Ignoramus', this pamphlet was entered at Stationers' Hall on 18 December 1809 by John Hodgson, who is identified as its author in a handwritten note on the title-page of the copy at BL 7891.bbb.56.(6). 'Musicus Ignoramus' attacked the musical temperament proposed by Charles 3rd Earl Stanhope, which Kollmann had criticised in *La Belle Assemblée*, but the pamphlet contains nothing to suggest that Kollmann was involved in its creation.

[15] See note 12 above and Isaac, p 82.

which the music example apparently was engraved before it was transferred to a metal block,[16] Bulmer on this occasion seems to have printed the vignette from a wood block whose relief areas were cut on the basis of handwritten music notation rather than punched music symbols.[17]

Each number of *The Quarterly Musical Register* consisted of three separately printed portions: eighty pages of letterpress text, four foldout sheets of engraved music printed on one side only, and a wrapper. It is not known who engraved or printed the plates of musical examples.[18] The wrapper—a single sheet that made four pages when folded—was printed from type and the wood block that contained the first page's vignette.

In the British Library copy of *The Quarterly Musical Register* the text pages and music pages of each number have been lightly sewn into its folded wrapper. Presumably each number was so sewn when it left Becket & Porter's shop, as this was a customary way of supplying English periodicals to the public at that time. Sewing holes are visible in the Royal College of Music copy, although this has been bound and now lacks the wrappers.

Journal wrappers commonly were discarded in this era, so it is not surprising that most extant copies of *The Quarterly Musical Register* have no wrappers.[19] Usually a publisher of a journal issued a title-page for, and index to, a volume after its last number was printed. Collectors then would have this title-page, the individual numbers and the index bound as a book, without the wrappers that initially had enclosed the separately issued numbers.

The music example on the title-page of the wrapper is an 'ænigmatical canon' that interested readers could try to solve at their

---

[16] See pages 87–88 above.

[17] I am very grateful to Michael Twyman for examining the British Library copy of *The Quarterly Musical Register* and for advising that a wood block probably was used to print the vignette onto its wrappers. The unevenness of the printed music symbols in the vignette demonstrates that they were not formed from music punches.

[18] Presumably this was not W. Bulmer & Co., as 'there is no evidence that Bulmer ever printed engraved plates' (Isaac, p 140).

[19] The locations of the surviving wrappers are noted in section III.2 below.

leisure, much as people today attempt to work out crossword puzzles.[20] Kollmann aimed this challenge at people who had access to his *An Essay on Practical Musical Composition*, in which he gave very general guidance for solving such canons.[21] In *The Quarterly Musical Register*'s second number he said that he would be happy to receive and 'to notice' readers' solutions to this canon, suggesting that no acceptable solutions had been communicated to him by then.[22]

Example 5 is a solution to the canon that satisfies Kollmann's title-page clue 'Canon 4 in 1; and Counterpt. in the 8, 10, and 12'. The music in the title-page vignette is in the alto part, a counterpoint at the octave is in the tenor part, and counterpoints at the 10th and 12th are in the soprano and bass parts respectively. *Example 5* accords with Kollmann's further direction that 'when resolved, its four parts together make a quadruple counterpoint in the octave; and its highest and lowest part alone, a counterpoint in the tenth and twelfth'.[23] However, readers of this book are encouraged to find a solution that makes better music.

The last page of the first number's wrapper was filled by an advertisement for an exhibition of a mechanical musical instrument called 'the panharmonicon'. Its inventor, Joseph J. Gurck, had brought it to London before 18 November 1811, when it was advertised as having 'just arrived from Vienna, to be seen at Wigley's Exhibition-Room, Spring-gardens'.[24] During his London visit Gurck—who spelt his surname 'Gurk' in England—claimed that he had shown this instrument to Haydn before his 'last illness and death' in 1809, and that

---

[20] Crossword puzzles were first published more than a century later.

[21] See *QMR p 80*. In *EPMC*[1] Kollmann wrote (p 68): 'By the resolution of a Canon I understand, the art of unriddling its subject, or of discovering the replies for which it is calculated, when the author has not explained it sufficiently or not at all. ... [T]he only way of resolving a Canon that is without all explanation, is: to try in what intervals, at what distances, in what motion, and by what sort of length in the notes, one can find out some of its replies; and then to see whether the replies discovered make a subject with a complete harmony or not'. Kollmann's algorithm, in other words, was to try all potential solutions until a satisfactory solution was found or every potential solution had been considered.

[22] *QMR p 160.*

[23] *QMR p 80.*

[24] Advertisement, *The Times*, 18 November 1811, p 1.

Example 5. A solution to The Quarterly Musical Register*'s 'ænigmatical canon'*

Haydn—in a letter written to Gurck the next day—had named it 'the panharmonicon'.[25]

---

[25] According to Gurck's large advertisement in *The Times*, 28 November 1811, p 4. I am grateful to Armin Raab of the Joseph Haydn-Institut for advice that no correspondence between Gurck and Haydn is extant. It is plausible that they met, as Gurck had served as an assistant to Rev. Joseph Niemecz (Father Primitivus), a maker of musical automata who was chaplain and librarian to Prince Nikolaus II of Esterházy at Vienna, in whose court Haydn was music master. See Sonja Gerlach, 'Haydn's works for musical clock (*Flötenuhr*): problems of authenticity, grouping and chronology', in Jens Peter Larsen *et al.*, *Haydn Studies: Proceedings of the International Haydn Conference, Washington, D.C. 1975*, New York, 1981, p 126–129; and Arthur W. J. G. Ord-Hume, *Joseph Haydn and the mechanical Organ*, Cardiff, 1982, p 115, 121–123 and 131–135.

Gurck asserted in his *Quarterly Musical Register* advertisement that he was a 'member of the Imperial and Royal Academy of Arts and Sciences at Vienna'. In another advertisement he described himself as a 'Member of the Austrian Imperial Academy of Arts'.[26] As no organisation with a name like this existed in Vienna in 1811, it is plausible that he invented this credential.[27] If he were inclined to impress the public by fabricating a false credential, he might also have made up the story of his letter from Haydn. It is relevant to add that Johann Nepomuk Mälzel had used the name 'panharmonicon' for a mechanical musical instrument that he exhibited in Paris in 1807.[28]

Gurck probably met Kollmann in November or early December 1811 and sought advice about ways to attract Londoners to pay 2/6 to see the panharmonicon.[29] Kollmann presumably then mentioned the advertising opportunity offered by his forthcoming journal.

Kollmann's investment in *The Quarterly Musical Register* suggests that he would have had Bulmer print at least one hundred copies of the first number. Most of them probably were thrown away after they were read or when it became clear that the journal had ceased publication. Therefore it was possible in 1907 to describe *The Quarterly Musical Register* as 'little-known'.[30]

---

[26] *The Morning Post*, 28 December 1811, p 1.

[27] I thank Stefan Sienell of the Österreichische Akademie der Wissenschaften (which was founded in 1847) and Ferdinand Gutschi of the Akademie der bildenen Künste Wien for this information, and for advising that no record has been found that Gurck belonged to the latter academy or to the Vienna Konservatorium (now part of the Universität für Musik und darstellende Kunst).

[28] See *Athenaeum* v 2 no. 9 (September 1807) p 285. According to Arthur W. G. Ord-Hume, *Barrel Organ: the story of the mechanical organ and its repair*, South Brunswick, New Jersey, 1978, p 173, it is 'unclear' whether Mälzel's panharmonicon 'preceded or succeeded' Gurck's. Both panharmonicons were 'orchestrions' designed to mimic the sound of many conventional musical instruments. As Mälzel lived in Vienna from 1792, he and Gurck must have been aware of each other.

[29] Promotional expenses for this exhibition included advertisements in *The Times* on 18, 20, 22, 28 and 29 November 1811, and on 4, 10 and 20 December 1811.

[30] 'Notes on an old musical journal: *The Quarterly Musical Register*', *The Musical Times* v 48 no. 776 (1 October 1907) p 645-648. This article—which printed extracts from the *QMR* and also (not entirely accurately) Kollmann's 3 February 1812 letter to Charles Burney, reproduced in the frontispiece to this book—was unsigned

3. THE SECOND NUMBER (1 APRIL 1812)

It is not obvious why Kollmann chose someone other than Bulmer & Co. to print the letterpress text of the second number. However, as the third number (announced on the second number's wrapper) never appeared, it seems likely that sale of the first number fell much below Kollmann's expectations and did not provide the income on which he had counted to pay for the second number's production costs. Furthermore, no advertiser booked space on the second number's wrapper.[31] He therefore had to economise, and one way to do this was to hire a cheaper printer.[32] Bulmer had the deserved reputation of being a 'fine printer' and presumably charged accordingly. As the wood block containing the wrapper's music example was already made, Kollmann could pass it to someone else.

The letterpress text of the second number was printed by 'Collins' of the 'Memoranda Office', 9 Queen Street, Golden Square.[33] Shortly afterwards—probably between April and June 1812—'Collins' printed the letterpress text of the second edition of Kollmann's *An Essay on Practical Musical Composition*.[34] By that time Collins had changed the name of his business to 'Memoranda Printing Office', and this name, but not 'Memoranda Office', appears in a few other

but almost certainly was written by Frederick George Edwards, the editor at that time of *The Musical Times*, who wrote signed articles for that journal on Bach's music in England and on Samuel Wesley.

[31] Kollmann's interest in attracting advertisements was noted on the first page of each wrapper and also in an advertisement announcing *QMR1* in *The Morning Post*, 27 December 1811, p 2. These notices said that advertisements and 'useful communications' for the journal were to be sent to Becket & Porter.

[32] Kollmann's economising also may be reflected in the circumstance that four advertisements of the first number were published in newspapers (see page 246 below), but no newspaper advertisements of the second number have been located.

[33] Both Bulmer & Co. and Collins set colophons including their names at the bottom of the second page of *The Quarterly Musical Register* wrapper but did not print their names on the journal's text pages.

[34] The list of Kollmann's works printed in that edition (*EPMC*^{2}, p [68]) said that two numbers of *The Quarterly Musical Register* had appeared and that the journal was 'to be continued', indicating that Kollmann was intending to publish its third number when *EPMC*^{2} was typeset.

contemporary publications. Although the name suggests that Collins printed memoranda books, no evidence of this has been found.

At 9 Queen Street, Golden Square, someone called 'C. F. Collins' published a book entitled *Truth: containing the Case of the Seven Princes of Britain* that was printed by 'Collins' of the Memorandum Printing Office at the same address. The book's author, who used the pseudonym 'Fingal', dated his preface 'To the public' 11 April 1812.[35] In 1813, at the same address, C. F. Collins published a booklet entitled *Letters to His Royal Highness the Duke of Sussex, relative to His Majesty* by Francis Armstrong, who revealed on the title-page that he was the author of *Truth*.[36] By this time the name 'Memorandum Printing Office' seems to have been abandoned, as the imprint in this booklet reads: 'Printed by C. F. Collins, No. 9, Queen Street, Golden Square, London'.

C. F. Collins seems likely to have been related to Thomas Collins, who had been a master printer at Harvey's Buildings, Strand, but was declared bankrupt in May 1811.[37] Evidence for this assumption is found in copies of Joseph Corfe's collection *The Beauties of Handel*, which was published by Thomas Preston in three volumes that were reissued several times. In one issue a letterpress page headed 'Advertisement' and dated 25 June 1803 bears the colophon 'T. Collins, Printer, Harvey's Buildings, Strand'.[38] In a later issue a letterpress page headed 'Index to Handel's Songs, vol. II' bears the colophon 'Collins, Memoranda Printing Office, No. 9, Queen Street, Golden Square'.[39] It is conceivable therefore that C. F. Collins was Thomas's son Charles, who was apprenticed to his father in 1797[40] and may have joined him subsequently in business, as volume 2 of Frederick Dudley's novel *Amoroso* was printed in 1810 'by and for

[35] Copy at BL 8132.ee.3.(2).

[36] Copy at BL 1414.d.7.

[37] Thomas Collins's bankruptcy is reported in *The Times*, 8 May 1811, p 4.

[38] Copy in National Library of Australia, MUS MUSM 137231.

[39] Copy in Point Ellice House, Victoria, British Columbia, PE975.1.8989a-b.

[40] D[onald] F[rancis] McKenzie (ed.), *Stationers' Company Apprentices 1701–1800*, Oxford, 1978, p 83.

T. Collins and son, Harvey's Buildings, Strand'.[41] Following Thomas Collins's bankruptcy he or his son presumably was eager for work in 1812 and offered Kollmann an attractive price.

Preston also arranged the printing and sale of the only other work known to have the imprint 'Collins, Memoranda Printing Office': the letterpress portion of John Gunn's *An Essay with Copious Examples towards a more easy and scientific method of commencing & pursuing the study of the piano forte*, printed on paper watermarked '1812'.[42] It is conceivable that Preston, who had published Kollmann's edition of Bach's *Chromatic Fantasy* in 1806, recommended Collins to Kollmann.

The different typesetting styles of Bulmer and Collins in *The Quarterly Musical Register* are readily seen in their setting of numerals. To print the numeral one in page numbers and in the body of the text, Bulmer used type resembling 'I', whereas Collins's glyph resembles '1'.[43] Further, Collins used a font of numerals of uniform height which he set on a common baseline, whereas Bulmer's zero, one and two are half-height; his three, four, five, seven and nine descend below the baseline of his half-height numerals; and his six and eight have the same baseline as his half-height numerals but rise above their top.

The music printed in the second number also differs graphically from that in the first number, suggesting that Kollmann changed engravers as well as typesetters. For the music examples in the first number an F-clef punch was used that produced a filled circle at the clef's lower opening. The second number's engraver used a different F-clef punch that made, in the corresponding place, a hook which was punched approximately perpendicular to the staff lines. Clearly, Kollmann did not consider it essential to preserve graphic consistency from the first number to the second.

In both numbers of *The Quarterly Musical Register* the letterpress text and engraved music were printed on paper watermarked

---

[41] Copy in University of California at Los Angeles library, PR4629.D86a.

[42] I thank Niki Pollock for information about the Glasgow University Library copy of this work, shelfmark Sp. Coll. A.x.56. The colophon has the 9 Queen Street, Golden Square address.

[43] Exceptionally, Bulmer used type having the '1' shape to print dates and currency on the wrapper.

'1810'. As no change of paper from the first to the second number has been discerned, it seems likely that Kollmann or Becket & Porter bought sufficient paper for at least two numbers of the journal before the first number was printed. The wrappers of both numbers were printed on unwatermarked paper.

The second number included articles by correspondents on the state of music in Bath, Edinburgh and Bristol. The latter two contributions were described as extracts from letters to the editor, suggesting that Kollmann had not solicited them. The names of his correspondents have not been discovered.

4. The Projected Third Number

On the wrapper of the second number Kollmann announced plans for the third number of *The Quarterly Musical Register*, due to appear on 1 July 1812. It would include an article on 'the present musical season in London', a review of William Crotch's recently published *Elements of Musical Composition*,[44] and 'An Analysis of Sebastian Bach's Preludes and Fugues'—a reference to Bach's '48'. Albert Schweitzer, who implied that Kollmann had published this analysis, presumably saw the Berlin copy of the second wrapper and inferred incorrectly that the third number had been issued.[45] As no manuscript of the third number has survived, the extent of Kollmann's preparation of it cannot be known.

---

[44] The publication of this work was reported on *QMR p 157*.

[45] Albert Schweitzer, *J. S. Bach*, Leipzig, 1908, p 294 fn. 27: 'Anno 1812 veröffentliche Kollmann 'An Analysis of S. Bach's Praeludes [sic] and Fugues' (The Quarterly Musical Register.)'.

THE QUARTERLY MUSICAL REGISTER,

No. I.

JANUARY 1, 1812.

WRITTEN AND COLLECTED

BY

A. F. C. Kollmann.

Canon 4 in 1; and Counterpt. in the 8, 10, and 12.

See page 80.

LONDON:

PUBLISHED FOR THE EDITOR,

BY BECKET AND PORTER, 81, PALL-MALL,

By whom all useful Communications (post paid) and Advertisements will be regularly attended to.

Price Three Shillings.

CONTENTS of No. I.

No. II. will contain

A Retrospect of the State of Music in Germany.

The Life of Mozart, and an Account of his Works.

The Conclusion of the above Art. V. VI. VII.

A Quarterly Catalogue of Musical Publications, and Inventions; an Account of Public Performances, &c. &c.

London: Printed by W. Bulmer and Co. Cleveland-row, St. James's.

THE QUARTERLY MUSICAL REGISTER.

JANUARY, 1812.

I. *Introduction.*

THE present Periodical Work is intended to promote a more *general*, and more *certain* acquaintance, with all that is *useful*, and *interesting*, in the study and practice of Music, than can be obtained from the Treatises, Magazines, and other sources of public information hitherto known; and the Editor flatters himself, that the pains which he has taken in musical studies, and researches, during a great part of his life, and an extensive correspondence, will enable him to conduct it to the satisfaction of the public.

The *importance* of publications of this kind has long been universally acknowledged; for they are one of the best means of supporting the cultivation of an art or science, viz: by rendering the best masters and productions of it known, and encouraged; by creating a useful emulation among those who excel in it; and by preventing many errors, and false pretences, from gaining upon the Public, as fast as otherwise they might have done. And even the degree of success, which such works meet with, seems to indicate the more or less flourishing state of their respective art or science.

The latter may be concluded from the list of *former similar publications*, which we give in the next article For the greatest part of them have been carried on, with little intermission, in Germany, as the former principal seat of musical learning, and musical art. But during the last twenty years they have also continued, and increased in number, in England; and this in proportion to the increasing more general study, and cultivation of Music in this country than before.

The reason why this work appears under its *Editor's* name, like most of those former works just mentioned; and not, like the modern Magazines and Reviews in general, with the name of the *Publisher* only, is; because it will be allowed that there is a great difference between a work only *collected* by an Editor, who himself is not involved in its contents, like the parties whose merits or productions are examined in it; and one *written* as well as collected, by an Author, whose own works ought to come under a similar investigation as those of other Authors, with which they often must be compared. For in the former case, nothing more is necessary, than the name of a *Publisher*, who can be made responsible for any thing *illegal* in the work. But in the latter case, being that of the present work, it is proper to let the *Editor himself* be known, in order to convince the Public, and every party called in question, that he is willing to be answerable even for every *impropriety*, which may be found or imagined in the work.

The *Public* therefore may be certain, that by this work, nothing can be imposed on them, through false commendation; nor any thing be prejudiced in their opinion, by misrepresentation: and that mistakes will not only be carefully avoided, but also rectified, as soon as discovered.

And on the same grounds every *individual* stands assured, that his merit, publication, or invention, will be noticed in a *fair* and *liberal* manner. To which we may be permitted to add: that though in regard to *doctrines*, and to cases of a *general* importance, it will be our duty to the Public to be very particular; we shall, in regard to all *harmless* productions, endeavour to render our criticisms rather instructive, and encouraging, than humiliating to those whom they concern.

II. *A Chronological List of the Periodical Musical Works, of the Historic-critical kind, which have existed before the present Musical Register.*

THE following ist, and brief Account, of periodical musical works, is abstracted from *Dr. Forkel's Allgemeine Literatur der Musik,* (Universal Literature of Music,) Leipzig, 1792. A valuable work in one volume octavo, of which frequent notice will be taken in the present work.

Matheson's, Critica Musica, (Musical Critic,) German. Hambro, 1722. In all two volumes in quarto.

Mitzler's, Neu eröfnete Musicalische Bibliothek, (Newly opened Musical Library,) German. Leipzig, from 1739, to 1754. Four annual courses in octavo.

Mitzler's, Musicalischer Staarstecher, (Musical Oculist,) German. Leipzig, 1740. Weekly numbers, amounting to one volume in octavo.

Der Musicalische Patriot, (The Musical Patriot,) German. Brunswick, 1741, and 1742. Published in weekly numbrs, quarto.

Scheibe's, Critischer Musicus, (Critical Musician,) German. Published in single sheets at Hambro, 1737; and a new improved edition of it at Leipzig, 1745, octavo.

Marpurg's, Kritischer Musicus an der Spree, (Critical Musician on the Spree,) German. Berlin, 1750. Fifty numbers in quarto.

Marpurg's, Historisch Kritische Beyträge, (Historic-critical Magazine,) German. Berlin, from 1754, to 1760. Five volumes in octavo.

Lougier's, Sentiment d'un Harmoniphicile, &c. French. Paris, 1756. Only two numbers.

Marpurg's, Kritische Briefe über die Tonkunst, (Critical Letters on Music,) German. Berlin, 1760, and 1763. Two vols. each consisting of four parts, quarto.

Hiller's, Wöchentliche Nachrichten, (Weekly Musical Accounts,) German. Leipzig, from 1766, to 1770. Four annual courses in quarto; with an Appendix.

Deutsches Museum, (German Museum,) German. A general Literary Magazine, 1772 et seq. which contains only occasional Musical articles. Octavo.

Wieland's, *Deutscher Mercur*, (German Mercury,) German. A similar work as the above. From 1773, et seq. Octavo.

Journal de Musique, par une Sociétié d'Amateurs, French. Paris, 1773. Four numbers, octavo.

The New Musical and Universal Magazine. London, 1775, and 1776. Octavo.

Forkel's, (Dr.) Musicalisch Kritische Bibliothek, (Critical Musical Library,) German. Gotha, 1778, and 1779. Three vols. in octavo.

Vogler's, (*The Abbé*) *Betrachtungen der Mannheimer Tonschule*, (Reflections on the Musical School at Mannheim,) German. Mannheim, 1778, et seq. Three annual courses, in octavo.

Wahrheiten die Musik betreffend, (Truths concerning Music,) German. Frankfurt, 1779. Two parts, octavo.

Meusel's Miscellaneen artistischen Innhalts, (Miscellanies concerning the Arts,) German. Erfurt, from 1779, o 1783. Thirty numbers in octavo. This work is only partly on Music.

Museum für Künstler und Kunstliebhaber, (Museum for Artists, and the lovers of the Art,) German. Mannheim, from 1787, to 1789. Nine numbers in large octavo; also but partly on Music.

Det Almindelinge Dansc Bibliothek, (The Universal Danish Library,) Danish. Copenhagen, 1780, for August. This seems to be an extensive general Magazine, which only contains occasional Musical articles.

* *The European Magazine*, from 1782, et seq. This contained, till within a few years past, musical articles written by Dr. Busby; and also occasionally some by other Authors.

Reichardt's Musicalisches Kunstmagazin, (Magazine on Music as an Art,) German. Berlin, from 1782, to 1783.

Four quarterly numbers in folio; and No. 5, 6, were published in 1787, and 1788.

Cramer's (Professor at Kiel) *Magazin der Musik*, (Magazine of Music,) German. Hambro, 1783, and 1786, two annual courses in octavo. A continuation of it appeared at Copenhagen a few years later. Four numbers.

Eschstruth's, (Baron) *Musicalische Bibliothek*, (Musical Library,) German. Marburg, 1784. Two numbers in octavo.

The Analytical Review contained, in 1788, some Reviews of Musical Compositions, by Mr. Busby, (now Dr.) which were not continued long.

Musicalische Realzeitung, (Royal Musical Gazette,) German. Speier, from 1788, to 1790.

Musicalische Correspondenz, (Musical Correspondence,) German. This is a continuation of the preceding work under another title. 1790, et seq.

N. B. As Dr. Forkel's quoted work, from which the above abstracts have been made, (except the European Magazine and Analytical Review,) was published in 1792, we shall now specify the works of a similar nature which have been published since, as follow:

Musicalisches Wochenblatt, (A Weekly Musical Publication,) German. Berlin, 1792. Twenty-four numbers in quarto.

Musicalische Monatschrift, (A Monthly Musical Magazine,) German. Berlin, 1792. Six numbers in quarto, from July to December.

The Monthly Review, from 1796 till near the present time, contains Reviews of the Musical Treatises published; which are ascribed to Dr. Burney.

The Critical Review, 1796, et seq. the same.

The British Critic, from 1796, to the end of 1799, also the same. But from August 1800, till March 1807, those Reviews are written by Dr. Callcott. And the Review of Dr. Callcott's Musical Grammar, in April and June 1807, is by Mr. S. Wesley.

The Monthly Magazine, from 1796 to the present time, contains Reviews of Practical, as well as Theoretical Musical works, by Dr. Busby. And also occasional Musical Articles by other Authors.

Allgemeine Musicalische Zeitung, (Universal Musical Gazette,) German. Leipzig, from October 3, 1799, et seq. continued in weekly numbers.

Berlinische Musicalische Zeitung, (The Berlin Musical Gazette,) German. Published by *J. F. Reichardt*, Maitre de Chapelle to H. M. the King of Prussia. Berlin, from 1805, et seq. Mr. R. is since Maitre de Chapelle to the King of Westphalia.

* *The Musical Magazine and Review*, from 1808 to 1811, consists of Musical Compositions and Reviews, by Dr. Kemp; and also contains occasionally some Compositions and Articles by other Authors.

The Beau Monde, which was published for a few years, contained Musical Reviews by an Amateur.

The Repository of Arts, also contains Musical Reviews by an Amateur.

La Belle Assemblée, contains occasional Musical Articles by different Authors; and also in every number a piece of Music.

The Philosophical Magazine likewise contains occasional Musical Articles, some of which, on the calculations of Temperaments, are by Mr. Farey.

N B. Should any thing remarkable be omitted in the above list, we shall notice it whenever it may come to our knowledge.

III. *A Retrospect of the State of Music in Great Britain, since the Year* 1789.

Since the above year, in which Dr. Burney published the last volume of his General History of Music, that art is become not only *far more general* in this country than it was before; but also *much improved* in some, though not in an equal degree in all its departments.

As the former is universally allowed, we need not enlarge upon it; and may immediately proceed to an enumeration, and examination of the latter, or of the *improvements* which have taken place in the different musical departments.

We shall endeavour to bring our remarks under the four general heads, of Musical *Knowledge*,—*Composition*,—*Performance*,—and *Invention*, as follows:

I. In regard to Musical KNOWLEDGE, it is certain, that at the beginning of the period in question, the *study* of music was excessively difficult and perplexing. For the improvements of its *doctrine* had not kept pace with those of its *practical use;* and an immense number of new chords and progressions, which genius had from time to time introduced in composition, could not be systematically accounted for by any of the *treatises*, or private *methods* of *teaching*, then known in this country. The consequence of which was; that but few professional musicians ventured into the labyrinth of such a study;—that ladies and amateurs were positively disadvised by their masters, from attempting it; —and that the art of composition began more and more to be considered as a mere *natural talent*, which neither *can* be taught, nor *need* to be taught. But since the above time an amazing *progress* has been made in the theoretical musical department of this country, as will appear from the following particulars:

First, a much greater number of musical *treatises* have been written and published in England, during the time in question, than at any former similar period. And most of them are of a more practical nature, than the generality of former treatises have been. For their principal object is to shew the *use* that can be made of the sounds of our modern scale; when most former treatises dwelt too much upon the mere *philosophy* of them.

The said treatises divide themselves into *two opposite*

classes, viz. first, those of *Mr. Kollmann*, which depend on two New Systems of Harmony; and, secondly, those of *all the other theoretical Authors*, which depend more or less, either on the system of Rameau, or on a still more ancient system. The nature of those opposite systems and doctrines will be particularly investigated, in reviewing the Treatises themselves, to the number of which shortly will be added a new work by *Dr. Crotch*, entitled Elements of Musical Composition.

Secondly, a general acquaintance with *all* the English and foreign musical books come to any notice, has been introduced into this country, by the importation of *Dr. Forkel's* Allgemeine Literatur, quoted at the beginning of Art. II.; as will be farther mentioned.

As a *third* proof of the increasing musical knowledge in this country, may be considered the public *Lectures on Music*, which have been read in London these several years, viz. first, we believe two seasons by *Dr. Crotch*, and one season by *Dr. Callcott*, at the Royal Institution; then by *Mr. Samuel Wesley*, at the same place, and at the Surry Institution; and last year also by *Dr. Kemp*, at the Russell Institution, and the Pantheon; besides the established annual lectures at Gresham College, by *Mr. Stevens*. And we find that this season those at the Surry Institution will be read by *Dr. Crotch*.

As a *fourth* proof of the increase of musical science, we should wish to consider the numerous degrees of Bachelors and Doctors in Music, which have been granted by the Universities of Oxford and Cambridge. But as the exercises, by which those degrees have been obtained, are only deposited at their respective Universities, and in general not published, it is difficult to form a true idea of them, or to appreciate their merit. However we shall take the first opportunity to try, if we can be permitted a copy of some of them, or at least a perusal of them, in order to give our Readers an account of them.

Whether the recent numerous complaints of the imagined great imperfection of our modern scale, in regard to *temperament*, and the different attempts that have been made to establish an *artificial* temperament, also prove an increase of musical knowledge, or rather a *deficiency* of it in that department, we do not wish to decide in the aggregate. But we shall give the temperaments lately proposed, and particularly the mechanical tempering apparatus proposed by *Mr. Hawkes*, *Mr. Loeshman*, and the *Rev. Mr. Liston*, an examination in a subsequent article. (Art. VII.)

II. Concerning the *Art* of musical COMPOSITION, we presume to observe *in general:* that though numerous works have still been published in this country, as well as abroad, in which there is *no* musical *art;* and even sometimes but *little taste* or *sense*, England can boast, during the period in question, of *master works*, equal at least, and in some instances superior, to any of the same kind produced abroad. But as not all the departments of composition have been cultivated in an equal degree, we shall offer a few remarks on the different *departments in particular*, as follows:

On the theory of composition, which has been produced by *Mr. Kollmann*, in his Essay on Practical Composition, and in his Twelve Analyzed Fugues, it would be improper to offer any *opinion*, as he is the writer of this Retrospect. But a description of the plan, and contents of those works, we may be allowed to give in subsequent articles.

In regard to *scientific* compositions, we have observed above, that the exercises for musical degrees, which ought to be composed in *five* and *eight* real parts, and which, if their authors meant to *deserve* the rank of Graduates, ought to shine forth with *uncommon* art and science, are not published. And it will be allowed, that very few *new* compositions, of the truly scientific kind, have appeared But as a proof, that the Public has not yet lost its relish of such music, we mention, that Clementi's Practical Harmony, * seems to have taken very generally; and that Sebastian *

Bach's works take more and more, in proportion to their becoming known.

The other branches of composition we shall endeavour to consider under the denominations of *Sacred; Theatrical;* those for *Concerts;* and those for *Voices*, and for the different sorts of *particular Instruments.*

Among *Sacred* compositions those for *Cathedrals* rank foremost. Concerning these it is generally allowed, that their ancient dignified solemnity and true sacred style has rather been neglected of late; and that in a similar manner as the Church style hung heavy upon ancient operas, the improved Theatrical style has retaliated upon sacred compositions, and brought into them a levity which ought to be removed again. But we presume, that to see the golden age of chathedral music return, it would be necessary to restore first, the golden age of its professors; and to let their salaries keep the original proportion, to the encreasing price of all commodities; in order to enable them to study and compose with the same *leisure* and *inspiration* as the ancient masters.

A learned gentleman has favoured us with the following remarks on the same subject: "Of Cathedral music in England the last twenty years, there is little within my knowledge that is deserving of the title. Since the days of Dr. Boyce, Cathedral music I think has much declined. It is a species of music, which too often rewards the composer with only posthumous fame; and I think we write in this country now more for money than for fame, either posthumous or contemporary. Musical students too generally make their first efforts of composition in this style; and when they have learned in it to handle the elements of harmony, they generally apply their improved efforts either to Glees, or Theatrical music, or to any species more immediately productive of lucrative rewards of their acquirements. They have attempted too to introduce into Church music, what they call greater expression; but their expressive passages too often become mere feeble prettinesses, and their attempts at imitation are too theatrical.

"The best collections of Anthems published within the last twenty or thirty years are:

"Dr. Boyce's two volumes. His own compositions within collection.

"Dr. William Hayes's. Last Professor but one at Oxford.

"Dr. Nares's. King's Chapel.

"Mr. Stafford Smith's twenty Anthems.

"Dr. Dupuis's.

"Dr. Crotch's.

"Mr. Kent's of Winchester.

"Dr. Clarke's of Cambridge.

"I have heard Dr Beckwith, the late Organist of Norwich Cathedral, spoken of as a good organ player, and composer. I believe there are some anthems of his published, but I have never seen them. I do not know that the late Dr. Cooke, of Westminster, has *published* any Church music, but I have heard there is some, in the good style of his glees, which are certaintly the last glees that have been written in *parts* in this country."

But though compositions for the Cathedral service claimed our *first* attention, in regard to the sacred art that can be displayed in them; those of Psalmody for Churches deserves our *greatest* attention, on account of the effects they are calculated to produce on the greater part of the nation. Concerning these, the late Lord Bishop of London justly observed, in his Primary Visitation Charge: "Parochial * Psalmody was originally intended to be a part of divine worship; and of praise, adoration, and thanksgiving to the Almighty; in which of course the whole congregation, as being all equally interested, were to take an equal share. And when this is done with propriety and judgment, it has a most noble and edifying effect; and forms one of the grandest scenes of unaffected piety, that human nature can afford. It would therefore add greatly to the solemnity, dignity, and beauty of our public worship, if this part of it was restored to its ancient purity and simplicity, and general Congregational Psalmody universally revived."

Yet, how can an object of so great a national importance, as the above, be gained, without an entire *reformation* of the musical *compositions* of English Parochial Psalmody? In all the collections of those compositions we know, the *melodies*, which should be as simple, and of as narrow a compass as possible, too generally consist of large intervals, and require a compass of voice, beyond that of numerous persons, who wish to join in the praise of the Lord, as well as others: and too many of those melodies are in three crotchets, or *tempo di minuetto* time, which, when performed and sung the least lively, renders them calculated more for * inspiring the congregation to dance to them, (like Charles the Ninth of France, to his favourite 129th psalm;) than to heighten and support public *devotion*. And the *harmonies* also in most of those collections, are very far from being correct, and calculated for the *sacred* purpose they are to answer.

Concerning the sacred compositions for *Chapels*, nothing can be said in general, but that *some* of them are quite the opposite to what they *ought to be*.

Under the denomination of Sacred Music also come *Oratorios*, which have been composed during the time in question, by *Dr. Busby* and *Dr. Arnold*. Both these gentlemen did not meet with the success they might perhaps have found, had not a great deal of the chance of it been taken away by Handel; which also Haydn has experienced in his *Creation*. But one thing, which we suppose to have been particularly disadvantageous to both of them, is the nature of their *text*. For in Dr. Busby's oratorios it had not that historical and religious interest, found in all the texts of Handel's oratorios; and in Dr. Arnold's *Woman of Shunem*, it rendered an insignificant history, worse, by imitating the poetical by-thoughts, of the text of Haydn's Creation, without containing any of its majestic prominent features. We learn that a new oratorio, entitled *Palestina*, has been composed by *Dr. Crotch*, on words from the celebrated Prize Poem by Mr. R. Heber; and is intended to be performed this spring.

In regard to *Theatrical* compositions, those for the Italian *Opera* claim the first rank. This department has been kept up in its usual respectability; and the operas expressly composed for this country by *Winter*, with those by *Mozart* recently introduced, are particularly deserving the distinguished applause they have met with. But we beg leave to observe, that though it was very proper to have *Italian* operas, as long as nothing equal to them could be produced in the *English* language, this seems to be no longer the case. For in point of *composition* there can be no obstacle, because most of the modern greatest opera composers understand English, and any Italian opera might also be translated; and as to singers, this country has lately possessed talents equal to the best of Italy. And if only the *encouragement* was the same to those who can sing English, as to those who cannot; more than sufficient able singers would form themselves for an equally good *English* opera, as for the best Italian. The greatest Italian singers also would be very desirous to learn to pronounce English properly, if without it they could not have a lucrative English engagement. And what an effect truly fine *English* operas would have, may be concluded from *Artaxerxes*, and its never failing general applause. This also we learn to have been experienced with an opera at Petersburg, which, during the reign of the late Emperor Paul, and by his Majesty's command, was composed in the Russian language, by *Himmel*, Maitre de Chapelle to the King of Prussia, and which is said to have met with an applanse never equalled by that of any of the best Italian operas, in that metropolis.

Concerning the compositions for the other *Theatres*, we are sorry to observe, that some of them have not been so respectable of late, as at the time when *Dr. Arne*, *Dr. Arnold*, and *Mr. Shield,* flourished in that department, and when almost every song made such lively impressions on all the hearers, as still to live in their memory. But we conceive that as the composition of a vocal piece is of the same importance in it, as its vocal and instrumental performance; the proprietors of theatres would find it much their interest, to provide eminent composers for those pieces, as well as able and favourite actors and performers.

Under compositions for *Concerts,* we comprehend Symphonies, and Concertos. In both kinds an amazing progress has been made. The twelve *symphonies* composed here by *Haydn* for Mr. Salomon's concerts, exceeded every thing of that sort known before; and those by *Pleyel,* for the Professional Concerts, also were exceeding fine, though not quite equal to them. *Clementi's* symphonies, composed about that time, were heard with credit in the same concerts with those of Haydn. And *Woelfl's* are heard with great applause at present. The *Concertos,* published for the Piano Forte, by Cramer, Dussek, Steibelt, and Woelfl, also are so much superior to all the former ones, in regard to the *principal* part, as to admit of no comparison; but the accompaniments to some of them are too insignificant in the solos, and so as quite to loose sight of the *concerting* nature of the piece. This has been particularly attended to, in all the concertos by *Mozart.*

Under the denomination of *Vocal* compositions, we comprehend here, those of Catches, Glees, Canzonets, and all sorts of Airs by themselves. Of *Catches,* we wish to have nothing to say. But *Glees* have hitherto formed a very respectable branch of British musical composition; and may be expected to maintain that respectability, as long as so considerable a number of professional musicians are constantly growing up by the performance of good music in parts, at the Cathedral Schools. The *Canzonets* by *Haydn,* particularly the first book, are, as he calls them himself in the title, *original;* and we also may call them very *fine.* Those by other authors, published since, cannot be compared to them. In regard to all other more *simple airs*, published either as single songs, or in collections, we suppose, that there are few instances, of an author's having kept himself popular with them for such a number of years, as *Mr. Dibdin*, and *Mr. Hook*.

But one thing we have observed, which we can not approve of, viz.: the *modernizing* of *ancient* national airs, so as to take away their original characteristics. For the only improvements that can be allowed in them are: the filling up of their harmonies with such chords, as the ancients may be supposed to have used, at the time those pieces were composed; and the removing of striking incorrections that may be found in them. Whenever a composer is inclined to do more to such pieces, he ought rather to set new ones in imitation of their style, than to *destroy* those monuments of antiquity, by *altering* them.

In regard to compositions for the different sorts of *particular instruments*, mentioned before, we shall consider those for the Organ, for the Piano Forte, for the Harp, and for all the other instruments in general.

Though very fine compositions for the *organ* have been published by *Mr. S. Wesley*, and by other able masters, they are still for manual keys only, and the use of obligato pedals is * not yet promoted by them. But a true idea of the latter begins now to become pretty general, by the increasing circulation of Sebastian Bach's Organ Trios, and of his other works for the Organ, published by Messrs. S. Wesley and Horn.

Compositions for the *Piano Forte*, originally written *in* England, or *for* this country, have been exceedingly numerous and respectable. And to these have been added importations of almost all the valuable publications for that instrument, existing abroad. We may therefore venture to say, that this country at present possesses as complete a store of the best works for the piano forte, as can be found any where else.

One of the most extensive collections of works, *arranged*

for the organ or piano forte; will be that of the Overtures and Choruses of Handel, by *Dr Crotch;* of which those from Esther, Deborah, and Athalia, are already published.

Compositions for the *Harp*, have been written, and imported into this country, in proportion to the increasing cultivation of that instrument. But as the best *performers* on the harp have not yet been found equally great *composers* for it, that department of composition still seems to offer a fair chance for celebrity, to those who have genius, and like to set about it in the right manner.

For all the *other instruments*, few original compositions have been published, in proportion to those for the piano forte.

III. The third principal object of this Retrospect, as pointed out at the beginning, is: the state of Musical *Performance*, during the time in question. This we shall endeavour to consider, first, with regard to *public* musical performances; and, secondly, with the regard to the *art* of vocal and instrumental performance itself.

Under the head of *Public Performances*, which are remarkable in the musical period in question, those in *Commemoration* of *Handel* at Westminster Abbey, rank foremost, as the most grand, exquisite, and unique performances in their kind, ever recorded. As they have been ably described by * Dr. Burney, in his well known publication for that purpose, we need not repeat any thing of what he has said. But we may add, that we were particularly struck in them, with the beautiful difference, between a *piano* on many instruments, and one on a solo instrument only. For here a comparison may be allowed, because the former sounds nearly as soft to the ear, as the latter ; but in a grand *forte*, the same comparison would not be admissible, because a solo instrument can not sound as loud to the ear, as many instruments together. Yet though every thing was combined in those performances, that could produce the highest and most noble effect, we presume, that if the Coronation

Anthem, or other similar chorus, had been accompanied in time with *Cannons* on the outside of the Abbey, which would still have made a majestic addition to the effect. And that such an accompaniment is practicable, has been proved by the funeral music on the late King of Prussia, by *Himmel*, where * cannons are said to have been brought in with great success.

Important in their kind also have hitherto been the *Oratorios*, which are given in Lent by the Messrs. Ashley, viz: first, in themselves, because they are performed by a numerous band, and very able singers; and also on account of their being given at play-house price, which enables a number of persons to hear them, that would be deprived of them if they were given at the usual concert price.

Equally important in their kind, and perhaps still more so, are the concerts at what are called the *Country Music Meetings*. For besides the festive musical enjoyments, which they produce at places where they cannot be so frequent, as in, or near the metropolis, and to numbers of persons, who otherwise would be entirely deprived of hearing grand musical performances; they also create a social intercourse, which is extremely valuable in many respects.

As the musical performances at the *Cathedrals*, and the *Churches*, cannot undergo any material change in their forms, without an alteration of the established laws on which they depend, we need only observe, that the remarks we should have to make on them, follow from what we have said in regard to the *Compositions* for them.

The *Opera* has kept up its former respectability, under such changes as are unavoidable in concerns of that magnitude; and Madame *Catalani* has for some time enjoyed the honour, and the trouble of being the sole object of principal interest in it. But at present the principal characters of it are more numerous again, and the most celebrated operas can be performed. The musical band of the Opera also, under its present able leader, *Mr. Weichsel*, is both * numerous and very select. The great preparations, which according to public accounts are making, for the performance * of operas at the Pantheon also, will probably create a kind of rivalry, which cannot fail becoming advantageous to the cause of music, though it may not be equally so to the two opposite parties.

At the *other Theatres*, the musical characters have been supported by numerous vocal abilitles of the highest merit; and even such first rate talents as a *Mara*, a *Billington*, and a *Braham*, have graced the British stage.

In regard to public *Concerts* we have had the brilliant period, when Mr. Salomon's concerts, assisted by Haydn, and the professional concerts assisted by Pleyel, strove to outdo each other, by all the varieties of musical excellence that could be found. And as the discontinuance of them has been much regretted by the lovers of that kind of music, nothing would be more desirable, than the re-establishment of similar concerts, by such a combination of men of merit, and of influence, as might ensure their permanency.

The concerts of *Ancient Music* have been removed from their former small rooms in Tottenham-street, to the new and elegant Opera Rooms; and from thence to the rooms at Hanover-square. They are carried on with that vigour and success, which may be expected from the royal and noble patronages they enjoy. And if any improvement might still be wished for in them, it would be an extension of their performances to a greater *variety* of ancient first rate works, than have hitherto been introduced; as an abundance of them might easily be found.

The *Vocal Concerts*, which have long been annually given by Messrs *Harrison*, *Knyvett*, and other professional gentlemen, prove what Mr. Kollmann says in chapter X. of his Essay on Practical Composition, viz: that vocal music is the principal branch of music in general, because the text conveys a more distinct meaning and interest to our understanding; and consequently vocal music produces a more lively entertainment, both to our ear and mind, than can be expected from instrumental music alone. For these concerts have at all times been frequented more than the best miscellaneous concerts, except those of ancient music; and of the benefits for the Royal Society of Musicians, and for the new Musical Fund.

The concerts which have been given for several years, at the houses of some of the *Nobility* and *Gentry*, can, we presume, not sufficiently answer their *musical* purpose. And as they also must be a great inconvenience in a house which has not been expressly built for such performances, it may be supposed that they will be given up again.

In regard to the *Benefit Concerts* which are annually given, it strikes us that of late, concerts are become frequent, in which the musicians are *expected* to perform *gratis*, for non-musicians. This certainly is highly unjust. For what would persons of any other art or employment say, if it should become a practice, to call upon them for a *day's earning*, towards a collection for some distressed musicians? particularly if, at the same time, it made them loose part of the chance of earning what they stand much in need of themselves. The latter is the case in these instances. For when the public, as it were, could not avoid attending those charity concerts; it too often prevents their supporting also the benefits of musicians, whose principal dependance is on them.

It is therefore our humble opinion, that if charity concerts for non-musicians are to be given, the performers ought to be offered their usual *payment;* though those who can afford it, and have a mind to do so, certainly are in the right if they exert the best of their vocal or instrumental abilities *gratis*. And we think it very hard, when singers or players are abused in the public papers, for not finding it convenient to give their *gratuitous* assistance on such occasions.

Concerning the state of the *Art* of musical *Performance itself*, as mentioned before; we shall consider it with regard to *Singing;* and to *Playing* on the Organ, Piano Forte, Harp, and on all the other instruments in general.

The Art of *Singing*, though it has been very generally *taught* and *practised;* and though numerous able Singers have formed themselves in this country alone; it seems not yet to be so generally *understood* as might be wished. It divides itself into two distinctly different departments, viz. that of *forming* and *cultivating* the *voice;* and that of making a judicious *use* of it.

The former, or the forming and cultivating of the Voice itself, is still too little known and attended to, though it is the principal part of the whole art, without which no true and great singing can be imagined as possible. For too many Teachers of Singing still make their Pupils believe, that the grand arcanum of forming the voice lies in the use of the Guidonian syllables Ut (Do) Re Mi Fa Sol La, either without or with the addition of Si after the La. With these syllables they make their Pupils sing a certain quantity of exercises, called, from the syllables Sol Fa, *Solfeggios;* and when a certain time has been passed away with those Solfeggios, or Sol-Fa's, the voice is considered as *formed*, though in most instances it is only *spoiled*.

The latter, or art of making a judicious *use* of the voice, also is still too generally misunderstood. For the chaste style of true Cathedral singing, is frequently considered as consisting in an *inanimate dryness*, and this as the only real style in which *Handel's* songs ought to be sung. Every judicious grace, therefore, which a *Braham* introduces in those songs, above the graces vulgarly adopted, is considered as a musical murder. On the other hand, in what are considered as songs of taste, the *graces* are looked upon as the principal thing; and many boast of singing a song with *Mrs. Billington's* graces, when they have not yet learnt so much as to *sound*, or to *sustain* one *pure* note of it. And in regard to one of the finest of all graces, the *shake*, the general creed is, that the more *open* it is the better; according to which error many shake with the *major third*, though it should be with the *tone*, or even the *semitone*, according to the degree of the scale on which it takes place.

As the art of singing is one of the most important musical departments, we shall particularly attend to it in our succeeding Numbers.

The art of *Organ Playing* in England, still labours under two very great disadvantages, viz. the want of *Organs* as they ought to be, and as they are in other countries; and such *salaries* for organists, as make great organ playing an object of study and speculation

In regard to *Organs*, it is remarkable, that throughout the whole British empire, and in the most opulent city on the face of the globe, London, there is, according to the best of our enquiries, *not one* organ equal to those which are *frequent* in the principal cities of Germany, Holland, and the Netherlands; and also, that the churches of many populous parishes in England, even some of the richest, not far from the metropolis, are *without any* organ; though a good organ, well played, is allowed as one of the most proper and most noble additions to the solemnity of divine worship, as well as the best means of supporting, and improving general Congregational Psalmody.

And in regard to the *Salaries* of organists also, it is strange that in general they are so much less than those abroad; where, for the mere playing on Sundays, and for a short attendance on Saturdays, the organist has a genteel competency; and all that he can earn besides, by teaching during the whole week, is for his particular encouragement.

There is consequently not the same enticement, for making organ playing a *particular study* in this country, as abroad. And yet numerous able performers on that instrument are found in England, among whom Messrs. *Charles* and *Samuel Wesley* deserve particular notice; the latter gentleman as one of the first *extempore* Fugue players on any given subject, of the present age.

The art of playing on the *Piano Forte*, is become so general, and has risen to such a perfection, that it may be considered as *amazingly improved*. For though before the period to which we confine this Retrospect, *Handel's* and *Scarlatti's* lessons were performed in this country, and though the late *John Christian Bach*, and *Schroeter*, contributed very much towards the introduction of a *naturally* melodious performance on *keyed* instruments; that *finer touch*, and higher degree of *expression*, which distinguishes good piano forte playing from that of the harpsichord, has been fully established by *Clementi*, *Cramer*, *Dussek*, *Woelfl*, and other great modern masters.

But as the unbounded execution of great performers, now and then enticed them to introduce extravagant difficulties; inferior ones began to consider those extravagances as the true essence of modern playing; and could not be persuaded, that they might become good performers; unless they should be able to work through the double and quadruple chromatics; till they could master an uneven double shake; till they had distorted their hands for awkward stretches; and till they could venture on some uncertain skips. The absurd fashion also, of accelerating some, and retarding other whole passages, where the author has not prescribed it, seems to have originated in a misunderstanding of that judicious stretching of one or a few notes only, which great players introduce without varying the tempo of the whole passage.

The art of playing on the *Pedal Harp* is not only become much more *general* than it was twenty years ago, but has also been highly *improved*, by the able instructions and performances of a *Dizi*, *Marin*, *Meyers* senior and junior, and other masters of that instrument.

In a similar manner, the art of performing on *all the other* musical instruments is become more *general*, as well as generally *improved*. For England, and particularly London, has always possessed virtuosos of the first rank, on almost all instruments. But we are afraid, that in attempting to enumerate them, we should not be able to do justice to all merit; and therefore we will only mention, (in alphabetical order,) the names of a *Barthelemon*, *Bridgtower*, *Cramer* senior and junior, *Salomon*, *Viotti*, *Weichsel*, and *Yaniewicz*, on the violin, and of a *Cervetto*, *Crosdill*, and *Lindley*, on the violoncello.

The *Military Bands* of *Music* have been much enlarged, and the serpent, trombono, and the German flute as well as the different kinds of smaller flutes, have been introduced in them, which formerly were not generally used. England therefore has at present a great number of excellent performers on the different wind instruments, and it might be wished that their *music* were not so often drowned, by the drumming, and other *noise*, with which it is too frequently accompanied.

IV. The last principal objects of this Retrospect are: the musical *inventions* made during the period in question. As, in regard to these, it will not be in our power to give a *complete* list, we notice only those we can recollect; and shall be happy to add in our succeeding numbers, whatever of this kind may still come to our knowledge.

The greatest, and most important invention, we presume to be that of a new, complete, and natural *System of Harmony*, as set forth by Mr. *Kollmann*, in his New Theory, (the outlines of which will be given in our Art. V.) and in his second guide to Thorough Bass, (which will be noticed in our next Number.) This invention therefore deserves the particular attention of every well wisher to music. For, if it is what it professes, it *completes*, and thereby *simplifies*, the doctrine of Harmony, in such a manner, as perfectly to supersede all the other theories of that science, hitherto known. And as that work has been published upwards of six years, and to the best of our knowledge met with general *approbation*, without one attempt at a *confutation*, we consider it as established, and allowed to answer its purpose; though * some still adhere to the systems of harmony which it professes to confute. According to this invention, England, which formerly followed only the *French* system of Rameau, or the *German* system of Kirnberger, or also some more ancient, and still less perfect system, possesses now a musical system of *its own*, which already is introduced in Germany, by a translated edition of Kollmann's second Guide to Thorough Bass, and which probably will prevail, wherever it meets with an unprejudiced examination.

A second invention of importance in the doctrine of *harmony*, we believe to be that of a general rule, by which *double counterpoints* can be constructed so, as to become invertible in *more* intervals, than before; and even in *all* the intervals together, of the chromatic, as well as the diatonic scale; and this not only in the similar motion, but also in * reverse, retrograde, and reverse retrograde motion: as given by *Mr. Kollmann*, in his said New Theory, chap. XIV; and as practically proved by the two last of his Twelve Analyzed Fugues, Op. X. These counterpoints, which can not be found to have ever been taught, or practically introduced in composition, also follow from that author's new system; and are additional proofs of its natural simplicity, as well as perfect completeness.

In the *piano forte*, various inventions have been introduced as follows:

1. *Additional keys*, above the former high F three lines and a space over the treble stave; and below the former low F four lines under the bass stave. In regard to these, it is certain, that though any rational extension of the compass of the scale, is an improvement in an instrument, the modern rage for additional keys *without end*, seems to carry the art of invention too far in that respect. For no great composer for keyed instruments, or great performer on them, had reason to complain of their limited compass, even when they contained but five octaves, from F to F; and to them a good tone, with a mechanism that admits of a high

finished, as well as an expressive performance, always will remain the first consideration. To this must be added, that too great an extension of the scale of keyed instruments, renders their construction precarious in regard to an equality of tone throughout; as well as the instruments themselves too unwieldy for a removal, and too large for a room of a moderate size. It might therefore be wished that the compass of piano fortes would not be enlarged beyond *six* octaves.

2. Hammers with different sorts of *double actions.* These have been universally considered as real improvements of the piano forte.

3. Varieties of *dampers.* In regard to these, every good player knows how much there depends on dampers, which take away the sound perfectly, and promptly, without occasioning a noise, or jarring. Every *improvement* of this kind therefore, ought also to be considered as very useful and desireable.

4. Square piano fortes with the sound board extending over the whole instrument, have been made for some years by Messrs. Broadwood; and they seemed to depend on the principle of giving a firmness to the instrument, *at the top,* where it is particularly wanted. But their unremitted attention to the improvement of those instruments, seems to have made them discover a method, by which that support at the top can be dispensed with; for they have discontinued making them in the above manner.

5. Other sorts of square piano fortes, apparently on a similar principle as the above, have also been made by other manufacturers; one of which were those with a slender wooden beam *at the top,* along the lowest bass string, similar to that in front of the harp. This invention greatly improved the firmness of the instrument, without injuring its tone. But it has not been generally adopted.

A variation of the same principle seemed to be, Mr. * Hawkins's piano fortes, with a *metal frame,* all around the strings, as well as with a metal supporter along the midst of them; which however appeared as being too stiff for the necessary vibration, and as spoiling the tone.

And as another variation of that principle, we consider
* the square piano fortes by Mr. Scott, which were equally firm and closed up in front, as behind; and the keys to be pulled out, in a manner as at some organs. This construction seemed to be very natural, and not disadvantageous to the sound of the instrument. But the required sliding of the keys, apparently rendered the mechanism of the action less certain than otherwise. And we are not sure whether this kind of instruments is still manufactured.

* 6. A few years ago, a Mr. Riley of Hull brought out a patent piano forte constructed so, that the whole set of keys could be shifted towards the right or left, in order to transpose the same keys into a higher or lower scale. This was very useful for the accommodation of singers, though it could be of no advantage to good players; but we have also not heard of these instruments lately.

7. *Upright* grand piano fortes have been brought to a great perfection by several of the first makers; and they are very useful for saving room. But we must confess, that though in regard to a fullness of tone, we think them highly preferable to square piano fortes; we cannot, for several reasons, consider them as equal to horizontal grand piano fortes.

* 8. A smaller sort of upright piano fortes, with only two strings to each key, called *cabinet* piano fortes, have lately been brought forward by Messrs. Wilkinson and Wornum, but are also manufactured by the other makers. Whether they will be adopted as preferable to the square piano forte, time must shew.

In regard to musical *temperament*, three inventions have lately been produced, for the purpose of bringing into the scale of modern organs, and piano fortes, an artificial perfection, greater than that which can be produced by tuning alone. An examination of these will be found in Art. VII.

An apparently important invention in the *French horn, trumpet,* and *bugle horn,* has just been brought forward by Mr. Percival, military musical instrument maker. It consists in the simple introduction of six holes for the fingers; by the use of which, each of those instruments gives all the tones and semitones, we believe from near its lowest, to its highest note, and this as well in tune as any clarinet or other wind instrument. The finger holes are brought well under the hands; and as there are no keys to either of those instruments, they cannot easily be injured by being knocked about as in riding. What seems to be still more advantageous to this invention, is, that without the use of those finger holes the scale and treatment of the instrument remain the same as before; and that with the use of them the higher notes do not require the usual great force of blowing.

A similar invention as the above seemed to be that of a Mr. Weydinger from Vienna, who was in this country some years ago, with a trumpet that had keys to it, on which he performed in some concerts. But as he did not submit it to examination, no distinct description can be given of it.

A few years ago a Mr. Baldwin had invented a musical *notation with letters.* As far as we can recollect, the keys of the instrument were by that notation expressed by the letters of their usual denomination, over and under a single line, with marks of distinction for the different octaves, and with the addition of other characters for rests, the lengths of notes, and so forth. But as this invention was nothing more than an altered revival of what is called the ancient *tablatura,* which has been superseded by our modern notation, we suppose that the inventor has not published it.

Another invention of a similar *notation with letters* has just been published by a Mr. Rootsey. It deviates from the former, and the ancient tablatura, in not calling the notes by their usual name, but the twentv-four notes of two chromatic octaves together, by the twenty-four letters of the alphabet. This we shall give an examination in a subsequent article.

IV. *Of John Sebastian Bach, and his Works.*

It is remarkable, that the true merit of this great musician has remained unknown in this country, till within a few years past; though his countryman and contemporary *Handel* was perfectly acquainted with it ; though one of his own sons, the late *John Christian Bach*, flourished in this country a good number of years ; and though *Abel* called himself his pupil. But the reason becomes evident, when, in regard to *Handel*, it is considered, that Sebastian Bach was the *only* rival from whose competition he had any thing to fear, particularly in compositions for the organ, and in the performance on that noble instrument ; and it is known that though Bach highly regarded him, and endeavoured twice to meet him, on his tours to Germany, Handel both times avoided the interview. Concerning *John Christian Bach* also, it must be observed ; that he, as the youngest son of Sebastian, lost his father before he could receive any instruction from him, or form a true idea of his wonderful art ; also, that perhaps the tuition of his elder brothers, (by another mother,) was not kind and patient enough to create in him a predilection for his father's works ; and particularly, that he finished his studies in Italy, the religion of which country he also adopted, and became quite estranged to his father's great school of music. And in regard to *Abel*, it is probable, that as his principal instrument was not the organ or harpsichord, he could execute but few of Sebastian Bach's works, and therefore could not support his recommending of them, by his own performance.

In the year 1789 therefore, even *Dr. Burney* still de

scribed Bach thus: "Sebastian Bach is said, by Marpurg, to be many musicians in one: profound in science, fertile in fancy, and in taste *easy* and *natural.* To this part of the encomium many are unwilling to assent; as this truly great man seems by his works for the organ, of which I am in possession of the chief part, to have been constantly in search of what was new and difficult, without the *least attention* to *nature* and *facility*. He was so fond of full harmony, that besides a constant and active use of the pedals, he is said to have put down such keys by a stick in his mouth, as neither hands or feet could reach." (General History of music, vol. iv. page 593.)

The numerous and sublime examples therefore, from the works of J. S. Bach, which Mr. Kollmann gave in his Essay on Practical Composition, were for some time looked upon only as very *curious;* and the higher kind of *melodiousness* in them, with the *natural* progression of every part, in the most intricate combinations, seemed not yet to strike the generality of students; because few, or perhaps none of them took the trouble of having them transcribed, in order to *try* and *hear* the *effect* of them.

But one circumstance, which operated most surprisingly in favour of all the works of Sebastian Bach, and which ought not to remain unknown is, Mr. Kollmann's announcing in chapter XI. § 21, of the said Essay, an *analyzed* edition of those forty-eight preludes and fugues of Bach, called The Well Temper'd Clavier, one of which he inserted as a specimen; for this was immediately noticed in the *Allgemeine Mus. Zeitung of Leipzig*, vol. II. * No. 1, for Oct. 2nd. 1799, thus: "England is not unacquainted with the state of music in Germany. Even those higher departments of German art, in which we ourselves begin to be strangers, are so well known there, that an English organist can have the courage of publishing Sebas-bastian Bach's Well Temper'd Clavier, with Explanations; when but *a few years ago* an attempt of printing that work was made in vain, at *two* different places, in that great composer's own country." This created so great an emulation, that the said work, which had *never been printed before*, appeared in print about a year after, at *three* different places, viz: at Zurich, Bonn, and Leipzig; and it has since been printed at several other places.

But as numerous copies of the three first editions were imported in England, it made Mr. Kollmann relinquish his intended edition, and attempt those twelve Analyzed Fugues of his own, which he has lately published. However Messrs S. Wesley and Horn, are now publishing those Preludes and Fugues, with explanations, in four numbers, three of which are already printed, and will be noticed in our Reviews. These two gentlemen have also printed Sebastian Bach's Organ Trios; and the public is much indebted to Mr. S. Wesley, for being so indefatigable, in making those works to be known to *advantage*, by his able performance. Of the other editions of Bach's Preludes and Fugues mentioned above, one has been brought forward by Messrs. Wilkinson and Co., and the other but lately by Mr. Lavenu.

The great success which the printing of the above Preludes and Fugues met with, has encouraged more than one of their Editors, to undertake also an edition of the other principal works of Sebastian Bach, of the progress of which an account will be given in a succeeding Number.

As the above will be sufficient, to shew the manner, in which S. Bach's works are become more universally known and admired, upwards of half a century after his death, than at the time of his life; we shall now endeavour to give a brief account of that *greatest* of all musical *harmonists*, and *performers* himself. The data of these accounts will be taken from a book entitled *J. S. Leben*, &c. (J. S. Bach's Life, Art, and Works of Art,) by *Dr. Forkel*, Director of Music at Göttingen. Leipzig, 1802,— . . . pages in quarto with Bach's portrait. This work is so well written, and so replete with important musical remarks, that we are happy to learn, an English translation of it, by a very able hand, is in great forwardness.

John Sebastian Bach was born in the same year with Handel, and in the same part of Germany, viz: 1685, March 21st, at Eisenach in Thuringia, where his father, John Ambrosius Bach was musician to the court and city of Saxe Eisenach. All his progenitors, which are known as far as to the sixth generation, have been very musical, and several of them highly distinguished musicians. Our Bach himself was by nature endowed with a good understanding and a great genius, an amiable disposition, and above all with an uncommon perseverance in his studies and practices.

In the tenth year of his age Bach lost his father; his mother having been dead some years before. This put him under the care and tuition of an austere elder brother; where he seems to have been about three years, when that brother also died. He was then admitted as chorister at the institution of St. Michael's at Lüneburg, where great attention was paid him on account of his beautiful treble voice, and where he received a classical as well as musical education. With an indefatigable perseverence in the practice of the harpsichord, organ, and also of other instruments, Bach very judiciously united the *hearing* of the greatest masters on the organ, and of the best concerts of his time; and frequently made (on foot) long journeys for these laudable purposes. In the preparatory part of his life, therefore, nothing was wanting, that could be essential for forming a great musician.

Bach's first engagement was, like that of Handel, on the *violin*, for at the age of eighteen he accepted of the place of musician to the court of Saxe Weimar, on that instrument; which seems to account for his wonderful violin, and violoncello solos, that will appear in the list of his works. But the year following he was appointed organist to the new church at Arnstadt, where he began to lay the foundation of his unrivalled organ playing, in which he arrived to the highest degree of perfection about the thirtieth year of his age.

In the year 1717 Bach, who was then court organist at Saxe Weimar, was appointed Maitre de Chapelle to that court, which required him to compose sacred pieces. And as about that time Handel's master, (Zachau,) died, Bach received a vocation to be his successor, which he did not accept. In the same year Bach was invited by Volumier, Maitre de Chapelle to the court of Dresden, for the purpose of the trial of skill with a celebrated French musician, (Marchand,) mentioned by Dr. Burney, which he complied with, and obtained an undisputed victory.

Sometime after this, Bach accepted of the place of Maitre de Chapelle to the Prince of Anhalt Coethen, which he held about six years, during which time he made a journey to Hamburgh, where the celebrated organist Reinken, nearly an hundred years of age, paid him a high compliment on account of his organ playing.

In the year 1723, Bach was appointed Director of Music and Cantor, at St. Thomas's School, Leipzig, where he remained during the rest of his life ; and where, we believe, a great collection of his motetts, and other sacred compositions is still to be found in his own hand writing. He also received the titles of Maitre de Chapelle to the Duke of Saxe Weissenfels ; and of Composer to the King of Poland.

Bach's fame then so highly surpassed that of all his contemporaries, that though he lived in a part of Germany where at his time there were numerous excellent organists, we do not find one instance of an attempted rivalry, like the vexations Handel had to encounter in his opera affairs ; but all parties seem to have respected him as their musical sire, because he never let any one feel his superiority in a humiliating manner. And in the year 1747, when after repeatedly expressed desires of Frederick the Great, in whose service Bach's son Emanuel then was, he visited Potsdam, that monarch paid him the most uncommon attention, and also laid before him an intricate subject for a fugue, to extemporize upon, which Bach did in an astonishing manner, and published several compositions upon it, under the title of *Musicalisches Opfer*, (Musical Offering), dedicated to His Majesty, as will appear in the subjoined list of his works. Part of that work are those Canons of Bach given by Mr. Kollmann in his Essay on Practical Composition, Chap. IX.

But this was the last journey of Bach. For his unremitted perseverance in studying and composing had brought upon him a complaint in the eyes, which turned into a total blindness; and weakened by two unsuccessful operations, and by an attendant illness, he remained in a declining state of health about half a year, till the 30th of July, 1751, terminated his meritorious existence, in the sixty-sixth year of his age.

It must be added that J. S. Bach was married twice, and had a numerous family. All his sons had a great talent for music; but few of them have cultivated it. And as far as we know, the musical celebrity of the Bachs terminated in the children of the great *John Sebastian!*

Concerning the ART of this *Bach*, it certainly is true what Marpurg says in the passage quoted by Dr. Burney, as above, viz: that he was "*many musicians in one*, &c. &c." For in many points of view he appears as an exceedingly *great* musician. But as there is a difference between merely *maintaining* this in an enthusiastic manner, and *proving* it to every unprejudiced comprehension, we shall endeavour to do the latter as briefly as we can.

In regard to Bach's abilities as a *Performer*, we cannot offer better proofs than those which may be given of *Handel's* performance, viz: the nature of his works, and the unanimous testimony of all those who heard him.

From the nature of *all* the works of Bach it is evident, that he particularly excelled in a *natural* combination of *melodious* obligato parts; and all those who heard him, unanimously testify, that this was also the particular characteristic of his *organ playing*, on which noble instrument he produced effects, and varieties that are difficult to describe. For, on the *full organ* with thirty two foot, and sixteen foot stops, he disposed his obligato parts at such distances, and played in such sorts of notes, as must produce every part and note distinctly, without any thing like that confused noise, produced by the grasping of full chords in both hands, as is too frequently heard in mere manual organ playing. And in performances for *solo stops*, he generally played in *three* melodious parts only, viz: on two sets of keys, with different but well agreeing stops, and the pedals. Specimens of this beautiful kind of organ performances are his *organ trios*, one of which has been given by Mr. Kollmann, in his Essay on Practical Composition, and the others have since been printed by Messrs. S. Wesley, and Horn, as before observed.

With three melodious parts of the above description, Bach accompanied the plain melody of a psalm or hymn, when he gave it out to a congregation before it was sung; which formed a fourth obligato part on a third set of keys with a reed stop. Specimens of this most respectable kind of organ performance are published under the title of *Choral Vorspiele*, (preludes to give out a hymn or psalm,) as will appear in the list of his works. The inexhaustible stock of art and genius which he displayed in those preludes may be concluded, first, from the vast nnmber of beautiful changes which he produced with the quantity of solo stops in a great organ; secondly, from the different manner of introducing the given melody, as highest part, as one of the middle parts, or as bass; and thirdly, from the exquisite harmonious, melodious, and rhythmical varieties, which he knew to choose according to every particular plan, and purpose

But though Bach generally played in the described moderate number of parts, to let his performance be intelligible to common capacities, he was able to *extemporize* even *figues* in *six* obligato parts, as he has shewn before the King of Prussia, at the interview mentioned before; and that he was *familiar* with the art of composing in *eight* and more obligato parts, will appear from the list of his works.

From the above therefore it is evident, that no true idea can be formed of S. Bach's *organ playing*, except by hearing his works expressly composed for the *organ*, performed in the manner in which *he* played them, viz: those for the *full* organ, on a good *large* organ, and the pedal part on a double bass stop; those for *solo* stops, on as many sets of keys with different stops as they contain parts, and the bass part on a suitable double bass stop.

And it must be observed; that though many of Bach's pieces composed for the harpsichord, also have a fine effect on a manual organ, particularly most of his forty-eight fugues in the Well Temper'd Clavier, mentioned before: the list of his works will shew, that they do not come under the denomination of his *organ* pieces; because they are deficient in *his* principal requisite for such pieces, being a part for obligato *pedals*. And consequently their effect cannot give an idea of his organ playing; unless an obligato part for the *pedals* be still selected from their bass part, and performed on a double bass stop.

Concerning Bach's abilities as performer on the *harpsichord*, it might perhaps be supposed, that one who is so familiar with the deep and heavy touches of a large organ, and with a true organ style, could not be equally great in the brilliancy, expression, and style calculated for stringed instruments. But the nature of all his compositions for the *Clavier* (harpsichord and clavichord,) as well as the unanimous testimony of all the writers on that subject, convince us of the contrary; which is also proved by his uncontested victory over the elegant harpsichord player Marchand, mentioned before.

That he must likewise have been a great performer on the *violin*, follows not only from his first appointment, which was as violin player; but also, and particularly, from his *solos* for that instrument. And his solos for the *violoncello* prove, that he also had the greatest practical knowledge of *that* instrument.

With regard to Bach's musical THEORY, it is certain, that, though his practical employments as composer, and performer, had not left him leisure to dispose of the unbounded store of his knowledge and experience, in treatises; no musician ever known has evinced a *clearer conception* of the true *art* and of all the *mysteries* of music, both in general, and with regard to all particular considerations, than *he*. And also: no musical SCHOOL ever known, has been more respectable and produced a greater number of first rate masters than *his*. For, besides those numerous distinguished musicians who have been his immediate pupils, so many others, among whom Mozart shines foremost, have formed themselves according to his works; that without partiality, his school may be considered as the principal source, from which Germany has drawn its musical *art*, for near a century past.

As COMPOSER in general, Bach has been equally *voluminous*, as *unrivalled* in his kind. The former will appear from the subjoined list of his works; and the latter evinces itself in every one of those works, except a few juvenile or mere occasional ones.

The principal characteristics of all his compositions are: the highest degree of *harmonious art*, which he acquired by a perseverence in study during the greatest part of his life; and an unaffected *noble originality*, which seems to have been favoured by the nature of all his appointments.

The *works* of Bach may be divided into those *published* by himself, or not long after his death; and those which have *not* been published till late, when a complete edition of all of them has been taken in hand at more than one place, and is eagerly wished for by all, who have a feeling for the improvement of music as an art.

I. Those *published* long ago are as follows :

1. *Clavierübung.* Part I. consisting in Preludes, Allemands, Courantes, Sarabands, Gigues, Menuetts, &c. In the new Leipzig edition, this work is entitled, Exercices pour le Clavecin.

2. *Clavierübung.* Part II (Exercices pour le Clavecin.) Containing a Concerto in the Italian style ; and an Overture in the French style ; for a harpsichord with two sets of keys.

3. *Clavierübung* Part III. (Exercices, &c.) Containing *Vorspiele*, or the giving out of Hymns, for the Organ ; and four Duetts, (pieces in two obligato parts only,) for the harpsichord, which are a complete harmony throughout.

4. Six *Chorale* (Hymns) of divers kinds, for an organ with two sets of keys, and pedals.

5. *Clavierübung.* Part IV. (Exercices, &c.) Containing an *Air* with *thirty variations*, for a harpsichord with two sets of keys, as mentioned before.

6. Five Canonical Variations, on the Christmas Hymn, *Von Himmelhoch*, (Behold I bring you good tidings ;) for an organ with two sets of keys and pedals. They are in divers intervals, similar to those of the preceding work.

7. *Musical Offering*, (as mentioned before,) dedicated to Frederic II. King of Prussia. Consisting in an Fugue ricercata in three parts ; a ditto in six parts for one performer ; divers Canons ; and a trio for the German flute, (that King's favourite instrument,) with a violin, and bass. The whole composed on the subject which his Majesty laid before Bach to extemporize upon.

8. The *Art of the Fugue.* Consisting in twenty-three periodical and canonical Fugues, on *one subject*, the last with two additional subjects ; and a Hymn for three sets of keys and pedals.

9. An hundred *Hymns* in four parts. Published in two

books by his son Emanuel Bach. And four more books of ditto, published by Kirnberger.

II. Those works, which have *not* been printed before.

A. Works for the harpsichord, without accompaniments.

1. Six Preludes for the use of beginners.

2. Fifteen Inventions, in two parts.

3. Fifteen ditto, in three parts; also called Symphonies.

4. The Well Temper'd Clavier, part I. and II. Each part consists in 24 Preludes and Fugues, being one in every major, and minor key. This is the work mentioned near the beginning of this article.

5. A Chromatic Fantasia and Fugue. This is the beautiful piece, printed with some additions of Mr. Kollmann, by Preston.

6. A Fantasia. This is like an Allegro of a Sonata.

7. Six Suites, containing Preludes, Allemands, Courants, Sarabands, Gigues, &c.; also called English Suites.

8. Six lesser Suites, containing Allemands, Courants, &c. also called French Suites.

B. Works for the Harpsichord, with accompaniments.

1. Six Sonatas for the harpsichord with a violino obligato.

2. Many single Sonatas for the harpsichord, with accompaniments for the violin, flute, viola da gamba, &c.

3. Concertos for the harpsichord, with numerous accompaniments.

4. Two Concertos for *two* harpsichords, with accompaniments, for violins, tenor, and violoncello.

5. Two Concertos for *three* harpsichords, with the same accompaniments, which are also concerting among themselves.

6. A Concerto for *four* harpsichords, with the above accompaniments.

C. Works for the Organ.

1. Grand Preludes and Fugues, for manuals and obligato pedals.

2. Vorspiele, (Preludes,) on various Hymns.

3. Six Sonatas, or Trios, for two manuals, and obligato pedals.

D. Works for Bow Instruments.

1. Six Solos for a violin, without any accompaniments. These are a most unique work.

2. Six Solos for a violoncello, without any accompaniment. These are similar to the preceding ones.

E. Vocal Works.

1. Five complete annual courses of Church Pieces, (like Cantatas,) with Recitatives, Airs, and Chorusses,) for every Sunday and other festival.

2. Five Passions, among which there is one for two Choirs.

3. Many Oratorios, Masses, Magnificat and single Sanctus; also pieces for Birth-days, Name-days, and Funeral Pieces; Wedding Masses, Evening Pieces; and several Italian Cantatas.

4. Many Motetts, for one and two Choirs. N. B. Of those for two choirs there are at present only eight extant.

The above list seems to comprehend upwards of five hundred *vocal* pieces, most of which we believe to have been with accompaniments for various instruments; and most of them may be considered respectable *works*, and not as mere single and small pieces. If to this we add the preceding great number of works for the organ, harpsichord, and other instruments; and also consider the amazing art displayed in most of them, we cannot but look with astonishment upon the great character before us.

And though it must be lamented, that many of the works of Bach have been lost; those still to be found are more than sufficient to delight and instruct the musical world in their turn. For though we acknowledge him as the most *scientific*, and yet most *naturally* rich composer ever known, *he himself* was too *good* and too *modest* a man, to expect that he should monopolize *all* musical regard.

We shall therefore value Bach, as Bach; Handel, as

Handel; and every great musician according to his particular merit; and recommend to all students of genius, to follow the example of Mozart, who, though he carefully attended to the *principles* of Bach, tried to make *his own use* of them.

V. *An Account of the Theoretical Works of A. F. C. Kollmann, Organist of His Majesty's German Chapel at St. James's.*

In Art. III. we have observed, that the musical treatises, lately published in England, divide themselves into two distinctly different classes, viz: first, those by the author before us, which *profess* introducing a *new system*, according to which harmony can be explained more completely, as well as more simply, than by any other known method; and secondly, those by all the other theoretical authors, which still depend on former opposite systems, and thereby counteract the immediate general adoption of Kollmann's new system, though none of them attempt to *confute*, or even to *dispute* it.

It must therefore be an object of the first importance to musical students, to know the real difference, between the doctrines of those two opposite classes of treatises, as well as the nature of the particular treatises of each class. For without that knowledge they are in danger of losing both time and expense, by studying treatises which do not answer their intended purpose; and perhaps even of being entirely deprived of that improvement, which they wished to make, and which they might have made, had they been acquainted with works calculated to give the desired instruction. And as no review or other publication has yet examined those works in the above point of view, we flatter ourselves, that the comparative, and faithful account we shall endeavour to give of them, in this, and other articles, will be so much the more welcome to the public.

Concerning the works now before us, we beg leave to observe, that as Mr. Kollman is the Editor of this Musical Register, we shall offer no other remarks on them, than any Author may with propriety make on his own works, either in a public lecture, or advertisement, or in a preface to them; and leave the right of *judging* of their merit, in regard to doctrines, as well to plan, and execution, to the discerning reader.

They are as follows:

I. An Essay on Musical Harmony. London, 1796. 146 pages of text, and 40 plates of examples, in folio. *Dale*, and the *Author*.

The purpose of this work is: to teach the *grammatical* part of the science of music in general, according to *Kirnberger's* system, which had not yet been publicly introduced in England. And the remaining or *rhetorical* part of the same science is contained in a succeeding work of that Author, entitled an Essay on Practical Composition.

This Essay on Harmony is divided into eighteen chapters, and subdivided into sections, and articles, the heads of which form an introductory List of Contents, calculated to give its readers a general idea of the whole, as well as to direct him where to find every particular doctrine. But as the whole of that list of contents would be too long for insertion, we have only selected the outlines of it, which are as follows.

Introduction. On the study of music, in general.

Chap. I. Of the Scale. I, of the scale in its natural state, or of the scale of nature; II, of the modern scale, and its temperament; III, of the modern diatonic, (major and minor,) chromatic, and enharmonic scale.

Chap. II. Of Intervals. I, as simple and compound; II, as fundamental and inverted; III, as major, minor, superfluous and diminished; IV, as consonances and dissonances, with their greater or lesser consonancy, or dissonancy.

Chap. III. General Rules concerning the use of intervals in harmony and melody; I, in harmony: their construction one over another, and which of them may be omitted, or doubled, if required; and their succession one after another, with regard to consonances, and dissonances; II, in melody, or in a single part.

Chap. IV. Of Chords in general. I, as essential concord, discord, and their Inversions, with their fundamental progression; II, as accidental chords, or suspensions, anticipations, and transitions; III, as complete and incomplete chords; IV, as anomalous chords.

Chap. V. Of the Triad and its Inversions. I, as perfect, major and minor, with its inversions; II, as diminished, with its inversions; III, as anomalous triads, with their inversions.

Chap. VI. Of the Chord of the Seventh, and its Inversions; I, as fundamental; II, as diminished; III, as anomalous; with their Inversions.

Chap. VII. Of Accidental Chords. In general, and as suspensions, anticipations, and accented or unaccented transitions, (transient notes.)

Chap. VIII. Of the Signatures of Chords in Thorough Bass. I, in general, with regard to simplicity, and certainty; II, with regard to every particular class of chords.

Chap. IX. Of Cadences. As perfect: imperfect; interrupted; and continued, or organ points.

Chap. X. Of Modulation. I, as natural; II, as abrupt, by the change of major and minor, by omission, and by enharmonic changes

Chap. XI. Of Time. I, as movement; II, as simple or compound measure.

Chap. XII. Of Rhythm. I, with regard to sounds indifferent in themselves; II, in regard to musical sounds; III, the particular qualities of each sort.

Chap. XIII. Of simple Counterpoint. I, as plain, in four, and in fewer or more parts. II, as figurative, and with regard to the different sorts of figurations.

Chap. XIV. Of Double Counterpoint. I, in the octave; II, in the tenth; III, in the twelfth; IV, in the fourteenth; V, in the ninth, eleventh, and thirteenth; VI, that in one part or melody only; VII, reverse, retrograde, and reverse retrograde counterpoint.

Chap. XV. Of Imitation. I, in regard to the interval in which it takes place; II, as strict, or free; III, as similar, or reverse; IV, as retrograde and reverse retrograde; V, with notes by augmented or diminished length: VI, as varied; VII, as periodical, and canonical.

Chap. XVI. Of Variation. I, that of the same harmony, and melody; II, that of different harmonies to the same melody; III, that of different melodies to the same harmony.

Chap. XVII. Of Fancy, or extempore performance. As free; and limited.

Chap. XVIII. Of the ancient Ecclesiastical Modes. Their nature; and their use in modern composition.

As the greatest object of consideration, in regard to all the above doctrines, is the *system* of harmony on which they depend, and this has not been publicly investigated; we shall endeavour to point out the particulars of it, as follows:

The basis of this system is: that the regularity of a harmony cannot be judged of by its *individual* chords only, but must be decided by the regular *connection* between those chords. And in that respect it resembles the system of a language, which also does not depend merely on the proper spelling of every word, but chiefly on the regular combination of words into phrases, and sentences.

In its fundamental principle, therefore, this system is perfectly true. But its inventor (*Kirnberger,* a pupil of Sebastian Bach) applied that principal only to his *essential* chords, * and to *prepared* suspensions. And though all unprepared suspensions, and all anticipations, and passing notes, which did not produce an irregular fundamental progression, were by his system also *allowed;* they did not come under a positive rule, which made them a real part of his *system*, but were to be passed over unnoticed.

To the above must also be added: that though Kirnberger *taught* all the natural species of the fundamental concord and discord; he did not establish a general systematical rule of musical *mode*, from which they follow, and by which *any* natural species of them is allowed the *same treatment*, as all the other species of the same chord. For he taught the diminished Triad as a chord which may only take the progression of a chord of the seventh, which was an *exception* from the general rule of Triads, that ought not to be admitted in a system which shall be complete.

Kirnberger's system also does not establish a general systematical rule for *all* the *chromatic* species of chords; and therefore his chord of the diminished seventh is not an essential chord of the seventh, and is not allowed to take the fundamental progression of a perfect cadence, but must always take the progression of a chord of the fifth and sixth. From this deficiency in his system arise his *anomalous*, or irregular chords, which also ought not to be admitted in a complete system.

The perplexities which the above produces in the doctrine of harmony, appear from the work before us. For though it is far more methodically arranged than Kirnberger's own works; no less than three quarters of the number of accidental notes useful in music, are by it left without a positive systematical rule.

However, as that system of Kirnberger most effectually removes the infinitely greater perplexities of Rameau's chords by supposition, it has been very generally, and very deservedly adopted in Germany, in preference to the doctrines of Marpurg, who was one of the greatest followers of Rameau. And the Essay before us also has met with very general, public as well as private, approbation.

But though, as far as we know, not a single musical writer or reviewer has noticed any of the above mentioned imperfections of the system in question; and though Mr. Kollmann allows, that he himself was not struck with them when he wrote the Essay before us; he mentions in the New Theory, Chap. I, that the unremitted consideration he has since given the science of harmony, made him discover them. And he continues: "I have therefore made it my particular study, to find out a simple method, by which *every note* that is useful in music, might have *as positive a rule*, as it denotes a *positive sound*. And the result has been, that I discovered the system which I presume to offer in the present work." (NB. In the New Theory alluded to.)

We need therefore not enter into more particulars of the work before us, because the system on which it depends has been superseded by that new system just mentioned. But we beg leave to observe, that those who possess it, and have an opportunity of comparing its doctrines with those of the work we are now going to describe, will find that comparison very improving; particularly as it is facilitated by as nearly the same arrangment of the two works, as their different systems would permit.

II. A New Theory of Musical Harmony, according to a complete and natural system of that Science. London, 1806. 92 pages of text, in a smaller type than the preceding work, and 36 plates of examples; in folio. *The Author.*

This work is divided into seventeen chapters, as follows:

Chap. I. Of the *System* proposed in the present work. By a *system* of harmony the author understands, "a certain method, according to which the rules of harmony are derived from general leading principles;" and he reduces all the systems of harmony hitherto known, to *three* different kinds, viz: first, those by which all the intervals and chords are considered and explained according to their mere *individual appearance;* like those ancient systems of astronomy by which the globe of the earth is considered as a fixed central body; and all the other heavenly bodies as moving round it, as *appears* to be the case. Concerning this sort of systems the author says: "they could be found sufficient for the explanation of harmony only so long, as but a small number of chords and progressions were allowed as regular; and they have been almost universally laid aside, wherever the doctrine of a fundamental bass is become known; though they still find some adherers, like many other ancient errors, that have been confuted."

Secondly, those systems, which depend partly on mere *appearances*, and in other respects on the *proofs*, of intervals and chords, like the system of Rameau and his followers; that of Tartini; and numerous others. Concerning these, as well as the above first kind of systems, the author says: "the more harmony is *explained* according to them, the more *perplexing* it becomes." And this will appear to be the fact from the works depending on them, which we shall examine.

Thirdly, those systems, which entirely depend on *proofs.* The only former one of that kind, is the system of Kirnberger, described under the preceding Essay on Harmony; and to it now is added the system of the New Theory before us, which, as we have observed, supersedes it. The particulars of this system will appear from the nature of the whole work.

Chap. II. Of the Musical Scale. Here the Author endeavours to establish, that the succession of notes, produced by the division of a string into aliquot parts, and by the natural notes of a French Horn, is a *Scale of Nature.* From this scale therefore he derives in § 14, the following fundamental principles of his system: first, its fundamental note, with the repetition of it in the *octave*, or ratios 1, 2, shew the compass in which nature produces all its other intervals. Secondly, its *harmonic division* of the octave, or ratios 2, 3, 4, shews the fundamental notes, of the essential concord, and discord: and the foundation to the authentic and plagal mode, on which a regular answer to the subject in fugues depends. Thirdly, its next division of the octave shews all the *harmonics* of a fundamental note, as the only *essential* intervals in music. Fourthly, its next division of the octave shews the *diatonic means* between those harmonics from which all accented and unaccented *passing* notes arise; Fifthly, its still smaller division of the octave shews the *chromatic means* between the diatonic degrees, from which the most natural rules for chromatic harmonies and melodies arise. And its last division of the octave of which we can form a distinct idea, is that into *enharmonic means* between the chromatic, which, however, are not expressed in modern composition, though some writers on music have insisted more upon minutia of that kind, than upon a perfect doctrine of the common chord.

From that scale of nature Mr. Kollmann derives our *modern scale;* and shews, in § 21, that it consists of the ratios of nature 8, 9, 10, (C, D, E,) and their mere transposition to the fifth of the scale, (G, A, B,) with an equal fourth (F,) to the key note, as the octave of the key note (C,) is to the fifth. And the chromatic semitones between the five diatonic tones, he derives from the mere transposition of the ancient tetrachord of the Greeks. This derivation of our modern scale, shews the most probable manner, in which the sixteen semitones of a chromatic octave of nature have been reduced to the twelve semitones of our modern octave. And these twelve semitones in an octave, when properly distributed by tuning, constitute that wonderful *compound* of *twelve* diatonic major and minor scales, of *equal* use in harmony and melody; as well as of twelve *chromatic* scales, of the same equal use; besides the equivocal treatment of every note, by which it has the effect of an *enharmonic* progression.

Chap. III. Of a Musical Mode. By a musical mode the Author understands: "a proper use of the sounds of a musical scale, both in harmony and in melody." And from the rules of it, he derives his chapter of Modulation.

As we presume the doctrines of this chapter to be

important, we shall endeavour to shew the particulars of them as clearly as brevity will permit.

From the *equal* use of the twelve notes of a chromatic octave it follows ; first, that every one of them must be useful as *key note* to the same diatonic, and chromatic, scale, and mode, as all the others. This seems to be generally allowed. But the author also gives the *same use* to every *diatonic interval* of a major and minor scale ; and this we do not know to have been allowed by any former writer. For
* though, in a set of variations by Mozart, and in Handel's
* Lessons, vol. II, page 43, double 5, and at page 58, natural ascending and descending progressions, from every degree of the diatonic scale to its octave are found ; the *same treatment* has never been allowed before, to *every chord*, in those different species of an octave.

This appears even from *Kirnberger's* diminished Triad, and chord of the diminished Seventh ; and so late as from Dr. Callcott's Musical Grammar.

But the *simplicity* which this doctrine of a *general* musical mode brings into a doctrine of harmony, is very great. For it removes all the former individual distinctions, between chords with major or minor, perfect or imperfect, intervals as *different* chords ; and reduces all of them to mere different species of the *same* chord, calculated for the *same* treatment, in *harmony*, and *melody*. And the simple rule, which follows from this general rule, for all *chromatic* notes, intervals, and chords, will appear in the next chapter.

The nature of the ancient *ecclesiastical* modes, also, is explained in a similar manner as the above modern modes.

Chap. IV. Of Intervals. Here the *distances* from one degree of the diatonic scale to another, including their extremities, are explained, first as essential, and accidental ; and secondly, as consonant and dissonant, intervals.

The *essential* intervals, as fixed in chap. II. § 14, are the harmonics of a fundamental note, viz. : the major or minor third, and perfect fifth, of a *key note ;* with the minor.

seventh, to the major third and perfect fifth, of the *fifth* of the key note. But according to the rules of a musical mode in chap. III, *every* degree of the natural scale may carry *every* such interval in that major or minor state, in which the scale produces it; and from this follows the *minor fifth*, on the seventh of the major, and on the second of the minor scale, as *equal* in *treatment* to the *major fifth* on all the other degrees of the diatonic scale, though not equal to it in perfection.

All the intervals, which are not treated as harmonics of a fundamental note, are by the system before us called *accidental;* and the immense variety of them which is useful in composition, are reduced: first, to the mere *syncopations* of the essential ones; and secondly to those diatonic and chromatic *means*, which the scale contains *between* the essential intervals or harmonics. And the said *chromatic* means are disposed of by the very simple rule: that whenever a natural note is to ascend or descend a *whole* tone, the intermediate semitone may be introduced, either *after* the first note as chromatic *mean*, or immediately *added to it*, as its chromatic higher or lower *extremity*.

A *Consonance*, by the system in question, is an interval which satisfies the ear *in itself*, without the assistance of a succeeding interval; and a *dissonance* that, which does not satisfy the ear in itself, but only with the assistance of a resolution.

The *consonances* of modern music are: the fundamental note, and its third, and fifth, on all the degrees of the diatonic scale; and this includes the said minor, or imperfect fifth, as consonance. The *dissonances* are: first, the seventh of a fundamental note, as the only *essential* dissonance; and secondly, all the said accidental intervals, as *accidental* fore or after notes, with all the chromatic extremities of those intervals.

And all the above remains the same, in any *inversion* of

an interval, when the fundamental note is made the higher, as well as in their fundamental state.

Chap. V. Of the use of Intervals in Harmony and Melody. Here it is shewn, in regard to the construction of one interval *over* another; first, which intervals may be *doubled;* and secondly, which may be *omitted*, if required.

With regard to the succession of one interval *after* another, the progression *to*, and *from* an interval is distinguished.

In the progression *to* an interval, the erroneousness of the ancient rule of *preparing* an interval, is shewn; and a distinct rule for *connecting* consonances as well as dissonances, is substituted in its place.

In the progression *from* an interval, the rules of disallowed fifths, and octaves are explained; and exemplified from cases in which they are very offensive to the ear, to those in which they are more and more tolerable. And the resolution of dissonances is shewn with regard to their *ascending* as well as descending progression.

All the above is then applied to melodious progressions in *one single part* only.

Chap. VI. Of Chords in general. By a chord Mr. Kollmann understands: *two* or *more*, *notes* or *intervals*, one over another, so that they are heard at once. The chords of the work before us, are, like the intervals of which they consist, divided into *essential* and *accidental*; and into *concords* and discords. And each of those sorts may be either fundamental, or inverted; complete or incomplete.

Chap VII. Of the Fundamental Concord and its Inversions. This is the chord which, in the Essay on Harmony, was called the Triad, which term Dr. Callcott has adopted in his Musical Grammar; but in the New Theory the term common chord, or simply chord is used. It is a *fundamental* chord, because its lowest note is the root, and its two other notes are the harmonics of that root, according to the explanation given in chap. II. And it is a *concord*, because all its three notes are consonances. But though this definition is strictly applicable only to the *major* chord of a *key* note; according to the rules of a musical *mode* it extends to all the other species of it, on the six other degrees of the natural scale, even to that chord of a minor third and minor or imperfect fifth, called in this work the *imperfect* chord, and in the Essay on Harmony the *diminished* triad.

This *imperfect chord,* which takes place on the seventh of the major, and on the second of the minor scale, produces that finer gradation between concords and discords, which would be lost if it were not admitted as a systematical concord; and in the latter case, a whole degree of the minor as well as major scale would be without a fundamental chord, which certainly must occasion a very great awkwardness in natural modulation.

As the common chord consists but of three essential notes, a bass, third, and fifth, it admits only of *two inversions,* viz: the first, which is that when the original third is made the bass, and which produces what is called a chord of the *sixth;* and the second that when the original fifth is made the bass, which produces a chord of the *fourth* and *sixth.* In both these inversions, which may take place with every species of that chord, the combination remains a concord; and every note of them is treated according to what it is in the fundamental chord.

Any *chromatic* species of these chords also, remains the same as its respective natural chord; only that the accidental note ought not to be doubled, and must ascend when sharp, or descend when flat.

Chap. VIII. Of the Fundamental Discord, and its Inversions. This is the chord of the third, fifth, and seventh, which when it takes the progression of a perfect cadence, or of the interrupted cadence, is called the chord of the *essential* seventh, in distinction from those similar chords where the seventh is only an *accidental* fore or after note. Its principal *species* takes place on the fifth of a key note, both in major and minor; but it must also be allowed on a the other degrees of the natural scale, which produces in all, four natural species of it, that may all be treated in the same manner.

The seventh of this chord, as essential dissonance, must descend one degree; and the third, as leading note, ascend one degree: both of them ought also not to be doubled. But the bass and fifth of this chord, as consonances, may be doubled; and ascend as well as descend, according to circumstances.

As this chord consists of four essential notes, it admits of *three inversions*, viz: those when the original third, or fifth, or seventh is made the bass. In all those inversions, which may take place with every species of this chord, every note is treated according to what it is in the fundamental chord.

Any *chromatic* species of these chords also, remains the same as its respective natural chord; only that the accidental note ought not to be doubled, and must ascend when sharp, or descend when flat. This simple rule likewise includes the whole doctrine of the chord of the diminished seventh, and its inversions.

Chap. IX. Of Accidental Chords. Under this denomination the Author brings all those chords, which arise as it were accidentally, when the essential chords are drawn one into another by *syncopation*, or linked together by their diatonic and chromatic means, as *transient notes*. And it is principally by *this doctrine*, and by the doctrine of a Musical *Mode*, (Chap. III.) that his system has obtained its completeness and natural simplicity.

Both syncopations and transient notes, produce the *same sorts* of accidental combinations, though not in the same manner, for both produce them by the *suspension*, or *interruption*, of one or more notes of the essential chords. But syncopation does it by the mere retarding or anticipating of some of the *essential* notes; and consequently without the introduction of any new note; when transient notes come in as the diatonic and chromatic *means* between the essential notes. And to shew how this explores all that can be done with the notes, of the modern scale, the author has taken particular pains to explain it distinctly ; and also has shewn the application of it to organ points, and their inversions, with the cases which follow from them.

Chap. X. Confutation of the Doctrine of Chords by Supposition. These are the chords which Rameau invented, with a view to derive all the chords of modern music from a construction of third upon third, in the same manner as the fundamental concord and discord arise. And the author says ; "As the doctrine of chords by supposition has been very generally adopted, and is still continued by some writers on harmony, though Kirnberger's general rule of *suspension* so effectually confutes it : I think it proper, for the purpose of establishing the system I propose in this work, to give a faithful description of it, and to compare it candidly with the doctrine of accidental chords, advanced in the preceding chapter."

The doctrine of those chords is then given as distinctly, as that of the author's own accidental chords ; and no less than 231 chords by supposition are enumerated, which ought to be known in regard to all their different diatonic and chromatic species, and which certainly would amount to more than *a thousand* different chords, each of which admits of various regular and irregular treatments, so that the perplexities of that doctrine, when properly examined, become almost *infinite*.

And in § 26 of that chapter the author says ; "Upon the fairest calculation therefore, the *thousands* of rules which are required for the doctrine of chords by supposition, as far as it hitherto goes, do not explain *one-twentieth* part of what has been taught in the preceding chapter, under the *four* simple general rules given there at § 4, and § 16, with the few remarks added to them."

To the above he adds in § 28 "To continue therefore chords by *supposition*, after all I have shewn above, would be the same as declaring them chords by *opposition* to reason and common sense. And with equal propriety the doctrine of chords by *addition*, of which I give a description at chap. XI, § 15, might be adopted, and carried to the same extent, and uncertainty, as that by supposition."

Chap. XI. Of Fundamental Progression. In the preceding part of the work has been shewn the manner in which all harmony *arises* from *two* fundamental chords; and in this chapter it is shewn, how the regularity or irregularity of a harmony can be *proved*, by the *progression* of those two chords, when reduced to them.

This is particularly important, because the *same* chord may appear like different chords; and *different* combinations of intervals denote the same chord: and in composition the doubling or omitting of intervals, as well as their treatment like consonances or dissonances, depends upon the knowledge of their fundamental harmony.

The author therefore gives two general rules, on which all fundamental progressions depend; and then shews the particulars of fundamental progressions, a fifth, fourth, third, second, and seventh, descending; with the changes of the fundamental chord on the *same* bass note; and with the *inversions* of all those progressions, and the progression of *accidental* chords. To this he adds abstracts from the works of six esteemed ancient composers of this country, viz.: Tye, Tallis, Farrant, Morley, Bird, and Orlando Gibbons, as proofs, that though they seem almost in every bar to *contradict* the general rules given by him, they evidently *confirm* them.

Chap. XII. Of Modulation. By this the author understands: "the playing or composing according to the major or minor mode, of one key alone, or of different keys in connection." He then treats of modulations that remain in the *same* key and mode, according to the principles pointed out in the chapter of a musical mode; where his Rule of the Octave, and other accompaniments of the bass scale, will be found depending on three principles of modulation, which we do not know to be found in former treatises.

And when he proceeds to modulations in which the key and mode is *changed*, he shews the particulars of *natural*, and of *abrupt* changes. The latter, by the change from major to minor, or the contrary; by omission; and by enharmonic changes. The end of the chapter also shews modulations in the ancient Ecclesiastical modes, with examples of double chants.

Chap. XIII. Of Simple Counterpoint, shews the application of all the preceding doctrines, to the *harmonizing* of a *single part* or melody, by setting one or more parts to it. And by *simple* counterpoint is understood: the *simple correctness* of a composition in parts; without regard to its invertibility.

The Author begins according to the method of Sebastian * Bach, with *plain* harmonies in *four* parts, to make the pupil familiar with the treatment of *complete* chords, as the most natural beginning of that study. He then proceeds also to *fewer*, as well as *more* than four parts, according to the rules for the omission, and for the doubling of intervals, given in Chap. V.

All the varieties of this kind are exemplified, by harmonizing the *same plain melody*, as highest part, as one of the middle parts, and as bass.

From those plain harmonies he proceeds to *figurate* harmonies, and shews: how any single part or solo, or any part of a harmony, can be reduced to various *divisions*, viz. first, so as to retain the effect of *one* melody only; and secondly, so as to create a regular harmony of *two*, *three*, and *four* parts *in one*.

As the *opposite* to the dividing of a plain harmony in the above manner, he also shews by twelve pages of examples, first from Plate XIV. to XIX., and then at the end, how the most intricate figurate harmonies can be *reduced to the plain chords* on which they depend.

In Chap. XIV. Of Double Counterpoint, it is shewn, how

any two or more parts, of a plain, or figurate harmony, can be calculated so as to admit of *inversions;* and how those inversions serve to combine a stricter *unity*, with an infinite number of interesting *varieties*, than can be done by mere *simple* counterpoint.

The term double counterpoint in the above *general* sense, denotes any invertible harmony, that consists of three, and four invertible parts, as well as that of two. But in a *particular* sense, a *double* counterpoint consists of *two;* a *triple* counterpoint of *three;* a *quadruple* counterpoint of *four* invertible parts; and so forth.

To the infinity of beautiful and interesting harmonious varieties, which offer themselves in the rules of double counterpoint, the way is shewn by the *same* subject or plain melody, by which *simple* counterpoints have been explained in the preceding chapter. And the heads of this chapter are as follows: I. Double counterpoints with regard to the *interval* in which the inversion is made; viz. that in the octave; and those in the twelfth, tenth, and fourteenth, as *principal* counterpoints, from which those in the eleventh, thirteenth, and ninth, arise as *derivatives;* each in all those species of the diatonic octave, which follow from the Author's rule of a musical mode; and those in *more than one* principal interval. II. Double counterpoints with regard to the number of *invertible* and other *parts;* where it is shewn, in what manner a double, triple, and quadruple counterpoint, can be set without the addition of other parts, or with other parts as *accompaniments.* III. Double counterpoints with regard to the *sort of motion* in which the inversion shall be made, viz. in the *same*, in *reverse*, in *retrograde*, and in *reverse retrograde* motion,

However two particulars are not distinctly mentioned in the chapter before us, viz.: *first*, that in a similar manner as the counterpoints of the twelfth, tenth, and fourteenth, may be considered as principal ones, and those of the eleventh, thirteenth, and ninth, as derived from them; the three latter counterpoints also may be constructed as principal ones, and the former as derived from them; and *secondly*, that the third general rule given by the author in § 13 of that chapter, raises the doctrine of double counterpoint to a completeness, never attained by it before.

Both these particulars we presume to be fully established by the last four of the author's *Twelve analyzed Fugues.* Op. X. the first of which (No. IX,) is invertible in the eleventh; the second (No. X,) in the thirteenth, eleventh, and ninth; the third (No. XI,) in all the intervals of the diatonic scale; and the last (No. XII,) in all the intervals of the chromatic scale: all as principal counterpoints; and in reverse, as well as in the original motion.

Chap. XV. Of Imitation, and Variation. By *imitation* the author understands, the introduction of the *same*, or of a *similar* subject, in another part of the harmony; but without regard to a certain attached part, as in double counterpoint. And the heads under which he brings the doctrine of it, are: Imitations on the different *degrees* of the *scale; strict* or *free* imitations; those is similar, reverse, retrograde, and reverse retrograde *motion;* those with regard to the similar, augmented, or diminished *length* of the *notes* in which they shall be made; and *varied* imitation.

By *variation* he understands: the *same* piece, or subject, brought into *another* form; and he brings all the sorts of variation, hitherto known, under three different denominations, viz. first, the *same harmony and melody*, in different forms; secondly, *different* harmonies, to the *same* melody; and thirdly, different *melodies*, to the same *harmony*, He also shews: that a certain subject, or phrase of a piece, may be varied as well as a whole piece.

Chap. XVI. Of Time and Rhythm. In the preceding chapters of the work musical harmony has been explained with regard to *sounds;* and now the author also shews that harmony, which must be attended to in their duration.

By *time* he understands: first, a certain degree of *slowness* or *quickness*, called the *movement* of a piece, which is indicated, by the terms, Adagio, Andante, Allegro, &c.; and secondly, the different sorts of equal timed *measures*, expressed by bars. In the latter or measures the author follows the distinct and methodical classification of Kirnberger, as in his Essay on Harmony; which has not yet been adopted by other English writers on that subject.

By *Rhythm* is understood, a certain metrical order, similar to that of speech, in verse. He distinguishes *simple* rhythm, or *periods*, with all their useful rhythmical varieties, from *compound* rhythm, or *sections*, and whole pieces, with all the compound rhythmical varieties useful in them.

Chap. XVII. Conclusion of the Work. In this final chapter the author endeavours "to give the reader a more complete idea of the system of the work, than he could well do in the first chapter; and to bring the particulars of it into a narrower compass, than that of all those chapters, in which they have been explained." And then he analyzes * the example given as a *vignette* on the title page, to prove the *completeness* and natural *simplicity* of his system.

Mr. K. also answers the important question: whether it is not arbitrary, to reduce all harmony to *two* fundamental chords; and if it cannot with equal propriety be reduced to *one*, or to *more* than two? And in § 14 he observes: "that though he flatters himself of being the first who *teaches* the system he proposes, it is remarkable that it *has existed* in the natural feelings of all the good writers and composers hitherto known; in a similar manner as America existed all the time, before it was discovered by Europeans. For all the good treatises and compositions we have, shew that their authors *felt* what this system proves to be regular or irregular, though they did not *explain* it according to a perfect system; and that the more acute their natural feelings have been, the less their compositions trespass against the rules of this system."

The conclusion is made with an analysis of intricate harmonies according to the author's system, which *cannot* be reduced to their natural roots according to any former system, except by numerous arbitrary rules for exceptions, suppositions, and additions, which ought not to be admitted in any system that shall be called complete, and natural.

An account of the other Theoretical works of the same author will be given in our next, viz. of his Essay on Practical Composition, a second edition of which is ready for the press; and of his first, and second, Practical Guide to Thorough Bass.

VI. *Review.*

A Musical Grammar in Four Parts: I. Notation, II. Melody, III. Harmony, IV. Rhythym. By Dr. Callcott, Organist of Covent Garden Church. London, 1806. One Volume in octavo. *Birchall.*

The reason why we examine this work prior to several others that have been published before it, is, the greater attention which has been paid to it, on account of the author's particular activity in the musical profession, as well as of his vocal compositions, which are deservedly admired, and some of which have gained the prize-medals given by the society of noblemen and gentlemen, called the Glee Club. And it is not without a mature consideration of the *propriety* of this article that we have resolved to offer it. For though it is true, and we sincerely lament, that Dr. Callcott suffers under an affliction, which prevents his attending himself to his cause; it must be observed, that a second edition of the work has been published, under the combined auspices of three professional musical gentlemen, who thereby have made its cause their own; and who will be sufficient to guard it against any supposed injustice or misrepresentation.

The design of the work before us, as expressed in its

Preface, is: "to compress in a small volume, the leading principles of Practical Music." &c. And Dr. C. adds: "The author takes this public method of announcing, that he has not abandoned the design formed nine years ago, of compiling a *Musical Dictionary.* His original plan merely professed to comprehend an abridgment of *Walther, Rousseau,* &c., but when the friendship of Mr. Kollmann (Organist of the German Chapel at St James's,) had assisted him with some valuable treatises, he found it necessary to relinquish the idea of immediate publication; and unwilling that many more years should elapse, without shewing the world in what manner his researches had been conducted, he ventures to lay before the public a specimen of what may be expected from his labours."

As Dr. Callcott himself agitates the idea of his announced Dictionary, we may be excused for confessing, that we think it rather extraordinary in an author to *promise* a work, and after keeping the public *nine* years under an obligation for such a promise, to *perform* no more than laying before them a specimen of what may be *expected (sine die)* from his labours; when all he promised was to *compile* a Dictionary of *one* volume in *octavo;* and when there is a proof that this may done in a few years: because we learn from the preface to *Koch's* Musical Dictionary, (German,) which certainly is very extensive, and very elaborate, that in January, 1800, the Editor made him the first offers for writing it, and in 1802 it was published.

However, the "specimen of what may be *expected* from nine years of Dr. Callcott's labours," is the Musical Grammar before us, which therefore we shall endeavour to give a careful examination.

The second edition differs from the first in three particulars, viz. first in the compression of the numbers of its articles, by *Mr. Jousse;* which cannot be admitted as an improvement of the work, because those numbers were not in the least disadvantageous to the first edition, and the altering of them renders references, and comparing of the two editions difficult Secondly, in adding the chords, or parts of the score, to numerous examples; by which *Mr. Horsley* has really improved those examples, to students. Thirdly, in altering some of the examples on Rhythm, by Mr. *S. Wesley*, on which alterations we shall offer some remarks in their respective places. As in other respects those two editions are alike, we shall examine them in connection, and make our references only to the Chapters, and Sections, which still correspond.

The *Introduction* of the first edition begins with a list of seventy-two Treatises, quoted in the work, (eight pages,) which certainly shews a considerable portion of literary research But as the work professes only, " to compress in a small volume, the leading principles of Practical Music;" and as most of those quoted works are not in the hands of its readers, and many of them even in foreign languages, we should have preferred finding in their place a more distinct doctrine by Dr. C. *himself*, than the incessant interruptions in reading the work, by useless annotations, concerning the doctrines of *other* authors.

To give our readers a specimen of the nature of those annotations, we take the very outset of the work, where after these few words: " five lines drawn over each other form a *staff*," Dr. C. already inserts by means of a note: " Sir John Hawkins (vol. i. p. 427,) writes the word *stave* for staff.—Dr. Burney, vol. ii. p. 87: The regular *staff* of four lines was not generally used in the church till the thirteenth century." How strange is this, to quote two voluminous musical histories, for the mere purpose of proving that the term *stave* should be *staff*; and even how confusing to students, to mention a *regular* staff of *four* lines, when it shall prove that *five* lines are a staff. In this manner the work is at almost every, even the most trifling opportunity, interrupted with similar quotations and other annotations.

A list of contents is then given, according to the heads mentioned in the title.

PART I. entitled "The *Notation* of Music," fills more than a third part of the whole work, with things which other authors suppose to be known by those who will *study* music, viz. with explanations of the "staff, clef, notes, sharps flats and naturals, graces, characters, &c." As these are no objects of any particular importance, we need not enlarge upon them; and we only observe: that we cannot agree to the author's doctrine of musical *measures*, because he still adheres to the former confusion of too many *individual* distinctions, and disregards the more simple, and more certain classifications of Kirnberger and other great masters, as adopted by Mr. Kollmann in his Essay on Harmony, Chap. XI, and in his New Theory, Chap. XVI. But we must also add: that what is said in the first part of the work concerning the *tune*, *time*, and *accent* of notes, belongs more to a *theory* of music, than to its *notation*.

PART II. entitled "*Melody*," treats of "intervals; consonant and dissonant intervals; the genera; keys or scales, and their two modes, major and minor; the qualities of the notes which compose the scale; and of ancient signatures."

This general title *Melody* we do not find applicable to most of the doctrines introduced under it. For though *intervals* may be considered with regard to a succession of their two terms one *after* another, as in *melody*; they undoubtedly are elements of chords, and consequently of *harmony:* and therefore their two terms ought principally to be explained as one *over* another. *Consonant* and *dissonant* intervals also, can be explained more distinctly, according to their use in harmony, than in melody. The genera, or diatonic, chromatic, and enharmonic scales of modern music, are in this part of the work explained, only with regard to their *notation*, and to the *intervals* peculiar to them; but no rules are given concerning their use in *melody*. The twelve major and minor *keys* or *scales* also, are explained only in the manner just mentioned And what *transposition*, the French *terms* "tonic, dominant, subdominant, leading note, mediant, submediant, supertonic, superdominant, and the ancient *signatures*," have to do with *melody*, we are not able to guess.

As the doctrine of *intervals* is the most essential part of this chapter, because they are the elements of chords, harmony, and modulation, we are sorry to find, that Dr. Callcott does not explain them according to a system, by which their different diatonic and chromatic *species*, and their *consonancy* or *dissonancy*, with the *use* that can properly be made of them, in regard to *progression*, and to the *doubling* or *omitting* of some of them, might be derived from *simple*, general leading principles, without any *exception*; as in Kollmann's New Theory; (See our Art. v;) but that he embarrasses the doctrine of them with individual considerations, which render it in a high degree *uncertain*, and *perplexing*.

With regard to the diatonic *species* of intervals, he only allows the third, sixth, seventh, and second, as major and minor, but not the fifth, and fourth; though a complete musical mode allows and requires the two latter in both those forms, as well as the four former. His *fundamental* and inverted intervals, he does not derive from the order, in which nature produces them, as the *harmonics* of a fundamental note; but according to the *diatonic* series, so that the second, third, and fourth, are fundamental, and the fifth, sixth, and seventh, their inversions. (See his Part II, chap. i. sect. iv.) His *consonances* and dissonances he considers only according to their individual contents: without regard to those numerous cases, in which a major or minor third and sixth, a perfect fifth and fourth, and even a perfect octave, or unison, is an undoubted *dissonance;* or those in which the major or minor seventh, and the bass of the major or minor second, is an undoubted *consonance.* And equally uncertain is his doctrine of the chromatic, and enharmonic intervals; and of their use.

One principal confusion in the author's doctrine of intervals also arises, from what he calls the *qualities* of the notes which compose the scale, in Chap. V. For he considers the different notes of the diatonic scale only as dominant, subdominant, &c. of the tonic or *key note*, according to the French school; without having that general rule of a musical mode, by which *every note* of the scale can be made a substituted key note, and have its dominants, mediants, &c, in the same manner as the key note; only in other major or minor species, according to the natural notes of the diatonic scale. This brings upon his doctrine of intervals, chords, and modulation, a constraint, which he endeavours to remove by allowing *irregular* chords and modulations, or *licenses*. But this is nothing more than an attempt, to confirm one uncertainty, by a number of others; as will more fully appear from his doctrine of chords, in the next part of the work.

PART III, entitled "*Harmony*," treats "of the triad; of the dominant seventh; of discords; of cadences; of sequences; and of licenses."

Chap. I. Sect. 1. "Of the consonant and dissonant triads," begins thus: "Two or more melodies, heard at the same time, form harmony; and the different combinations in harmony are termed *chords*." This is the same, as deriving the parent from the child; or a syllable, from a word. For in Part II., Dr Callcott professed to treat of *melody;* when in the whole of it he treated only of *intervals*, and of the other particulars mentioned above; without giving rules for the application of what he shewed, to melody. And here he professes to treat of *harmony*; when what he advances is nothing more than his doctrine of *chords*, and of their progression; without the least attention to a combination of melodies in those chords, or of *harmony* which arises from such a combination of *melodies*.

The work then continues: "The union of any sound with its *third* (major or minor) and its *perfect fifth*, forms the harmonic triad, or common chord." This definition contains two inaccuracies, viz. first, that *any* sound, with its said third and fifth, is called a triad; when only a *fundamental* note can carry that most essential chord of harmony; and when also an incomplete chord of the seventh, or of the fifth and sixth, or a mere accidental chord, can have the said *form* of a triad, and yet require the *treatment* of that incomplete essential, or accidental discord, which it really is, according to its connection. Secondly, that the *perfect* fifth only, is allowed in forming a triad; when all composers, and Dr. Callcott himself, make frequen use of the imperfect fifth in that chord; and when, in the course of his succeeding explanations, he not only introduces the *imperfect*, but also the *extreme sharp* fifth, as forming a triad.

The distinction which is then made between *consonant* and *dissonant* triads, according to Marpurg's arrangement, concerning which Dr. C. says in a note that it "seems most agreeable to the *theoretical* doctrine of harmonics," arises from his uncertainty in the doctrine of intervals we have mentioned before. For, as he makes no difference between an imperfect fifth of a *fundamental* note, which may be treated like the perfect fifth; and an imperfect fifth of the *third* of a fundamental note, which is the *seventh* of what he calls the root, and not a fundamental *fifth*: he considers a triad of the minor third and imperfect fifth, as a *diatonic dissonant* triad; and that of the major third and extreme sharp fith, as a *chromatic dissonant* triad. And from the former, (the diatonic dissonant triad,) he derives two *altered* triads, when its third is flattened, or sharpened; of which he says they "are very seldom used."

The confusion of doctrine which arises from the above distinctions, will appear through the whole remainder of this third part of the work before us; and as one present

F

instance of it we only notice the remark, that the two altered triads "are *very seldom used*." Is that a rule from which a student can learn *any thing* concerning their use?

After having substituted the term *root*, for *fundamental* bass, which terms are synonymous, Dr. Callcott says: "The roots of the two consonant triads are easily understood, as every *radical* base must have its *perfect* fifth," &c. The uncertainties which lie in this explanation are important, and therefore it will be necessary for us to shew the particulars of them, as follows:

Dr. C. makes no distinction between a triad on a *key note*, and one on all the *other degrees* of the diatonic scale. The *former* undoubtedly must always have a *perfect* fifth, and always has it, except in those cases where that fifth is to ascend a whole tone, and the intermediate semitone is added to it by a sharp; or where it is to descend a whole tone, and the intermediate semitone is taken from it by a flat; or also where its bass is made accidentally sharp, or flat, for the same reason. But the *latter*, (a triad on the other degrees of scale,) may have an *imperfect* fifth on that degree of the scale, where the natural notes of the scale produce it; which is on the seventh of the major, and on the second of the minor scale. This triad, with an imperfect fifth, instead of being an *irregularity*, which can only be allowed by license, and in sequences, is one of the greatest *beauties* in modern harmony; because it produces that fine gradation from perfect consonancy to perfect dissonancy, which otherwise would be lost; and may be compared in harmony, to what half shade, or half light, is in painting. And without allowing this triad, *all* the liberties of progression, which a triad with a perfect fifth may take, there would be an end to all the regular liberties of modulation, imitation, and double counterpoint, found in the works of all great composers.

However the only stumbling block in regard to this triad seems to lie in the term *perfect* fifth; which, if it was made *major*, would immediately remove all difficulties, and render a *minor* fifth as allowable, (where the scale produces it,) as a minor *third*. As we shall have occasion to resume this subject, we need not farther dilate on it in this place.

In Sect. II the author shews the *inversions* of the triad; the definition of which he gives thus: "When the lowest note, instead of being the *root*, is the *third* or *fifth* of the triad, such change is termed *inversion*." This certainly is very indistinct. For no rule has yet been given in the work by which a bass note as *root*, can be distinguished from one that is *not* a root; and here is mentioned a lowest note as *root*, or as third or fifth of the *triad*. In the general acceptation of the word also, inversion denotes the turning of *upside down*; and here it is said "such *change* is termed inversion."

In proceeding to the inversions themselves the author says: "The chord of the *sixth* is the first inversion of the triad, when the lowest note becomes the third of the harmony, instead of the roof." Here the student might understand thus: "third of the *harmony*, instead of the *root*." But the intended meaning is: *third* of the root, instead of *root* itself He then continues: "In the practice of counterpoint, the octave of the lowest note is either omitted, or if four parts are requisite, the sixth or the third may be doubled;" the particulars we must object to in this explanation, are, the "practice of *counterpoint*," which is entirely out of the question in that place; the expression that the octave is *omitted*, when it has not been shewn that the octave is allowable at all; and that the *sixth* or *third* may be doubled, when the *bass* also may be doubled.

When in speaking of the first inversion of the diatonic triad B, D, F, Dr. C. says: "the *sixth* is never doubled, but the octave preferred, when four parts are requisite, it is an error, which arises from his mistaking the root of that chord."

In the explanation of the chord of the *fourth* and *sixth*, we find the same inaccuracies, as in that of the chord of the sixth. For the fifth of the harmony instead of the root, is here mentioned, as the third of the harmony instead of the root was mentioned before and also the triad, the Harmony, and the root, are spoken of as of different things, hough these terms seem intended to denote the same thing.

Sect. III, treats " of the direct and contrary *motions*, and the rules for their *use* in harmony." Here Dr. C. distinguishes the *direct* and *contrary* motion ; but the former might have been more properly termed *similar* motion. And one principal kind, the *half* motion, where one part moves, and the other remains stationary, he entirely omits.

The three rules also given in this section, are so indistinct, that it would have been much better not to have them inserted, than to perplex a student with them.

Sect. IV. " Of Harmonical *Progression.*" Here " the term *progression* is used, in contradistinction to the term *modulation*, to signify that succession of triads or perfect chords, which, by being confined to the scale of the original key, only admits of the tonic and its two attendant harmonies, (chords,) occasionally interspersed with the relative tonic and the two harmonies, (chords,) attending on that scale ; whether the original mode be major or minor." By this explanation the author seems to understand, a modulation which remains in the same key and mode. And therefore what he says concerning *attendant*, and *relative* harmonies, (chords,) is a mistake.

In a similar manner as in a preceeding section he does not distinguish a *triad* of the key note, from that on the other degrees of the scale ; he now does not distinguish a *modulation* in one key only, from that in several keys in connection This is evident, from his speaking of attendant and relative *keys*, when they are nothing more than different degrees of the *same* scale.

Whatever therefore appears in this section, depends on the

mistake just pointed out; and shews, that Dr. Callcott does not allow *every* degree of the diatonic major and minor scale, to carry the *same* chords, and take the *same* progressions, as that of the key note. And according to this mistake he has curtailed the examples of the motions of the radical bases, (of fundamental progression,) which are taken * from *Koch's* Lexicon, at the end of sect. IV. so as to keep out of them the imperfect triad, which they contain, because it would not have agreed with his doctrines.

Chap. II, treats "of the *Dominant Seventh*, (with) its inversions, (and) Resolution; and of Modulation.

Sect. I, Of the *Dominant Seventh*, begins: "When a minor seventh is joined to the major triad, a chord of four different sounds is formed; and as this only occurs when the fifth of the key is the base note, the harmony is called the dominant seventh."

The imperfections contained in this definition, are as follows: 1, a chord of the seventh on the fifth of the *key*, is separated from those on all the *other degrees* of the major and minor scale, which, in all respects, depend on the same rule and have the same treatment, as that on the fifth of the key, though their progression does not produce a final close. 2, a chord of *four* different sounds is mentioned, without saying whether all of them are essential, or some of them accidental; and on this distinction depends so very much in the doctrine of chords, as will farther appear.

The author then continues: "the note which forms the discord in this harmony, (chord,) is the subdominant, or fourth of the scale; and being a minor interval, requires the part in which it is heard, to descend one degree."

In this we have to notice; 1, the mentioning of the note which forms the *discord*, (dissonance of the chord) when it has not yet been said that the chord itself is a *discord*. 2, that this note is not called by its real name, the *seventh*; but the *subdominant*, or *fourth* of the scale; the meaning of which no student can guess, without being told, that what is the seventh here, makes a fourth to the next fundamental note. 3, that this note is required to descend, because it is a minor *interval;* though according to the French school, from which these terms are derived, it is called the minor *dissonance*, in distinction from the *major* dissonance, which must ascend.

Concerning the *third* in this chord, the author says: "the major third of the dominant, which is also the sharp seventh, or leading note of the scale, must ascend." Here it will be perplexing to a student, how the *third* of a bass, called the dominant, can be the sharp (major) *seventh* of the scale; when before, the *seventh* was called the *fourth* of the scale. But in both cases the scale of the *final* bass note is understood, to which the resolution is made.

So far Dr. Callcott has nearly followed the French school of Rameau and Rousseau; but now he deviates from it, by saying: "the dominant seventh is used, like all other discords, either by *transition*, *addition*, or *suspension*; and must in all cases be *resolved*, that is, taken away, by the descent in the part in which it is found." This passage is of the greatest importance in the work, for the following reasons: 1, because no difference is made between that most essential of all dissonances, the seventh as harmonic of a *fundamental* note; and a seventh by mere *transition*, *addition*, or *suspension*. 2, a *descending* resolution of the seventh only is mentioned, though in the three latter capacities it may regularly *ascend* as well as descend. 3, the examples which are given of a seventh by transition, by addition, and by suspension, are a mistake, because each of them contains the *essential* seventh of the fundamental discord. The erroneousness also of the ancient rule for *preparing* dissonances, which the author here adopts, has been shewn in Kollman's New Theory, Chap. V, § 9.

Concerning the other *species* of this chord, the author says: "there are several other sevenths, used in harmony, upon the different *triads* of the scale, (whether consonant or dissonant,) in both modes. These sevenths, although not exactly chords of the dominant, are nevertheless used in its place, to avoid modulation; as will be hereafter explained in the fifth chapter of this part; on sequences." Here again the essential sevenths are built upon *triads;* which is a mistake, because they stand on their own root, and not on the root of a triad. The author also allows those species of this chord which take place on all the other degrees of the scale but the fifth of the key note, only by *license;* and yet they are one of the most essential things in natural modulation. And he says that they are used to *avoid* modulation; though they are the principal means of producing it: but confines his term modulation only to the *changing* of a key and mode, and does not apply it to modulations in the same key.

Examples of four species of the above sevenths (chords of the seventh) are then given; the first of which does not shew its resolution at all; the second shews its resolution indistinctly, for the guides after the first chord may denote a chord of the sixth, as well as a chord of the fourth and sixth; and those after the second chord shew a resolution into an interrupted cadence, which has neither been explained, nor is mentioned in that place. In the third example Dr. Callcott takes refuge to the French doctrine of a *double employ*, (or to two different roots of the same chord), because he has no systematical rule for *one* positive root of it; and in the fourth example he shews only *one* resolution of the chord, though it has *three*, by means of which, and their inversions, *any* chord of that nature may in *one step* proceed to any of the twelve major and minor keys, as is practically shewn in Kollmann's Rondo on the chord of the diminished seventh.

Sect. II, treats of the *Inversions* of the dominant seventh, which are as inaccurately defined, and as imperfectly explained, as the inversions of the triad in Chap. I. Under the *first* inversion, or chord of the fifth and sixth, it is said:

that "in practice the octave of the bass is *omitted;*" but it should have been said: that neither the bass, as leading note, nor the fifth, as seventh of the root, ought to be *doubled.*

Under the *second* inversion, or chord of the third and fourth, Dr. C. makes the strange observation, "that as the *Fourth* is not pleasing to the ear, it is usually omitted." But how is it possibie to say, that the fourth of this chord, which he himself allows to be the *root,* is not pleasing to the ear, when unquestionably it is the *most* pleasing note of the chord, and may be *doubled* in preference to the three other notes of it?

Under the *third* inversion, or chord of the second, we find the former incorrect idea of a *triad,* as root of the chord of the seventh, repeated thus: the lowest note becomes the discord, (dissonance,) and the *triad* commences on the next degree above."

Sect. III "Of the *Resolution* of the dominant Seventh." Though in Sect. I. Dr. C. has already shewn the resolution of this chord of the seventh, not only in regard to the seventh, and third, but also with regard to the progression of its bass; he introduces in this place some cases not yet mentioned. But now his definition of that resolution is incomplete; for he only says: "the descent of the part in which the dominant *seventh* is found, is called its resolution;" and takes no more notice of the resolution of the *third* as leading note, or of the progression of its bass. He also adds: "that descent (of the seventh) is either a tone or a semitone, according to the *mode;*" without noticing, that in whatever case it may be, the essential seventh descends a *diatonic degree,* which also includes all the other natural species of that chord.

He then says: "this resolution of the seventh occasions two apparent irregularities, viz. 1, the *four* sounds of the dominant, followed by the *three* of the triad in which the last harmony is weakened by two parts becoming *unison.*" But how can there appear any irregularity, in the strictest regularity, merely because two parts of a chord meet in the unison, or (which is the same,) in the octave? "2, The omission of the fifth in the tonic triad, when the antecedent dominant is taken without the octave to the base." Here the octave of the bass of the chord of the seventh is apparently considered as essential in that chord, though it is only a replicate of its bass. To this is added: "when, however, instead of the octave, the fifth or third of the dominant itself is omitted, the subsequent triad can be taken complete," &c. This confirms our observation that the octave had been considered as omitted; and the omission of the *third* as leading note, can only be allowed in those cases, where a combination of melodious parts renders it necessary; in the example given there is no apparent reason and excuse for it.

In Kollmann's second Guide to Thorough Bass, (Chap iv. § 5,) the above cases are expressed thus: "when a chord of the seventh is taken *complete* in four parts, its regular resolution produces the succeeding fundamental chord *incomplete*, that is to say, without the fifth; and it is the same on the contrary. For when a chord of the seventh is taken with the *octave*, instead of the *fifth*, it produces the next fundamental chord complete."

Dr. C. then shews cases in which the resolution of the essential seventh, or of its inversion the second, is thrown into another part of the harmony. But he does not mention, that this can only be allowed in cases, where a combination of *obligato melodies* renders it both necessary and inoffensive. This also must be observed respecting the cases of some more unusual licenses found in Haydn's Sonatas, Op. 40, which he exemplifies; because the student remains uncertain whether they are allowable in general, or only in particular cases?

Under the resolutions of the *Inversions* of the dominant seventh the work says: "I. The *first* inversion, or chord of the fifth and sixth, resolves by the base ascending a semitone. II. The *second*, or chord of the third and fourth, resolves by the base descending a tone. III. The *third*, or chord of the second and fourth, resolves by the base descending a semitone." These explanations are indistinct. For it is not sufficient in those resolutions, that the bass proceed as pointed out; it is particularly necessary to know *to what chord* it proceeds. This is at I, and II, to the Triad; and at III, to a chord of the sixth. The author also omits that the chord at II, may ascend to a chord of the sixth, as well as descend in the above manner.

Concerning the other species of the chord of the seventh, the work adds: "The other *sevenths*, when used in *sequences* have *similar* inversions; and the same *method* of resolution is *generally* applicable to them all." Here Dr. Callcott carries his individual distinctions so far, as to allow the fundamental discords of *six* degrees of the diatonic scale, with their inversions, only in *sequences;* and yet in all compositions, even *in all his own* that are not too short, they are used without sequences. He also speaks only of *similar* inversions of his other sevenths, as those of his dominant seventh; and yet they are perfectly *like* them. Why he says the same *method* of resolution, and not distinctly the *same resolution*, it will be difficult to guess; but it seems intended as a provision for the numerous cases of uncertainties which follow. And for the same reason, the term is "*generally*" applicable to them all, appears to be introduced.

[*To be concluded in our next Number.*]

VII. *Remarks on the Artificial Temperaments of Organs, and Piano Fortes, invented by Mr. Hawkes, Mr. Loeshman, and the Rev. Mr. Liston.*

The three inventions in question depend on the position, that our modern diatonic-chromatic scale cannot be tuned so as to become good, and equally useful, in all the twelve major and minor keys; and that without some artificial contrivance, for the purpose of a better temperament, it must either be out of tune in all the keys, or perfect in some, and intolerable in others.

It is therefore necessary, before we examine the quality of those temperaments themselves, to consider the propriety or impropriety, of the above position. This we shall endeavour to do, by shewing the nature and purpose of our modern scale; and the temperament it requires, if it shall answer its purpose.

Concerning the *nature* of our modern scale, it has been shewn in Kollmann's New Theory of Musical Harmony, Chap II. § 24, that the twelve semitones in an octave, and their replicates, called the diatonic chromatic scale, are of so wonderful a constitution, that, when properly tuned, they form a *compound*, of *twelve* diatonic and chromatic scales of the same use, *in one*.

This *compound* nature of our scale answers the following * great purposes. First, that every one, of its twelve notes, can be made a *key note*, of an equally constituted, and equally useful, diatonic chromatic scale, as that of the gravest note. Secondly, that every one, of the seven notes, of a modern diatonic scale, can carry the *same natural chords*, and take the same harmonious and melodious *progressions*, as the key note. And thirdly, that even the different *species* of diatonic octaves, intervals, and chords, which follow from the second case, can be substituted for the principle species, and be allowed its treatment.

According to the above system of our scale, every one of its notes is calculated to serve in *different capacities*. For the note C, may either be a key note; or a natural diatonic second, third, fourth, &c. of another key note; or arise from a sharp before B, or a double flat before D, as a chromatic note; or it may be treated like B sharp and C, or D double flat and C, in immediate succession, as by an enharmonic change; and in all these different capacities, *every one*, of the other eleven notes of an octave, also is calculated to serve.

The condition, on which, as has been said, the above numerous and important varieties in the use of our modern scale depend, is; its being *properly tuned.* Concerning this it must be observed, that there is a small difference, between the *strict* perfection of every interval, in a scale considered *individually*, and that *moderate* perfection, which must be allowed in our modern scale, as the described compound of twelve equally useful scales, in *one.* And the manner of producing by tuning, that moderate individual perfection, which constitutes the grand general perfection, of the compound scale in question, is called tempering the scale, or *temperament.*

To decide, whether the required temperament of the modern scale can be produced by mere *tuning;* or whether it requires some *artificial* contrivance, like those before us? it is necessary to ascertain the degree of *imperfection*, required in every individual scale, to produce the desired perfection of a compound scale. For this purpose it must be considered, that if every one of the twelve notes in an octave shall have as good a second, third, fourth, &c. as all the others, it is indespensably necessary, to dispose of those twelve notes either at *equal*, or at such nearly equal distances, as may pass for equal.

As it is impossible, to judge by the ear, of that equality of distances, in a succession of such small intervals as semitones; and as no other interval forms a circular succession through all the twelve notes of an octave, but the perfect *fifth*, and *fourth*; the former of which fortunately is the best interval to be ascertained by the ear, next to the perfect octave; we ought to calculate a circular succession of twelve perfect fifths, (six of which must be taken in the perfect octave below,) to see how much the last of them differs from a perfect octave of the beginning note. And here it appears, that the last of those fifths *exceeds* the said perfect octave, by the ratio 531441 : 254288, called a * *major comma.*

If therefore all the notes of the scale shall have equally perfect fifths; each of those fifths must be *one twelfth* of the said major comma flatter than mathematically perfect.

But by *Kirnberger's* temperament, which has been adopted by a great number of the best musicians in Germany, *half* a *minor* comma in flatness, which is nearly half a major one, is allowed as tolerable in a *perfect* fifth, without destroying its quality as a perfect fifth and *consonance.* The above *twelfth* of a major comma, therefore, is so extremely small a deficiency, in the strictness of a perfect fifth, as to come into no consideration at all. And this has been admitted by the first mathematical calculators, such as Euler, Sulzer, Marpurg, Sorge, Chladni, &c.; as well as by the greatest practical musicians, such as all the Bachs, Matheson, Kirnberger, Fasch, Vogler, &c.

Concerning all the diatonic and chromatic seconds, thirds, fourths, &c. contained in our modern scale, both calculation and experience teach us, that if every perfect *fifth* is good, as above, those other intervals also are good. And thus *every* interval of this compound scale is calculated, to serve in all the various capacities, mentioned before.

The *regular* liberties, of melody, harmony, and modulation, which follow from the described *compound* state of our modern scale, are as it were incalculable; for in *every* consideration, *every* note, interval, and chord of it, comes so near to perfection, that like all other things in the world which are considered as perfect, it may be called *virtually* perfect, though not *strictly* so.

This however the inventors of the artificial temperaments before us, will not allow, as has been mentioned at the beginning of this article. For they consider the best equal or unequal temperament, which can be produced by tuning alone, as rendering the modern scale so *imperfect*, as to make it offensive to the ear. And they also object to one note's serving in the *different capacities* mentioned before. We shall therefore examine the propriety of those two objections, as follows.

Concerning the *first*, viz: that our modern scale is too *imperfect* without an artificial temperament, for being good and equally useful in all keys, it is evident: either that those inventors *never heard* a properly tempered scale; or that they must have accustomed their ear to an over sharpness of some, and over flatness of other intervals, which *prejudices* them against that degree of perfection, on which the described nature of our diatonic chromatic scale depends. For with all the great calculators, and practical musicians mentioned before, it has never been a question, whether that scale can be tempered sufficiently by tuning alone? but only, whether an *equal* distribution of the described major comma, would be preferable to an *unequal*, or not? and with regard to the latter, *which* unequal distribution would be the most useful, and the most easy to be produced in tuning. To
* this must be added: that the old organs in Germany are a semitone higher in pitch, than concert instruments, which requires the organ part of performances with an orchestra to be transposed a semitone lower, viz. from D to D flat, from A to A flat, &c., and that this is constantly done in many churches, without offending the ear of the most attentive hearers.

The *second* objection pointed out before, viz.: that *one* and the *same* note cannot properly be used in the described *different capacities;* and particularly, not in the capacity of
* two intervals whose difference in calculation is the *enharmonic diesis*, depends on prejudices more erroneous than the above. For the inventors of the temperaments in question seem to think, that because on the violin, G sharp and A flat, D sharp and E flat, &c. are taken in a different manner, and because the ear *admits* of a small difference between the former and the latter, of each sort, such difference is *essential* in modern harmony; and that a *medium*

between the one and the other, which the ear very willingly accepts for both, ought not to be allowed, though on that medium depends the grand object of the *compound scale* described before. And they are not aware of the infinite *confusion* which their proposed temperaments would bring into the whole theory and practice of music, if the possibi- of their general adoption were supposed.

From what has been said above we presume it to be evident, that the artificial temperaments before us are not only *unnecessary*, to render our modern scale calculated for all its intended purposes; but that their general adoption would be the greatest *mischief* that can be imagined in music. However, to do those temperaments all the justice in our power, we shall now examine the *nature* of them, to enable the public to judge, whether they recommend themselves by some *particular merit*, or not.

They divide themselves into two different classes, viz: two which produce a certain alteration in the different notes by *additional* pipes in the organ, or by additional strings on the piano forte; and one which produces a similar alteration chiefly by a mechanical apparatus which alters the pitch of the *same* pipes, though we learn that it also requires some additional pipes. Whether this latter temperament is intended to be applied to the piano forte also, we have not yet ascertained.

With regard to the two former temperaments, which are those of Mr. *Hawkes*, and Mr. *Loeshman*, it appears, that in the Piano Porte they require *double* the fixed number of strings, for those notes which shall be altered by them, such as from F sharp to G flat, from G sharp to A flat, and so forth. To and from each of those two sets of strings the hammers are shifted by means of pedals. And as in a grand piano forte double the number of three strings would make *six* strings for every key, these two inventors satisfy themselves with twice two, or *four* strings to each key.

[*To be concluded in our next Number.*]

VIII. Explanation of the Musical Pieces given in this first Number.

At page 2, 3, of the plates, see a *Musical Definition*, being a humourous essay on the following three lines:

> There are great numbers of *Players ;*
> Yea even many *Composers ;*
> But few *Musicians* among them.

The words of the first and second line contain mere general remarks, without regard to any particular person. But the last line alludes to John Sebastian Bach, the beginning of one of whose fugue subjects, (that of No. 1 in the first part of his Well-temper'd Clavier,) introduced by right and reverse imitation in the introductory symphony, and to the last line of the words; and treated as a Fughetta, in the final symphony.

At page 4, 5, of the plates, see a diatonic, chromatic, enharmonic, *Cancrine Minuett*, with two variations; every second part of which arises from taking the first part backwards, i. e. in cancrine, or retrograde motion. The subject, or first part alone, of the minuett, has been given on the title page of the author's four Sonatas, Op. II ; and as an example of retrograde motion, in his Essay on Harmony, plate 34.

And on the title-page of this No. 1, see an ænigmatical *canon* by the Editor, on the same subject of Bach, part of which has been introduced in the above Musical Definition. It consists of four parts in the one given, and is intended for those of our readers, who may be inclined to seek the solution of it, which may be found according to the rules given in the author's Essay on Practical Composition, Chap. IX, § 25 ; and the proof of which will be: that when resolved, its four parts together make a quadruple counterpoint in the octave; and its highest and lowest part alone, a counterpoint in the tenth and twelfth.

A MUSICAL DEFINITION

Written and composed by A. F. C. Kollmann.

-si - cians, Mu - - si - - - - - - cians a - - mong them. But few - - Mu - si - cians, Mu
- si - - cians a - - - mong - - - - - - them.
Fughetta
rallent

Menuetto Cancrino, Diat. Chrom. Enharm. con Variaz. By A. F. C. KOLLMANN.

Var: II

To be published by Subscription,

A SECOND EDITION

OF AN

ESSAY ON PRACTICAL MUSICAL COMPOSITION,

WRITTEN,

AND MOST HUMBLY DEDICATED BY PERMISSION, TO

His Majesty,

BY A. F. C. KOLLMANN,

ORGANIST OF HIS MAJESTY'S GERMAN CHAPEL, ST. JAMES'S.

Mr. KOLLMANN respectfully acquaints the Public, that a Second Edition of the above Work, which has been out of print these seven years, is now ready for Publication, with considerable Additions and Improvements; and that it will be put to press, as soon as one hundred copies are subscribed for.

The Contents are as follows:

Introduction:—Of the Method according to which Harmony and Composition should be studied. Chapter I.—Of the Plan for a piece to be composed. Chap. II.—Of Sonatas, without and with Accompaniments; including Solos, Duos, Trios, &c. Chap. III.—Of Symphonies, and Overtures. Chap. IV.—Of Concertos. Chap. V.—Of Fugues in General. Chap. VI.—Of simple Fugues. Chap. VII.—Of Double Fugues, or Fugues of two and more Subjects. Chap. VIII.—Of Canons in general. Chap. IX.—Of the Construction and Resolution of Canons. Chap. X.—Of Vocal Music in general, and with regard to Recitatives, Airs and Chorusses. Chap. XI.—Of Instrumental Music, with regard to every particular Sort of Instruments, and to any Combination of different Instruments. Chap. XII.—Of Style and National Music.

The Work will make one volume in Folio, as before.

Price to Subscribers, One Guinea and a Half; to be paid for on delivery. To Non-Subscribers, Thirty-six Shillings.

The Names of Subscribers will be received by the Author, MR. KOLLMANN, *(Friary, St. James's Palace;)* and at the principal Music-sellers. Where may be had, lately published by the same Author:

	£	s.	d.
A New Theory of Musical Harmony, . .	1	11	6
A Second Practical Guide to Thorough Bass, .	0	10	6
Twelve Analyzed Fugues, with Double Counterpoints in all Intervals, for two Performers on one Piano Forte or Organ. Op. X. . . .	0	15	0
The Melody of the Hundredth Psalm, with Grounds and Directions for an Hundred different Harmonies, in four parts, . . .	0	3	0
A Rondo on the Chord of the Diminished Seventh, shewing the immediate Progression of that Chord to all the twelve Major and Minor Keys, .	0	1	0

TO THE NOBILITY AND GENTRY.

Mr. J. J. Gurk, Member of the Imperial and Royal Academy of Arts and Sciences at Vienna, has invented, and brought to perfection, after seven years labour, besides considerable expence, a most singular and curious Musical Instrument, called by *Dr. Hadyn,*

THE PANHARMONICON.

It performs by means of Barrels, moved by Clock-work, Pieces of Haydn, Mozart, and other eminent Composers: on real Trumpets, French Horns, Bassoons, Clarinets, German Flutes, and an Organ Flute Stop; accompanied by Kettle Drums, large and small Drums, Cymbals, and Triangles, when required: so as to produce an amazing effect, like that of a Band composed of Performers on those Instruments.

The *Panharmonicon* is exhibited at *Wigley's Rooms, Spring-Gardens,* every afternoon, from One to Two, and from Three to Four; and every Evening from Seven to Eight, and from Nine to Ten. And the general approbation which it has met with from those of the Nobility, Gentry, and distinguished Musicians, who have already heard it, makes the Inventor flatter himself, that not one admirer of Music in this Metropolis will refuse himself the satisfaction of hearing it.

Admission Half a Crown.

THE QUARTERLY

MUSICAL REGISTER,

No. II.

APRIL, 1, 1812.

WRITTEN AND COLLECTED

BY

A. F. C. Kollmann.

Canon 4 in 1; and Counterpt. in the 8, 10, and 12.

See page 160.

LONDON:

PUBLISHED FOR THE EDITOR,

BY BECKET AND PORTER, 81, PALL MALL,

By whom all useful Communications (post paid) and Advertisements will be regularly attended to.

Price Three Shillings.

CONTENTS of the Work.

No. I.

No. II.

No. III. will contain,

The Conclusion of the above Articles, IX, XIII, XVII.
The State of the present Musical Season in London.
A Review of Dr. Crotch's Elements of Composition.
An Analysis of Sebastian Bach's Preludes and Fugues
An Account of A. F. C. Kollmann's Practical Works, &c. &c.

Collins, Printer, Memoranda Office,
No. 9, Queen Street, Golden Square.

THE QUARTERLY MUSICAL REGISTER.

No. II. APRIL, 1812.

IX. *A Retrospect of the State of Music in Germany, since the beginning of the last Century.*

In attempting the present Article, we think it expedient to extend our remarks to a greater period of time, than that of the Retrospect of the State of Music in Great Britain, given in our No. I; in order to introduce such particulars of an earlier date, as will deserve to be noticed.

We shall endeavour first to point out the *state of music* itself, in Germany; and then to shew the *causes* of its former particular cultivation in that country.

I. The state of music itself we shall again consider with regard to Knowledge,—to Composition,—to Performance,—and to Inventions, as follows:

1. The musical *Knowledge* of Germany, at the beginning of the last century, was already in a very respectable state; and it has still been improved since that time.

The former appears from the musical *writings* of that country; which we shall consider under the heads of historical, theoretical, and critical works.

General musical *Histories* have been published in Germany by *Printz*, Dresden, 1690, 31 sheets in quarto;— *
by *Marpurg*, Berlin, 1759, 33 sheets in quarto;—and by *Dr. Forkel*, vol. I. Leipzig, 1788, 504 pages in large quarto; and vol. II. 1801, 776 pages ditto; both with a long introduction, and several plates. Vol. III. which will con-

clude the work was not yet published, when the communication with Germany became interrupted. Concerning these musical histories we must observe, that the first already was very good for the time in which it appeared; that the second, by Marpurg, does credit to its celebrated Author, but extends only to the time of Pythagoras; and that the last is all that can be expected in its department. For it not only shews Dr. Forkel as a man of the most extensive historical knowledge, and literary research; but also as a *musician* of the greatest penetration.

To the above *general* histories may be added, *Dr. Forkel's* Allgemeine Literatur der Musik, (Universal Musical Literature) as the work repeatedly quoted in our No. I. Leipzig, 1792, 540 pages in large octavo. It gives the most complete account known, of all the musical writings come to any notice, in all languages; and from it are selected the literary accounts of the present article, with the addition of such remarks as we thought necessary for our purpose. Also the same Author's Life of John Sebastian Bach, quoted in Art. IV. p. 30.

Of the *Biographical* kind, the following are the most respectable publications during the period in question:

Mattheson's Grundlage einer Ehrenpforte, (Foundation of a Triumphal Arch) Hamburgh, 1740, two alphabets and 4 sheets in quarto. This contains interesting biographies of 148 distinguished musicians.—*Hiller's* Biographies of 19 others, Leipzig, 1784, 320 pages in octavo.—*Gerber's* Biographical Lexicon, part I. from A to M, Leipzig, 1790, 32 sheets in large octavo. Part II. which was to conclude the work, and also to contain a complete list of engravings on musical subjects, was expected to appear in 1791, and has probably been published.—Besides the above collections, numerous musical biographies have also been published singly, and in periodical works of miscellaneous contents, of which we only mention that of Fash, late musician to Frederick the Great, written by *Zelter*, Berlin, 1801,

62 pages in quarto, with Fash's portrait, as a very interesting tract.

The principal musical *Dictionaries* are: *Walther's* Lexicon, Leipzig, 1732, 43 sheets in octavo, and 22 plates. It contains musical biographies, and explanations of musical terms, and is a much-esteemed work. But the continuation of it, which was also ready, has not been published.—*Sulzer's* Theory of the Fine Arts, Leipzig, 1773, 2 vols. in octavo; and a new edition, augmented with numerous literary references, by Capt. Von Blankenburg, Leipzig, 1786, 4 parts in large octavo. The musical articles of the first part are known to have been written by Kirnberger, and those of the second part by his pupil Schulz.—*Koch's* Lexicon, Frankfurt-on-the-Main, 1802, 60 sheets in large octavo. This is a very complete and well-written explanation of musical terms, and principles; but it does not contain any biographies. *

The *theoretical* works which we think entitled to the notice of our Readers, we will classify under the heads of *acoustics; calculations; temperament; practical music; harmony; thorough bass;* and *composition;* according to Dr. Forkel's arrangement, in the Universal Literature mentioned.

On *Acoustics* in general, the following are the principal works: *Mattheson's* Phys. Klanglehre, (Physical Doctrine of Sounds) Hamburgh, 1748, 167 pages in octavo.—*Beltz's* Abhandlurg Vom Schalle, &c. (Treatise of Acoustics) Berlin, 1764, 139 pages in quarto; which gained a prize from the Royal Society of Arts at Berlin, in 1763.—*Dr. Chladni's* Entdeckungen, &c. (Discoveries concerning the Theory of Sounds) Leipzig, 1787, 78 pages in quarto.—The same Author's *Acoustic*, (Treatise on Acoustics) Leipzig, 1802, 302 pages in quarto, with 36 pages of introduction, and 12 plates. This is a very valuable work, which deserves to be translated into the English language. We shall therefore give the heads of its contents as follows:

Introduction. PART I. Of the doctrine of sounds in general, or of arithmetical acoustics. *Sect. I.* Of the original ratios of sounds; or of intervals, chords, scales, and the arithmetic and harmonic division of the octave. *Sect. II.* Of the necessary modifications of intervals, or of temperament; with calculations of equal, and unequal temperaments. PART II. Of the laws of vibrations which are peculiar to sounding bodies. *Sect. I.* General remarks on the different kinds of vibration. *Sect. II.* Vibrations of strings. 1, transversal vibrations, harmonic notes, and rattling notes; 2, longitudinal vibrations. *Sect. III.* Vibrations of a stretched membrane. *Sect. IV.* Vibrations of the air itself, as in the voices of human beings, and other living creatures; and in all kinds of wind instruments. *Sect. V.* Vibrations in a straight staff; 1, six cases of transversal vibrations; 2, three cases of longitudinal vibrations; 3, spiral vibrations. *Sect. VI.* Vibrations of bent staves, as in a fork, a ring, and in bendings of other forms. *Sect. VII.* Vibrations of a plate; 1, general remarks and principles; 2, vibrations of rectangular plates in general, and with regard to three different cases; 3, vibrations of square, or other rectangular plates, with numerous experiments, and their calculations; 4, vibrations of a round plate; 5, ditto of eliptic plates, with calculations; 6, vibrations of sexangular plates; 7, those of a semicircular plate; 8, those of triangular, and of some other forms of plates; 9, on the practical musical use of sounding plates. *Sect. VIII.* Vibrations of a bell, or of bent plates in general. *Sect. IX.* Of combinations of different kinds of vibrations, with regard to all the preceding cases in strings, in the air, in staves, and in plates. *Sect. X.* Of swinging and undulating vibrations combined. PART III. Of the propagation of sounds, by means of the air, and of other elastic fluids. *Sect. I.* Numerous particular cases of this. *Sect. II.* The same, by means of water or similar fluids, and of solid bodies. PART IV. Of the perception of sounds. *Sect. I.* Of human hearing; 1, of the construction, and the functions, of our hearing organs; 2, the particulars of our hearing itself, with regard to noise, sound, distance, and direction. *Sect. II.* Of the hearing of different kinds of animals. The whole of the above important contents are treated of in a very clear and masterly manner; and numerous works of other Authors, which treat of the same or of similar subjects, are quoted, and very liberally mentioned. The Introduction describes the Author's two musical instruments, on entirely new and original principles, which we shall mention under Inventions. And a well-engraved portrait of him is given on the title-page.

The principal treatises of Musical *Calculations* are:

Sorge's Rational Rechnung, (Calculations of Musical Ratios) Lobenstein, 1749, 308 pages in octavo.—*Marpurg's* Anfangsgründe, (Elements of Theoretical Music) Leipzig, 1757, 146 pages in quarto. It teaches the addition, subtraction, copulation, comparation, æquiparation, and mediation or division of ratios, with regard to different, equal, and unequal temperaments.—Partly on those calculations are: *Klein's* Versuch, which will be mentioned under * Practical Music; *Koch's* Lexicon, which has been mentioned page 83; and *Dr. Chladni's* Acoustic, described above.

The treatises on *Temperament* are:

Werkmeister's Mus. Temperatur, (Musical Temperament) Frankfurt, 1691, 96 pages in quarto.—*Sinn's* Temperaturapractica, Werningeroda, 1717, 23 sheets in quarto; which explains temperament, arithmetically and geometrically.—*Sorge's* Dialogue on the Temperaments of Præ- * torius, Printz, Werkmeister, Neidhard, Silberman, and Teleman, Lobenstein, 1748, 86 pages in octavo;—ditto Investigation of Schröter's Temperament, 1754, 38 pages in octavo;—ditto Guide to Temperament, as a vindication against that of Fritz, 1758, quarto.—*Fritz's* Anweisung, (Guide to Temperament) Leipzig, 1757, three sheets in quarto.—*Kirnberger's* Gleichschweb. Temperatur, (Construction of an Equal Temperament) Berlin, 1760, one sheet in quarto.—*Marpurg's* Mus. Temperatur, (Essay on Musical Temperament) Breslau, 1776, 20 sheets in octavo; it demonstrates different, equal, and unequal temperaments, by harmonical calculations; and to it is added, an Appendix on *Rameau's* and *Kirnberger's* Fundamental Bass;—ditto several other explanations of temperaments and their calculations, in his Histor. Crit. Beyträge, 1778.—*Schröter's* Letzte Beschäftigungen, &c. (Last Musical Occupations, with Six Plans of Temperaments) Nordhausen, 1782, 52 pages in quarto. Besides the above entire works on temperament, explanations of it also from part of several other treatises.

Among the treatises on *Practical* Music, we begin with those on *Singing;* the principal work of which is: *Hiller's* Anweisung, &c. (A Guide to the Art of Singing Musically Correct) Leipzig, 1774, 224 pages in quarto; and Part II. (A Guide to the Art of Singing Musically Graceful) Leipzig, 1780, 152 pages in quarto.

The principal treatise on the *German Flute* is: *Quantz's* Versuch, &c. (Essay on the Art of Playing the German Flute) Berlin, 1752, 45 sheets and 24 plates, in quarto. This highly-esteemed work was also published in Dutch, at Amsterdam, 1775.

For the *Violin*, the principal German work has been: *Mozart's* Versuch, &c. (Essay on the Art of Playing the Violin) Augsburg, 1756, 35 sheets in quarto; and an improved edition, 1770. The author was the father of the celebrated W. A. Mozart.

For *Keyed* Instruments, the following treatises are remarkable: *C. P. E. Bach's* Versuch, (Essay on the True Manner of Playing the Clavier) Berlin, 1753, 15 sheets in quarto; second edition, 1759; third edition, 1780. N. B. Part II. will be mentioned under Thorough Bass.—*Marpurg's* Anleitung, (Guide to the Art of Playing on the Clavier) Berlin, 1765; second edition, 11 sheets in quarto, with 18 plates; Part II. will also be mentioned under Thorough Bass.—*Türk's* Clavierschule, (School for the * Clavier) Leipzig, 1789, 54 sheets in quarto, with 12 lessons for practice.

The principal treatise of a *System of Harmony* is *Kirnberger's* Wahren Grundsätze, (True Principles of Harmony) Berlin, 1773, 115 pages in quarto. It elucidates that system of harmony, which has been described in our No. I. p. 43.

Among the works on *Thorough Bass*, we have to notice, *Heinichen's* Generalbass, (Guide to Thorough Bass) second edition, Dresden, 1728, 129 sheets in quarto.—*Mattheson's* Kleine General Bass Schule, (Lesser School of Thorough Bass) Hamburgh, 1735, 30 sheets in quarto.—*Sorgen's* Vorgemach, (Guide to Thorough Bass) * Lobenstein, 1745, 432 pages in quarto, with numerous plates.—*Marpurg's* Second Part to the Guide mentioned under Keyed Instruments; treating of accompaniment, Berlin, 1761, 52 pages, and 4 plates in quarto.—*C. P. E. Bach's* Second Part to the Essay mentioned under Keyed Instruments; treating of accompaniment and free fancy, Berlin, 1762, 44 sheets in quarto.—*Schroeter's* Generalbass, (Guide to Thorough Bass) Halberstadt, 1772, 223 pages in quarto.—*Kirnberger's* Generalbass, (Principles of Thorough Bass) Berlin, 1781, 88 pages in quarto, and 25 plates.—*Türk's* Ditto, Halle and Leipzig, 1791, 308 pages in octavo.—*Kollmann's* Practische Anleitung, (A Second Practical Guide to Thorough Bass). A German translation of this work, with the addition of the original English text, Offenbach, 1808.

As musical *Encyclopedias*, though not written in alphabetical order, we have to select: *Mattheson's* Newly-Opened Orchestra, with notes by Keyser. Hamburgh, 1713, 15 sheets in duodecimo.—Ditto Kern Mel. Wissench. (Kernel of the Science of Melody) Hamburgh, 1737, 25 sheets in quarto.—Testimonies to the same, 1738, two sheets.—Ditto Der Vollkomne Kapellmeister, (The Complete Chapel Master) Hamburgh, 1739, 131 sheets in folio, or three vols. The great merit of Mattheson, in the improvement of music as an art and science, is universally acknowledged in Germany; and this last is one of his best works.

The principal treatises of musical composition are:

Werkmeister's Anleitung, &c. (Treatise on Composition including Simple and Double Counterpoint, Fugue, Canon, and Extempore Performance,) Leipzig, 1702, 142 pages in quarto.—*Fux's* Gradus ad Parnassum, Vienna, 1725, 279 pages in folio. An Italian translation of it, by Manfredi, at Carpi, 1761; a German translation of it, by Mitzler, with annotations, Leipzig, 1742; a French translation, by Denis, Paris, 1773; and an English translation, in which the name of the author is spelt *Feux*, by Preston, without mentioning the year of the publication. This is the best work of its kind, for the time it was published; but it has since been superseded by the treatises of Marpurg and Kirnberger.—*Spiess's* Mus. Tractat, (Musical Treatise) Augsburg, 1746, 66 sheets in folio.—*Riepel's* Tactordnung, (Rhythmopoeia) Regensburg, 1754, 79 pages in folio.—Ditto Tonordnung, (Modulation in General) Frankfurt, 1755, 130 pages in folio.—Ditto Tonordnung, (Particular Modulations) Frankfurt, 1757, 84 pages in folio.—Ditto Bertrügliche Tonordnung, (Deceptive Modulation) Augsburg, 1765, 103 pages in folio.—Ditto Counterpoint, Regensburg, 1768, 21 sheets in folio.—Ditto Bass Schlüssel, (Bass Clef) or Rules for Setting a Bass to Compositon, Regensburg, 1776, 84 pages in folio. All these works of that author have been much esteemed.—*Marpurg's* Handbuch, (Guide to Thorough bass, and to Composing in 2, 3, 4, 5, 6, 7, 8, and more Parts) Berlin 1755, 100 pages in quarto; Part II. 1755, 205 pages; Part III. with an Index to the whole, 1758, 341 pages; an Appendix, 1760, nine sheets;

each part with plates. This work treats on harmony in a masterly manner, but according to Rameau's system, concerning which it is certain, that the more harmony is *explained* by it, the more *perplexing* it becomes; and nothing would be more desirable than an English translation of this work, for the purpose of comparing its doctrines with those of Kollmann's New Theory.—*Kirnberger's* Kunst des Reinen Satzes, (Art of Perfect Harmony) Berlin, 1774, 250 pages in quarto; Part II. in three divisions, 1776, 1777, and 1779, in all 573 pages. This work also treats of harmony in a masterly manner, according to the system adopted in Kollmann's Essay on Harmony, as mentioned in our No. I. Art. V.—*Vogler's* Ton Wissenschaft, (Treatise of Harmony and Composition) Manheim, 1776, 86 pages in octavo.—*Koch's* Versuch, &c. (Essay of a Guide to Composition) Rudolstadt, 1782, 374 pages in octavo; Part II. Leipzig, 1787, 464 pages. This is a well written work; but the doctrine of the chords rather inclines to Em. Bach's individual consideration of them, than to Marpurg's or Kirnberger's system.—*Kalkbrenner's* Theorie der Tonkunst, (Theory of Music) Part I. Berlin, 1789, 40 pages and 13 plates in quarto. Whether Part II. has been published, we have not had an opportunity of ascertaining.—*Albrechtsberger's* Anleitung, &c. (Guide to Composition) Leipzig, 1790, 440 pages in quarto. This work still treats of intervals and chords, according to their individual contents, without regard to a fundamental bass, like Fux's Gradus ad Parnassum, mentioned above; and therefore its doctrines have been superseded long before they were published. But at the end, it contains the scales, and a brief explanation of the instruments used in an orchestra, which may be of some use to young composers.—*Knecht's* Elementarwerk, (Elementary Work of Harmony and Thorough Bass) Augsburg, 1792, 200 pages in quarto, and 52 plates. This treats of intervals and chords, according to the principles of

Rameau and Marpurg, with the only difference, that the ninth, eleventh, and thirteenth are derived from a nine, eleven, and thirteen of the ratios, according to Vogler's doctrine, and not from one, two, or three thirds by supposition. But this by no means improves the doctrine of a chord of the nine, eleven, and thirteen, with their inversions.

Under the head of treatises on *Particular Branches* of Musical Composition, we have to notice *Marpurg's* Abhandlung von der Fuge, (Treatise on the Fugue) Part I. Berlin, 1753, 26 sheets and 62 plates in quarto; and Part II. 1754, 20 sheets and 60 plates. A French translation of it, entitled Traité de la Fugue, was published at Berlin, 1756. This is the most profound, and most masterly work of its kind, in the German language.

The principal works on *Vocal* Composition are: *Marpurg's* Anleitung, (Guide to Vocal Composition) Berlin, 1758, 206 pages in quarto.—*Riepel's* Dialogues on Singing, Regensburg, 25 sheets in folio.—*Kirnberger's* Singcomposition, (Guide to Vocal Composition) Berlin, 1782, 85 pages in folio.—*Rellstab's* Versuch, &c. (Essay on the Combination of Musical and Oratorial Declamation) Berlin, 1786, 14 sheets in folio.

On *Melody*, a work has been published by *Nichelmann*, entitled Die Melodie, (Melody, with regard to its Nature, and its Qualities) Danzig, 1755, 175 pages and 22 plates in quarto. The purpose of this excellent work is to prove, that only those parts of a composition please above the rest, where not only the melody expresses a sentiment, but where also the harmony coincides with it, and supports its effect.

The *critical* musical works, which have been published in Germany, may be divided into *periodical*, and *single* ones. The former have been enumerated in our No. I. Art. II.; and alluded to in the Introduction, Art. I. as a proof of the influence which such works have on the cultivation of music. And it will be unnecessary to enlarge on the latter, though several of them also are respectable.

2. The art of musical *Composition*, as the second object of consideration pointed out at the beginning of this Article, was already in a high state of respectability at the commencement of the last century; and it has still been much improved in point of taste, but also much neglected in point of solidity, and in the department of the fugue, and of double counterpoint.

The former, or the high *respectability* of German composition, at the commencement of the period in question, appears from the following particulars:

First, the art of *rich*, and *scientific* harmonious combinations, in canons, fugues, and imitative pieces in a fixed number of obligato parts, was already very high, and very general, in Germany, before the time of Handel and Sebastian Bach. For though those two great musicians were contemporaries, and countrymen, they studied under different masters, in a different manner; and yet they acquired a *similar* greatness, as harmonists, from the *German* school only, and Handel not from the Italian school, which only improved his *taste* but not his harmonious *art*.

Secondly, the compositions for all kinds of *instruments* also, contained rational, and not mere awkward or whimsical difficulties; and they are still esteemed as very improving lessons for modern practice. This appears particularly from Sebastian Bach's pieces for the Organ, Harpsichord, Violin, and Violoncello; and also from Handel's and Teleman's pieces for those instruments.

Thirdly, even the state of *theatrical* music in Germany, was far from being indifferent: for Dr. Burney mentions in his General History, Vol. IV. p. 577, that "Operas, (either Italian or German,) were established in the principal cities of the empire during the latter end of the last century," or near the year 1700. And as the chief part of them was set to music by Keiser, they must have been very good;

for, according to the opinion of so great an authority in that department, *Hasse*, "Keiser was one of the greatest musicians the world ever saw." (See Dr. Burney's Tour through Germany, Vol. I. p. 350.) This must chiefly be understood with regard to his dramatic compositions, in which Hasse found much more elegance, clearness, and grace, than were to be found in most modern compositions, even at the time when operas had been, and were still in the most flourishing state in Germany. And *Marpurg* also, in a certain comparison between Handel and Sebastian Bach, which we may introduce at another opportunity, speaks highly of Keiser as a composer of operas.

That about the middle of the century in question, the musical compositions of Germany had arrived at their utmost height, appears from Dr. Burney's General History, as well as from the account of Sebastian Bach's works we have given in our No. I. Art. IV. For at that time all the harmonious arts flourished in the greatest perfection, and were blended with natural melodiousness. The best *Italian operas* were composed by German masters. And instrumental compositions became tasteful, both for keyed instruments, and for those used in an orchestra.

But, as we have already observed, the study of composition as a *harmonious art*, has since been much neglected; and the lighter style of theatrical compositions is become so general, that not many attempts at concerting obligato parts, and at a regular fugue, are met with in modern German compositions. However, fine and tasteful *expression* has still been studied, and successfully displayed in the works of Emanuel Bach, Mozart, Haydn, Winter, Pleyel, Dussek, Woelfl, Beethoven, and of numerous other great masters, which are not sufficiently known in England. Among the latter we find Mr. Reichardt, who has distinguished himself not only as a great Composer, but also as one of the most able musical Critics. (See our No. I. Art. II. near the end.)

3. The musical *Performance* in Germany, as the third

particular pointed out at the beginning of this Article, has been very general, and highly respectable, during the whole period of time in question. This we shall endeavour to shew with regard to theatrical music; to concerts and smaller parties; to church music; to the organ; to the clavier; and to all other instruments.

Concerning *theatrical* music we have already observed, that *operas* German or Italian, were established in the principal cities of Germany, before the beginning of the last century. One of those cities was Hamburgh, where Handel assisted in the performance of operas, and composed an opera himself as early as 1705. The respectability of those * operas follows from the testimony, which Hasse gave of Keiser, as quoted above. Most of the other cities we suppose to have been those where the principal courts of Germany resided; and their opera establishments and performances have in general been both grand and excellent. For as the whole expense was defrayed by the court, viz. theatre, compositions, and performers, there could be no risk to proprietors, as by the opera in London; and the only concern of the managers was, to render the whole as exquisite, as the large sums granted for it would permit. The musical court establishments for this purpose, and for all the concerts at court were as follows: one or two composers, called Chapel Masters, who had the management of the whole vocal and instrumental department; one or two leaders, called Concert Masters; with a proportional number of able performers for every instrument, according to the required strength of the orchestra; and the most able singers that could be engaged.

As every individual of such a court establishment had a good salary, and as the Composers had full power to make a piece rehearsed and executed as they directed, the performances of operas in Germany generally have been highly finished; and intricate vocal pieces in three, four, and more parts could be performed in them with the best success. The

Leaders also enforced the greatest exactness in the instrumental performance; and we learn respecting the celebrated Pisendel at Dresden, that he even marked the bowing over the parts of the different stringed instruments, so that the motions of all the bows were as uniform as the notes which they executed. However the vocal parts of those theatrical pieces called *Operattas*, being plays that are spoken, with intermixed songs for one, two, and more performers, like the English Love in a Village, have not been so early brought to a state of general respectability in Germany, as early as real operas: and it is but since the time of *Hiller's* composing them, and giving them a popular interest, and a natural melodiousness, that the style of them has also been greatly improved.

A new species of theatrical vocal pieces also have been introduced by *Mr. Reichardt*, which he calls *Liederspiele*, (Lyric Plays;) and which consist of simple airs throughout, including duos, &c. without any recitatives, or simple speaking. They have been occasioned by his observing, that the public shewed too great a partiality to bravura songs, and did not much applaud those airs of simple expression, which ought to be particularly cultivated. And they are said to have met with great success. We conceive that short dramatic pieces of this kind, in one act, might be written and composed for social amusement, with the accompaniment of a Piano Forte only; where they would be both improving as vocal exercises, and more entertaining than mere songs, without regard to a historical or dramatic connexion.

[*To be concluded in our next Number.*]

---

* X. *A Parallel between* RAPHAEL *and* MOZART.

THOUGH a Biography of *Mozart* has been published, and prefixed to the text of the Requiem, by Mr. John Ashley, London, 1801; and though two other biographies of him also have appeared in Germany, one in Schlichtegroll's Necrolog, and the other singly, by Mr. F. Niemtshek, Prague, 1798: there still are found numerous accounts of him, which will shew his great and amiable character in a fairer light than is said to have been thrown upon it by the first of the said German publications. These we shall endeavour to lay before our Readers as occasion permits: and we make the beginning with the present parallel between the above two great Artists, which, we presume, will be as interesting to the lovers and professors of *painting*, as to those of *music.* It is written in German by Mr. *Frederic Rochlitz*, of Leipzig, and dedicated to his friend *Matthisson*, (a favourite German poet, many of whose productions have been set to music by Mozart, as well as by other composers); see the Leipzig Allgemeine Mus. Zeitung, No. 37, for June 11th, 1800. It begins with a short Introduction, as follows:

"A certain social amusement, which obliges its members to trace the similitude that may be found between two persons, or other given subjects, allotted to me the task of drawing a parallel between *Raphael*, and *Mozart;* and I own, that the apparent difficulty of that task distressed me at the first setting out; but in proceeding I discovered, to my own surprise, such a quantity of resemblances, that I consider the peculiarity of some of them, (even if they might be called accidental,) as sufficient to apologise for this intrusion on the attention of the Public.

"But I think it necessary to add, that though the particulars which I offer are historically true; the similitudes pointed out, are not intended to dispute certain *dissimilarities*, in the two great characters before us, which have been left unnoticed."

As in our whole existence, there depends so much on the respective physical and moral constitution of those to whom we owe that existence, it is remarkable, that both *Raphael* and *Mozart*, descended from very *handsome parents*. And as with regard to a certain situation in life, or *to what*, and in *what manner* we apply our faculties, there depends so much on the occupation of those, whose care and influence gives our spirit and mind its direction and support, it must be observed, that *Raphael's* father was a Painter, and *Mozart's* father a Musician. Both those fathers honoured, and loved their art; both pursued it zealously, and perfectly understood the true principles of it; both also, though they did not possess a high genius, or any thing more than genuine and well-cultivated nature, still knew how to teach others, and consequently also their sons, the rules of their art. And that is sufficient. For genius may be compared to a fertile ground, which, when properly tilled, manured, and sown, cannot fail yielding a plentiful crop, as long as no irresistible causes prevent it.

Raphael zealously, and with simplicity of heart, copied the pictures of his father, and those of Petro Perugino; *Mozart* practised the strictly regular pieces of his father, and the uniform works of most of the esteemed German composers of his time.

Two great men had begun to diffuse a new spirit over the age in which these two youths lived, and to exercise over their respective art a powerful, and almost arbitrary dominion. Exalted, but mysterious; bold, but without a tender taste; mighty, but without gentleness; were the spirit and the works of those great men. *Michael Angelo*, and *Sebastian Bach*, are the names of these heroes, between whom perhaps not only a resemblance might be traced, but a continued parallel might be drawn. *Raphael* became acquainted with Angelo's, and *Mozart* with Bach's works; and both were so enraptured, that the one abandoned his former manner of painting, and the other his former manner of composing.

But the obscure and deliberate manner of those two great masters, was irreconcileable to the juvenile fire of our two young Artists; and though they tried to adopt it, both of them, (particularly Mozart,) became harsh, extraneous, quaint, and confused. They made several attempts in this style, but without giving it a finish, and in most instances without even completing the works they began. Proofs of both may still be found, in *Raphael's* altar-piece of the church of the Santo Spirito at Sienna; and in some concertos, as well as several masses by *Mozart*, which he still composed at Salsburg, or soon after.

However, the beneficent and milder light of a finer taste now began to rise in the era of both our young Artists. For though they did not shun the gloomy sanctuary of those two oracles; and on the contrary, still valued and studied their works, to acquire a true knowledge of their art: they introduced the intricacies of that art more sparingly, and with better judgment; they followed the impulse of their heart, studied effect, and tried more to raise our spirit through a noble and sweet simplicity, than to overload it with the mazes of a misapplied intricacy. And now they began to please, when before they had only surprised; they conquered more by beguiling than by assaulting the ears of their hearers. The age then had the choice between the dictating Minerva, and the milder Apollo; they decided in favour of the latter, and now most of the artists also laid the laurel at his feet. *Leonardo* da *Vinci*, and his party, at the time stood foremost among those painters; and *Hasse*, with some Italians, among whom also there was a Leonardo,—*Leonardo Leo*—among those musicians.

The majority of painters, at the time of young *Raphael*, and the majority of musicians, at the time of young *Mozart*, now eagerly, and almost exclusively imitated these new patterns: but they themselves did otherwise. They were too lively impressed with the original spirit of former times, and felt themselves strong enough to act according to its impulse; but they also did justice to the charms of the new period, and made use of what is natural, true, fine, and charming in its style. And now arose in both of them, that independent original Genius, that heavenly gift, which, not merely like a growing child, gradually increased in strength; but which, like a man, nourished by substantial aliments, and strengthened by beneficent, animating cordials, presented itself in them, with all the energy of perfect maturity; and they themselves were now, in the principal points, arrived at the meridian of their art. Nothing more therefore could be wanting for both of them, but an *opportunity* to employ their extraordinary talents to advantage; and such a *patronage*, as would procure them an easy and encouraging existence. And this they found. *Raphael* the former, in the Vatican, and the latter, principally in the Popes, Julius II. and Leo X.; and *Mozart*, both the former and latter, in the journies, of his happy, unsettled, independent life of an Artist.

And how do both of them now appear in their works? which is the true characteristic, the predominant, distinct, quality of them? It is *invention!* Here the resemblance between the genius of our two Artists is so striking, that I may be permitted dwelling a little, on a closer contemplation of them.

Invention is either *poetical*, or *artistic*. Poetical invention shews what a work of art shall be; artistic invention, the means by which it is to obtain its intended nature and qualities. The former is the idea of the work; the latter the manner of expressing that idea. All *invention* exclusively belongs to genius; but the *execution* of an invention, to talent, which will be examined in the sequel. The *poetical* genius suggests not only the principal idea, but also the most favourable moment, and the leading features, which are requisite for substantiating that idea: the *artistic* genius finds the most successful expression of it, within the limits of that art in which it acts; it regulates and treats every part of the whole, not merely so, as a true representation and expression of the idea requires, but particularly so as to beautify the subject of representation, and to heighten the expression of it.

These two qualities are united in a true artist; and nevertheless he may not yet be able to produce his conceived work of art. This requires divers abilities which he ought to learn, viz. the use of the pencil in a painter, the art of speech in a poet, the treatment of an instrument in a musician, and so forth. This is what I call *execution*. It is no more a property of genius, but of talent and experience. It is, like talent in general, the perfection, and facility, of successfully representing the said poetical and artistical invention, to our senses. Without this ability, genius would know how to produce much, but not produce any thing, at least nothing but rhapsodical, fragmentary sketches; without genius, our talent would be able to produce much, and yet produce nothing, at least nothing, perhaps, but imitations of genuine works of art, the manners of others, and copies of common nature. A talent may be exercised, and genius be rendered more acute—the former as execution, and the latter as ability: in this manner both are improved, but the former in quantity, and the latter in quality.

Both now, the said spirit of an art, and the execution of it, ought to be united in a perfect artist; however, if one might be admitted to rank before the other, it must unquestionably be the former before the latter,—the genius before the talent—the gift of heaven before an earthly acquisition. This, I presume, is the meaning of *Lessing*, when he says, *Raphael* would have been the greatest painter, even if unfortunately he had been born without hands. And in like manner it might be said, that *Mozart* would have been the greatest composer, even if he had never set a note.

But let us return to our subject—though indeed we are in the midst of it! for *invention*, richness, inexhaustible richness, success, invariable success in invention—in poetical and artistical—exactly are the first characteristic of *Raphael* and *Mozart;* and certainly are the means by which they have arrived at their eminence. By both of them we always find choice, noble, fine ideas; by the former a world of living figures, and by the latter a world of living musical thoughts, each of which is speaking, interesting, and appropriate in itself, and equally important in its connexion with the whole. All may be compared to the different limbs of a body, and to beautiful limbs of a beautiful body; all are judiciously arranged, so that nothing which can interest in itself, and add to the effect of the whole, remains unobserved; and even none of those limbs are disproportional, or incorrect. However, the latter must be understood only of Mozart's finished works of his mature age; and not of his juvenile ones, or of those, where circumstances sometimes obliged him, either to write in too great a haste, or to make his art stoop to meaner comprehensions, and to the arbitrary whims of the times.

Through this exalted peculiarity of the works of both our Artists, which immediately captivates the whole soul of every person, whether judge or not, if only he is not without all cultivation and sensibility, both rose above the age in which they lived. Both of them conquered by degrees those egotists, which, regarding nothing but themselves and what is their own, endeavoured to lessen their fame; with those, bigotted to antiquity, which condemned them; and with those envious, which, as they felt the impossibility of rising up to them, endeavoured to lower them to their level:—through the said peculiarity of their works, they gained for themselves a lasting fame; and for their arts, a new and higher rank. Both founded a new school, and with them commenced a new era of their art. But I shall not unnecessarily enlarge on their distinguished pupils; and only observe, that *Raphael's* Julio Romano painted too gloomy and black, and his J. F. Penni *(Il Fatore)* too wild and gigantic, and therefore indistinct and unpleasing; neither shall I make any remarks on those distinguished modern composers, who have formed themselves upon *Mozart's* principles, or else there might be traced some similarity between them and the pupils of

Raphael; and I only venture on some more particular observations, concerning our masters themselves.

Raphael, though he was great, and felt that greatness himself, still incessantly studied his art, and without self-sufficience, indefatigably endeavoured to raise it and himself to a higher degree of perfection; and so it was the case with *Mozart*. If this were not related in history, the least attentive chronological examination of both their works would prove it. *Raphael* lived in his art alone, and found in it all the enjoyment he was desirous of; even in his hours of recreation he drew light, though unfinished, but very expressive sketches; and *Mozart* did the same, as can be proved by many pieces which are published among his other works. *Raphael* was obliged by men and circumstances, to execute, in the latter period of his life, several grand, but more delightful and charming works, than it was is usual fancy; yet though he drew the history of Psyche, and Galatea, according to the ideas of those who ordered them, he executed them so, that throughout, the great and profound artist was discoverable; and the same *Mozart* did with his Magic Flute, Clemenza di Tito, and some lesser productions.

But both *Raphael* and *Mozart* had their little imperfections, like other human beings. Their works therefore have not in *all* respects arrived at the highest degree of perfection. And where is there to be found a mortal, who could perform *all* that his immortal spirit conceives, feels, and intends? Both of them seem now and then less successful in what we have called *execution*, but which ought not to be confounded with what is commonly understood by treating a thought or subject. Raphael was rather weak in shortening a scene, and not very strong in perspective; his colouring is not always good, it contains black shades, and red flesh, and sometimes his pencil is hard. The same is the case with Mozart. Several of his full compositions are overcharged, his modulations not unfrequently *bizarre*, his abrupt changes of the key often harsh; he seldom writes plaintive, without some single traits of secret grief, which it is not easy to describe in words, but which easily may be felt; he seldom writes tenderly, without some painful sighs of an ardent as passion. As far as in this respect Raphael ranks behind the soft Correggio, and the charming Titian, Mozart ranks behind the Italians of the middle age, and even behind *some* that are still living.

The uncommon *diversity* in the works of both our Artists, and this not only with regard to contents, but also to treatment, (though in all of them we find the above characteristics) must create astonishment; and it would, like the *number* of them, be almost incredible, particularly by the short life of those masters, and their having indulged themselves in divers excesses,—if it was not known, how both of them lived solely and entirely for their art; how they commenced their distinguished career so early; and their spirit was unconcerned about every thing, which they did not find in a great measure connected with their principal object. Any thing else they dispatched quickly, and often carelessly; their principal concern only engaged their whole, eager, and persevering attention. It is very remarkable, that notwithstanding the incessant pressing of their spirit from one subject to another, the crowded succession of new works, and the inviting advantages of new engagements, neither Raphael nor Mozart (in their riper years) offered to the world any work, done only superficially, and carlessly finished. Both of them worked with dispatch, but without over hurrying themselves; and this is visible in all the original scores of Mozart, in which he has most carefully expressed in *every part*, all that is material, even every piano and forte. And wherever we meet in their works with deviations from what has been considered as established rules, it is done with good reason; either on account of the imperfection of the rule, or as a proof, in which cases a small

Another beautiful feature in the character of both Artists, I cannot leave unnoticed, though it is generally known, viz. that both of them did justice to all other merit. For *Raphael* always testified the most lively regard for the works of his master *Petro Perugino*, and for those of his patron *Bramante*, though he exceeded them so much; out of repect for the former, he even preserved the ceiling, painted by him in the third chamber of Signatura; he openly expressed his regard for the mighty braving rival, *Michael Angelo*; and even supported the respectable *Julio Romano*, who exceeded his master in fire. And so also was *Mozart*. His conduct towards *Joseph Haydn*, his defending *Jomelli*, his veneration for *Sebastian Bach*, and *Handel*, his supporting and aiding respectable young artists, is too well known to require particulars.

In this manner our two Artists made use of their short, but crowded life, and both felt, towards the age of thirty-five, a decline of their bodily strength; whilst their mental powers still encreased their noble exertion, and thereby speeded the destruction of the former. *Augustin Chigi* then prevailed on *Raphael*, and other influence on *Mozart*, to undertake the above-mentioned works, of a more delightful and charming nature; and both of them became, through the good-will of their encouragers, involved in a still more sensual life. Their bodily strength became exhausted, but their spirits once more burst forth with redoubled strength and nobleness. Both felt the chilling hand of death, which already seized them, and tried still to raise themselves a monument for posterity. Both chose the *Transfiguration* — *Raphael* that of the Redeemer, *Mozart* that of the Redeemed. With the zeal of those who already perceive themselves attended by the shades of death, and who feel that they perform their last work, both of them exerted themselves to the utmost, and produced, as it were, the quintessence of their most sacred feelings. Both these transfigurations transfigured our Artists themselves.

The work of *Raphael* became the first of new painting, and that of *Mozart* the first of new religious music; though in both of them, many good judges find the effect of some of the parts a little too dark.

In finishing those works, both *Raphael* and *Mozart* died—and both in the thirty-seventh year of their age."

To the above parallel we have to add, concerning *Mozart*: that his works are as *numerous*, as they are masterly and pleasing. This appears from a chronological * list, made by himself, of those composed from Febr. the 9th, 1784, till November the 15th, 1791, and published, with the beginning of each, by *Mr. Andrè*, at Offenbach, on the River Main. It specifies no less than 145 larger and smaller works, to which his Requiem must still be added. And in a Preface, Mr. Andrè says: "Besides these, I possess about 250 original manuscripts, by Mozart; a chronological list of which, with the subjects, and necessary remarks, will also be published. The number of Mozart's compositions, which he has written in the short period of his life, is about 450; and, as they comprehend numerous Operas, Masses, Cantatas, Concertos, Sinfonies, and such voluminous works, we ought to be astonished at his extraordinary activity. It is very interesting to read his original scores, and to behold in the them the first sketch, and further expression of his ideas. Most of his scores, particularly those since the year 1770, are written and filled up throughout very distinctly and neatly, with small notes; and even the marks of expression are added to every part, &c."

As a chronological list of this description is very desirable, for the purpose of tracing the gradual progress of the genius of so great a master as Mozart, we shall endeavour to lay it before our readers, in a succeeding number, and to point out those of his works, which are printed in England.

XI. *An Account of the Theoretical Works of A. F. C. Kollmann.*

(Concluded from p. 40.)

CONCERNING these works we beg leave to repeat, that as they are by the Editor of this Musical Register, we shall offer no other remarks on them, but such as any author may with propriety make on his own works; and leave the right of *judging* of their merit to the discerning Reader.

III. An Essay on Practical Musical Composition, London, 1799, 126 pages of text, and 67 plates of examples, in folio. The Author.

Though this work has been out of print upwards of seven years, a new edition of it is announced as ready for the press, with considerable additions and improvements; and therefore we shall now state the nature of the first edition, leaving an account of the improvements to be made in the second edition, for a succeeding number.

The purpose of the work is to form an equally *systematical* doctrine of the practical, or rhetorical part, of the science of music in general, as the Author's Essay on Harmony, or particularly his New Theory, forms of the grammatical part; and to complete his doctrine of that science. It consists of an Introduction, and of 12 Chapters, as follows:

Introduction. Here the Author points out two faults, which he presumes to have discovered in the usual methods of studying musical treatises; and proposes a method, according to which, not only his own, but all musical treatises, should be studied, if they shall afford that instruction which is contained in their doctrines and examples.

Chapter I. Of the Plan for a piece to be composed, treats I. Of that *Plan* in general, with regard to its intended nature, and quality; to the purposes for which it is to serve; and to the means by which it can be made to answer its intended purposes in the best manner.

II. Of the *Particulars* in the said plan for a musical piece; 1, with regard to the length, and disposition of a piece; 2, to the modulation of a piece, in short pieces, and in longer, and long pieces; with several plans of modulation from short and longer pieces; 3, to the character of a piece, whether it shall be prescribed, or optional, with the means by which characteristics can be produced, and an explanation of the characteristics proper to be introduced in a piece of composition; 4, to the instruments, or voices, for which a piece is to be composed; and 5, to the number of parts, particular performers, &c.

Chap. II. Of Sonatas. An introductory article shews the particulars in which Sonatas, Symphonies, and Concertos, are alike; and also in what respects they are different; after which there is treated, I. Of *Sonatas in general*, the definition of which is: "A Sonata is a piece, chiefly calculated for *one* performer to each part; and it may be compared in instrumental music, to what an *air* is in vocal music."

II. Of the different *sorts of Sonatas* in particular, viz. 1, of Sonatas for *one solo instrument* only, such as for the Organ, Piano Forte, Harp, &c.; 2, of those for one or more *principal* instruments, with some others as *accompaniments*, and the latter as obligato, or ad libitum; 3, of those for one or more *principal* instruments, *without* accompaniments, viz. of concerting Duos, Trios, Quatuors, &c.

III. Of *Sonatinas*, and their different forms.

Chap. III. Of *Symphonies*, the definition of which is thus: "A Symphony is a piece calculated for *more than one* performer to each part; and it may be compared in instrumental music to what a *chorus* is in vocal music." From this definition, which shews a distinct difference between Sonatas, and Symphonies, are then derived all the other particulars of the latter.

I. Of Symphonies *in general*, viz. of characteristic Symphonies, including characteristic Overtures; 2, of free Symphonies, being such as are not to express any prescribed characteristics.

II. Of Symphonies for an *Orchestra;* with regard to subjects; to the distribution of the harmony among the different instruments; and to the number of real, and mere filling parts, introduced in them.

III. Of Symphonies for one, or only a few instruments.

Chap. IV. Of Concertos. They are defined thus: A Concerto is a grand instrumental piece, chiefly calculated to shew the abilities of a player, on a certain principal instrument. It consists of *Tuttis,* in which it resembles a Symphony, and of *Solos,* that are like the principal passages of a grand Sonata; and consequently may be considered as a compound of Symphony and Sonata." To this ought to have been added, that the ancient characteristic of a Concerto was that *concerting* emulation between the different parts, from which it has its name.

I. Of Concertos *in general;* 1, with regard to their length, and character; 2, the number, and nature of their movements; 3, the fancy cadence that is generally introduced in them.

II. Of Concertos, with regard to the principal, and other *instruments,* for which they are set, viz. 1, of those for one principal instrument, called simple Concertos; 2, those for two, or more principal instruments, called double Concertos, Concertantes, and Concerti Grossi; 3, those for one or more solo instruments, without any accompaniments.

Chap. V. Of Fugues in general. By a *Fugue* is understood, " A piece in which one or more subjects are imitated, according to some particular rules, which will be explained." The supposed origin, and gradual perfection of Fugues, is then shewn in a manner, as to give students an idea of their ancient nature, and characteristics; which facilitates the composing of them according to the improvements of modern harmony, and modern instruments. And general explanations are then given, I. of proper and improper

Fugues. II. of strict, and free Fugues. III. of simple, and double Fugues. IV. of Fugues with regard to the interval, in which the answer is made. V. of Fugues with answers in similar, reverse, retrograde, and reverse retrograde motion. VI. of Fugues in two, three, four, and more parts.

Chap. VI. Of simple Fugues, or Fugues on one subject.

I. *Particulars* of a simple Fugue, viz. 1, of the subject, being a short melody, with which it begins, and on the imitation of which, it depends. 2, of the answer, or reply to the subject; with the rules that follow from the authentic and plagal division of the diatonic octave. 3, of the order of the replies, with regard to its varieties, in the different sections of the Fugue. 4, of the counter harmony, or harmony which accompanies the subject. 5, of the intermediate harmony, or harmony between a preceding and succeeding subject or answer. 6, of the different sections of a Fugue, or the connected introduction of the subject and answer, in its different parts; with the intermediate harmony that belongs to it. 7, of the modulation of a Fugue, in general, and with regard to its different sections.

II. *Construction* of a whole simple Fugue, viz. 1, with regard to its sections. 2, with regard to the number, distance, and relation of its parts.

III. Fugues *analyzed* according to the above principles; being four Fugues on one subject, by the Author, and two by other Authors.

Chap. VII. Of Double Fugues, or Fugues of two or more subjects.

I. Of Double Fugues, or those of *two* subjects. These are explained, first as simple Fugues with a double Counterpoint; secondly as Fugues of two subjects, independent of each other.

II. Of Triple Fugues, or those of *three* subjects; with the varieties of principal, and mere occasional subjects, that are useful in them.

III. Of Quadruple Fugues, or those of *four* subjects; with regard to the varieties just mentioned.

IV. Of Quintuple and Sextuple Fugues, or those of *five*, and *six* subjects; with rules for the invention of subjects, calculated for such combinations.

Chap. VIII. Of Canons, or pieces in which the whole beginning part or melody, is imitated by the other parts.

I. Of Canons *in general*; with descriptions of simple and double; resolved and unresolved; finite and infinite Canons; those calculated for one, or more sorts of solutions.

II. Of Canons, with regard to the different sorts of imitations, viz. with descriptions of those in the same or different intervals; with greater or lesser strictness; in equal or contrary (reverse) motion; with equal or different length of the notes; and at equal, or unequal distances.

III. Of Canons, with regard to the *number* and *quality* of parts, viz. Canons for two or more parts, without any accompaniments; for any number of real parts, with one or more other as accompaniments; for two parts, which may be doubled by thirds; or for a certain number of parts to a given melody; with descriptions of each sort.

Chap. IX. Of the Construction and Resolution of Canons. I. Of their *construction*, with regard to *simple* and *double* Canons.

1. The construction of *simple* Canons. This is shewn, *first* with regard to the interval in which the reply is made, viz. in the unison, or second, or third, &c. above or below the subject; and in any combination of more than one of those intervals; also with regard to equal, or any variety of unequal distances, between the beginnings of the different replies. *Secondly*, the motion in which the reply is made, viz. when all the replies are made in the same motion as the subject; or some, or all of them, in equal, reverse, retrograde, or reverse retrograde motion, with all the useful intermixtures of those motions. *Thirdly*, the different lengths of notes, in which the reply is made, viz. in notes of the same length as those of the subject, or by simple and double augmentation, and diminution, with any useful in-

termixture of those different lengths of notes. *Fourthly*, the number and quality of the parts of a Canon, viz. real parts, with their duplicates in thirds, and mere accompaniments or filling parts.

2. The construction of *double* Canons, or Canons on more than one subject, with regard to all the particulars pointed out under simple Canons.

II. Of the *resolution* of Canons, in cases where they are partly explained, or entirely enigmatical.

III. A *survey* of all the Canons given in the work, according to the order in which they stand in the plates; the beginning of which is made with a general Canon in any interval above or below the unison, which modulates through all the degrees of the diatonic scale; and the others are: 1, ten Canons, by the Author, being all on the same subject, on which he has given the four fugues, analyzed near the end of Chap. VI. 2, three Canons, by Dr. Burney. 3, two Canons, by Kirnberger. 4, two Canons, by Eman. Bach. 5, three Canons, by Fasch. 6, one Canon, by Marpurg. 7, nine canons on the Royal Subject, by Sebast. Bach; taken from his work entitled Musical Offering, dedicated to Frederic the Great. 8, five Canons, by Bevin. 9, two, by Handel. 10, one, by Graun.

Chap. X. Of Vocal Music, or music for voices, without, and with instrumental accompaniments.

I. Of vocal music *in general*. 1, with regard to all human voices. 2, to treble, alto, tenor, and bass voices. 3, to the correspondence between the music and the text, viz. respecting the metre of the text, the nature of its words, and even the sort of letters in a word.

II. Of the *different sorts* of vocal music.

1, Of *Recitatives*, or musical declamation, without the form of lyric singing. They are divided into recitatives with a mere bass accompaniment; and those with an accompaniment of other instruments also. In both of them the particulars to be attended to are: their time and rythm, their modulation, and the declamation of their text, with those interspersed airs in strict time, called ariosos.

2. Of *Airs*, or pieces calculated for melodious singing. *First*, the inventing of a proper melody. *Secondly;* the supporting of a melody, with a proper harmony and accompaniment. *Thirdly*, the different forms in which airs may be composed, viz. the *plain song*; the *air*, itself, either as solo song, or as duet, terzet, quartet, &c. without, and with accompaniments; and the *bravura* song, with all its varieties of form, and of accompanients.

3. Of *Chorusses*, or singing in parts, calculated for more than one performer to each part, viz. as Chorusses in which the same words are sung at the same time, by all the parts; and as imitative Chorusses; both of which sorts may be either simple, or double; and also Semi-chorusses; with, or without instrumental accompaniments.

Chap. XI. Of Instrumental Music, or music composed either for any single instrument, or for any number and variety of instruments; without and with the addition of vocal parts.

I. Of instrumental music *in general*, with regard to every particular instrument; and to the combination of different instruments.

1. With regard to every particular instrument, there are explained: stringed bow instruments (the Violin, Tenor, Bass, and Double Bass); and wind instruments (the Hautboy, Clarinet, German Flute, Bassoon, Serpent, Trumpet, French Horn, and Trombono); viz. first, the nature of their sounds; and secondly, the passages for which each of them is calculated.

2. With regard to the combination of different instruments; or, which of them agree together; and which produce the best variety in their combination.

II. Of *certain sorts* of instrumental music in particular.

1. Of that for an orchestra, viz. first, what harmonies, melodies, and passages, are proper for an orchestra; and

secondly, what combinations of instruments are good in the whole, as well as in particular passages.

2. Of pieces for a military band; divided into pieces of duty, and occasional pieces.

3. Of pieces for the organ, in which there is to be considered: the nature of organ sounds; the temperament of its scale; the construction of the keys, or what is calculated for them; the different sets of keys; with the particular use and importance of the pedals.

Chap. XII. Of Style and National Music.

I. The different *Styles* of composition are divided into the Church Style; Chamber Style; Theatrical Style; and style for the Open Field, as in military music.

II. Under *national* music is considered: 1, national music in general, particularly with regard to Italian, German, French, and English national music; 2, characteristic national pieces in particular, viz. the Allemande, Bourée, Ciaconne, Courante, Gavotte, Gigue or Jig, Loure, Passecaille, Passepied, Pastorale, Polacca or Polonoise, Rigaudon, Sarabande, Siciliano, Waltzer; with explanations of the particular characteristics of each of these sorts of pieces.

IV. *A Practical Guide to Thorough Bass*, London, 1801, 76 pages in folio. The Author.

This work practically teaches the use of Chords, in the accompaniment of a figured bass, called a Thorough Bass; according to the system of *Kirnberger*, as adopted in the Author's Essay on Harmony. (See our p. 41.) But it is discontinued printing, on account of that Second Guide to Thorough Bass, an account of which will be given in the sequel; and therefore we shall briefly mention the heads of its contents, as follows:

Chap. I. Of the Scale.—II. of Intervals.—III. of Chords in general.—IV. of the Triad, or Common Chord.—V. of the two Inversions of the Triad.—VI. of the Chord of the Seventh.—VII. of the three Inversions of the Chord of the Seventh.—VIII. of Accidental Chords.—IX. of some other particulars, viz. of the signatures of chords, their number of parts, their highest and lowest position, &c.—X. of the accompaniment of a Recitative.—XI. rules for figuring a Bass, according to its upper parts.—XII. rules according to which the different Signatures of other Authors can be understood.—XIII. of Rameau's Chords by Supposition.—Practices according to the Doctrines of the preceding Chapters.—Six Thorough Bass Lessons, with a Solo Part for the Violin.—Thorough Basses, by six celebrated Authors, as studies of their different signatures.

V. A second Practical Guide to Thorough Bass. London, 1807, 54 pages in folio. The Author.

This work teaches the use of Chords, in the accompaniment of a figured Bass, according to the *Author's* own system of harmony, as set forth in his New Theory; and, we believe, in a more practical manner than the preceding work, as follows:

Chap. I. Introductory explanations, briefly treats of the diatonic and chromatic *Scale;* and of *Intervals*, as essential and accidental, as consonances and dissonances, with their inversions, and their natural and chromatic species; with examples.

Chap. II. Of the Fundamental Concord, or Common Chord, explains the terms fundamental and inverted, concord and discord; the difference between the inversions and positions of a Chord; which notes may be doubled, or omitted in the common Chord; the natural species of it; and its progression, so as to avoid consecutive fifths and octaves; to which are added examples and exercises for the practice of the common Chord, both in writing and performing it.

Chap. III. Of the two Inversions of the Fundamental Concord. Here the first inversion, or Chord of the Sixth, and second inversion, or Chord of the Fourth and Sixth, with their natural species, and their regular treatment, are explained, and exemplified; and practices are added, first for each of those Chords by itself, and then for both Chords and the common Chord, intermixed.

Chap. IV. Of the Fundamental Discord, or Chord of the Seventh. Here the treatment which the Seventh and the Third of this Chord require, are explained and exemplified; with its different species; and its progression in the perfect and interrupted cadence: to which practices, for writing as well as performing, are also added; and a simple rule for the Chord of the Diminished Seventh is shewn.

Chap. V. Of the three Inversions of the Fundamental Discord. These are explained as Chord of the Fifth or Sixth; Chord of the Third and Fourth; and Chord of the Second: with their different species, and treatment; with the addition of practices, for each Chord by itself, and for all the three and the Chord of the Seventh intermixed.

Chap. VI. Of Accidental Chords. These are shewn as arising accidentally, when mere *forenotes*, or *afternotes*, or both, are introduced in the essential Chords explained in the four preceding chapters. I. forenotes (or suspensions) are shewn as arising either from the mere prolongation of a preceding note, or from an accented passing note. II. afternotes, as arising from the anticipation of a succeeding note, or from an unaccented passing note. To this is added, a simple rule for all the Chromatic Species of Chords; and a similar rule for Organ Points, and their inversions.

N. B. As the doctrine of all the above chapters is abstracted from the Author's New Theory, from Chap. II. to IX. a clearer idea of it may be formed from our p. 46, to 53; and a comparison between the Author's doctrine of Accidental Chords, and the doctrines of Chords by Supposition, and Addition, of other Authors, may be made from our p. 53.

Chap. VII. Of the Signatures of Chords. Here it is shewn, first, which are the most *simple*, and most *distinct* signatures, according to the Author's system, and secondly, how the different signatures of other Authors can be understood.

Chap. VIII. Of the Progression of Chords. The knowledge of this is necessary, for the purpose of understanding not only the signatures of other Authors, but also wrong or imperfect signatures; and the regular progression of Concords, and of Discords is shewn. Concerning the latter, the Author explains and exemplifies what is called the rule of the octave, according to his new system (see our p. 54, chap. XII.); and also shews *abrupt* progressions by the interrupted cadence; and gives a simple rule for *sequences*.

Chap. IX. Of other Particulars, viz. the number of Parts in chords; the number of Chords in every bar; how high and how low the Chords may be taken in thorough bass: and how a Recitative is to be accompanied.

Chap. X. Practice of Thorough Bass, according to all the preceding doctrines. This consists first of six thorough bass lessons, with a solo part for the Violin; and then of abstracts from works of six celebrated Authors (Emanuel Bach, Handel, Corelli, Geminiani, Rameau, and Tartini), to shew how their signatures of thorough bass must be understood.

In our next number will be given an account of the Author's *Practical* Works.

XII. Review of Dr. Callcott's Musical Grammar. *
(Concluded from p. 59.)

Sect. IV. of *Modulation.* Here Dr. Callcott limits his * term Modulation to the mere *change* of the *key*, by the use of his dominant seventh; or by a perfect cadence from the chord of the seventh on the fifth of the key, to the key note.

He first explains modulations (changes or digressions) *from* the *Major Scale*, viz. to its fourth, fifth, sixth, third, and second; which he introduces under his French terms, subdominant, dominant, submediant, mediant, and supertonic. One thing which struck us, in the explanations of these changes of key, was, his saying, that a modulation to the fourth only requires *two roots;* that to the fifth, *three;* and that to the submediant, *four* roots; to the last of which he adds, "previous to the alteration of its signature." For in all the three of those changes he introduces the same number of fundamental chords; and we were at a loss how to account for those different *roots.* But we believe that we have found his meaning of them, viz. in Kollmann's Essay on Harmony, under the examples of the different *species* of *medial cadences*, arising from a systematical use of those species of the chord of the seventh, which Dr. Callcott only allows in sequences. (See his previous Sect. III.) For at Kollmann's plate XI. No. 24, we find that the second species, viz. the intervals of the minor triad and minor seventh, require one more chord of the seventh, which, including the resolution, makes three *roots*, till a final close arises; and as that close is there made on G, Dr. Callcott considered that G as the fifth of the C scale, without perceiving that the whole phrase is in G, and the close on the *key note* of its scale. The whole therefore might be made in C, a fifth lower, without any accidental sharp on the root before last.

The second case, or where Dr. C. mentions *four* roots, we find at Kollmann's Plate XII. No. 2, viz. the intervals of the major triad and major seventh, which chord requires two more natural chords of the seventh, and which, including the resolution of the last, makes *four* roots, till a final close arises; and as that close is there made on A, Dr. C. considered that A as the *submediant* of C, without perceiving that the whole phrase is in A minor, and consequently the last close also on the *key note.*

His first, or subdominant modulation, therefore, as he did not find any close in F, in the quoted examples by Mr. Kollmann, he gave only *two* roots; though it has *three* on the same grounds, on which his G has them. And his mediant modulation, and supertonic modulation, he gives no roots at all; because no closes on E, and D, are found in the quoted examples, though those given include them.

Dr. Callcott then proceeds to modulations (changes or digressions) *from* the *minor* scale, to its fourth, fifth, third, sixth, and seventh; which he also introduces under his French terms, except the seventh. And as no closes in these intervals, similar to the above, are found in Kollmann's quoted examples, we also find no number of roots mentioned under these changes of the key.

This section is concluded with the remark: "that the changes there given are the foundation of all *regular* modulation; and that in the chapter of *licenses*, a more *ample* explanation of *irregular* modulation will be found."

But we cannot approve the idea of teaching *irregular* modulation, when the principal object of a treatise ought to be that of teaching only what is *regular*, and how irregularities can be avoided. However, we conceive, that by the term irregular, the Author does not mean modulations which are contrary to rule, but only such as he cannot bring under a *general* rule, and which therefore he allows by particular rules of *licenses*.

Chap. III. Of *Discords*. It is strange, that in the preceding chapter, which treats of those *essential* Discords, without which no change of the key can be decided, Dr. Callcott avoided the term *Discord* as much as possible; and that in the present chapter, which treats only of those *accidental* Discords, on which nothing in modulation depends, and which might be called harmonious *graces* as well as Discords, he speaks of nothing but *Discords*. But we are sorry to observe, that the more he attempts to *explain* harmony, the more he involves the doctrine of it in new labyrinths of *perplexities*, as will appear from every part of the chapter now before us,

The introductory passage of it is expressed thus: "Discords are used in harmony, either by Transition, Suspension, Syncopation, or Addition."

* Sect. I. Discords of *Transition.* This term Transition itself is incorrect, and has, we believe, been first introduced in this country, in the sense in which it here appears, by Mr. Kollmann, who considered it as synonymous with *Transient.* But though he, as a foreigner, was in some measure excusable for it, as long as the meaning of it was clearly defined, it was noticed in the Monthly Review for September, 1796, p. 29, we believe by Dr. Burney, thus: "English Musical Writers do not use the term Transition in the sense in which Mr. Kollmann has taken it, but generally make it synonymous with modulation, or passing from one key to another." We shall therefore endeavour to shew the difference between the meaning of the terms Transition, and Transient, when they are used in a musical sense, as follows:

Transition denotes the *changing* or *passing itself*, from one chord, key, or mode, to another; and *Transient* the *intermediate* notes or intervals, *between* the chord, key, or mode from which we pass, and to which we proceed. To set therefore the plain chord of C major, and immediately after it, the plain chord of F minor, is a *Transition* from the former to the latter chord, and from a major to a minor chord; but this immediate progression contains *no Transient* notes, because in both chords all the notes are essential. And in passing from one position of the chord of C to another, on the same bass, or from one essential note of that chord to another, as in a solo part without a bass, by introducing between its essential notes, those diatonic, or chromatic means, which fill up part of the distance between them, or that whole distance, there is *no Transition*, because the chord remains the same; and the said intermediate, or passing notes, are *Transient* notes. See the following example of the latter case, where the capital letters denote the essential notes of the chord of C, and the small letters the Transient notes: C d E f G a G f E d C b C.

The described incorrectness of the term *Transition*, also

appears from Dr. C.'s own definition of it, thus: "Any note which passes by one degree *between* the other notes of the triad, forms a discord of transition; and if found on the weak part of the measure, is termed a *passing* note." And this period also contains the following other inaccuracies: first, "the *other* notes of the triad," should only be, the *notes* of it; 2, "the *triad*" should be, *any essential chord;* 3, "forms a discord of transition,"—is called transient, or passing; 4, "the *weak* part of the measure,"—the unaccented; 5, "*part* of the measure,"—*time* of the measure. But we should have thought it unnecessary to point out the above incorrections of mere *terms,* if the work before us had not been mentioned, in its preface, as a specimen of what may be expected from the Author's labours, in collecting a musical dictionary, the principal object of which we conceive to be, an *explanation of terms.*

The confusion of *doctrine* concerning the transitions in question, is very great. For at Chap. II. Sect. I. Dr. C. introduced the essential *Seventh* as transition; and here he speaks of passing notes between those of the triad, as transitions. In both cases, he shews what he calls the *root* of the combination; and does not notice that the root of the former is as different from that of the latter, as a question is from an answer. The erroneousness of what he says in a note, concerning the preparation of dissonances, has been shewn before. He introduces Marpurg's regular (unaccented) and irregular (accented) transitions, with the intermixture of both, and considers them as *different* from suspension, and syncopation; though his accented transitions are undoubted suspensions, and his retarding syncopations the same, as will appear from the succeding sections.

In *Sect. II.* Discords of *Suspension* are explained. Dr. C. begins with a note, thus: "While *Rameau* in France, 1722, was *confusing* his system with a *false theory* of these discords, &c." which of course entitles the reader to expect something very clear and correct. But he does not even give a *definition* of those chords; and immediately proceeds as follows:

I. Of the *Fourth.* "The fourth, accompanied with the fifth and eighth, is an appoggiatura, continued in the place of the third, on the strong (accented) part of the measure. It is generally prepared, and is resolved by descending one degree." To this we must make the following objections: 1, the 4, with a 5 and 8, is not always an appoggiatura, but admits of several other regular derivations, and of various regular treatments, different from that shewn. 2. from this it follows, that the fourth, with the 5 and 8, does not always suspend the third, and that consequently it may remain stationary, or ascend, as well as descend; and also resolve into chords, different from those shewn in the examples.

The fourth, as there explained, is what the French school calls the eleventh; but though the Author has adopted numerous terms of that school, he here deviates from its systematical order in the derivation of their intervals, and introduces the eleventh before the ninth, of which he says: "The *ninth*, accompanied with the third and fifth, is an appoggiatura, continued in the place of the eight. It is, like the fourth, generally prepared, and always resolved."

The uncertainties contained in this explanation, are as follows: 1, the ninth of the root is not distinguished from that of the third, fifth, and seventh of the root. 2, it is not said, whether the resolution ought to take place in the same, or in the succeding essential chord, though this is the mark of distinction between a ninth as appoggiatura, and one that is an essential note. 3, it is not shewn that the 9 may regularly ascend, as well as descend. 4, it is also not mentioned into what chord the 9 must, or may resolve. The confusion of doctrine which arises from these uncertainties, is so great, that it would fill several pages to shew the particulars of them.

Dr. C. then introduces an example of the "double suspension of the fourth and ninth, and of the seventh and ninth," which he only says "frequently occurs." But the seventh as suspension, has not been explained at all; and observing merely that a thing frequently occurs, is not yet establishing a rule for the propriety of it. He also says, "The chord of the ninth has two inversions; one figured with a seventh, followed by its resolution, the sixth on the third of the root; the other figured as fifth and sixth on the fifth of the root." But where can a learner find his *chord* of the ninth, when the *ninth* only has been explained?—and where his doctrine of the *root*, when no real doctrine of it is offered in the whole work?

The Author then still adds: "The following tonic pedal or organ point, is a very important study for the chords of *suspension;*" and yet in a note to it he says: "The Abbé Roze shews clearly, that these passages form a species of *supposition*;" when before, he has called Rameau's doctrine of chords by supposition, a *false theory* of suspensions.

III. Of the *Appoggiaturas* of Suspension. Under this denomination, Dr. Callcott brings those suspensions, which, as he thinks, have a greater freedom in their resolution. The cases of these appogiaturas which he mentions, are first: "Any part of the dominant seventh may be retained on the tonic base, and afterward proceed according to its proper motion." But in this there is not the least freedom in the resolution; and the case ought to have been provided for by a general rule of suspension. Secondly, "The ninth also *may* resolve by ascending into the tenth, and the sharp seventh or leading note *must* resolve by ascending into the eighth." In this case also, there is no freedom of resolution, for it ought to be included in a general rule of suspension; and the whole proves the imperfection of the doctrine of that part of the work.

IV. Of *Anticipation*, &c. This, we are sorry to observe, is one of the most unsuccessful parts of the work before us. For Dr. Callcott introduces anticipations as a part of his doctrine of *suspensions*, though they are exactly the *opposite* to it; and though he himself calls the postposition of Dr. Pepusn, which he introduces under the head of anticipations, the *reverse* of them. Nothing therefore can be more contradictory, than what he advances in that respect.

Sect. III. Discords of *Syncopation.* Here the above confusion is continued as follows: the Author says, "the term syncope, or syncopation, signifies the division, or *cutting through* a note by a bar, or accent, expressed or understood." But in the example he gives, there is no such *dividing* of one note; it exhibits the *tying together* of *two* essential notes, and *no* syncopation. All the real syncopations, therefore, which have appeared in his prepared suspensions, in his postpositions, and in his anticipations, he does not notice; and what he exhibits here as syncopations, is a mistake. This mistake is raised to an excess, by his following observation: "The German Authors, previous to the writings of Kirnberger, 1774, seem to have classed the discords of suspension, with those of syncopation; but his arrangement of chords into *essential* and *accidental*, establishes that difference between them, which is adopted in this work." For Kirnberger's syncopations perfectly agree with those of all former good writers on the subject; and Dr. C. perfectly misunderstands him.

Sect. IV. Discords of *Addition.* Concerning this kind of Chords, it must be observed, that they were invented by Rameau, with an idea of giving the imperfect cadence (that from the fourth to the key note), a similiar dissonant Leading Chord, as the perfect cadence (that from the fifth to the key note). As this could not be effected with a chord of the seventh, and yet the leading Chord must be fundamental, he introduced it in the sixth as an *irregular* dissonance, which must resolve ascending, and called the *added*, or supernumerary sixth. This sixth Mr. Kollmann has proved, by Kirnberger's examples, to be a mere *passing* note.

But Dr. Callcott defines his chords of Addition thus: "When any Discord (dissonance), which has not been heard in the preceding harmony (chord), is united to the perfect triad, it is termed in this work a Discord of *Addition.*" According to this definition, every dissonant note, which has not been heard in the same part of the preceding chord, or which, according to the usual term, has not been prepared, is a Discord of Addition; and all the previous explanations of discords are again confounded in this new manner. For even the unprepared *essential* seventh becomes, by this explanation, a mere *added* seventh; and the Author has no mark of distinction between Rameau's chord of the fifth and sixth, where the added *sixth* is a dissonance, and the essential chord of the fifth and sixth, where the *fifth* is the dissonance. He also makes no difference between his added Sixth as *afternote* to the essential, his added Ninth as *forenote* to the essential, and his added Seventh as the *essential* note itself. Some particulars of this doctrine, see as follows:

1, Dr. C. says: "The Discords of Addition are the Seventh, the Ninth, both on the dominant; and the Sixth on the subdominant;" but just before he had made *any* unprepared dissonance a Discord of Addition. 2, under the added Sixth, he says: "As the dominant harmony is distinguished from that of the tonic by its added Seventh, so the subdominant is distinguished from the tonic, and from the dominant, by its added Sixth." This would be the same as Rameau's doctrine of that chord, if the *essential* seventh was not classed among mere *added* or accidental dissonances: but now it is erroneous in a high degree. 3, concerning the *resolution* of the added sixth, he says: "This discord may resolve two ways, viz. into the tonic, (on its second inversion) or into the dominant harmony;" and adds in a note: "Rameau has resolved it also into the tonic base, as an irregular cadence." But this last is the principal case for which the *added* sixth has been adopted, as we have before observed; the first resolution seldom is into an essential 4 and 6, as inverted triad, but into a 4 and 6 as double suspension of a triad on the same bass, which in that case immediately succeeds; and the second resolution is into this latter triad itself. From this it follows, that the first and second resolution on the chord before us, which the Author gives as the *real* ones, are *no* resolutions of the *added* sixth, but of the *essential* fifth and sixth; and that the last resolution *is* the *real* one, if a chord of the *added* sixth should be understood or allowed. 4, what Dr. C. then adds concering the derivation of this chord from *two* different *roots*, according to the major and minor mode, is still another proof of the confusion of his doctrine, which he adopts for the purpose of not allowing the diminished or imperfect triad. (See our No. I. p. 66.) 5, his doctrine of the added Ninth, is as imperfect as that of his added Seventh and sixth.

Chap. IV. Of Cadences. The general definition of them is given thus: " A cadence in harmony consists of *two* distinct chords; the last of which is generally accented, and is used to terminate the sections and periods of musical Rythm." Though the whole of this definition is very inaccurate, we shall only notice the words " is *generally* accented," for this is an uncertain rule, which admits of exceptions; and such ought not to be found in a perfect doctrine.

Dr. C. divides his cadences into *radical*, and *medial*. By the former he understands those in which both chords are fundamental; and by the latter, those in which the first chord is inverted. But this distinction already is erroneous. For *medial* cadences are the opposite to *final*. The latter are those which *always*, and not only *generally* end in the *accented* time of the measure; and the former, those which take place before the final ones, or, as it were, in the midst of a progression, from which the term *medial* arises. These medial cadences therefore are unaccented, when only one of them precedes the final cadence; or alternately accented and unaccented, when more than one of them precedes the final cadence.

In both, the final and the medial cadence, not only the leading chord, but both chords may be *inverted;* and this does not alter the cadence in any other respect, than that it renders the progression less conclusive, than when fundamental. From these inversions of the different cadences, arises the possibility of setting long periods, without making every progression in them a striking close, and the period like a verbal period, composed of nothing but short phrases of two or three words, and crowded with full stops, colons, and interrogations. For what can all harmony be else, than a progression from one cadence to another? And is not this evident, when it is reduced to its roots, or to a regular fundamental bass? But we shall now proceed to the Author's explanation of his cadences themselves.

Sect. I. Of *Radical* Cadences. These are divided into the perfect, imperfect, false, and mixt; with the plagal, and authentic cadence.

Of the *perfect* cadence, Dr. C. says: "It consists of the Dominant Harmony, followed by that of the Tonic;" and "the first or leading harmony is always major." The remarks we have to make on this explanation are as follows: 1, by the *harmony* of a note he always denoted its triad, and here the example of the dominant harmony contains the chord of the seventh; 2, but Dr. C. says, that this harmony is always *major;* is that not speaking of it as of a triad? 3, the perfect cadence on a key note only is shewn; and all its species on the six other degrees are not mentioned, because they would prove medial cadences as above explained, which the Author does not allow; 4, in these medial cadences, the third of the leading chord may be minor as well as major, contrary to the rule given; 5, the fifth also may be minor, and the seventh major, in some of those leading chords, which is not mentioned at all.

Of the *imperfect* Cadence it is said: "It consists of the tonic, followed by the dominant without its added seventh, and is the former cadence reversed." Here it appears, that in the preceding cadence Dr. C. really considered the leading chord as a common chord, and its Seventh only as an *added* note, though it is the modern third harmonic of the root, and one of the most essential notes in harmony. What he says in a note, concerning Rameau's added sixth, proves his great confusion in the doctrine of *added* notes. And when he considers this cadence only as the reverse of the perfect cadence, it is a great error; for its final chord always is the fundamental concord, and cannot be the discord, except when the progression is to continue. He also adds: "the second or final harmony is always major." But though ancient composers generally end even their minor pieces in major, to render the end less depressed than otherwise, this does not constitute a rule that it *always* must be so; and the last chord of this cadence may be minor as well as major, even at a final close. The medial cadences of this kind, which take place on all the other degrees of the scale, are not mentioned; for in them the last of the two chords *must* be minor as well as major, if the progression shall not be chromatic.

III. Under the denominations of the *false*, and IV. of the *mixt* Cadence, the Author introduces one of his most favourite errors, viz. that a *gradual* progression from one fundamental concord to another is allowable. But whenever that progression seems to take place, either the first, or the second chord, or both of them, only *appear* like common chords, and are either incomplete other chords, or some of their notes are accidental fore or afternotes to the essential ones into which they must resolve. (See Kollmann's New Theory, Chap. XII. § 21, and seq.) In the *false* cadence before us, therefore, the first or leading chord is an incomplete chord of the seventh, and the cadence is more properly called an *interrupted* cadence, because it is a mere interruption of the perfect Cadence. And the mixt Cadence either is a mere other species of the former, one degree of the scale lower; or the first chord is an incomplete fifth and sixth; or the first chord a triad, and the second an incomplete chord of the seventh: or similar other explanations may be given those progressions; except that on which the Author insists. Here again it is not shewn, that these cadences are allowable on *every degree* of the scale.

What is then added, concerning the *plagal*, and the *authentic* cadence, must be understood according to the remarks we have made on the imperfect, and perfect cadence.

Sect. II. Of *medial* Cadences. The erroneousness of the term *medial*, in the sense in which it here appears, has been shewn at the beginning of this chapter. And all that is introduced under this head is imperfect, in a similar manner as the preceding doctrine of radical cadences.

Chap. V. Of Sequences, begins thus: "Any similar succession of chords in the same scale, ascending or descending diatonically, is, in this work, termed a Sequence." But this definition is indistinct. For sequences are those harmonious progressions, where a short clause of two or more chords is carried from degree to degree higher, or lower; and they may be as numerous, as the clauses that can be formed for that purpose. (See Kollmann's second Thorough Bass, Chap VIII. § 16.)

The Author then continues: "All sequences are particularly distinguished by the *irregularity* of making the Leading Note a temporary Root, to avoid modulation out of the original scale." But this pretended irregularity exists only in the imperfection of his doctrine, and not in the treatment of that chord, for which he has no systematical rule. (See our No. I. p. 66.) And this fundamental concord, and discord, on that degree of the scale where it has a *minor* fifth, (see the quoted page at the bottom) is not used to *avoid* modulation *out* of the key; but to *enable* us to *remain* in the same key: because, without those two chords, a whole degree of the diatonic major and minor scale would be unfit for general modulation, which would be as bad as throwing away a whole case of a Declension, or a whole tense of a Verb, in a language.

The particulars of this chapter are then brought under the heads of dominant, mediant, inverted, simple, compound, and irregular sequences. But these individual distinctions are as useless, as it would be to give a particular name to every passage, in all other kinds of composition.

Chap. VI. treats *of Licenses.* Of this term the Author gives no definition; but, from the preceding doctrines, we know, that under licenses he comprehends those cases in harmony, which he considers as allowable irregularities. They are brought under the following heads:

Sect. I. Of *Pedal Harmonies.* These are generally called Organ Points; being a holding bass note, (for which the *organ* is particularly calculated) with a series of chords over it, that seem to take irregular progressions. They might have been reduced to the most simple rule, according to the note made concerning the Abbé Roze's doctrine, at the end of *the Ninth*; (Chap. III. Sect. II.) but the Author does not notice it here, where it would have been in its principal place: and, without giving a general rule, speaks of a *tonic pedal*, a *dominant pedal*, the *thirteenth* of Marpurg, &c.

Sect. II. Of the *extreme sharp sixth; Sect. III.* Of *partial modulation;* and *Sect. V.* Of *chromatic* modulation; shew how a doctrine can be confused by individual distinctions; when the whole might have been brought under one simple general rule, as in Kollmann's New Theory, Chap. IV. § 23, 26; and second Thorough Bass, Chap. VI. § 18.

Sect. IV. Of the *Rule of the Octave*, we are sorry to find very erroneous. But our space will not allow us, this time, to enter into the particulars of it.

Sect. VI. Of *Enharmonic* modulation, also does not lay down simple general principles, on which those modulations depend.

Part IV. Rhythm. Though it has been our painful

duty to shew the imperfections of doctrine, contained in the work before us, in Part II. entitled *Melody*, and Part III. entitled *Harmony;* we now can have the satisfaction of speaking in terms of approbation, and even of vindicating some Articles of the part before us, against the objections made to them by Mr. S. Wesley, in the British Critic * for June, 1807, and against the alterations made by that Gentleman in the second edition of the work.

This part IV. treats of Accent, of the Musical Foot; Cæsure; Phrase; Section; and Period. There is a little difference between this arrangement, taken from Koch's Musical Dictionary, and the arrangement of Kollmann's doctrine of Time and Rhythm, adopted from Kirnberger's works, which we do not find so important as to require our enlarging upon it. But we must repeat our objection to the Author's doctrine of musical *measures*, on the grounds mentioned before; (p. 62.) and shall now examine this part of the work, with regard to the alterations made in its examples by Mr. S. Wesley.

Though this Gentleman allows the importance of the knowledge of *Accent*, he does not think, that the appellations of *trochaic*, *iambic*, &c. musical feet, are appropriate to measures with notes of *equal* length; nor that the *same* metrical foot can properly be represented by *different* sorts of notes. But it appears to us, that he takes the terms *long* and *short* syllables of a metrical foot, in too strict a sense; which, if it were necessary to be attended to, would lay vocal compositions under a great constraint, and prevent the introduction of those *varieties* of expressing the *same* words, by which rhythmical *genius* maintains its high rank above mere *mechanical* rhythm. This will appear from the following particulars:

In Art. 504, of the original edition, Dr. Callcott ingeniously introduces a series of notes of equal length, without any division into measures; and, in the three succeeding articles, he shews, how, from those notes, there arise trochaic, iambic, dactylic, anapæstic, and amphibrachic rhythms, by the mere variety of placing the bar, and with it the accent; but, in the corresponding articles of the second edition, (Art. 467, 468) Mr. S. Wesley does not preserve the *same length* of the notes, and *alters* their length according to the idea of *long* and *short*, instead of *accented* and *unaccented* syllables. To this must be added, that, in Art. 508, (first edition) Dr. C. shews the variety of *harmony* which arises from the three last examples, by the mere different placing of the bar; and Mr. W. even alters those examples, to bring in the imagined variety of long and short notes, contrary to the Author's purpose, who in that case was very right. We also cannot approve of the omission of Art. 506, and 509, (first edition) in the second edition.

In *Sect. IV.* Of Emphasis, again two of the original articles are omitted, without any apparent reason.

The above alterations have depended only on the general idea of short and long syllables, or times of the measure, instead of accented and unaccented; in Chap. II. now, of the musical *Foot*, *Sect. I.* alterations begin to be made, according to the particular idea, that the *same* foot of a text, ought not to be expressed *several ways*. The good and very useful varieties, therefore, of the examples in Art. 539, 540, 546, 548, (first edition) are reduced to the one arbitrary idea of long and short syllables only. The whole original page 249, also is omitted in the second edition, without any assigned or striking reason. And in Art. 514, 515, (second edition) the examples are left unaltered, though they are contrary to the rule of long and short syllables before insisted upon.

As we do not find any other alterations made in this Part IV. of the work, except the addition of three examples at the end of Sect. III. Art. 685, (first edition) we must only observe: that, though Dr. Callcott shewed the *similarity* between musical rhythm, and the rhythm of speech, he did *not limit* the latter to notes of a certain fixed proportion of length, but allowed, that the *same* words may be set to music with notes of several rhythmical *varieties*. And in this respect, he has the works of all great composers on his side. We trust also, Mr. S. Wesley himself will allow, that if the same text were set to music by several good composers, every composition might probably contain rhythms different from the others, and yet they all might be right, according to the particular point of view in which the text was taken by each of those composers.

Finally, we beg leave to add, concerning the work in the aggregate: that, though we could not in justice approve of the doctrine of those two principal parts of it, entitled *Melody*, and *Harmony*, nor of the first chapter of Part IV. which treats of *Accent*, we have been happy to find that last part, entitled *Rhythm*, more successful than the others. Concerning the incessant quotations of the works of other Authors, we must also observe, that we are sorry not to find the principal work, from which we know Dr. Callcott to have derived the greatest part of his literary musical information, nor its author, mentioned as much as once; we mean *Dr. Forkel's Allgemeine Mus. Literatur*, (see our p. 3, and p. 82.) And with regard to those eight works, which Dr. C. enumerates at p. 16 of the introduction to the first, and p. 334 of the second edition, and concerning which he requests the favour of any communication: it appears that the Titles also are taken from the quoted work by Dr. Forkel, who gives more information of them, and, we believe, calls only one of them scarce, and deserving to be reprinted.

XIII. *On the Origin, Progress, and present State of Music in Bath,* 1812. *By Favour of a Correspondent.*

At the commencement of the last century, Bath was a place of very little importance, (comparatively speaking) to what it now is.—Its Buildings were miserably poor and mean, and its Amusements were of a very low cast, such as drinking, smoking, and gambling in the ale houses,—with cudgel playing, cock fighting, grinning through horses' collars, hopping in sacks, and bowling. In fair weather, a Fiddle and a Hautboy played on the green, to such as liked to dance.

In the year 1702, Queen Anne paid the city a visit, to which she brought many persons of distinction in her train of attendants. The Duke of Beaufort undertook to regulate the amusements of the superior orders in society, and prevailed upon the company to remove their Dancing Parties from the Green to the Town Hall; on which Captain Webster was appointed to be Master of the Ceremonies. A Band of five wretched performers played to the Ladies and Gentlemen during their promenades in the Orange Grove, which was the fashionable place of resort in fine weather.

At this time, Mr. Nash made his first appearance, and occasionally assisted the Master of the Ceremonies in his official capacity, until the year 1704, when Captain Webster fell in a duel; on which Mr. Nash was appointed to succeed him. A disappointed Physician had endeavoured to prejudice the company against the efficacy of the waters, by publishing a pamphlet, wherein he boasted of having thrown a Toad into them, which had poisoned the springs. Mr. Nash undertook to cure the bite of the doctor's tarantula, and happily succeeded, by the establishment of a Band of Music in the Cross Bath pump room; which band consisted of seven good performers, who were paid One Guinea per week each for their services. This band was afterwards removed to the Pump Room, which was built at the King's Bath; and the number of performers was increased to ten.

On the recommendation of Mr. Nash, in 1708, Mr. Harrison built a Suite of Rooms on the Walks; to which the Balls were removed from the Town Hall. The great influx of company, (amongst whom were the Princess Amelia in 1728, and the Prince of Orange in 1738) was such, as to call for more extensive accommodations than Mr. Harrison's Rooms could supply; and, in 1728, other Rooms were built upon the Walks, by Mr. Thayer, which were successfully rented by Mr. Lindsay and Mr. Wiltshire; to which Rooms, and Mr. Harrison's, the company alternately resorted. In the year 1742, it was found necessary to make certain regulations to be observed by the company; they were published by Mr. Nash, and were indiscriminately enforced by him, over all ranks and conditions, with the utmost rigour.

In 1747, a new species of entertainment was added to those of Balls, Plays, &c. which was that of Breakfast Concerts, at the Rooms. This favourite amusement was supported by a subscription amongst the Gentlemen, who presented tickets to the Ladies; which tickets did not amount individually to more than 1s. 9d. each, and which covered the expense of the Breakfast and the Concert. Notwithstanding the subscriptions and expenses were so moderate, at the annual close of the accounts a very handsome surplus remained, which was generally given to one of the public charities. These Breakfast Concerts continued until the time of Mr. Nash's death, which happened on the 13th of Feb. 1761.

In 1763, a select party of twenty Gentlemen established an *Evening Concert* at Wiltshire's Rooms. Their subscription was one guinea each, which entitled every Member to two admission tickets for Ladies. This concert was of very short duration, as it produced much clamour amongst such of the company who could not gain admittance.

This induced Mr. Linley, in 1764, to open a public subscription, at half-a-guinea each, for fifteen *concerts*, at which he lead, supported by the Pump Room Band, and such Ladies and Gentlemen as were pleased to take seats in the orchestra. *This Concert* was so well received, as to induce Messrs. Richards and Herschel, to set up another; but in which they did not succeed.

About the year 1770, Miss Linley (afterwards *Mrs.* * *Sheridan*), made her first appearance at her Father's Concerts; and sang so divinely sweet, as to charm all who heard her. Exclusive of her great powers, Mr. Linley procured the first professional talents which London could supply; and his selections were such, as gave a meridian splendour to the Bath Concerts. They are now spoken of with rapture, by some who recollect them; amongst whom is the venerable Doctor Harrington, whose opinion may be safely relied on, as he is a man as justly celebrated for his elegant musical compositions, as he is for his learning, and goodness of heart.

In 1771, the New Rooms were built, in the upper part of Bath, to which Mr. Linley removed his Concerts; whereby he opened a door to opposition. For Mr. Wiltshire engaged his rooms to Mr. Rauzzini and Mr. Lamotte. They established a series of twelve Concerts, at a guinea subscription, with considerable effect. Mr. Linley, being thus strongly opposed, and having been refused the Abbey Organ, for which he applied on the death of Mr. Chilcott, he quitted Bath in disgust, and engaged himself in the management of Drury Lane Theatre.

This was the commencement of a New Æra in the Taste of the Bath Audience, which had hitherto been accustomed to the sublime strains of Handel, Corelli, Geminiani, and other masters in the old school. Mr. Rauzzini had been the first serious singer at the Opera, where he was deservedly a great favourite, on account of his fine voice, and elegant action. His talents were not confined to the executive departments of the stage; but he was also eminent as a Composer. Notwithstanding he was so good a Singer, and so graceful an Actor, the capricious taste of a British audience called for something new. To this caprice the managers were compelled to bend; and Mr. Rauzzini was dismissed to make room for novelty.

Thus circumstanced, he had no other means of support,

but by giving Lessons in singing, and undertaking the direction of a Concert at Bath; for both of which he was most happily qualified. His colleague, Mr. Lamotte, was a performer on the Violin, in the first style of excellence; but he soon quitted Mr. Rauzzini.

No sooner had Mr. Linley left Bath, than Mr. Rauzzini removed his Concerts to the Upper Rooms, where he continued to conduct them to the time of his death. In the * course of his 12 concerts, he gave three Choral Nights inclusive, at his usual terms, until the latter part of his life, when he reduced them to nine in number, and raised his subscription to three guineas and a half for one ticket, not transferable, with two, transferable to ladies only; and two guineas for a single ticket, not transferable, and six shillings door money.

His Band consisted of two principal first Violins, two principal second, four first Repienos, four second Repienos, four Tenors, two Violoncellos, two Double Basses, one Bassoon, two Oboes, two Flutes, two Horns, one Trumpet, a pair of Drums, (an Organ on Choral Nights) and a Piano Forte. Independent of this band, he procured from London, Singers and Solo Players, of the first celebrity. Many of the Singers had been his pupils, and seemed happy to exert themselves in the employment of their old Master. He kept an open table for them, which was covered daily with all the delicacies, which the season and Bath could procure. He died on the ninth of April, 1810.

The expensive style in which Mr. Rauzzini had treated his performers, and the difficulty of procuring so much excellence, deterred the professional men at Bath from embarking in Concerts for the following season. Several professors from London hovered about; but Mr. Ashe secured the Upper Rooms, and Mr. Lanza the Lower Rooms, where they both embarked. Mr. Richards, with the Band, were engaged for Mr. Ashe on Wednesday nights, as was Mr. Windsor, to preside at the Piano Forte. Mr. John

Loder, with the same Band, were engaged for Mr. Lanza on Friday nights; Mr. F. Lanza presided at the Piano Forte. Mr. Ashe's Concerts commenced on the 21st of November; and Mr. Lanza's on the 23d.

From three guineas and half subscription, Mr. Ashe rose his to five and half, and eight shillings door money, without any choral night, for nine concerts. This subscription was eagerly filled, under an assurance from Mr. Ashe, that Madame Catalani and Mr. Bartleman, were engaged to sing at his concerts. But neither Madame Catalani, nor Mr. Bartleman, did make their appearance at one of these concerts; which created great dissatisfaction amongst his subscribers. The Name of Catalani had so far ran away with the public opinion, that Mr. Ashe's subscription instantaneously filled.

But Mr. Lanza was not so fortunate, who had announced twelve intended concerts, with a five guinea subscription for three tickets, and five shillings door money. Both concerts were kept up with very great spirit, but Mr. Lanza's receipts did not keep pace with his expenditures. He stopped at the tenth concert, whereby Mr. Ashe was left without a competitor for the ensuing season.

On the 27th of November, 1811, his first concert took place, on the same terms as the preceding season, with a positive assurance on his part, that Madame Catalani was under an engagement to him, to sing at every one of his concerts. She sung at his first, his third, and his fourth subscription concerts, most divinely, and also at his own benefit on Christmas Eve, but not afterwards, for she was obliged to go to London, to fulfil her engagements at the Opera. She would have gratified the Bath subscribers on the fifth night, but was prevented by a most severe cold.

Madame Catalani was the great attraction to those concerts; and to be deprived a second time of her angelic strains, produced strong sensations of offence among the subscribers to whom Mr. Ashe had fully committed himself, under a positive engagement for her singing at the whole of his concerts. Had she been prevented by sickness, every favourable allowance would have been made; and the public would have felt very sensibly for the affliction of a most amiable woman. But when the subscribers were told she had left Bath, and was gone to sing in London, they had just cause to complain.

On seeing his Room so full as it was, during the subscription nights, Mr. Ashe presumed he might have a similar attendance at one concert more; and announced it for the 31st of January, at which he had engaged a very eminent Performer from London, to sing; but so indignant were the company, at having been disappointed, that only 25 persons made their appearance, who had their money returned; and the band who had assembled, were abruptly dismissed. And thus ended the Bath Concerts this Season.

Independent of the *Concerts*, there are other musical establishments in Bath, which demand particular attention. They are the *Theatrical Band*, the *Pump Room Band*, and the *Harmonic Society*.

The *Theatrical Band* consists of nearly the same performers as are engaged at the Concerts and Pump Room; but under a different Leader, who is Mr. John Loder. Mr. Loder's abilities and execution are such as would do credit to a leader of the first Orchestra in England. Under his auspices, the business of the Theatre is conducted with the utmost correctness.

The *Pump Room Band* originally consisted of seven performers, who played from 8 o'clock till 10 in the mornings, during the seasons, which generally lasted 30 weeks. They were encreased in number, to ten performers, as was observed in a preceding part of this account. Their pay was a guinea per man, per week; the fund for defraying which, arose from the subscription to the Balls. About the time of Mr. Nash's death, the Band consisted of Messrs. Fleming, Linley, Herschel, Richards, Rogers, Eve, Milgrove, Shaw, Peck, and Dr. George. Now they consist of Messrs. Daniels, I. Perry, Mumford, Chubb, White, Lyne, Ashley, Rogers, A. Herschel, and Philpot.

Their time of performance is now from 1 till 3; but their number of weeks is reduced from 30, to less than half the number. Not a shilling is added to what they were paid 100 years ago; and they give up every day, two hours of the best part of their time, from their more lucrative professional pursuits. Were it not for the liberality of the Corporation, this Band would inevitably be lost to the Public. Here it may be asked, how comes this to pass? The answer is, what is every body's business, is nobody's business. The Public have been supine, of which the Renters of the Rooms have taken advantage. Instead of paying the full amount of the 30 weeks, under the direction of the Master of the Ceremony, and the Subscribers, out of the Ball money, the Renters have undertaken to carve for themselves, and to allow only £50. from the Upper Rooms, and 30 from the Lower Rooms; leaving the Band and the Public beyond this, to shift for themselves. The Corporation of Bath, under these circumstances, came forward, very handsomely, with £50. per Annum in addition; and a book is laid down in the Pump Room for a few adventitious subscribers.

Had Mr. Nash been living, this would not be suffered. Considering the utility of this band, it certainly deserves a much better fate. The Renters of the Rooms are not so much to blame, as the Company who support them. They should insist upon something being done, to support that, which is the foundation of their most rational amusements. For the Pump Room Band is the best school for music, when the practice of ages has given the best possible effects to the works of the old masters; and where the minds of the afflicted may be amused, and diverted for the moment, from the reflections on their unfortunate situations.

To complain of an evil without pointing out a remedy, might deserve severe animadversion; in order to guard against which, it is here recommended, that every person subscribing to the Balls and Concerts, shall add only Half-a-Crown to the money already advanced, towards the support of the Pump Room Band; which would not only restore the weeks to their original number, but also be adequate to pay each performer Two Guineas, instead of one, for their services.

It is also further recommended, that the Pump Room Orchestra shall be made to project from the wall, instead of following the recess; that it be divided with a curtain, for such Amateurs as might feel disposed to take up repieno instruments unseen, which would not only strengthen the Band, but make it a first-rate school for instrumental music.

The *Harmonic Society* is an institution, which reflects honour upon the City of Bath, not only from the superior excellence of its annual performances, and the respectability of its members; but from the regulations by which it is governed. The first of which is: "The Society having been established for the promotion of Harmony, in its general signification, it is unanimously resolved, that no political discussion, personal altercation, or improper behaviour, can be suffered to take place; and no indecent song, or sentiment, shall be permitted to be sung, or spoken at the meetings, on any account whatever. The least infringement on this rule, (under the opinion of a majority of the members present) shall subject the party offending to immediate expulsion, never to be admitted again, either as a Member, or a Visitor."

The Society was founded by the Rev. *J. Bowen*, on the * 18th of December, 1795. None but Noblemen, Gentlemen of independant Fortune, and those of the Liberal Professions, are admissible as Members, which is by ballot.

On the 5th of April, 1799, H. R. H. The Prince of

WALES honoured the Society with His presence; and on the 12th, He was graciously pleased to signify his pleasure of becoming a *Member*. On the 29th of December, 1803, He was further graciously pleased to signify his pleasure of becoming PATRON of the Society; with permission for each Member to wear a Garter-blue Ribband, with an embroidered Plume over a Lyre, with the motto of "*Curarum dulce lenimen.*" THEIR R. HIGHNESSES THE DUKES OF YORK AND CUMBERLAND, have also been graciously pleased to become Members; whose names are followed by a list of seven hundred of the principal Nobility and Gentry.

The Meetings of the Society are held on Friday evenings, at their room in the White Hart; commencing on the last Friday in November, and ending the last Friday in February. The chair is taken precisely at half past 7 o'clock, by some Nobleman, or Gentleman, appointed by the Committee as President for the week. Fourteen Glees, interspersed with Chorusses, are sung by the professional members, who are the best singers to be procured in Bath, or its vicinity. Their names are: Messrs. A. Loder, Garbett, Burke, Cole, Gattie, Leonard, Comer, Winter, Kirtchel, Chatterly, Masters Beachamp, Wood, and Milsom. Mr. A. Loder accompanies the Glees on the Piano Forte. The singers consist of three Sompranos, three Counter Tenors, three Tenors, and three Basses; by whom the glees are given in a style of excellence, now very rarely to be met with elsewhere.

At half-past nine the ballot for new members takes place; each of whom pays three guineas for the first season, and two guineas for every succeeding season, provided he is in Bath; but if absent, no arrears are called for. At 10 o'clock the Members and Visitors sit down to a cold supper, for which, and their wine, each pays five shillings. All extras are paid out of their general fund. Before supper the following grace is sung; the words by the Rev. * Mr. Morgan, the music by Mr. C. Wesley.

"Seu edamus, seu bibamus,
"Seu quid aliud faisamus,
"Deo gratias agamus,
"Ejusque Laudes concinamus, Amen."

After supper, Byrd's "Non Nobis" is sung; then three toasts only, accompanied with appropriate Glees. The Toasts are: "The King and Constitution;"—"Our Patron, the Prince Regent;"—and "Success to Harmony;" after which are sung such Songs, Duets, Catches, or Glees, as may be called for by the President, until 12 o'clock, when the meeting breaks up with "God save the King," verse and chorus, all standing.

Every member who has paid his subscription, has the privilege of introducing to the meetings one or more visitors, by taking out tickets from the secretary, who attends in the room from 12 till 4 o'clock on Fridays, for the purpose of issuing them; which ticket takes the visitor to hear the Glees; but if he stays to sup, 5s. more is to be paid.

Once in the season the Ladies are entertained by the Society, at the lower assembly rooms, with a grand Gala, consisting of a Concert, a Supper, and a Ball; to which only 400 can be admitted. This entertainment is conducted by a President, Vice President, and twenty Stewards. To defray the expenses of which, tickets are taken out by the Members, at 15s. each, who must write on them the names of the parties making use of them, as well as their own; which effectually prevents improper persons from being admitted. This is confessedly the most splendid entertainment given at Bath, where every thing is conducted with as much order, and ease, as if the party sat down to sup in a private family.

The business of the Society is conducted under the orders of the Founder, Mr. Bowen; and a Committee of twelve members, who are annually elected at a general meeting.

To the above may still be added, that upon the whole there is *much music* going on in Bath. For scarcely a house is to be passed without hearing some vocal or instrumental practice. But we must not be too hasty, in estimating the value of the Quality, from the appearance of Quantity. Professors of the very first abilities may give their lessons, and enforce them by the most elegant examples; yet they would want bread if they did not give way to a vitiated taste, which is introduced for the purposes of astonishment, more than calming the passions, and amending the heart. This wretched taste is become general; and that it should prevail in Bath, is no more than what can be expected.

Here are private musical parties out of number, in small, crowded, hot rooms; where singing, piano fortes, harps, fiddles, flutes,—clattering of cups and saucers, barking of lap-dogs, talking over card tables,—loud laughing, and silly conversations, are jumbled together in the room itself; when from without, it is still accompanied by the thundering raps at the door, and the porter's bawling out the names of the parties squeezing in. All this is called a Concert, to which every body must go, if they wish to be considered as people of fashion. Or if they go to the Public Concerts, their tongues are not to be kept quiet, unless it be when a Catalani sings, or a Lindley takes up his Violoncello.

A very remarkable instance of depraved taste in the audience, happened a few years back, at one of Rauzzini's Concerts. A celebrated performer on the Violin was rapturously applauded and encored, for a paltry Contra Dance, which he gave with much conjuration as a finale to his solo. On the same evening, the 8th of Corelli was hissed, although given in a style of excellence by a Band, very rarely to be met with.—Such is modern Taste!!!

A ray of hope, however, displays itself from the Throne, and gives us reason to think, that this taste is the short-lived Child of Fashion; and that we may yet be witnesses to better things. Our adored and venerable Monarch knew what good music was, and He encouraged it. So does his amiable Son, our beloved Prince Regent. Their examples united, must infuse into the minds of their subjects, a disposition, to feel the sublime Powers of Harmony, in every sense of the word.

N. B. In our next will be given an account of the Organs, Organists, Teachers of Singing, of the Piano Forte, and Harp; and of the Professors of other instruments, Organ Builders, Instrument Makers, Music Sellers, &c.; with their places of residence. *

XIV. Abstract from a Letter to the Editor, dated Edinburgh, Jan. 21, 1812.

Sir,

I should be very willing to give you, from time to time, an account of the state of music, and of musical occurrences in this part of the Island, if music, either in theory or practice were on a respectable footing amongst us. But alas! it is far from being so. Scotland, however renowned for her Poets, Historians, Philosophers, and Warriors, has yet made very little progress in the fine arts. Except our beautiful national melodies, which of late years have been rendered doubly interesting by the exquisite accompaniments of Haydn, and the charming Verses of Burns, we have nothing to boast of, that can be called musical Composition: for though our dance tunes are lively and full of spirit, and much prized by the Natives, who, like most other nations, are passionately fond of dancing, yet those tunes cannot be dignified with the name of Composition.

With respect to the Practice of Music, it is confined almost entirely to the fair sex. The very few Gentlemen who play the Flute, Violin, or Violoncello, take to it too late in life to attain any proficiency. Fathers in general have an absurd prejudice against their sons' learning music, thinking it would lead them to idleness and dissipation: though to men of fortune, and all those who have much leisure, instrumental music always appeared to me the best possible resource against *ennui*, and an antidote to dissipation.

Every man, however, who can afford to buy a Piano Forte, has his daughters taught to play a little; and, among the higher ranks, the French Harp, as well as the Piano Forte is beginning to be pretty common. We have a few young Ladies who can play and relish Haydn, Mozart, and Beethoven; but in general, they are contented with superficial music, and perform it but poorly: while in vocal music, with some very few exceptions, they are still much more in the infancy of the art.

We had, for above half a century, a weekly concert, upon a most liberal and agreeable footing. It was supported by a subscription of the Nobility and Gentry, no tickets were sold, but were given to every genteel stranger that applied for admission. In the outset of the establishment, such of the Subscribers as could play a little, made part of the Orchestra, but those fell off as the music became more intricate; and, during a good many of the latter years of the institution, the performance was entirely professional. From various causes it was given up twelve years ago; and since that time we have had six or eight Concerts annually, chiefly from Mr. Corri, who generally engages a Singer or two, and a Concerto player from England; and in this way we have opportunities of hearing most of the great performers by turns.

You will perceive, from the foregoing short account, that good Music is yet quite an exotic in Scotland; and that it is impossible from this quarter to make any communications at all interesting to the musical Cognoscenti. In the Highlands, there is nothing like music, they are prodigiously fond of the great, noisy, and utterly inharmonious bagpipe!

We have in Edinburgh two good public Organs and a good Chamber one by Snetzler; the rest are but so so. You know, I presume, that in the established Church of Scotland, there are no organs, nor instruments of any description! you will not be at all surprised, therefore, when I tell you, that our psalmody is wretchedly bad: indeed worse cannot easily be conceived, — —.

I am, Sir, &c.

XV. *Abstract from a Letter to the Editor, dated Bristol, Feb.* 14, 1812.

Sir,

Notwithstanding there are many lovers of music in Bristol, and that private musical parties are frequent here, it is perhaps the place of all others in which public Concerts (and indeed public amusements in general) are least encouraged. For the last twenty years past, different professional men of this city have given Concerts, by subscription or otherwise, and have declared it to be a losing concern. Of late years, Mr. Ashe (now conductor of the Bath Concerts) has repeatedly brought forward concerts here, most of which, as well as those conducted by a resident musician, have been by no means destitute of attraction; and yet, very rarely indeed has a crowded room been witnessed on such occasions; and not unfrequently have these performances been so thinly attended, as to bring to one's mind the *Wall Lectures*, read at some Universities.

The *Assembly Room*, where the Concerts are held, (which has for the two last years been let out for public dinners, for sales by auction, and for exhibitions of every kind) is admirably calculated for Music: but too small to contain a sufficient number of persons at the *usual price*, (even when filled) to leave a great profit, after the charges of an expensive Concert have been defrayed. But as the complaint has generally been of the *superfluity*, and not of the *want* of room, this has hitherto been of little consequence.

The building is now turned into a *Theatre*, being fitted-up with Boxes, and a Gallery; by which alteration it will not only hold half as many persons again, than it was formerly capable of accommodating, but it will serve as well as ever for a Concert Room, the Stage being a temporary one, which can with little trouble be removed, and an excellent Orchestra (also temporary) substituted in its place.

In endeavouring to account in part for the *little support* given to Concerts here, and which is matter of astonishment to most people, when the extent, and flourishing state of the City, and also the immense wealth of some of its inhabitants are considered, it must be remarked, that those Merchants, whose great incomes in a peculiar manner give this place the denomination of *rich*, (though their families learn Music) are not themselves musical; and are seldom seen at entertainments of this nature.

The real *Amateurs*, though constant attendants on these occasions, are not sufficiently numerous of themselves, to make an amusement of this kind answer. The inhabitants of Clifton, in the immediate neighbourhood of Bristol, who consist chiefly of that class of society, which may be supposed to possess a taste for every elegant art, or science, would doubtless contribute greatly to the support of Concerts here, were it not for the vicinity of Bath (which is within twelve miles of this place); and, being so near, these people are in the constant habit of going over to the Bath Concerts; consequently they care less about encouraging music in Bristol.

The *Theatre* here is esteemed to be as elegant (though not as large) as any out of London. When there is any *extraordinary* performance here, such as by a Braham, Cooke, or Jordan, it is as well attended as any place can possibly be. But at other times, though open but once a week, (except at the commencent, and conclusion of the season) the attendance is but very indifferent. Alone, this Theatre would not answer; but, in connexion with that of Bath, (as the same Performers, Scenes, &c. serve for both places) the managers find it a profitable concern.

The *Orchestra*, both of the Theatre and Concerts, is composed (in addition to the above-mentioned Bristol) of the Bath Musicians; and the Concerts are sometimes strengthened by some selected from the Military Bands of Regiments stationed here.

Of the *Cathedral* Music I cannot say any thing, having no opportunity of attending the service there The Choir, however, is but a small one, and the emoluments attached to the office of Organist there, are not any thing like so great, as those belonging to the same office in other Cathedrals. The Organ is a fine one, and sounds to great advantage in that building, which is one of the best for music imaginable. If there be any fault in this respect, it is in there being rather too much echo. It is remarkable for being the only Cathedral in England, which has the roof of equal height in every part.

There are several good *Organs* in Bristol; among which, that in the church of St. Thomas was praised by Handel, who tried it when he passed through this city. But the one most worthy of notice, is that belonging to St. Mary Redcliff, the finest Parish Church, in the estimation of all * judges who have seen it, in the Kingdom. This instrument, built by Harris and Byfield, both for its size, and quality of tone, is scarcely inferior to any Organ in the Country. It has three Diapasons, (two open and one stopped) in the great organ. The Bass extends to C, the lowest notes of the modern Piano Fortes, with additional keys, in the Bass. The *lowest Octave* may also be played by Pedals, which put down the keys of the great organ. There is likewise a stop for putting down the octaves (below) of all the notes played.

The Swell of this organ originally went down to C, on the second space in the Bass, and the low notes of the Reed Stops were, as I am told, very fine. It now however extends only to G, on the fourth space. The pitch of that instrument has been lately raised; and it is generally thought, that it would sound to great advantage, if the organ gallery was lowered a few feet. As it is now, the greater part of the organ is above the cieling of the side aisles, whose roof is greatly below that of the middle aisle, in which the organ stands; the sound of course cannot spread itself over the Church, as it otherwise would.

A Gentleman of the name of Antes, who died not long * since, belonging to Bristol, has invented a machine for turning over the leaves of Music, and turning them back again by the same method. He has also improved the Sound Posts of Violins, and Violoncellos, for which he expected to get a Patent just before he died. He was a great mechanical genius, and deserves this our public notice.——&c.

XVI. Remarks on the Artificial Temperaments, &c. invented by Mr. Hawkes, Mr. Loeshman, and the Rev. Mr. Liston.

(Concluded from p. 74.)

THE imperfect and complicated state of an instrument of the above description, and its inferiority to the usual piano forte, is palpable. For, instead of endeavouring to increase its *tone*, and the *simplicity* of its mechanism, our Inventors decrease the former, and render the latter complicated in a high degree. Instead of simplifying the *performance* on keyed instruments, they render their instruments even unfit to be played upon by any person, who is not perfectly *acquainted* with the use of the pedals, according to their intention, and also fluent in the *practice* of using them as required; and young ladies who are not yet tall and strong enough to reach those pedals, and to move them with facility, also are as good as being prohibited performing on that kind of instruments.

How perplexing the use of those pedals is, we have seen even in gentlemen, who publicly recommended and shewed that use; and the perpetual and vexatious embarrassments which arise, either from using wrong pedals, or from obstructions in the mechanism of them, added to their rattling, and to the audible shiftings of sounds, are sufficient to deter any person who wishes to *enjoy* the performance of *music*, from the instruments before us.

Equally objectional also are those piano fortes, in point of *tuning*. For, instead of admitting *any* useful temperament, to which a tuner may be accustomed, or which a lover of music may prefer, two of the strings to each key are to be tuned, like what the *Inventors* call in tune for a certain number of keys; some of the other two strings, so as they call it sharp, and the rest, so as they call it flat; and the numerous tuners who are not acquainted with *that* perfection, and sharpness, and flatness, do not make the instrument answer the inventors' purpose. The same also is the case when the instrument gets *out of tune*, to which its double set of strings renders it more liable, than the usual piano fortes with one set of strings.

To all the above must still be added, the complicated mechanism of the instruments before us, which make them require constant attention to regulation and repair; the more unwieldy state of them than usual, and the greater trouble of moving them only from one part of the room to another, without doing some injury to them; and finally, the greater first price of them, with the continual expense for tuning and regulating them, which they require.

With regard to the *Organs*, according to the inventions in question, it is comparatively the same as with the described Piano Fortes. They must cost double the sum required for a simple organ of the same number and quantity of stops; they cannot but require constant attention to regulation; and the performance on them is as perplexing, and subject to all the vexatious embarrassments, as mentioned under the Piano Fortes.

Concerning the Organ of the Rev. Mr. Liston, Inventor

of the last temperament before us, we have not yet learnt all the particulars; and we believe, that the Essay on Perfect * Intonation, announced by that Gentleman, is not yet published. However, we know, that the above-mentioned apparatus, which is to be applied to the open end of the pipes, requires so high a degree of mathematical exactness, that it would be almost impossible, as well as too expensive, to use it with the lesser kind of stops, such as the Twelfth, Fifteenth, Sesquialtera, and Cornet; and that it can also not be applied to reed stops, and covered pipes. But the intended temperament of this organ also, is produced by means of pedals, similar to those in the two preceding temperaments; and, as far as we are able to judge, this invention seems to be still more intricate, and even less useful, than those others.

We flatter ourselves of having sufficiently proved two particulars, viz. *first*, that no artificial temperament, beyond that which can be produced by the mere *tuning* of the 12 semitones in an octave, is required in modern music; and *secondly*, that even if an artificial temperament was useful or desirable, the three inventions before us would be the least useful, and most awkward means of producing it, that can be imagined, And to the proofs we have offered concerning the latter, may be added, that neither of those three inventions is calculated for *general* use, because they cannot be applied to *large* Organs, and that of the Rev. Mr. L. even not to all stops of a *small* organ.

The inventions in question therefore confute themselves. But, as the necessity, or at least utility, of temperaments of that kind, seems to have been a favourite idea of this country for a number of years, we presume still to offer a few remarks on the *consequences*, which would be unavoidable, if such a necessity or utility were really admitted, and if the above, or other similar temperaments were to become pretty general.

The *first* consequence would be, the abolition of our modern scale, as that wonderful compound of *twelve* Diatonic Chromatic Enharmonic scales *in one*, every note of which is calculated to serve not only in twelve times twelve, but in an almost infinite number of different capacities; and the return of the science of music to that state of *infancy*, where every note is considered only in one individual capacity, and not as a member of that grand compound, on which all the *simplicity* of a perfect doctrine of *harmony* and *modulation* depends. And that this abolition is *not necessary*, we have shewn at page 79.

Secondly, that difference between A flat and G sharp, D flat and C sharp, &c. &c. which violins and violoncellos *can* produce, would still be considered as *proper* to be produced; though it is indisputable that it *ought not* to be produced, if modern harmony and melody shall be as *simple* and *complete*, as it can be. For the more all Voices and all Instruments can *agree*, the better will be the effect; and this can only be done by their general and individual attending to as nearly *equal* a temperament as possible, which is the basis of that true *standard* scale, on which all modern music depends.

Thirdly, all kinds of Flutes, (perhaps even the Fifes) Hautboys, Clarinets, Bassoons, and Serpents, would also be considered as very imperfect, if they could not *produce* a difference between D sharp and E flat, &c. &c. though the greatest perfection in all those instruments must be, if they can *avoid* any such difference, and approach the happy musical period of a general agreement, by being tempered as *nearly equal* as possible.

Fourthly, the mere allowing of a better temperament than that which produces the great desideratum of modern music, a *standard scale*, would prevent, or at least retard, the general adoption of it. For the Violins, Tenors, and Basses would still temper in what was formerly called the *perfect* manner. The Flutes, Hautboys, Clarinets, and Bassoons, each according to their *natural key*. The French Horns, and

Trumpets, as *unnatural* as they could. The Organ, according to former *prejudices;* or according to one of the temperaments before us. The Voices, according to those instruments which predominate in their hearing. And can such a combination of temperaments be allowed as comparable to one of a *general agreement?* And would not that general agreement be produced by a *standard scale*, which the temperaments in question oppose?

XVII. *On the Abbé Vogler's System of Simplification in the Construction of Organs.*

In the preceding article, we have offered remarks on three recent inventions, which, if adopted, would render the construction of organs far more *complicated* than usual; and, in the present, we introduce to our Readers an attempt to render it far more *simple* than it has hitherto been. It is by the celebrated Abbé Vogler, one of the greatest organ players of the present age, who has seen and examined more organs than perhaps any other person; and who likewise professes having made organ building his study for many years. For, though it will appear that this invention also is carried to the extreme, it depends on principles which have attracted the attention of some of the greatest musical philosophers; and therefore we trust, that a description of it will be desirable in the present work. The Author's small tract, from which we have taken it, is entitled: *Data zur Akustic*, Leipzig, 1801, 38 pages in octavo.

The particulars proposed by that invention, are: first, a less expensive, and more judicious *arrangement* of those pipes which are introduced; and, secondly, an *artificial* graveness and fullness of the sounds, by which a great quantity of the pipes, that are otherwise required for the same effect, can be saved. By these means, the Inventor pretends to save *two thirds* of the usual expense of an organ, and still to produce *effects*, of fulness and of gradations in the piano and forte, which that instrument is not calculated for, in its usual construction.

I. Concerning the above *arrangement of the pipes*, the Inventor proposes the abolition of all front pipes; and ranking of the pipes according to their succession in the scale, or to the order of their respective keys.

The *former*, or abolition of all the front pipes, he proposes for two purposes, viz. first, to prevent that interruption in a general plan of architecture, which the usual form of organs makes in a church or other noble building, and to allow the case of the organ a form which corresponds with the unity of the whole, as well as with the style of the Altar, the Pulpit, and other parts of the edifice; secondly, to save the considerable expense of the usual grand front of an organ, as well as to give all the former front pipes a more full and certain supply of wind, than they can have through their wind conductors in a place distant and detached from the Wind Chest.

By the *latter*, or ranking of the pipes according to the order of their respective keys, he endeavours to produce the following advantages: first, a more simple mechanism, which renders the touch of the organ less heavy than usual; secondly, a better effect, than the instrument can have in its usual construction, to those who hear it close by, when F sounds here, F sharp in an opposite place, C in one corner, and C sharp in another, according to the former symmetrical distribution of the pipes.

By the *combination* of the above alterations, the Inventor also answers the purpose of being able to construct the *case* of an organ, so as to make it perfectly *enclose* the sounds on all sides; and to force them to *ascend* before they reach the ear, in a manner which unites and strengthens them, and which takes away their usual roughness.

Though all the above seems very plausible, it may be observed: first, that *hearing* an organ, which produces almost all the effects of a grand orchestra, and *seeing no pipes* which can be imagined as producing those sounds, or behind which numerous others can be supposed to stand, appears very unnatural; and that all the proposed advantages might be gained by a noble front of *false pipes*. Secondly, what has been mentioned concerning the rules of Architecture in a building, cannot be strictly attended to, even in *new* organs. Thirdly, the usual *symmetrical* order, in which the pipes of an organ are ranked, does not produce so striking an effect, even close by, as the Abbé V. thinks; and, at any distance, it is not perceptible at all. But fourthly, *enclosing* the sound on all sides of the organ case, except the top, seems to deserve attention; particularly in a building where this directs them towards a cupola, which strengthens them, as is described in the quoted tract.

II. The *artificial graveness* of organ sounds, mentioned before, depends on Tartini's doctrine of a *third sound* which two others *generate*, as their root or ratio 1, when their ratios are aliquot parts of it; and these aliquot parts are the ratios $\frac{1}{2}$ $\frac{1}{3}$ $\frac{1}{4}$ $\frac{1}{5}$ $\frac{1}{6}$ $\frac{1}{7}$ &c. of a fundamental note as ratio 1. As this principle, if it could be applied to that use which the Abbé V. endeavours to make of it, would be of the utmost importance in organ building and organ playing, we shall endeavour to give it our particular consideration.

It is unquestionable, that *any* two notes, whose ratios are *aliquot* parts of a common generator as their fundamental note, generate that fundamental note, as a third note, when they are *in tune*, and well *sustained*, in a *quiet* place of *good resonance*. But the ratios which are most calculated for the Inventor's purpose, are those most *simple* ones, which nearest approach to unity, and to each other, viz. $\frac{1}{3}$ $\frac{1}{5}$, $\frac{1}{5}$ $\frac{1}{6}$, $\frac{1}{6}$ $\frac{1}{7}$; and the reason why he omits among them $\frac{1}{2}$ and $\frac{1}{4}$, is: because the third note, which is generated by their assistance, is not so striking as otherwise, on account of its being a mere lower duplicate of one of them. But he allows: that when C two lines below the bass stave is sustained with its fifth G on the first bass line, the C an octave below the first is distinctly heard.

According to the above principle, G on the fourth space of the bass stave, with E on the first treble line, generate C two lines below the bass; E G on the first and second treble line, generate the same C; and the latter G, with that over flat B on the third treble line, which is the true harmonic Seventh of C, again generate the same lowest C.

But the Abbé V. maintains, that two notes of the above description generate their fundamental note so distinctly and fully, as to make that fundamental note alone to be heard, and their notes, as it were, lost in it; and that this would be the case with all organs, and in all kinds of organ performances. This experience, he says, is founded on the following arguments:

"When, on a monochord, the lowest violoncello C is divided into three equal parts, there arises the lowest violin G; and, when it is divided into five equal parts, there arises E on the first treble line. The C is the whole to its third part G, and to its fifth part E. In the same manner as the sound of the whole includes the notes of its $\frac{1}{3}$ and $\frac{1}{5}$; there also is heard the note of the whole, when only its third part and fifth part are sounded," &c.

But, though it is indisputable, that every sounding body which continues its sound, includes in its principal note one or more of its harmonics as secondary notes; our ear can distinguish it only in *full* and *grave* notes: and even then, the secondary notes are heard very *faintly*, in proportion to the principal note. And it is equally certain, that when two harmonics generate their fundamental note, as before described, that generated note also is not only very faint in proportion to its generators, but also requires a little time till it can be distinctly perceived; and therefore its use, in the manner proposed by the Inventor, is both against reason and experience.

The above will also appear, from the following explanation of the phenomena in question, taken from *Dr. Chladni's Akustic*, Leipzig, 1802, Art. 168 and seq. (See our p. 83.) *
"The generation of a lower note, when two higher notes *

are sounded together, may be produced with all sorts of sonorous bodies. For the ear perceives not only the proportion between the vibrations of the two sounding notes, but also the *coincidence* of those vibrations, in the same manner as it would feel an independent sound, whose vibrations should be equal to the times of those coincidences. We hear, therefore, the additional sound of a lower note, whose ratio is 1, when the two really given sounds are expressed by the lowest terms of their ratios. I shall exemplify this with dots, by two notes whose ratios are $\frac{1}{4}$ and $\frac{1}{5}$; the higher row denotes the vibrations of the more acute, the second row those of the more grave given note, and the lowest row the coincidence of both vibrations, at every fifth vibiation of the highest, and every fourth vibration of the second note, which coincidence is heard as a separate note, whose vibrations take place at those slower spaces of time.

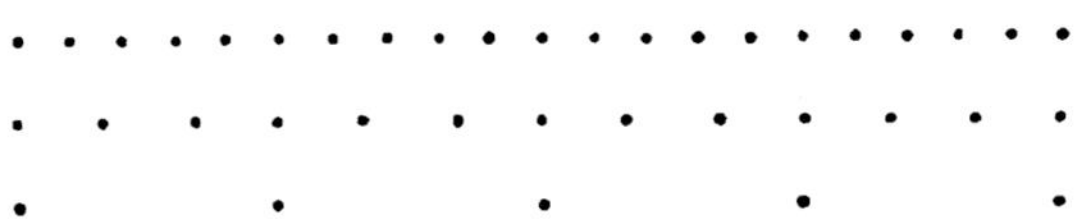

" If such a lower note shall be distinctly heard, it is necessary, that the two given notes continue, and have nearly the same strength; and that they are either perfectly in tune, or but a very little deficient in that respect: also that the greatest quietness prevail. It is most perceptible with the major third, when, as expressed by the above example of dots, the double octave below, of the lower note, is generated; but also with the minor third, when the generated lower note is two octaves and a major third below: and when the minor third is so flat, that it contains the proportion of 6 to 7, the generated lower note is two octaves and a fifth below the given lower note.

" When two given notes are related in such a manner, that the coincidences of their vibrations are very distant, this coincidence is heard only as single *beatings*, which, when an instrument is out of tune, or when it is tempered very unequally, are offensive to the ear. The more an interval approaches its arithmetical perfection, the less perceptible are those beatings; and they loose themselves at last in the sensation of a soft generated lower note. A *good temperament* therefore requires, that the necessary deviation from arithmetical perfection, is never carried so far, particularly not in *consonant* intervals, as to be heard like single beatings.

" This generation of a lower note has been made known, first by *Romieu*, who gave an account of it to the Society of Sciences, at Montpellier, in 1753; and then by *Tartini*, in his *Trattato di Musica secondo la Vera Scienza dell' Armonia*. Padova, 1754. The best remarks upon it may be found in the Recherches sur le Son, by *La Grange;* in *Miscellan. Tauriens*, tom. I. § 64; and in *Mathew Young's* Enquiry into the principal Phenomena of Sounds and Musical Strings, Part II. Sect. VI. of grave harmonic tones. *Sarti*, Maître de Chapelle, at Petersburgh, has made judicious experiments with this phenomenon, to determine the number of vibrations of a note; an account of which may be found in *Voigt's* Magazin, &c. No. I. p. 102. (German)."

[*To be Continued.*]

XVIII. A Quarterly Catalogue of Musical Publications, Inventions, &c. *

N. B. Publishers, Authors, and Inventors, are requested to send an early account of their productions, and also of works and inventions in hand, which will be attended to, gratis, in this catalogue.

I. Publications of *Theoretical Works.*	*s.*	*d.*	
Beale. A complete Guide to the Art of the German Flute.	8	0	
Crotch, Dr. Elements of Composition —— ——	18	0	*
Loder. General Instruction Book for the Violin ——	10	6	
Stevens. Treatise on Piano Forte Expression. ——	10	6	
II. Publications of *Composition.*			
Ashley. Twelve Duets for two Flageolets or Flutes ——	3	0	

		s.	d.
*	*Beethoven.* "Les Adieux, &c." Sonate Characteristique. P. F.	6	0
	——— "Anxiety of Absence." Ariette. Voice & P. F.	2	0
	——— "The distant Lover." ditto ditto ditto.	1	6
	Bottomly. Three Airs with Variations. P. F. ———	5	0
	Carnaby, Dr. Six Songs. Book I. ——— ———	10	6
	——— Six ditto. Book II. ——— ———	10	6
	Chappell and Co. National Melodies, as Rondos, &c. Nos. I. II. III. each. ——— ———	2	6
	Chianchettini, Veronica. Delassement Champêtre. P. F.	2	6
	Clarke, Dr. Love and Harmony. A Canzonet. ———	1	6
	Clementi and Co. Collection of Rondos, &c. P. F. No. 48.	3	0
*	*Cooke,* M. "Dear Grize." A Song in the Five Lovers.	1	0
	Cooke. T. "Dreary was the Day." A song in ditto. —	1	6
	Cramer. Favourite Sonate, P. F. with accompaniment for the Flute. ——— ——— ———	3	6
	——— New Grand Sonate. P. F. ——— ———	4	0
	Von Esch. Divertissement Turque, &c. P. F. ———	3	6
	Gildon. Favourite Duet. P. F. ——— ———	2	6
*	*Gilon* Grand Military March. P. F. or Harp. ———	2	0
	Haigh. "Juliana." Air arranged as Rondo. P. F. —	2	0
*	*Hodsoll.* Collection of Duets. P. F. No. 24. arranged by Rimbault. ——— ——— ———	2	6
	Holder, Mus. Bac. Oxon. Sonata. P. F. Op. 34. ———	3	6
	Hook. Introduction and Polacca. P. F. or Harp, with Flute accompaniment ——— ——— ———	2	6
	King. "Oh never." Glee for Three Voices. ———	3	0
	Knyvett. "O stay sweet Warbling Woodlark." Glee for four Voices. ——— ——— ———	2	0
	Kreusser. Sonata. P. F. ——— ———	4	0
	Mazzinghi. "Lochgyle." A Glee for four Voices. —	2	6
	——— "Robin Adair." Irish Ballad. Voice and Harp.	1	6
	Moore, Thomas, Esq. A Melologue upon National Music.	3	6
	Moore, J. "Lord Wellington." Pandean Air as Rondo. P. F.	2	0
	Mugnié. "Quand le bien aimé." With Introd. & Var. P. F.	5	0
	Netherclift. 24 Psalms and Hymn Tunes ———	2	6
	Panormo. "Utile Dulci" Divertimento. P. F. ———	4	0
	——— Neapolitan Villagers. Air with Var. P. F. —	2	0
	Parry. "The Reply." P. F. ——— ———	1	6

	s.	d.
Parry. " Munster House." Rondo. P. F. or Harp. —	1	6
——— " Robin Adair." Air ——— ———	1	6
Smith, Theodore. Duet. P. F. ——— ———	4	0
Taylor, Abraham. " The Soldier's Dream." Song with P. F.	2	0
Taylor, Samuel. 2d. Set of Six Divert. German Flute.	5	0
Latour. " La Replique." Divert. P. F. & Flute ad libit.	4	0
Walker. " Rans des Vaches." Trio with Accompaniments.	3	0
Webbe, S. Jun. " The Lord's Prayer." ———	1	6
Whitaker. Songs and Duets in " Up to Town." ———	6	0

III. *Inventions.*

Mr. *Erard,* of Great Marlborough Street, has produced his Patent * Harp, with pedals for Sharps and Flats to all the seven notes of the Diatonic Scale. This invention, if it perfectly answers its purpose, will be a great acquisition in its respective instrument.

Mr. *W. Bundy,* of Camden Town, London, has produced a Patent * Piano Forte, the invention of which consists in covering all the strings with platina wire, in order to add to their elasticity a greater specific gravity, than otherwise; which the inventor says, is found to encrease the purity and power of tone, in proportion to the quantity used of that heavy metal.

We are glad to find, that the Patent of *Mr. Riley's* piano forte, mentioned at p. 26, No. 6, has been sold to Messrs. *John Broad-* * *wood and Sons*; whose excellent manufactory certainly will produce it in the best perfection, for which it is calculated.

Two inventions at *Bristol,* have been mentioned, page 48.

IV. *Lectures* have been read, by *Dr. Crotch,* at the Surrey In- * stitution; and by *Dr. Kemp,* at the Great Assembly Room, Cateaton Street.

XIX. To the Editor of the Musical Register.

SIR,

I should esteem it a particular favour, if you, or any of your correspondents, could oblige me with information relative to some ancient English Airs I lately met with in a small book, published, I think, in the 17th century. I send you the initiatory lines of the words. * What I am desirous to see, or hear of, is the full complement of the harmony, as this publication only contained the mere melodies.

I am, Sir,

Your well-wisher,

An AMATEUR.

"Who doth behold my mistress' face."
"How now, shepherd?"
"When from my love, I looked for love."
"Begone, sweet night."
"Brave Man begins to rouse."
"With my love, my life was nested."
"You minor beauties of the night."

XX. *Explanation of the Musical Pieces given in No. II.*

* At Page 6 of the plates, see a ***Sacred Song*** for one or three voices, in the ancient ecclesiastical mode of D. This is neither the modern mode of D major, with two sharps, nor that of D minor, with one flat, but the mode of D without any sharp, or flat at the clef, called the ancient ***dorian*** mode, as explained in Kollmann's New Theory, and in his Essay on Harmony. But accidental sharps or flats, which do not obscure its characteristic modulations, are as allowable in this mode, as in the modern major or minor.

At page 8, see a ***Family Piece***, as Rondo for two Performers, the one to play with both hands, and the other with the right hand only It may be played either by the same performer throughout, or employ 3,4,5, and more performers, in the following manner: at 1 the first performer begins, and at 2 the second performer joins him. Where there stands 1 off, the first leaves the instrument, and the second takes the two lower staves, whom the third joins at 3. Where there stands 2 off, the second performer leaves the instrument, and the third and fourth play the beginning as 1, 2, before. Where the first left the instrument, the third now does the same; and the fourth and fifth performer continue, as indicated by 4, 5. Where there stands 4 off, the fifth and sixth performers play the beginning, as 1, 2, and 3, 4, have done it before, and end at the term ***Fine.*** N. B. instead of 5, and 6, the first and second performers may come in again; and to bring in ***more than six*** performers, the piece may be repeated. In the latter manner, a ***whole school*** may be agreeably employed by this piece.

Concerning the ænigmatical ***Canon*** on the title page, which has been explained at p. 80, the Editor will be happy to receive the solutions that may be found, by some of our Readers; and to notice them in this work.

A SACRED SONG FOR ONE OR THREE VOICES

In the antient ecclesiastical Mode of D.

The words by MERRICK

The music by A. F. C. KOLLMANN.

N.B. the second and third Voice as in the Piano Forte part.

2. Let faith |:* suppress:| each rising fear,
Each anxious doubt exclude;
Thy Maker's will has plac'd thee here,
A Maker wise and good.

3. He to thy |: ev'ry :| trial knows
Its just restraint to give;
Attentive to behold thy woes,
And faithful to releive.

4. Though griefs and |: troubles:| throng thee round,
Still in thy God confide;
Whose finger mark's the seas their bound,
And curbs the headlong tide.

* The words between dotted bars thus |:—:| are those to be repeated in the first line.

A FAMILY PIECE.

By A.F.C.KOLLMANN.

See the explanation at Page 160.

D.C. 4
D.C. 3
2 off
4
D.C.6
D.C.5
8
4 off

To be published by Subscription,

A SECOND EDITION

OF AN

ESSAY ON PRACTICAL MUSICAL COMPOSITION,

WRITTEN,

AND MOST HUMBLY DEDICATED BY PERMISSION, TO

His Majesty,

BY A. F. C. KOLLMANN,

ORGANIST OF HIS MAJESTY'S GERMAN CHAPEL, ST. JAMES'S.

Mr. KOLLMANN respectfully acquaints the Public, that a Second Edition of the above Work, which has been out of print these seven years, is now ready for Publication, with considerable Additions and Improvements; and that it will be put to press, as soon as one hundred copies are subscribed for.

The Contents are as follows:

Introduction:—Of the Method according to which Harmony and Composition should be studied. Chapter I.—Of the Plan for a piece to be composed. Chap. II.—Of Sonatas, without and with Accompaniments; including Solos, Duos, Trios, &c. Chap. III.—Of Symphonies, and Overtures. Chap. IV.—Of Concertos. Chap. V.—Of Fugues in General. Chap. VI.—Of simple Fugues. Chap. VII.—Of Double Fugues, or Fugues of two and more Subjects. Chap. VIII.—Of Canons in general. Chap. IX.—Of the Construction and Resolution of Canons. Chap. X.—Of Vocal Music in general, and with regard to Recitatives, Airs and Chorusses. Chap. XI.—Of Instrumental Music, with regard to every particular Sort of Instruments, and to any Combination of different Instruments. Chap. XII.—Of Style and National Music.

The Work will make one Volume in Folio, as before.

Price to Subscribers, One Guinea and a Half; to be paid for on delivery. To Non-Subscribers, Thirty-six Shillings.

The Names of Subscribers will be received by the Author, MR. KOLLMANN, *(Friary, St. James's Palace;)* and at the principal Music-Sellers. Where may be had, lately published by the same Author:

	£.	s.	d.
A New Theory of Musical Harmony, - -	1	11	6
A Second Practical Guide to Thorough Bass, -	0	10	6
Twelve Analyzed Fugues, with Double Counterpoints in all Intervals, for two Performers on one Piano Forte or Organ. Op. X. - - - -	0	15	0
The Melody of the Hundredth Psalm, with Grounds and Directions for an Hundred different Harmonies, in four parts, - - - - - -	0	3	0
A Rondo on the Chord of the Diminished Seventh, shewing the immediate Progression of that Chord to all the twelve Major and Minor Keys, -	0	1	0

THE
QUARTERLY
MUSICAL REGISTER.

THE EDITOR of this Periodical Work respectfully acquaints the Public, that the four Numbers, which are intended to be published yearly, viz. on the first day of the months of January, April, July, and October, will form an Annual Volume; and that a Title, and Index, will be given with the last Number.

Concerning its Contents, he begs leave to observe: that his first and principal object is, to bring the opposite Doctrines, of the Musical Treatises, recently published, under a fair public investigation; because on the improvement of Musical Knowledge undoubtedly depends that, of the Practice of Music, both in Composition, and Performance: and that Reviews of Compositions also will be given, according to the principles pointed out in the Introduction. (Page 2.)

With regard to the state of Music on the Continent, it will be found, that though the existing difficulty of correspondence deprives the Editor for the present of those regular communications, which he has to expect, as soon as the intercourse shall be open again; he is sufficiently provided, during the interim, with such important foreign articles, as will be equally interesting as new ones, and form an useful introduction to those succeeding occurrences, which will be noticed as soon as possible.

5. Notes to the Text of *The Quarterly Musical Register*

The following annotations amplify passages in *The Quarterly Musical Register* that begin on lines with asterisks in the outer margin of the facsimile. Italic numerals refer to this journal's pages. Each person mentioned in *The Quarterly Musical Register* is entered in the index at the end of this book.

p 4–6: Reviews in English periodicals at this time generally were printed anonymously, and Kollmann's identification of music reviewers here appears to have been the first public disclosure of their names. Several of his attributions have been confirmed. Charles Burney's contributions to *The Monthly Review* from November 1785 to June 1802 were marked by its editor, Ralph Griffiths, on his copy of the journal, now Bodleian Per. 3977 d.190.[46] According to Roger Lonsdale, Burney 'frequently arranged for his friends and relations to review for' *The Critical Review* and is known to have written at least one review for it.[47] John Wall Callcott told Kollmann that he was reviewing for *The British Critic* in Callcott→Kollmann, 30/4/1801, and listed his reviews in that journal from 1800 to 1802 in what is now BL Add Ms 27669 f 43^v–44^r. Samuel Wesley referred to his *British Critic* review of Callcott's *A Musical Grammar* in Samuel Wesley→Charles Wesley Jr, 21 March 1807 (*LSW* p 51–54; *SWSB* p 227–228).

p 6: Kollmann's information about this journal is incorrect. When first issued in March 1809 it was called *The New Musical Magazine, Review, and Register of valuable musical publications*.[48] From September 1809 (v 1 no. 7) the word '*New*' in its title was replaced by '*Royal*', in consequence of the journal receiving 'the immediate patronage' of the Prince of Wales. Its last number

---

[46] See Benjamin Christie Nangle, *The Monthly Review First Series 1749–1789, Indexes of Contributors and Articles*, Oxford, 1934; *ibid.*, *The Monthly Review Second Series 1790–1815...*, Oxford, 1955; and Roger Lonsdale, 'Dr Burney and the *Monthly Review*', *Review of English Studies* n.s. v 14 no. 56 (November 1963) p 346–358 and n.s. v 15 no. 57 (February 1964) p 27–37.

[47] Lonsdale, *op. cit.*, v 14 no. 56 (November 1963) p 347.

[48] A copy of v 1 no. 1–8 including the wrappers is at BL R.M. 8.a.2. A copy of all the numbers but lacking the wrappers is at Boston Public Library **M.167.4.

(v 2 no. 1) appeared in March 1810. Although several of Joseph Kemp's compositions were published in this journal, most of its engraved music was by other composers.

p 8: Kollmann's 'two New Systems of Harmony' are the ones he adopted in *An Essay on Musical Harmony* and *A New Theory* respectively. These systems are outlined in part I of this book.

p 8: The preface of William Crotch's treatise is dated 6 January 1812. It was published in time to be noticed on *p 157* of the second number of *The Quarterly Musical Register* (see the annotation to *p 157* on page 216 below).

p 8: Crotch gave courses of lectures on music at the Royal Institution from 1805 to 1807, followed by John Wall Callcott in 1808 and Samuel Wesley in 1809.[49] Wesley lectured at the Surry Institution in 1809 and 1811.[50] Richard John Samuel Stevens was elected to the musical professorship of Gresham College in 1801.[51] Crotch's lectures at the Surry Institution began on 4 February 1812.[52]

p 8: Kollmann had expressed his view that university exercises should be published in Kollmann→Callcott, 28/8/1800.

p 9: The first three volumes of [Muzio] *Clementi's Selection of Practical Harmony, for the Organ or Piano Forte; containing voluntaries, fugues, canons & other ingenious pieces, by the most eminent composers* were published in 1801, 1802 and 1811. The fourth and last volume was published *c*1815.[53]

---

[49] See Jamie Croy Kassler, 'The Royal Institution music lectures, 1800–1831: a preliminary study', *Research Chronicle* [Royal Musical Association] no. 19 (1983–1985) p 1–30 at p 14–16; and Samuel Wesley→William Savage, 28 February 1809 (*LSW*, p 98; *SWSB*, p 252).

[50] *SWSB*, p 39, 42.

[51] Mark Argent (ed.), *Recollections of R. J. S. Stevens, an Organist in Georgian London*, London, 1992, p 118–122.

[52] *A Journal of Natural Philosophy, Chemistry, and the Arts* [called 'Nicholson's *Journal*', after its founder, William Nicholson] v 31 (February 1812) p 160.

[53] Alan Tyson, *Thematic Catalogue of the Works of Muzio Clementi*, Tutzing, Germany, 1967, p 103.

p 9–10: England's awakening interest in J. S. Bach's music is discussed extensively in *EBA*.

p 11–12: Kollmann's quotation is taken, but not verbatim, from Beilby Porteus, *A Charge delivered to the Clergy of the Diocese of London, at the Primary Visitation of that Diocese in the year MDCCXC*, London, 1790, p 17. Kollmann omitted Porteus's acknowledgement that he had borrowed the phrase 'forms one of the grandest scenes of unaffected piety that human nature can afford' from John Brown, *A Dissertation on the Rise, Union, and Power, the Progressions, Separations, and Corruptions, of Poetry and Music*, London, 1763, p 214.

p 12: Kollmann's story that King Charles IX danced to the tune of the 129th psalm has been repeated subsequently, notably by Carl Engel, 'The literature of national music (continued)', *The Musical Times* v 19 no. 428 (1 October 1878) p 531–535 at p 532, and again in his *The Literature of National Music*, London, 1879, p 37. However, corroboration of this story in sources prior to 1812 has not been found, and Engel, who owned at least one work from Kollmann's library (see page 180 above), might have got this story from *The Quarterly Musical Register*.

p 13: In 1803, Reginald Heber won, for his poem 'Palestine', Sir Roger Newdigate's Prize for the best verse composition by an Oxford undergraduate. Crotch's oratorio received its first performance at the Hanover Square Rooms in London on 21 April 1812.[54]

p 13: von Winter's operas first performed in London are *La grotta di Calipso* (1803), *Il trionfo dell'amor fraterno* (1804), *Il ratto di Proserpina* (1804) and *Zaire* (1805). All were written to librettos by Lorenzo Da Ponte.

p 13: Mozart's operas *Così fan tutte* and *The Magic Flute* received their London premieres in 1811.[55]

---

[54] Jonathan Rennert, *William Crotch (1775–1847), Composer, Artist, Teacher*, Lavenham, Suffolk, 1975, p 52.

[55] William C. Smith, *The Italian Opera and Contemporary Ballet in London 1789–1820*, London, 1955, p 107–111.

p 13: An English opera house was established by Samuel James Arnold (son of Dr Samuel Arnold) at the Lyceum Theatre in 1809.[56]

p 13: *Artaxerxes*, by Thomas Augustine Arne, was first performed in 1762.

p 13: Himmel's opera *Alessandro* was first performed at St Petersburg in 1799. From 1795 he was Kapellmeister to King Frederick William II in Berlin, where he collaborated with the dramatist August Wilhelm Iffland—who was appointed director of the Prussian national theatre in 1796—on a plan to develop a national opera there. Kollmann inscribed a copy of his 1799 *An Essay on Practical Musical Composition* to Himmel. As Iffland and Kollmann apparently had been classmates at the Hannover Lyceum (see pages 7–8 above) it is plausible that Kollmann's connection with Himmel arose through Iffland.

p 15: Few English organs at this time had pedals.[57] Charles Frederick Horn and Samuel Wesley therefore adapted Bach's organ trio sonatas for 'three hands upon the piano forte' in their edition of BWV 525–530 (London, 1809–1810). The only other work by Bach that Wesley and Horn edited jointly was the '48' (London, 1810–1813).

p 16: Charles Burney, *An Account of the Musical Performances in Westminster-Abbey, and the Pantheon ... in commemoration of Handel*, London, 1785.

p 17: Himmel's 'Trauer-Cantate zur Begräbnisfeyer seiner Köninglichen Majestät Friedrich Wilhelm II' was composed shortly after the king's 1797 death.

p 17: The violinist Charles Weichsel led the Opera orchestra at the King's Theatre, Haymarket. The famous soprano Elizabeth Billington was his sister.

p 18: Performances of Italian operas began at the Pantheon theatre on 27 February 1812 but lasted there for only a short time.[58]

---

[56] See Michael Kassler (ed.), *Charles Edward Horn's Memoirs of his Father and Himself*, Aldershot and London, 2003, p 38–41.

[57] See Charles W[illiam] Pearce, *The Evolution of the Pedal Organ and matters connected therewith*, London, 1927, especially p 30–33.

[58] Smith, *op. cit.*, p 113–119.

p 23: *A New Theory* appears to have had only one review before 1812 by someone other than Kollmann himself (see page 89 above), and its content was not discussed by other writers in publications before 1812. However, Kollmann's assertion that his theory should be considered established because no attempt had been made to confute it disregards the alternative hypothesis that his theory was ignored by other authors during this time, perhaps because they found it difficult to understand.

p 24: Kollmann defined 'reverse motion' as 'that, in which every ascending interval becomes descending; or the contrary'.[59] The word 'inversion' is commonly used for this concept today. The four forms of motion mentioned by Kollmann—similar, reverse, retrograde, and reverse retrograde—later became a fundamental part of Arnold Schoenberg's twelve-note-class system.

p 25–26: Kollmann is referring to John Isaac Hawkins, who made pianos in London and Philadelphia.[60]

p 26: On 10 November 1801 the music theorist Antonius Bemetzrieder, Robert Scott, John Scott and Alexander Scott received English patent subsequently numbered 2552 for a new way of making piano fortes. Such pianos afterwards were manufactured in London by Scott & Co.[61]

p 26: On 28 November 1801 Edward Ryley received English patent subsequently numbered 2562 for a mechanism that moved a keyboard so that its Middle C key could sound any semitone within an octave, thereby eliminating a player's need to know how to transpose music.

p 26: On 8 April 1807 William Southwell received English patent subsequently numbered 3029 for a 'cabinet pianoforte'. Rights to this invention were acquired by Wilkinson & Co., who manufactured these 5½-feet-tall instruments under Southwell's inspection from 1808. That company ceased trading at the end of 1810, when George Wilkinson of Wilkinson &

---

[59] *NTh*[1], p 68.

[60] See Martha Novak Clinkscale, *Makers of the Piano, 1770–1820*, Oxford, 1993, p 138–139.

[61] Rosamond E. M. Harding, *The Piano-Forte: its history traced to the Great Exhibition of 1851*, Cambridge, 1933, p 404. As mentioned on page 134 above, English patents were not numbered until the 1850s.

Co. established the piano manufacturing firm Wilkinson & Wornum with Robert Wornum II.[62]

p 27: Thomas Percival was a partner in the firm of musical instrument makers Köhler & Percival. He was a son-in-law of the German Chapel porter John Conrad Köhler, from whom Kollmann probably learned about Percival's accomplishments. Köhler, a warehouseman, apparently was a relative (perhaps a brother) of John Köhler I, the founder of Köhler & Percival, who came to London from Germany before 1782, became musical instrument maker to the Prince of Wales and Duke of York, and subscribed to Kollmann's 1799 *An Essay on Practical Musical Composition*.[63]

p 27: Anton Weidinger visited England in 1803.

p 27: Kollmann's recollection that Baldwin's notational scheme had letters written 'over and under a single line' indicates that he saw it not later than Baldwin's June 1803 visit to London. Charles, 3rd Earl Stanhope became interested in the scheme then and shortly afterwards it was modified substantially.[64]

p 27–28: Samuel Rootsey's *An Attempt to Simplify the Notation of Music* was published late in 1811 (its dedication page is dated 1 October 1811). Bulmer, whose company printed this work, probably showed it to Kollmann. Kollmann's plan to examine it 'in a subsequent article' in *The Quarterly Musical Register* did not eventuate.

p 28: Although Charles Burney called Abel 'a disciple of Sebastian Bach' who had acquired his 'musical science' under 'his great master Sebastian Bach',[65] Kollmann's doubt whether Abel had been a pupil of Bach is consistent with

---

[62] Michael Kassler, 'Broderip, Wilkinson and the first English edition of the "48"', *The Musical Times* v 147 no. 1895 (summer 2006) p 67–76 at p 75. Robert Wornum II was the son of Robert Wornum, publisher of Kollmann's music *c*1792

[63] See John Conrad Köhler's will, court copy in National Archives, PROB 11/1548, and Lance Whitehead and Arnold Myers, 'The Köhler family of brasswind instrument makers', *Historic Brass Society Journal* v 16 (2004) p 89–123.

[64] See Michael Kassler, 'Earl Stanhope's "letter-music"', in Michael Kassler (ed.), *The Music Trade in Georgian England*, Aldershot, forthcoming.

[65] Charles Burney, *A General History of Music*, v 4, London, 1789, p 678–679.

the absence of documentary evidence of this. Bach was a godfather of Abel's sister Sophia Charlotta and knew Abel's parents.[66]

p 28: As Kollmann acknowledged on *p 30*, much of the information about Bach in this article, including the report that Handel had avoided him, was obtained from Forkel's biography of Bach.[67]

p 28: J. S. Bach died soon after John Christian Bach's fifteenth birthday.

p 28: Abel's principal musical instrument was the viola da gamba.

p 29: Kollmann's plan to publish an analysed edition of the '48' is discussed in section I.13 above. The notice of this plan in the *Allgemeine musikalische Zeitung* (cols. 5–9), signed 'F—l', was written by Forkel.

p 30: The edition of the '48' by Samuel Wesley and Charles Frederick Horn was published in four books. Book I appeared in September 1810, Book II in 1811 before 22 May, and Book III in 1811 not earlier than October but before Kollmann wrote this passage. Book IV was published about July 1813. Copies of Books I–III (but not Book IV) of the Wesley/Horn edition, inscribed by Wesley 'To Mr Kollmann, with S Wesley's respects', were sold as lot 64 in the 30 January 1877 Puttick & Simpson sale of items from Kollmann's library, described in section I.30 above. The present location of these copies is not known. The Wesley/Horn edition of the '48' and the Horn/Wesley edition of Bach's 'trio' sonatas are discussed in detail in *EBA*.

p 30: The first English edition of multiple preludes and fugues of the '48' was published by Broderip & Wilkinson. Book I was advertised as 'new piano forte music' in *The Times*, 14 June 1802, p 1. Broderip & Wilkinson had subscribed for six copies of Kollmann's *An Essay on Practical Musical Composition*, in which Kollmann announced his plan to edit the '48', and may have decided to capture the English market for the '48' before he could produce his edition. Book I of the Broderip & Wilkinson edition comprised the first twelve preludes and fugues of part 2 of the '48'. Although re-

---

[66] Werner Neumann and Hans-Joachim Schulze (eds), *Fremdschriftliche und gedruckte Dokumente zur Lebensgeschichte Johann Sebastian Bachs 1685–1750*, *Bach-Dokumente* v 2, Kassel, 1969, p 76.

[67] J[ohann] N[icolaus] Forkel, *Ueber Johann Sebastian Bachs Leben, Kunst und Kunstwerke*, Leipzig, 1802.

engraved, its text was copied from Simrock's edition published in Paris and Bonn, in which part 2 of the '48' (BWV 870–893) was considered to be the first part and part 1 (BWV 846–869) the second part.[68] The firm, which became Wilkinson & Co. in January 1808 following Francis Fane Broderip's death, reissued Book I (without changing its title-page) between July and November 1808. About that time they also issued Book II, which included the remaining preludes and fugues of part 2. They never published part 1 of the '48'.[69]

p 30: Lavenu's two-volume edition of the '48' was advertised as 'new music' in *The Morning Post*, 26 April 1811, p 1.

p 31–40: The portions of Forkel's book that Kollmann translated in this article come principally from the second chapter (a chronological survey of Bach's life) and the ninth chapter (a list of Bach's works).[70]

p 43–46: Kollmann's recognition that *An Essay on Musical Harmony* (based upon Kirnberger's system) was incomplete and needed to be rectified by *A New Theory* is discussed in section I.18 above.

p 48: Kollmann's reference probably is to variation 7 of Mozart's twelve variations for piano in E♭ major, KV 354. According to Kurt von Fischer (ed.), *Wolfgang Amadeus Mozart Kritische Berichte, Serie IX, Werkgruppe 26, Variationen für Klavier* (Kassel, 1962, p 45), at least three editions of this set of variations were published in London before 1812.

p 48: 'double' is a now obsolete synonym of 'variation'. Kollmann is referring to the fifth variation of *The Harmonious Blacksmith* (HWV 430) and to the passacaglia of HWV 432. The page numbers given by Kollmann establish that he was referring to the edition entitled *Suites de Pieces pour le Clavecin.*

---

[68] I am grateful to Yo Tomita for this advice.

[69] Michael Kassler, 'Broderip, Wilkinson and the first English edition of the "48"', *op. cit.*

[70] Michael Kassler, 'The English translations of Forkel's Life of Bach', *EBA* p 169–209, details efforts to translate Forkel's biography in the early nineteenth century. *Table 2.1* of that chapter (*ibid.*, p 195) shows that Kollmann's Englishing of Forkel's text in *The Quarterly Musical Register* differs significantly from the first complete English translation published by T. Boosey & Co. in 1820.

Composées par G. F. Handel ... Second Volume, London, printed and sold by Harman [or Hermond] Wright, *c*1794.[71]

p 50: Kollmann was one of the first English writers to use the word 'triad'. John Casper Heck had used the word earlier in his *The Art of Playing Thorough Bass*, London, *c*1775, p 20ff.

p 55: In *A New Theory* Kollmann contrasted 'the method of Sebastian Bach', in which students learn to write four-part counterpoint before writing counterpoint in fewer parts, with that of Fux, who taught that students should first learn to write two-part counterpoint and then proceed to three and more parts.[72] 'In two parts', Kollmann noted, 'not one chord can be complete; when in four parts, every chord may contain at least all its principal notes.' For a student it is therefore 'much more natural and easy, to begin with complete than with incomplete harmonies'.

p 58: Kollmann said (*NTh*[1], p 81) that the vignette on the title-page of *A New Theory*, reproduced in ***Figure 6*** facing page 142, 'shews the whole system' of that work. Some readers must have been confused by the vignette, because in the second edition of *A New Theory* Kollmann explained that its music 'is to be considered, not as a score of six parts intended to be performed together; but each of the five parts over the bass, as a separate specimen, of the manner in which the notes of the modern diatonic chromatic scale can be introduced, according to the system' of that work (*NTh*[2], p 76). The lowest staff depicts the fundamental concord and discord—the two 'roots, from which all harmony arises'. The staff next above it 'shews one part of the said fundamental chords'. The third and fourth staves from the bottom contain the same two notes as the second staff displaced in time by two different types of syncopation. The fifth staff from the bottom shows the introduction of diatonic forenotes and afternotes to those two notes: the introduced 'accidental' notes are printed in smaller size than the essential notes. The top staff shows, amongst other things, chromatic accidental notes introduced between diatonic notes shown on the fifth staff.

---

[71] Copy at Coke 3539, described in William C. Smith, *Handel: A Descriptive Catalogue of the early Editions*, Oxford, 1970, item no. 9 on p 250-251. I am indebted to Katharine Hogg and Colin Coleman of the Gerald Coke Handel Collection, the Foundling Museum, London, for locating and examining this copy and confirming that the phrase 'Double 5' is found on page 43 of this edition.

[72] *NTh*[1], p 56–57.

p 59–74 and p 115–131: Kollmann's thirty-three-page review of Callcott's *A Musical Grammar* (henceforth called *Grammar*[1]) is the longest and most detailed published discussion in Georgian England of a book on music theory. Their substantial correspondence on music-theoretical matters between 1798 and 1806, summarised in section III.4 below, had exposed areas where they disagreed.

p 59: *Grammar*[1] was entered at Stationers' Hall on 29 March 1806 by its proprietor, Robert Birchall.[73] On 26 August 1805 he agreed to pay Callcott £105 for its copyright and to publish 1,500 copies of it, of which 100 were 'allowed the author for his friends'.[74] Callcott promised in this agreement to give Birchall 'every preference' to buy the copyright of any future editions of this work.

p 59: Callcott's affliction led to his admission on 30 May 1808 to a private lunatic asylum at Fishponds, near Bristol, run by Dr Joseph Mason Cox.[75]

p 59: Birchall entered the second edition of Callcott's *A Musical Grammar* (henceforth called *Grammar*[2]) at Stationers' Hall on 8 May 1809.[76] Its introductory 'Advertisement' noted (p ix) that *Grammar*[2] had not 'received the advantage of being revised' by its author, and identified the 'three professional musical gentlemen' responsible for revising the work: [Jean] Jousse, [William] Horsley (who became Callcott's son-in-law in 1813), and S[amuel] Wesley. Wesley's alterations, made to the fourth part of the book on rhythm, were said (*Grammar*[2], p x–xi) to be 'the most important' and to have been made in response to criticisms of that part in a review of *Grammar*[1] in *The British Critic* (v 29 (April 1807) p 398–407 and (June 1807) p 597–605). As Kollmann pointed out in *QMR p 5* and *QMR p 129*, and as confirmed in

---

[73] Michael Kassler, *Music Entries at Stationers' Hall, 1710–1818*, Aldershot, 2004, p 562.

[74] The agreement between Birchall and Callcott is in the Newberry Library, Chicago, Case ms folio V 209.52, f 12^r.

[75] H. Temple Phillips, *The History of the Old Private Lunatic Asylum at Fishponds, Bristol, 1740–1859*, Master of Science thesis, University of Bristol, 1973, p 262. I am indebted to Richard Hunter for this reference.

[76] Kassler, *Music Entries at Stationers' Hall*, p 628.

Wesley's correspondence, this anonymous criticism of *Grammar*[1] was written by Wesley himself.[77]

p 60: The 'List of treatises quoted' (*Grammar*[1], p [ix]–xvi; *Grammar*[2], p [327]–334) makes clear that Callcott's references are to Johann Gottfried Walther, *Musicalisches Lexicon*, Leipzig, 1732, and to Jean-Jacques Rousseau, *Dictionnaire de Musique*, Paris, 1768.

p 60: *Grammar*[1], p vi. The 'original plan' that Callcott mentions is his *Plan of a practical Dictionary of Music, compiled from the most approved Treatises, the authentic mss. of Dr Arnold, Dr Boyce ... to be published early in the year 1799*, London, 1798.[78]

p 60: Heinrich Christoph Koch, *Musikalisches Lexikon*, Frankfurt, 1802.

p 60–61: Kollmann's report of the changes to Callcott's book made by Jousse, Horsley and Wesley is taken from the 'Advertisement' on p [ix]–xii of *Grammar*[2].

p 67: Kollmann's quotation (in which Callcott's word 'root' has been misprinted 'roof') is from *Grammar*[1], p 150. The confusion that Kollmann identified was noticed before *Grammar*[2] went to press, as its corresponding passage (p 154) replaces 'lowest Note' by 'Base Note'.

p 69: As Kollmann reports, Callcott silently excised the first three notes from Koch's fundamental bass C F B E A D G C and the last three notes from his fundamental bass C G D A E B G C (Koch, *op. cit.*, p 492), in order to avoid having B as a fundamental bass note. In Koch's examples, this fundamental bass note supports the diminished triad {B, D, F}.

p 75–79: Kollmann's advocacy of equal temperament was criticised by some contemporaries. In particular, John Farey→Alexander Tilloch, 4 June 1812, printed as 'Further remarks on the Rev. Mr Liston's "Essay on Perfect Intonation"...', *Philosophical Magazine* v 39 no. 170 (June 1812) p 414–423, wrote (p 421–422) that

---

77 See the note to *QMR p 4–6* on page 197 above.

78 A copy of this work, which is dated 'London, 1st March 1798' at its end, is in Cambridge University Library, shelfmark MR 416.d.75.3(7).

> The commendable disposition shown by the people of this metropolis, for encouraging an extension and improvement of the Musical Scale of *Keyed Instruments* ... seems in a particular manner to have alarmed the German Organist Mr Kollmann, for the fate of his modern 'scale of nature', or 12 sounds only in the Octave, placed at equal distances, on which his 'new Theory' appears entirely built, that he so pompously and incessantly compares with the best writings of British Musicians, to their disadvantage, in his Quarterly Review [i.e., the *QMR*]; which '*wonderful* compound of *twelve* Diatonic Chromatic Enharmonic scales in *one*!', it is admitted by Mr K. must be abolished, as the first consequence of the establishment of the 'artificial *Temperaments*' of Hawkes, Loeschman, and *Liston*!, and therefore, he takes especial pains to cry them all down as useless and absurd.
>
> What a lamentable case! that the progress of Science and Improvement in one of the most delightful of arts, should render the sale less certain, of the voluminous works of this profound Theorist!, who, to the honour, or disgrace rather of the age, broadly asserts, that violins, violoncellos, and voices, *ought not* to make *any difference* between A♭ and G♯, D♭ and C♯, &c.!!, but should use, 'as nearly *equal* a *temperament* as possible', or in other words, 'follow the (his) true *standard scale*, on which all modern music depends'.

Nevertheless, by 1885 equal temperament had become 'firmly established' in England.[79] The twelve-note-class system subsequently developed by Arnold Schoenberg depended upon equal temperament. Recently, electronic sound synthesis has made alternative temperaments easy to realise, and debate on the appropriateness of equal temperament has been resumed.[80]

p 77: Two numerals have been transposed in the second term of this ratio: it should read '524288'. Today this musical interval is called a 'Pythagorean comma'.

p 78: Kollmann's statement 'that the old organs in Germany are a semitone higher in pitch, than concert instruments, which requires the organ part of performances with an orchestra to be transposed a semitone lower' presumably was true only of some such organs, as pitch levels before

---

[79] Alexander J[ohn] Ellis, 'The history of equal temperament', appended (p 548–549) to the second edition of *On the Sensations of Tone as a Physiological Basis for the Theory of Music* (London, 1885), his translation of Hermann von Helmholtz, *Die Lehre von den Tonempfindungen...*, Braunschweig, 1877.

[80] See, for instance, Ross W. Duffin, *How Equal Temperament ruined Harmony (and why you should care)*, New York, 2007.

standardisation in the late nineteenth century appear to have varied widely and by much more than a semitone.[81]

p 78: An 'enharmonic diesis' is an interval approximately a quarter-tone in size.[82]

pl 4: The highest note in the first beat of bar 9 was erroneously engraved as D. It has been corrected in ink to E on all copies seen (Boston Public Library, British Library, Manchester Central Library and Royal College of Music). This correction presumably was made before copies of *QMR1* were sold.

p 81–82: Kollmann is referring to Printz's *Historische Beschreibung der edelen Sing- und Kling-Kunst*, Marpurg's *Kritische Einleitung in die Geschichte und Lehrsätze der alten und neuen Musik* and Forkel's *Allgemeine Geschichte der Musik*. A third volume of the latter work never appeared. The sizes of the first two books are given in terms of quarto sheets, each of which contained eight pages.

p 82: Although French troops occupied the Duchy of Braunschweig-Lüneburg in 1803, contact between London and the University of Göttingen remained open until 1806,[83] when Napoléon I's Berlin decree followed by his 1807 Milan decree blockaded English ships and forbade communication with England. After the dissolution of the Holy Roman Empire in 1806 the duchy's territories became part of the Kingdom of Westphalia in 1807, ruled by Napoléon I's brother Jérôme-Napoléon Bonaparte.

---

[81] See the articles by Alexander J. Ellis and Arthur Mendel in *Studies in the History of Musical Pitch*, Amsterdam, 1968.

[82] See Thomas Busby, *A Complete Dictionary of Music*, London, [1801], s.v. 'enharmonic'; and *Grammar*[1], p 118.

[83] Graham Jefcoate, 'Wilhelm Philipp Best und der Londoner Buchhandel: Ein deutscher Diplomat im Dienst der Universitäts Göttingen im 18. Jahrhundert', *Leipziger Jahrbuch zur Buchgeschichte* v 6 (1996) p 199–210 at p 200. Both Best and his son George August Best worked for the German Chancery in St James's Palace and were responsible for acquiring books in London for the University of Göttingen library, including Kollmann's *An Essay on Musical Harmony* and the first edition of his *An Essay on Practical Musical Composition*.

p 82: 'two alphabets': Mattheson's book has a main alphabetical sequence of biographies followed by an alphabetically arranged 'Zusatz' [adjunct] which contains biographies that were added after the main sequence was finished.

p 82: Kollmann is referring to Hiller's *Lebensbeschreibungen berühmter Musikgelehrten und Tonkünstler neuerer Zeit.*

p 82: The second volume of Gerber's lexicon appeared in 1792. Kollmann endeavoured to collect material for a new edition of Gerber's lexicon between 1800 and 1803.[84] Kollmann's uncertainty whether the second volume had been published suggests that he had no direct communication with Gerber and presumably sent autobiographical and other information to him via Johann Anton André.[85]

p 83: Sulzer's work was entitled *Allgemeine Theorie der schönen Künste.* Christian Friedrich von Blankenburg's *Litterarische Zusätze zu Johann Georg Sulzers Allgemeiner Theorie der schönen Künste* was published in three volumes between 1796 and 1798, not (as stated) in 1786.

p 85: However, Kollmann does not mention Klein's 1783 *Versuch eines Lehrbuchs der praktischen Musik in systematischer Ordnung* in his discussion on *p 86–87* of German treatises on practical music.

p 85: Sorge's 'dialogue' is his *Gespräch zwischen einem musico theoretico und einem studioso musices....*

p 87: A copy of Türk's *Klavierschule* with the ownership inscription 'A. F. C. Kollmann' on its title-page is in Glasgow University Library, Sp. Coll. U.e.13.

p 87: 'Sorgen' is a misprint for 'Sorge'.

p 88: A partial English translation of Fux's *Gradus*, entitled *Practical Rules for learning Composition*, was printed by Peter Welcker *c*1769.[86] The author's

---

[84] Kollmann→Callcott, 26/7/1800 and subsequent letters in section III.4 below.

[85] See Kollmann→Callcott, 14/1/1803, and page 66 above.

[86] It is said to have been 'lately published' on the title-page of John Casper Heck's *The Art of Playing the Harpsichord*, another work printed by Peter Welcker that was advertised in the *Public Advertiser*, 15 January 1770, as 'published this day'.

name was spelt 'John Joseph Feux'. The edition by John Preston that Kollmann mentions was—except for its title-page—a later impression from Peter Welcker's plates.[87] Kollmann's pupil Arnold Merrick, in his translation of Johann Georg Albrechtsberger's *Methods of Harmony, Figured Base, and Composition* (London, 1834), said that the English translator of Fux's *Gradus* was John Casper Heck,[88] but this assertion has not been confirmed.

p 89: Only part 1 of Christian Kalkbrenner's *Theorie der Tonkunst* was published.

p 89: Kollmann is referring to Albrechtsberger's *Gründliche Anweisung* [not *Anleitung*] *zur Composition.*

p 92: The page reference is to the second 'corrected' edition of Charles Burney, *The Present State of Music in Germany, the Netherlands and United Provinces...*, London, 1775.

p 92: The comparison of Handel and Bach mentioned by Kollmann almost certainly is the anonymous letter dated 27 February 1788 to the *Allgemeine deutsche Bibliothek* published in v 81 no. 1 (1788) of that journal.[89] In the first edition of *The Bach Reader* Hans T. David and Arthur Mendel suggested that Kollmann had written this comparison,[90] but Dragan Plamenac pointed out the impossibility of this, because the author of the comparison claimed to have witnessed Bach meeting the composer Conrad Friedrich Hurlebusch, and Bach died six years before Kollmann was born.[91] Presumably Kollmann's

[87] Susan Wollenberg, 'The unknown "Gradus"', *Music and Letters* v 51 no. 4 (October 1970) p 423–434.

[88] In a footnote on v 1 p 232.

[89] Reprinted in Hans-Joachim Schulze (ed.), *Dokumente zum Nachwirken Johann Sebastian Bachs 1750–1800*, *Bach-Dokumente* v 3, Kassel, 1972, p 437–445. An English translation is in Hans T. David and Arthur Mendel (eds), *The Bach Reader*, New York, 1945, p 280–288. The passage about Reinhard Keiser reads, in their translation (p 282): 'As an opera composer there was another great man besides Handel: Kaiser [Keiser], who, be it mentioned in passing, in the beauty, novelty, expression, and pleasing qualities of his melody, need have no fear of comparison with Handel.'

[90] David and Mendel, *op. cit.*, p 280–281.

[91] Dragan Plamenac, 'New light on the last years of Carl Philipp Emanuel Bach. 2. The author of the anonymous comparison between Bach and Handel (1788)',

attribution of the comparison to Marpurg reported information he had learned from an unidentified German source. However, no evidence has been found that Marpurg was present at a meeting of Bach and Hurlebusch.[92]

p 93: Handel's operas *Almira* and *Nero* were produced in Hamburg in January 1705 and February 1705 respectively.

p 94: The comic opera *Love in a Village*, with music written or arranged by Thomas Augustine Arne to words by Isaac Bickerstaffe, was first performed at Covent Garden on 8 December 1762.

p 94: Because the third number of *The Quarterly Musical Register* was not issued, the conclusion of this article was never published.

p 94–95: On the wrapper of *QMR1* Kollmann announced that *QMR2* would contain 'The Life of Mozart, and an Account of his Works'. After *QMR1* had gone to press Kollmann evidently chose to defer the article he had announced until 'occasion permits' (*p 95*), and to include the present article in its place.

p 95–104: The essay 'Raphael und Mozart', published in the *Allgemeine musikalische Zeitung* v 2 no. 37 (1800) col. 641–651, was signed by Rochlitz, who was then the editor of that journal. Kollmann translated the entire essay, excluding some footnotes. Although only the first two paragraphs of his translation appear within inverted commas (*QMR p 95*), it extends to the second paragraph on *QMR p 104,* which ends with inverted commas. Kollmann's entire translation was reprinted, without acknowledging him or the *QMR*, as 'A parallel between Raphael and Mozart', *The Harmonicon* n.s. no. 28 (April 1830) p 148–150. *The Harmonicon* said that the translation was supplied to them on 16 March 1830 with a letter from a correspondent identified as 'T. G.'. Although Kollmann correctly named the author of the essay 'Frederic Rochlitz, of Leipzig' (*QMR p 95*), 'T. G.', in his letter to *The Harmonicon*, which that journal published as a foreword to the translation, called him 'George Rochlitz, of Leipzig'.

The Musical Quarterly v 35 (1949) p 565–587. Plamenac suggested (p 579–587) that the comparison was written by Carl Philipp Emanuel Bach.

[92] In Kollmann→Callcott, 24/10/1798, Kollmann said that he knew a man who had taught Marpurg's son, the violinist Johann Friedrich Marpurg. This teacher has not been identified, but the remark indicates a connection between Kollmann and the Marpurg family.

p 104: Kollmann is referring to, and translating from, the preface ['Vorerinnerung'] to Johann Anton André's *Thematische Verzeichniß sämmtlicher Kompositionen von W. A. Mozart, so wie er solches vom 9ten Februar 1784 an, bis zum 15ten November 1791 eigenhändig niedergeschrieben hat*, Offenbach, 1805. André presumably sent a copy of this lithographed publication to Kollmann, as lot 88 of the 1877 sale of items from Kollmann's library (see section I.30 above) included 'Mozart, André's Thematic Catalogue'. Kollmann's phrase 'the beginning of each' refers to the musical incipit of each composition printed in André's catalogue.[93] Kollmann's plan to publish a chronological list of Mozart's compositions 'in a succeeding number' of *The Quarterly Musical Register* did not eventuate.

p 105: As noted on page 193 above, Collins appears to have printed the letterpress section of the second edition of *An Essay on Practical Musical Composition* within a few months after he printed *QMR2*.

p 105: The two faults are: that a treatise is studied only by reading its pages consecutively; and that a student expects 'powers which no Author can give it; I mean the powers of rendering him perfect in the theory and practice of what the book teaches'.[94]

p 115–131: See page 206 above for the annotation to *p 59–74 and p 115–131.*

p 115: Kollmann did not so limit the term 'modulation'. He defined it as 'the playing or composing according to the major or minor *mode*, of one key alone, or of several keys in succession'.[95] Accordingly, for him, a modulation could remain entirely in a single key and mode.

p 118: Kollmann earlier had criticised Matthew Peter King for misusing the term 'transition'.[96]

---

[93] In 1841 André published another thematic catalogue listing all Mozart manuscripts then in his possession. See Henning Bey, 'Johann Anton Andrés Studien als Beitrag zur Mozart-Forschung', in Jürgen Eichenauer (ed.), *Johann Anton André (1775–1842) und der Mozart-Nachlass...*, *Offenbacher Studien* v 1, Offenbach, 2006, p 79–101 at p 94–97.

[94] *EPMC*^{1}, p xv–xvi.

[95] *NTh*^{1}, p 49.

[96] *Vindication*, p 6. See page 70 above.

p 129–130: Kollmann's objections to Wesley's changes were considered by Callcott during a period of release from the lunatic asylum at Fishponds, when he asked his son-in-law William Horsley to inform Wesley that 'the three first pages of the 4th part' of *A Musical Grammar* would be restored in the third edition of the work 'as they stood in the first edition'.[97] Kollmann's criticisms in *The Quarterly Musical Register* of Wesley's alterations to the fourth part of *A Musical Grammar* apparently led to a break in their relationship.[98]

p 134: Elizabeth Ann Linley married Richard Brinsley Sheridan in 1773. He subsequently became a famous playwright and politician.

p 135: Rauzzini died on 8 April 1810.

p 139: The Harmonic Society was founded by Henry Harington, not Bowen. Although both served on the committee that regulated the affairs of the Society in 1797, its Rule X that year specified a toast to 'Dr Harington, the founder of this Society'.[99]

p 140–141: The music of the Latin grace 'Seu edamus' was composed by John Charles Clifton (Clifton→editor of *The Harmonicon*, 28 February 1828, *The Harmonicon* part 1 (April 1828) p 73; the music is printed on p 74–75). The erroneous attribution of this music to Charles Wesley Jr presumably is related to the circumstance that Clifton had been Wesley's pupil (see Clifton's biography in the 1824 Sainsbury *Dictionary of Musicians*, v 1 p 165–167).

p 143: The promised continuation of this article on music in Bath of course did not appear.

p 147: The organ at St Mary Redcliffe was built in 1726 by Harris & Byfield, a partnership of John Harris and John Byfield I.

---

[97] William Horsley→Samuel Wesley, 8 January 1816, BL Add Ms 11730 f 77; *SWSB* p 344–345. The third edition of *A Musical Grammar*, in which these passages were restored, was entered at Stationers' Hall on 19 March 1817.

[98] Their estrangement is indicated in letters from Wesley to Vincent Novello between 1816 and 1825, in which Wesley calls Kollmann 'our old phlegmatic German', 'our phlegmatic Theorist', 'the infallible Lutheran Pope', etc. (*ibid.*). See Michael Kassler, 'The English translations of Forkel's Life of Bach', *op. cit.*, p 200–207.

[99] This rule is printed in *A Selection of favourite Catches, Glees, &c. as sung at the Harmonic Society, in the City of Bath...*, Bath and London, 1797, p 16–17.

p 148: John Antes's invention of a page-turning mechanism was reported in 'Kurze Nachrichten', *Allgemeine musikalische Zeitung* v 3 no. 41 (1801) col. 739–740. His letter to the editor of that journal about his improvements to musical instruments was published there in v 8 no. 42 (1806) col. 657–662. As Kollmann received this journal and could have read these articles,[100] some of this paragraph may have been written by him rather than by his Bristol correspondent. Antes died at Bristol on 17 December 1811.[101]

p 150: Liston's *An Essay on Perfect Intonation* is described as 'just published' in John Farey→Alexander Tilloch, 16 May 1812, printed as 'On the Rev. Mr Liston's euharmonic organ, and his "Essay on Perfect Intonation", just published...', *Philosophical Magazine* v 39 no. 169 (May 1812) p 373–376.

p 152: The correct title of Vogler's booklet is ***Data zur Akustik***. Vogler was in London in May 1783[102] and again in May 1790,[103] but evidence that he met Kollmann has not been found.

p 155: '168' is a mistake for '186'. Kollmann's translation is from sections 186–188 of Chladni's *Die Akustik*, Leipzig, 1802, p 207–209.

p 155–157: Subsequent research has confirmed that difference tones are not present in the acoustic signal but are perceived because of nonlinearity in the auditory system.[104]

p 157–159: Remarkably, none of the items in this 'quarterly catalogue' was entered at Stationers' Hall between January and April 1812.[105]

---

[100] See Kollmann→Callcott, 23/3/1800.

[101] For Antes's work in England see Karl Kroeger, 'John Antes at Fulneck', *Moravian Music Journal* v 30 no. 1 (spring 1985) p 12–18.

[102] See Vogler→Sir Joseph Banks, 30 May 1783, BL Add Ms 8095 f 235.

[103] Vogler's organ concerts at the King's Theatre, Pantheon, were advertised in *The Times*, 22/5/1790 p 1, and 29/5/1790 p 1.

[104] See, for instance, Sally Arnold and Robert Burkard, 'Studies of interaural attenuation to investigate the validity of a dichotic difference tone response recorded from the inferior colliculus in the chinchilla', *Journal of the Acoustical Society of America* v 107 no. 3 (March 2000) p 1541–1547 at p 1541.

[105] Music entries at Stationers' Hall during this quarter are listed in Michael Kassler, *Music Entries at Stationers' Hall*, *op. cit.*, p 671–672.

p 157: Crotch's book was advertised for sale in *The Times*, 2 March 1812, p 2. The *British Review, and London Critical Journal* reported (v 3 no. 6 (June 1812) p 507) that Crotch's book and William Seaman Stevens's book were published between March and May 1812.

p 158: Beethoven's 'The distant lover' was entered at Stationers' Hall on 31 August 1810 by Clementi, Banger, Collard, Davis & Collard. They entered his 'Anxiety of absence' on 31 October 1810 and his 'Les adieux' on 28 January 1811. As works entered at Stationers' Hall generally were first printed just before their entry there,[106] the Beethoven publications listed by Kollmann presumably were reprinted early in 1812 from plates engraved a year or two earlier. Engraved music at this time commonly was printed in small batches,[107] and the Clementi firm probably had these publications reprinted because their stock of copies from earlier impressions had sold out.

p 158: The opera *The Five Lovers* was composed by Thomas Simpson Cooke. 'M. Cooke' appears to be a mistake, as the next catalogue entry attributes to 'T. Cooke' a song from the same opera.

p 158: 'Gilon' is a mistake for John Gildon. Copies of his *Grand military March*, op. 29, published by Thomas Preston with watermark 1811, are at BL h.1458.j.(3.) and h.721.z.(7.).

p 158: 'Hodsoll' refers not to a composer but to the London music seller William Hodsoll.

p 159: On 2 May 1810 Sebastian Erard received English patent subsequently numbered 3332 for 'further improvements on pianofortes and harps'. These improvements included the harp described by Kollmann, whose 'double action' pedals enabled the sound of a string—and, simultaneously, the sounds of strings pitched one or more octaves above or below the pitch of that string—to be sharpened by one or two semitones.

---

[106] Alan Tyson, *The Authentic English Editions of Beethoven*, London, 1963, p 139–140.

[107] For instance, fifty copies of a work by Haydn were printed *c*1786 from engraved plates, and *c*1817 a further twenty-five copies of it were printed from the same plates. See William Sandys and Simon Andrew Forster, *The History of the Violin*, London, 1864, p 312.

p 159: William Bundy received English patent subsequently numbered 3436 on 2 May 1810 for this 'improvement on stringed musical instruments'.

p 159: John Broadwood & Sons manufactured a transposing piano forte in 1808, but it is not obvious that this instrument relied upon Ryley's patent. Broadwood's 1808 piano transposed only downwards, whereas Ryley's invention enabled transposition up as well as down.[108]

p 159: Crotch's course of lectures began on 4 February 1812.[109] Kemp's lectures started on 28 February 1812.[110]

p 159–160: The publication to which 'An amateur' referred presumably was *Cantus, Songs and Fancies, to three, four, or five parts ... as it is taught in the musick-school of Aberdeen*, Aberdeen, 1682, as this work includes melodic settings of all the songs whose initial lines were quoted. 'Brave Man begins to rouse' is a misprint of 'Brave Mars begins to rouse'.

p 160: Kollmann probably took the text of his 'Sacred song' from Hymn VII in Richard Sandilands, *Psalms, Hymns, and Anthems, selected for the use of Ebury-Chapel, near Sloane-Square, Chelsea,* Chelsea, 1792, p 100. Sandilands officiated at the Kollmanns' marriage (see page 30 above) and they presumably owned this book, as Kollmann acknowledged setting another text from it, 'Praise the Lord Jehovah praise', in *An Essay on Musical Harmony*.[111] Hymn VII in Sandilands's volume consists of the same four verses of James Merrick's poem that Kollmann set in his 'Sacred song', except that Kollmann substituted 'and troubles' for 'unnumber'd' in the first line of verse 4, so that the text repetition in this line would be a two-syllable word, 'troubles'. The verses in Sandilands's volume and Kollmann's 'Sacred song' are verses 15=18, 16, 17 and 19 of James Merrick's 'The trials of virtue' in his *Poems on sacred Subjects*, Oxford, 1763, p 20–25, except for the first word in verse 1. This word is 'Ah' in both Sandilands's volume and Kollmann's song; in Merrick's poem it is 'Then'.

---

[108] The 1808 Broadwood & Sons transposing piano forte is described, pictured and discussed in the context of Ryley's patent in Rosamund E. M. Harding, *The Piano-Forte: its history traced to the Great Exhibition of 1851*, *op. cit.*, p 277–278.

[109] Advertisement, *The Times*, 27 January 1812, p 1.

[110] Advertisement, *The Times*, 26 February 1812, p 1.

[111] *EMH*, p 87 and plate 20 no. 2.

~ III ~

SOURCE DOCUMENTS

1. Kollmann's *c*1823 Autobiography

The undated manuscript of Kollmann's autobiography was written for Sainsbury & Co., proprietors of *A Dictionary of Musicians, from the Earliest Ages to the Present Time...* (London, 1824).[1] A compiler of that dictionary made numerous alterations to this manuscript before sending it to the printer, who consistently misspelled Kollmann's surname as 'Kollman' when setting the article about him.[2] The manuscript, now in the Moldenhauer Archive, Northwestern University Music Library, Evanston, Illinois, USA, is transcribed here by that library's kind permission.

Augustus Frederic Christopher Kollmann, Organist of His Majesty's German Chapel St James's

Mr K. was born March 21st 1756, at Engelbostel, a Village near Hannover, where his Father was Organist and Schoolmaster. Though he was intended for a similar Station in Life, he benefited by the opportunity of learning latin with the son of the Pastor of that place; and at the age of fourteen years he for two years frequented the Gymnasium at Hannover, in the second class.

After that time, he was for five years more partly with his parents, and the other time at Hannover, learning music of J. C. Boettner, an able Organist in J. S. Bach's style, and also french.

In 1779 he was admitted into the Academy (improperly called Seminary) for intended Schoolmasters, to the Electorate, now Kingdom of Hannover,[3] where he learnt that methodical, and systematical manner of teaching, which has been very advantageous to him, not only

---

[1] Sainsbury & Co. were literary agents. See Leanne Langley, 'Sainsbury's *Dictionary*, the Royal Academy of Music, and the rhetoric of patriotism', in Christina Bashford and Leanne Langley (eds), *Music and British Culture, 1785–1914: Essays in Honour of Cyril Ehrlich*, Oxford, 2000, p 65–97.

[2] *A Dictionary of Musicians...*, v 2 p 22–23.

[3] The former Electorate of Hannover became the Kingdom of Hannover at the Congress of Vienna in October 1814.

for school instruction, but also in teaching music, and particularly in writing his musical treatises: and during that time he constantly heard, and assisted the said Mr Boettner, on the Organ of the principal church (Marktkirche,) also entirely officiated for him six weeks, during an illness.

At the end of 1781 he went to Lüne, a protestant establishment for noble ladies still called a Convent,[4] near Lüneburg, where he was appointed organist and schoolmaster, and had the encouragement of meeting with much approbation. But His late Majesty[5] commanding, that a person should be sent by the Hannoverian Government, to fill the place of Organist and Schoolmaster at the Royal German Chapel St James's, Mr K. was called away from the said place; and according [to] his new appointment, arrived in London Septemb. 1st 1782.

Though the said School took him up part of four days every week, it left him sufficient time for attending to musical pursuits; and it has been discontinued, since the demise of Her late Majesty Queen Charlotte.[6]

With regard to music, Mr K. applied himself in this country principally to its theoretical department, but also to practical composition, and for instructing his musical Pupils.

His works, divide themselves into three classes, viz. first, Theoretical works, and other musical writings; secondly, Theoretico-practical works, being compositions with theoretical explanations; and thirdly, Practical works only. A distinct account of the Contents of the said first class, is given in that author's *Quarterly Musical Register, Nos. I & II.* The second class[7] comprehends the following works: and they are as follows:

An Essay on Musical Harmony, folio, London 1796.

---

[4] The name 'Kloster Lüne' was retained after the originally Roman Catholic convent ['Kloster'] converted to Protestantism. See Carl Wünsch, *Kloster Lüne*, Munich, 1966, p 8.

[5] King George III died on 29 January 1820.

[6] Queen Charlotte died on 17 November 1818.

[7] Kollmann meant to write 'the first class'.

A New Theory of Musical Harmony, folio, London 1806; and a second improved edition of it, 1812.[8]

An Essay on Practical [Musical] Composition, folio, London 1799, and a second improved edition of it, 1812.

A Second Practical Guide to Thorough Bass, folio, London 1807. N.B. this supersedes the first Guide, and is not a second part of it.

The Quarterly Musical Register, Nos. I, II, Octavo, 1812.

'Bemerkungen' Remarks on what Mr J. B. Logier calls his New System of Musical Education, in the *Musicalische Zeitung* of Leipzig, Octob. 1821; and *A Sequel* to the same, in the said *Zeitung*, February 1822.[9]

The second class, or Theoretico-Practical works, are:

Twelve Analyzed Fugues for Two Performers, with Double Counterpoints in all Intervals, and Introductory Explanations. Op. X. Second edition Lond. 1823.

The Melody of the Hundredth Psalm, with examples and directions for an hundred different harmonies in four parts. Op. IX. London 1809.

An Introduction to extemporary Modulation. Op. XI. Lond. 1820.

The First Beginning on the Piano Forte, according to an improved method of teaching Beginners. Op. V. Lond. 1796.

An Analyzed Symphony, for the P. F. Viol. & Bass, Op. VII. Lond. 1789.[10]

A Rondo on the Chord of the Diminished Seventh. One sheet, 1810.

Of the third class the princ[ipal] work is: *A Concerto for the Piano Forte and an Orchestra, with the Cadences, as performed in public by Master Kollmann*, Op. VIII. 1804.

---

[8] Kollmann should have written '1823' instead of '1812'.

[9] Kollmann's dates are a month early. His articles in the *Allgemeine musikalische Zeitung* appeared in November 1821 and March 1822.

[10] Kollmann should have written '1798'.

2. Literary, Musical and Artistic Works by A. F. C. Kollmann

Kollmann's literary, musical and artistic works are listed in this section in their estimated chronological order. In each entry the opus number (if any) that he gave to the work appears at the top left, followed (in bold) by a short title of the work and sometimes (in italics) by the abbreviation used in this book to refer to the work.

At the top right of each entry is the date assigned to the work. If the work was printed, this is the date when it appears to have been first published. A date following the acronym 'ESH' it is the day when the work was entered at Stationers' Hall, which is taken to be its publication date.[11] For works not entered at Stationers' Hall and for unprinted works the assigned date either is stated in the work or has been chosen for a reason explained in the entry. Subsequent lines in each entry give further information about a work, including locations of copies and a chronological citation of contemporary reviews (if any).

The following abbreviations are used in entries:

1st perf	first performance of the work
c/sig	the 'control signature' written in ink on copies of the work by its proprietor, who owned the work's copyright
ded	the work's dedicatee
engr	the work's engraver
instr	the voices or instruments for which the work is composed
imp	impression (i.e., the set of copies printed in a single batch during which the plates or the type were not altered)
later	copies from an impression after the first impression
pr	the work's printer
pub	the work's publisher
ref	an explanation of a reference in the work's title
text	the initial words of the work's vocal text

[11] This presumption is justified in Michael Kassler, *Music Entries at Stationers' Hall, 1710–1818*, Aldershot, 2004, p xxi. The full text of entries of Kollmann's works at Stationers' Hall (except for his 1820 *An Introduction to extemporary Modulation*) is presented in that book.

The following symbols designate repositories of copies:

BL	British Library, London
Bodleian	Bodleian Library, University of Oxford
Coke	Gerald Coke Handel Collection, The Foundling Museum, London
CUL	Cambridge University Library
Fétis	Fétis collection, Bibliothèque Royale de Belgique, Brussels
GUL	Glasgow University Library
K	Private collection of Jamie and Michael Kassler, Northbridge, NSW, Australia
LC	Library of Congress, Washington
Newberry	Newberry Library, Chicago
NLS	National Library of Scotland, Edinburgh
NYPL	New York Public Library, New York City
Pendlebury	Pendlebury Library of Music, University of Cambridge
RAM	Royal Academy of Music, London
RCM	Royal College of Music, London
Riemenschneider	Riemenschneider Memorial Bach Library, Baldwin-Wallace College, Berea, Ohio, USA[12]
Rowe	Rowe Music Library, King's College, Cambridge
SBB	Staatsbibliothek zu Berlin—Preußischer Kulturbesitz
Sibley	Sibley Music Library, Eastman School of Music, University of Rochester, New York
UBC	University of British Columbia, Vancouver
Wits	University of the Witwatersrand, Johannesburg

[12] '*Kenney*' followed by numerals refers to the copy in this library so numbered in Sylvia W. Kenney (ed.), *Catalog of the Emilie and Karl Riemenschneider Memorial Bach Library*, New York, 1960.

Op. 1 **Sechs geistliches Lieder** *c*1784

title *Sechs geistliches Lieder mit neuen vierstimmigen Choralmelodien, welche zugleich mit dem bloßen Generalbasse beygefüget worden*

ded Queen Charlotte

pr Leipzig, Johann Gottlob Immanuel Breitkopf

copies **GERMANY** Stadtbibliothek Leipzig II/1/4°67 (Carl Ferdinand Becker's copy)
UK BL F.1120.ss [no wmk]

c/sig none

remarks AFCK's name spelt 'August Friedrich Christoph Kollmann' and 'Erste Ausgabe' printed on the title-page. Opus number assigned by AFCK after work printed. Date proposed because the publication's typography is similar to that used in the edition by C. P. E. Bach of J. S. Bach's *Vierstimmige Choralgesänge* printed by Breitkopf in four volumes from 1784 to 1787, and the vignette on the work's title-page is the same as that used in the first of those four volumes but differs from the vignettes used in the last three of those volumes.[13]

review ['Wk.', i.e., Daniel Gottlob Türk], *Allgemeine deutsche Bibliothek* v 107 part 2 (1792) p 441–442

Op. 2 **Four Sonatas** ESH 5/7/1788

title *Four sonatas for the harpsichord or pianoforte with an accompanyment for a violin*

engr Samuel John Neele (title-page plate); J. Scherer (music plates)

sold by [George] Smart's music warehouse and 'all other music shops'

copies UK Bodleian Mus. Instr. I, 136(6); BL g.161.f.(5.); CUL Mus.3.54(4); GUL Cb3-f.8

c/sig AFCK monogram

review [Thomas Busby], *Analytical Review* v 1 (August 1788) p 486

A Characteristic March ESH 9/3/1791

title *A characteristic march, with the sentiments that are expressed in it, as perform'd by the Third Reg.^{t} of Guards*

instr for keyboard; also parts for two German flutes

sold by 'all music shops'

copies UK Bodleian Mus.Instr.I.136(12); BL g.149.(20.); CUL MR340.a.75.50(9); GUL Cb3-f.15

c/sig AFCK monogram

[13] I am grateful to Hans-Joachim Schulze for this dating reason.

A Characteristic March [in score for a band] *c*9/3/1791

remarks No copies located. Advertised on the title-page of the preceding work as 'the present march in score for a band'. It could be had for 1/6, whereas the preceding work sold for 1/–. Presumably published about the same time as the preceding work.

Op. 3 An Introduction to the Art of Preluding 1792

title *An introduction to the art of preluding and extemporizing, in six lessons for the harpsichord or harp*
ded Miss Craufurd
pub Robert Wornum
copies AUSTRIA Bibliothek Hans Kann [private library], Vienna
UK RCM H386/6 [no wmk]
USA Folger Shakespeare Library M1585.H6C7 Cage;
LC MT68.K64 Case; Yale MT68.K81
later UK BL f.133.ff.(2.) [wmk 1797]
c/sig none
remarks The incorrect date '1779' for this work was printed on page 1 of AFCK's 1820 *An Introduction to Extemporary Modulation*. On the BL and K copies of that work this date was altered in ink to '1792', presumably by AFCK himself.

The Prussian Battle March *c*1792

title *The Prussian battle march, translated and adapted for England*
text 'Rage and attack us in vain'
instr voice and keyboard; includes optional part for German flute
pub Robert Wornum
copy UK BL G.385.c.(6.)
c/sig none
remarks The title-page announces as 'just published' AFCK's *Introduction to the Art of Preluding*. A sticker pasted over Wornum's name on the BL copy identifies H[ugh] Andrews as a subsequent seller of this work.

Charming Sally *c*1792

title *Charming Sally. A Scotch song written by a lady*
text 'The birks and braes where nature plays and wakes to joy'
instr voice and keyboard; includes optional part for German flute
pub Robert Wornum
copies IRELAND National Library Add. Mus. 9489
UK private collection

c/sig none

remarks Date suggested because Wornum appears to have published AFCK's music only about this time. This probably is the 'Scotch song' by AFCK that Wornum said, in his publication of J. W. Häßler's song 'To Myra', was just published for 6/–. The lady who wrote the words has not been identified.

Op. 4 Six Sonatinas for the Piano Forte *c*1792

title *Six sonatinas for the piano forte*

ded The Countess of Loudoun (Flora Mure-Campbell, from 1786 Countess of Loudoun, from 1804 Lady Moira)

pub Robert Wornum

copy UK BL h.1226.m.(17.)

c/sig none

remarks Date suggested because Wornum appears to have published AFCK's music only about this time. The sixth sonatina is stated to have been 'used as a Troop for his Majesty's third Reg[imen]t of Guards' (i.e., it was played as a signal for the regiment to assemble for marching).

A Prelude and Minuet 1792?

title *A prelude and minuet* [for the harp]

pub Robert Wornum

remarks No copies located. The work is listed for sale at 1/6 in Wornum's *A Catalogue of Music* (BL 7896.h.40(19)), which has wmk 1802. Date suggested because Wornum appears to have published AFCK's music only about this time.

A New March ESH 19/6/1795

title *A new march composed for the Corps of Light Horse Volunteers of the Cities of London and Westminster*

instr two versions: one for piano forte or harp; the other for a military band

pr/sold by J[oseph] Dale

copies CANADA McMaster University D 625
UK Bodleian Mus. Instr. I, 136(3); BL g.133.(34.); CUL MR340.a.75.45(7)

c/sig AFCK monogram

remark The version for a military band includes the statement 'as performed before their Majesties at Windsor'.

An Essay on Musical Harmony *(EMH)* ESH 18/1/1796

title	*An essay on musical harmony, according to the nature of that science and the principles of the greatest musical authors*
ded	Charles Burney, Mus. Doc.
pub	AFCK and Joseph Dale
pr/sold by	J[oseph] Dale
copies	**AUSTRALIA** K; University of Sydney RB 4696.92 **BELGIUM** Fétis 6508 **CANADA** UBC MT50.A2K8 **FRANCE** Conservatoire de Paris 99094038 and 99094967 **GERMANY** Bach-Archiv Leipzig Rara II, 163; Berlin SBB 4° Mus. Gk 347 (Georg Poelchau's copy); Göttingen SUB 4 MUS IV, 2170 **SWITZERLAND** Zürich Zentralbibliothek Mus Jac C 35 **UK** Birmingham University r f ML 444; BL 50.f.5 (King George III's copy) and g.304.(1.) and 558*.e.17; Bodleian 1745 c.2(1) (Stationers' Hall deposit copy) and fol.θ.333(1) (William Seward's copy); Coke 732; CUL MR580.a.75.7; Edinburgh University special collections O*.16.68; GUL Sp. Coll. RF 28 and A.x.53; Lambeth Palace G81.3 K83C (Stationers' Hall copy deposited at Sion College); Liverpool Central EX 266-2; NLS Music press 1/1 (imperfect); Pendlebury XRa.852.17B.X1 and XRa.852.17B.K2; Rowe 55.10[1] RES; RAM 9.76* (Richard John Samuel Stevens's copy); RCM D325/1 (Amelia Comer's copy); Southampton University FOLIO ML 3813 **USA** Boston University Theology Library, Hymn Society collection; Brown University MT50.A2K8; Harvard Mus.310.4.15; Illinois Urbana XQ.781.3 K833E; Johns Hopkins MT50.K64; LC MT50.A2K8; Michigan MT50.K82 1796; Riemenschneider *Kenney* 229; Stanford MT50.K81 (lacks the music examples); UC Berkeley fMT50.A2.K6 case X (bears the ownership stamp 'W, Ling' [sic], probably of the composer and organist William Ling); Yale MT50.K81 1796+
c/sig	A. F. C. Kollmann, except University of Sydney copy has: JD 07 [presumably indicating the seventh of Joseph Dale's copies]
reviews	[Charles Burney], *Monthly Review* n.s. v 21 (9/1796) p 27–30 [Charles Burney?], *British Critic* v 8 (9/1796) p 322–323 [Charles Burney?], *Critical Review* 2nd ser. v 18 (9/1796) p 88 [Thomas Busby], *Monthly Magazine* v 3 no. 13 (1/1797) p 44; v 7 no. 5 (6/1799) p 389–390; v 7 no. 6 (7/1799) p 477 [Johann Nicolaus Forkel], *Göttingische Anzeigen von gelehrten Sachen* no. 115 (21/7/1798) p 1137–1142 [John Wall Callcott], *British Critic* v 16 (8/1800) p 169–172 and (10/1800) p 393–397

Op. 6 The Shipwreck ESH 22/10/1796

title *The shipwreck, or loss of the Halsewell East-Indiaman. Being a grand instrumental piece adapted to the piano-forte with an accompaniment for a violin and violoncello*

ded Baron Ernst Ludwig Julius von Lenthe, 'His Majesty's minister from the Electorate of Hanover'

sold by Corri, Dussek & Co., London and Edinburgh, and 'all other music shops'

copies **AUSTRALIA** K
UK Bodleian Mus. Instr. I, 136(7); BL g.161.(5.);
CUL MR340.a.75.46(11); GUL Cb3-f.15

later **IRELAND** National Library Add. Mus. 7150 [wmk 1805 and p [14] blank; in the first impression p [14] announces the 'just publish'd' *EMH*]

c/sig A. F. C. Kollmann (K, Bodleian, BL, GUL copies);
AFCK monogram (Ireland copy)

ref The *Halsewell East-Indiaman* was wrecked off the Dorset coast on 6 January 1786. Almost 200 people were killed.

remarks Published as a set of three parts. The piano part lists 'things expressed' in the composition.

review [Thomas Busby], *Monthly Magazine* v 8 no. 4 (1/11/1799) p 814

Op. 5 The First Beginning on the Piano-Forte ESH 10/12/1796

title *The first beginning on the piano-forte, according to an improved method of teaching beginners. Containing an explanatory introduction, the rudiments of the art of playing on key'd instruments, & a series of progressive lessons and sonatinas.*

sold by Corri, Dussek & Co., music sellers to the royal family, London and Edinburgh, and 'all other music shops'.

copies UK Bodleian Mus. Instr. I, 240(2); BL e.140.(6.);
RCM H586; Rowe 31.97.(3) RES

c/sig A. F. C. Kollmann

remarks Advertised as 'new music' in *The Times*, 27/12/1786 p 2, and as 'just published' in *The Times*, 23/5/1797 p 2. On the title-page AFCK's *The Shipwreck*, op. 6, is announced as available for purchase. Although *The Shipwreck* has a higher opus number, the Stationers' Hall entry dates suggest that it was printed before op. 5.

review [Thomas Busby], *Monthly Magazine* v 7 part 1 no. 3 (1/4/1799) p 226

new ed. First movement of Sonatina III in Margery Halford (ed.), *Introduction to the Keyboard Sonatina*, Van Nuys, California, 1984, p 18–19.

My friend and pitcher 1797

title *Nachahmung des Engländischen Liedes: My Friend and Pitcher*
text 'Ich frage nichts nach Ruhm und Geld'
pr The text and folding plate of music are printed in *Musenalmanach 1797* (Göttingen, J. C. Dieterich; reprinted Hildesheim, 1979) p 156–157. Both the text and the music are attributed to 'A. F. K. Kollmann'.
remark This music is not the same as J. W. Häßler's setting of the English-language poem 'My friend and pitcher' (by John O'Keeffe) that was published by Robert Wornum in London *c*1792.

EPMC proposals 2/1798

title *Proposals for publishing by subscription, a new theoretical musical work, entitled An Essay on Practical Musical Composition, written, and most humbly dedicated, by permission, to His Majesty*
copy UK BL 1879.cc.13.(56.) (with AFCK's handwritten note on the back saying that 'Her Majesty' and 'Their R. H. The Princesses'—i.e., Augusta, Elizabeth, Mary and Sophia Matilda of Gloucester—had subscribed)
c/sig none
remarks Work is a single sheet, dated 2/1798. Presumably published near the end of that month, as AFCK's *Analyzed Symphony*, op. 7, is said in the work to have been 'just published'. Advertised, with a notice that the proposed *Essay* has been 'honoured with the subscription of her Majesty and their Royal Highnesses the Princesses', in *The Times*, 12/7/1798 p 2 and 3/12/1798 p 2.

Op. 7 Analyzed Symphony ESH 3/3/1798

A symphony for the Piano-Forte, a violin, and violoncello; with analytical explanations of the subjects and imitations, the modulations, the counterpoint inversions, and the rhythmical order it contains
ded Count John Maurice de Brühl, 'Minister from the Elector of Saxony, to His Majesty'
sold by Longman & Broderip and 'at all other music shops'
copies UK Bodleian 1745 c.2(3), and Mus. Instr. I, 136(6); BL g.161.(4.)
later UK Bodleian Tenbury c.7(3) [wmk 1815]
c/sig A. F. C. Kollmann (all copies except Bodleian Tenbury c.7(3)); AFCK monogram (Bodleian Tenbury c.7(3))
remark Published as a set of three parts.

review [Thomas Busby], *Monthly Magazine* v 8 no. 5 (1/12/1799) p 897
new ed. First movement printed in score in the Introduction, by Imogene Horsley, to the facsimile reprint of AFCK's *An Essay on Practical Musical Composition*, New York, 1973, p x–xxviii.

An Essay on Practical Musical Composition *(EPMC*[1]*)* ESH 21/6/1799

title *An essay on practical musical composition, according to the nature of that science and the principles of the greatest musical authors*
ded King George III
pr perhaps Sampson Low I, on the basis of 'sold by' below
sold by AFCK; [Joseph] Dale; Longman, Clementi & Co.; [George] Smart and 'at the other principal music shops', and at Mr [Sampson] Low's bookshop
copies **AUSTRALIA** K
BELGIUM Fétis 6773
CANADA UBC MT40.A2K77
GERMANY Berlin SBB 4° Gk 346 (Georg Poelchau's copy); Göttingen SUB 2 MUS IV, 1750
ITALY Bergamo Istituto Musicale Gaetano Donizetti, Fondo Piatti-Lochis no. 8796 (inscribed by AFCK to 'Mr Small' [perhaps the musician Robert Small])
JAPAN Tokyo Yomiuri Nippon Symphony Orchestra, Nanki coll.
SWITZERLAND Zürich Zentralbibliothek Mus Jac C 36 (inscribed by AFCK to 'Capellmeister [Friedrich Heinrich] Himmel');
UK Bodleian 1745 c.2(2) and fol. θ.333(2); BL g.304.(2.); CUL MR580.a.75.7 and MR580.a.80.12; GUL Sp. Coll. A.x.11 and Store HQ00953; Lambeth Palace G81.3 K83C; Liverpool Central EX 266-2; NLS Music press 1/1; Pendlebury XRa.852.17B.K1; RAM 9.76*; RCM D323 (owned by James William Windsor, a subscriber, who dated the copy 'Feby 1800 Bath') and LXX.B.2a; Rowe 55.10[1] RES (owned by John Woodall Jr, a subscriber); St Andrews s M1.A4M6;152
USA Harvard Mus. 310.4.15; LC MT40.K77 Case; Michigan MT50.K82 1796; NYPL Mus. Res. *MIB+; Pierpont Morgan Fuld Collection (sold by British Museum in 1818); Riemenschneider *Kenney* 230 (owned by Robert Lindley in 1809); Sibley MT40.K81 (owned by William Horsley, a subscriber); Syracuse University MT40.A2 K77f; Yale MT50.K81 1796+
facsimile New York, 1973, of text of *EPMC*[1] and the music plates of *EPMC*[2]
c/sig A. F. C. Kollmann

reviews [Thomas Busby], *Monthly Magazine* v 8 part 2 no. 1 (1/8/1799) p 561; v 8 part 2 no. 2 (1/9/1799) p 644; v 9 part 1 (20/7/1800) p 630
[Charles Burney], *Monthly Review* n.s. v 31 (2/1800) p 127–131
[Charles Burney?], *Critical Review* 2nd ser. v 28 (2/1800) p 219–220
[John Wall Callcott], *British Critic* v 17 (4/1801) p 399–400

Sun 1799?; <10/1799

remarks An engraving designed by AFCK and printed in London of a drawing whose main part has the shape of a sun. J. S. Bach's name is at the sun's centre, from which the names of other German composers radiate outwards. Under the sun is an Italian owl which cannot stand the light of German composition; also, an Italian capon and German cock are shown as if they were about to fight. No copy of the original engraving located. The sun portion only was re-engraved and printed, with commentary by Johann Nicolaus Forkel describing the original engraving, in the *Allgemeine musikalische Zeitung* (Leipzig) v 2 no. 5 (30/10/1799) col. 103–104. This second engraving is reproduced in *Figure 3* facing page 15 above. Forkel related the drawing to a dispute between Haydn and Felice Giardini that occurred while Haydn was in England (between 1791 and 1795).

Divertimento ESH 17/9/1799

title *A divertimento, for three performers on one piano forte, calculated also for the use of one performer only*
sold by AFCK and 'all music shops'
copies UK Bodleian Mus.Instr.I.136(14); BL g.130.(6.); CUL MRA.340.75.47; GUL Sp. Coll. Cb6-f.19
c/sig A. F. C. Kollmann
review [Thomas Busby], *Monthly Magazine* v 8 no. 3 (1/10/1799) p 738

***PGTB* Prospectus** 1/8/1800

remarks In AFCK→John Wall Callcott, 26/7/1800, AFCK said that he intended 'to publish a prospectus of a *Practical Guide to Thorough Bass*' on 'the first of August', presumably to solicit subscriptions. No copy of this prospectus has been located.

A Practical Guide to Thorough-Bass *(PGTB)* — ESH 14/2/1801

title *A practical guide to thorough-bass*
ded Hon. George Pomeroy
engr [John?] Barnes (title-page engraver)
sold by [Thomas] Hurst; Clementi & Co.; and 'all the music shops'
copies **CANADA** National Library MT49 K69 fol.
GERMANY Berlin SBB 4° Gk 348
UK Bodleian Mus. Instr. I, 136(4); BL g.302.(3.); CUL MR80.a.75.7(4); GUL A.x.54 and Cb3-d.20;| Lambeth Palace G81.3 K83T; NLS Music press 1; Pendlebury XRa.588.18A.K1; Rowe 51.119(2)
USA Baylor MT49.K816 P7 1801; Cornell MT49.K81; Harvard Houghton Mus. 403.6* and Mus.310.4.10 and Mus.310.4.15; Iowa FOLIO MT49.K69; LC NT49.K69 Case copy 2; Sibley MT49.K81p
later **USA** LC NT49.K69 Case copy 1; UC Berkeley fMT49.K66 case X [both copies have wmk 1803 and, at the bottom of p vi, AFCK's autograph annotation referring to his *Vindication* (the next work)]
c/sig A. F. C. Kollmann
reviews [John Wall Callcott], *British Critic* v 18 (10/1801) p 389–399
[Charles Burney], *Monthly Review* v 36 (11/1801) p 303–307

Vindication — 1801; >2/5/1801

title *A. F. C. Kollmann's vindication of a passage in his Practical Guide to Thorough-Bass against an advertisement of Mr M. P. King*
sold by AFCK and 'all the music shops'
copies **AUSTRALIA** K (inscribed by AFCK 'Mr [Charles] Bridgeman with Mr Kollmann's Compliments')
UK BL g.304.a.; GUL A.x.54; RCM LXX.B.16(3)
USA LC ML423.K75 Case
c/sig none
remarks Work, dated 1801, responds to the 'Advertisement' dated 8/4/1801 on p v–vi of the 'new [i.e., second] edition' of M[atthew] P[eter] King, *A General Treatise on Music....* After AFCK→Callcott, 2/5/1801, in which AFCK wrote that he 'shall answer' King but 'how soon and in what manner I do not wish to tell you at present'.
reviews [Thomas Busby], *Monthly Magazine* v 13 part 1 (1/3/1802) p 154
[Charles Burney], *Monthly Review* v 38 (6/1802) p 216–217
[John Wall Callcott], *British Critic* v 20 (11/1802) p 487–493
[Anon.], *Monthly Mirror* v 14 (12/1802) p 402–403

Key Prospectus 1/1803

remarks No copies located. In the preface to *NTh*[1], which was entered at Stationers' Hall on 21/5/1806, AFCK wrote that he 'first endeavoured to publish as a mere addition' to *EMH* a work that he had 'announced ... three years ago, under the title of a *Key* to a complete and natural System of Musical Harmony'. In AFCK→Callcott, 14/1/1803, AFCK said that he was enclosing 'a plan of my announced Key'. Callcott, writing anonymously in *The British Critic*, v 22 (8/1803) p 185, reported that 'Mr Kollmann has announced a new work, which is to prove the truth of Kirnberger's theory by examples, adduced from the earliest writers of counterpoint to the present times'. However, after this prospectus was published, AFCK abandoned his plan to write a work that he presumably would have called *Key to a Complete and Natural System of Musical Harmony*. Instead he produced *A New Theory*.

A Hymn with Various Harmonies 1803

title *A hymn with various harmonies to the same melody, translated from the German, & composed for one or four voices with an accompaniment for the piano forte or organ*

text 'The num'rous works of God proclaim'

pr/sold by Robert Birchall 'at his musical circulating library'

copies GERMANY Berlin SBB DMS 210682
UK RCM D226/5 (J. W. Windsor's copy)

c/sig none

remarks As noted on the title-page, AFCK mentioned this hymn in his chapter 'Of variation' in *EMH*, where he called its melody (p 119) 'a German hymn'. The idea of setting it 'with different harmonies to the same melody, for the purpose of expressing the words of every verse better than what could be done with the same harmony' (*ibid.*) had occurred to him before *EMH* was published in 1796. However, the incipits of the variations of this hymn given on *EMH* plate 36 differ from those in the present work.

Op. 8 **Concerto** ESH 31/12/1804

title *A concerto for the piano forte and an orchestra with the cadences. As perform'd by Master Kollmann* [GAK], *at his first public appearance, in the Grand Concert for the New Musical Fund (Opera House) and at the Nobility's Concerts*

sold by 'the principal music shops'

copies UK Bodleian Mus. Instr. I, 136(9); BL h.141.a.(8.) and h.277.(20.); CUL MR340.a.75.46(10); RCM LXII.E.12(7) (inscribed by James William Windsor 'from the author to J W Windsor'); St Andrews s M1.A4M6;262

c/sig AFCK monogram

ms An autograph manuscript of the full score was sold to W[illiam] T[homas] Freemantle as lot 79 in the 30/1/1877 Puttick & Simpson sale of items from AFCK's library. Its subsequent provenance and present whereabouts are not known.

1st perf 15/3/1804 by GAK at the New Musical Fund concert, King's Theatre, Haymarket

remarks Only the piano forte part printed, which included a piano reduction of the orchestral parts. The title-page states that parts for a full orchestra or in an arrangement without wind instruments were available in manuscript, but they have not been preserved.

NTh Prospectus *c*6/1805

remarks *The Eclectic Review* v 1 part 2 (7/1805) p 556 noted that 'Mr Kollman, organist of the German Chapel, at St James's, has issued a prospectus for publishing in folio, a Treatise on Musical Harmony'. No copies of this prospectus for AFCK's *A New Theory* have been located.

Chromatic Fantasy edition *c*5/1806

title *John Sebastian Bach's celebrated Fantasia Chromatica for the piano forte with some additions by A. F. C. Kollmann*

pr/sold by [Thomas] Preston

copies AUSTRALIA K (AFCK's preface printed upside down)
UK BL h.2997.(10.); RCM LVIII.B.24.(2.) (Susannah Ogle's copy); Pendlebury XRa.854.68B.C9 (Samuel Wesley's copy)

c/sig none

remarks The first English edition of J. S. Bach's BWV 903, including both the fantasy and the fugue. Published about the same time as *NTh*¹: the work's preface refers to *NTh*¹, and *NTh*¹ states (p 84) that the Chromatic Fantasy edition 'is now printed by Mr Preston'. Reviewed in *Monthly Magazine* a month before *NTh*¹.

review [Thomas Busby], *Monthly Magazine* v 22 part 2 no. 1 (1/8/1806) p 57

A New Theory (*NTh*^{1}) ESH 20/5/1806

title *A new theory of musical harmony, according to a complete and natural system of that science*

ded 'the president [Sir Joseph Banks] and council of the Royal Society [of London]'

pr W[illiam] Bulmer & Co.

sold by AFCK and 'all the principal musicsellers and booksellers'

copies **AUSTRALIA** K (text wmks 1805 and RG; music wmk RG)
AUSTRIA Gesellschaft der Musikfreunde in Wien 612/32
CANADA UBC MT50.K813
GERMANY Berlin SBB 4° Gk 350
SOUTH AFRICA Wits MT50.KOL [missing]
UK Bodleian fol.θ.333(3); BL 785.m.12; CUL MR580.a.75.7 and MR580.a.80.12; GUL A.x.12 and Cb3-d.20; Lambeth Palace G81.3 K83T; Pendlebury Xra.590.18A.K1; Rowe 55.8; Royal Society 47224 (AFCK's presentation copy, not inscribed by him)
USA Harvard Mus. 310.4; LC MT50.K82 1806 Case; NYPL Mus. Res. *MI+; Newberry folio V 54.4675

c/sig AFCK monogram

ms USA New York Public Library ms Drexel 4199.3, a two-page manuscript in AFCK's handwriting headed 'Five Double Chants in the antient Ecclesiastical Modes', wmk 1815. Its music is extracted from plates 23–24 of *NTh*^{1}, to which AFCK has added figured bass symbols.

remarks According to a report in the 2/8/1815 *Allgemeine musikalische Zeitung*, *NTh*^{1} had nearly sold out, and AFCK had completed the manuscript of an improved section edition of it. Although *NTh*^{2} did not appear until 1823 it is printed on paper with wmk 1817, suggesting that its production began about that time. This *Allgemeine musikalische Zeitung* report said that [Johann Anton] André had arranged for a German translation to be made of *NTh*^{1}, but no translation of it was ever published.

reviews [Thomas Busby], *Monthly Magazine* v 22 part 2 no. 2 (1/9/1806) p 170 [reprinted with minor alterations in Philadelphia in *The Literary Magazine, and American Register* v 6 no. 39 (12/1806) p 479]
[AFCK], *La Belle Assemblée* v 1 part 2 (12/1806) p 601
['Zero'], *Gentleman's Magazine* v 84 part 2 (8/1814) p 155–156

Knightsbridge ESH 14/6/1806

vol. title *Devotional harmony, containing psalms & hymns selected from various authors & adapted to favorite tunes from the works of [George Frideric] Handel, [Martin] Luther, [Thomas] Ravenscroft, Jer[emiah] Clark[e], Drs [William] Croft, [William] Boyce and [Samuel] Howard, etc., by L[eonard] B[enton] Seeley. ... Vol. II.*

pr/sold by L[eonard] B[enton] Seeley

remarks On p 150 of this volume is a hymn, KNIGHTSBRIDGE, by AFCK. Its music basically re-presents the first sung verse of AFCK's 1803 *A Hymn with Various Harmonies*. The text of KNIGHTSBRIDGE consists of the first and last three verses of that 1803 publication.

General Hutchinson's Waltz 1/12/1806

pr Composition no. 6, on the verso side of a sheet of engraved music headed 'Original country-dances, strathspey, and waltz. Composed (for the year 1807.) ... expressly and exclusively for *La Belle Assemblée* ... By eminent composers'. This sheet was issued as an embellishment to *La Belle Assemblée* v 1 part 2 no. 10 (11/1806), published on 1/12/1806. The title-page (p [503]) of this number announced that embellishments issued with the number included 'two German Waltzs, by Dr Kollmann, and Mr Andre'. However, p 558 of this number stated that 'an original Walz, by Dr [sic] Kollmann, is composed and given in the present number' but did not mention André, whose waltz does not appear in the embellishment.

ref John Hely-Hutchinson (from 1803 lieutenant-general, from 1825 2nd earl of Donoughmore [Ireland])

remark John Bell, publisher of *La Belle Assemblée*, advertised that these 'original country dances', including AFCK's, 'have been introduced into the most fashionable private and public assemblies in London, and are likely to become the rage of the season' (*The Times*, 1/1/1807, p 1). The spelling of Kollmann's name on the title-page was corrected during the print run.[14]

On thorough-bass 1/1/1807

pr *La Belle Assemblée* v 1 no. 11 (December 1806) p 600–602

remark An unsigned article, clearly contributed by AFCK because of its devotion to his published and forthcoming works and its lavish praise of his and his children's accomplishments.

---

[14] See page 90 above.

On the art of playing the piano-forte 1/2/1807; 1/3/1807

pr *La Belle Assemblée* v 2 no. 1 (January 1807) p 36–38 and v 2 no. 2 (February 1807) p 94–96

remark An unsigned article, clearly contributed by AFCK because of its high commendation of his work and of his son's pianistic achievements.

A Second Practical Guide to Thorough-Bass *(2nd PGTB)* ESH 23/3/1807

title *A second practical guide to thorough-bass*

ded 'Her Royal Highness Princess Sophia Matilda', i.e., Princess Sophia of Gloucester (daughter of William Henry, Duke of Gloucester and Edinburgh)

sold by AFCK and 'the principal music shops'

copies **AUSTRALIA** K
CANADA National Library MT49 K69 fol.
GERMANY Berlin SBB 4° Gk 349 (Georg Poelchau's copy)
ITALY Florence Conservatorio Luigi Cherubini
UK Bodleian Mus. Inst. I, 136(5) and Tenbury c.7(2); BL H.2878.(3.); Coke 734; CUL MR580.a.75.7(5) and MR580.a.80.12(2); GUL Sp. Coll. A.x.54; RCM D325/2 (Amelia Comer's copy); Lambeth Palace G81.3 K83T; RAM 9.77 KOLLMANN; St Andrews s M1.A4M6;190
USA Baylor MT49.K816 S4 1807; Harvard Mus. 310.4; LC MT49.K72 Case; NYPL Drexel 3251.2; Philadelphia Library Company Rare *Is Jous (b.w.) 7086.F.2; Sibley MT49.K81p.2

c/sig AFCK monogram

remark Advertised as published 'this day' in *The Times*, 22/6/1807 p 2.

review [Thomas Busby], *Monthly Magazine* v 23 no. 4 (1/5/1807) p 379

Review of Stanhope 6–8/1807

title *An essay on Earl Stanhope's 'Principles of the Science of Tuning Instruments with fixed Tones'*

pr *La Belle Assemblée* v 2 no. 18 (6/1807) p 321–323 and v 3 no. 21 (8/1807) p 99–101

ref A review of the mentioned booklet by Charles, 3rd Earl Stanhope which was published in 1806.

remark AFCK is named as the author of this essay.

Waltz for 1808 1/12/1807

title *An original waltz, by Mr Kollmann, for the year 1808, composed expressly & exclusively for* La Belle Assemblée, *& to be had only with that work*

pr on a sheet of engraved music included as an embellishment to *La Belle Assemblée* v 3 no. 25 (1/12/1807)

remarks Although the composer is named only as 'Mr Kollmann', the waltz can be ascribed to AFCK because of his connections with this magazine and the circumstance that GAK's op. 1 was not published until 1808. Also, the theme of this waltz is a variant of AFCK's *General Hutchinson's Waltz* entered at 1/12/1806 above.

Practical Guide/Practische Anleitung 5/1808

title *A practical guide to thorough bass / Practische Anleitung zum Generalbasse ... Englisch und Deutsch*

pr/sold by Offenbach am Main, Johann [Anton] André

copies AUSTRALIA K
AUSTRIA Gesellschaft der Musikfreunde in Wien 619/Schulen (inscribed to Ernst Ludwig Gerber by André on behalf of AFCK)
GERMANY Frankfurt Universitätsbibliothek Mus 141; André archive, Offenbach;[15] Würzburg Universitätsbibliothek 35/A 13.1
SWITZERLAND Zürich Zentralbibliothek Mus Jac B 32
USA Columbia MT49.K7; Florida State MT49.K75P7 1808; LC MT49.K7; Princeton Mendel OVERSIZE MT49.K7q; Yale MT49.K81 (owned by Johann Christian Heinrich Rinck and Lowell Mason)

c/sig none

ms GERMANY Staats- und Universitätsbibliothek Hamburg, ms 347/2b (a contemporary manuscript copy by F. C. H. Meyer of the German text and music examples of this work)

remarks Publisher no. 2601. A lithographed bilingual edition; the English text is that of *2nd PGTB*. The editor's note ('Anzeige') on p iii is dated 'Offenbach a/M, im May 1808'. Although not identified in the work, the editor was Johann Anton André, as the inscription from the 'Herausgeber' on the Gesellschaft der Musikfreunde copy is in his handwriting.

review [Anonymous], *Allgemeine musikalische Zeitung* (Leipzig) v 11 no. 25 (22/3/1809) col. 390–395

---

[15] According to Britta Constapel, *Der Musikverlag Johann André in Offenbach am Main...*, Tutzing, 1998, p 176.

Op. 9	**Melody of the 100th Psalm**	ESH 25/4/1809
title	*The melody of the hundredth psalm, with examples and directions for an hundred different harmonies in four parts*	
ded	'The Honourable Miss [Georgina] Charlotte Onslow'	
sold by	AFCK and 'the principal music shops'	
reviews	[Gottlieb Lewis Engelbach], *Repository of Arts, Literature, Fashions...* v 5 no. 25 (1/1811) p 47 ['Zero'], *Gentleman's Magazine* v 84 part 2 (8/1814) p 156	
copies	**UK** Bodleian Mus. Voc. I, 90(7); Edinburgh University; GUL A.x.12 and S.b.36	
later	**UK** Bodleian Tenbury c.7(6) [wmk 1815]	
c/sig	AFCK monogram	
remark	Example xxvi of this work reprinted inaccurately in W[illiam] H[enry] Havergal, *A History of the Old Hundredth Psalm Tune, with Specimens*, New York, 1854, p 66.	

Op. 10	**Twelve Analyzed Fugues *(TAF*[1]*)* 1-4**	ESH 28/12/1809
title	*No. 1 of a series of analyzed fugues with double counterpoints. Composed for two performers on one piano forte or organ.*	
sold by	AFCK and 'the principal music shops'	
copies	**AUSTRALIA K** **UK** RCM D1489/14 (lacks title-page, apparently Samuel Wesley's copy); St Andrews s M1.A4M6;151	
c/sig	AFCK monogram	
remarks	The title-page announced that this work 'will be completed in three numbers, each containing four fugues, and a sheet of introductory explanations' and that 'a title, and preface, will be given with the last number'. The title 'Twelve analyzed fugues' was first used on the title-page issued with the last number.	
reviews	[Thomas Busby], *Monthly Magazine* v 29 no. 1 (1/2/1810) p 74 [Joseph Kemp?], *New Musical Magazine, Review and Register* v 1 no. 12 (2/1810) p 202 and v 2 no. 1 (3/1810) p 17–18 [Anon.], *Le Beau Monde and Monthly Register* v 2 no. 13 (4/1810) p 457–458 [reprinted in Dublin in *Monthly Panorama* v 1 no. 6 (6/1810) p 383–384]	

Op. 10 **Twelve Analyzed Fugues *(TAF¹)* 5–8** ESH 18/4/1810
title *No. 2 of a series of analyzed fugues with double counterpoints. Composed for two performers on one piano forte or organ.*
sold by AFCK and 'the principal music shops'
copy UK St Andrews s M1.A4M6;143 (lacks title-page sheet)
review [Thomas Busby], *Monthly Magazine* v 29 no. 6 (1/6/1810) p 483

Op. 10 **Twelve Analyzed Fugues *(TAF¹)* 9–12** ESH 8/10/1810
title [of set of 12 fugues] *Twelve analyzed fugues with double counterpoints in all intervals, and introductory explanations. Composed for two performers on one piano forte or organ*
sold by AFCK and 'the principal music shops'
copy [of fugues 9–12 only] UK St Andrews s M1.A4M6;130
copies [of set of 12 fugues] SWITZERLAND Zürich Zentralbibliothek Mus Jac B 31
UK Bodleian Mus.Instr. I, 136(10) and Tenbury c.7(4); BL h.277.(17.); Coke 735; RCM LIX.C.21
USA LC MT59.K71T9
c/sig AFCK monogram
ms arr AUSTRIA Gesellschaft der Musikfreunde in Wien IX 23331, IX 23378 and IX 23383, a contemporary manuscript arrangement of fugues 1, 8 and 12 for string quartet
reviews [Thomas Busby], *Monthly Magazine* v 30 no. 4 (1/11/1810) p 361
[Gottlieb Lewis Engelbach], *Repository of Arts, Literature, Fashions...* v 5 no. 25 (1/1811) p 46–47
[Anon.], *La Belle Assemblée* supplement, n.s. v 2 no. 14 (1/2/1811) p 384

Rondo on the Chord of the Diminished Seventh ESH 3/11/1810
title *A rondo on the chord of the diminished seventh, shewing the immediate progression of that chord to all the twelve major and minor keys*
sold by AFCK
copies UK Bodleian Mus. Instr. I, 136(16); BL h.277.(21.); St Andrews s M1.A4M6;132
c/sig AFCK monogram
review [Gottlieb Lewis Engelbach], *Repository of Arts, Literature, Fashions...* v 5 no. 29 (5/1811) p 289

Quarterly Musical Register no. 1 *(QMR1)* 1/1/1812

title *The Quarterly Musical Register no. I.*
pr W[illiam] Bulmer and Co.
pub Becket & Porter
copies **BELGIUM** Fétis 4680 (AFCK's presentation copy to Charles Burney, includes AFCK→CB, 3/2/1812, lacks wrapper)
GERMANY Berlin SBB Mus. B 4610 (Georg Poelchau's copy)
UK BL C.190.aa.25; Manchester Central R780.5 Qd73 (lacks wrapper); Pendlebury XRb.856.18A.Q1 (lacks wrapper and the last page of engraved music); RCM XII.D.23 (lacks wrapper)
USA Boston Public Library **M.393.10 (lacks wrapper); NYPL Drexel 2210.3 (lacks wrapper)
facsimile in this book
c/sig none
adverts *The Morning Post*, 27/12/1811, p 2; *The Times*, 26/12/1811 p 3, 28/12/1811 p 2, and 1/1/1812 p 2
remark Includes articles by AFCK and others and two musical compositions by AFCK.
review ['Zero'], *Gentleman's Magazine* v 83 part 1 (4/1813) p 334–336

Quarterly Musical Register no. 2 *(QMR2)* 1/4/1812

title *The Quarterly Musical Register no. II.*
pr Collins, Memoranda Office
pub Becket & Porter
copies **GERMANY** Berlin SBB Mus. B 4610 (Georg Poelchau's copy)
UK BL C.190.aa.25; Manchester Central R780.5 Qd73 (lacks wrapper); RCM XII.D.23 (lacks wrapper)
USA Boston Public Library **M.393.10 (lacks wrapper); NYPL Drexel 2210.3 (lacks wrapper)
facsimile in this book
c/sig none
remarks Includes articles by AFCK and others and two musical compositions by AFCK. The *QMR2* wrapper listed some articles planned for the third number of this periodical, but that number was never issued.
review ['Zero'], *Gentleman's Magazine* v 83 part 1 (4/1813) p 334–336

An Essay on Practical Musical Composition, 2nd ed. *(EPMC^2)* 1812; >1/4/1812; ?<1/7/1812

title *An essay on practical musical composition, according to the nature of that science and the principles of the greatest musical authors. Second edition, with considerable additions and improvements.*

ded King George III
pr Collins, Memoranda Printing Office
sold by AFCK 'and all the principal musicsellers and booksellers'
copies **AUSTRALIA** K
BELGIUM Fétis 6774
GERMANY Berlin SBB 4° Gk 346[2]
UK Bodleian Tenbury c.7(5); BL i.37.pp; RCM E108
USA Arizona University MT40.K75; Harvard Mus. 310.4F; LC MT40.K77 1812; Stanford MT40.K81 1812; Yale MT40.K81 1812+ (Lowell Mason's copy)
facsimile New York, 1973, of text of *EPMC*[1] and music plates of *EPMC*[2]
c/sig AFCK monogram
remarks Published after 1/4/1812 because subscriptions for it were sought in *QMR2*, which is mentioned in this work; and presumably published before 1/7/1812, as work says that *The Quarterly Musical Register* is 'to be continued', but its third number, which was due to be published on 1/7/1812, never appeared.
review ['Zero'], *Gentleman's Magazine* v 83 part 1 (4/1813) p 334–336

South bridge 1812?

vol. title *A collection of psalm & hymn tunes, (some of which are original) in three & four parts; adapted to the various metres which are used in the established church & dissenting chapels in Scotland. Selected & adapted to general use, by David Wilson.*
text 'Let us sing to God above'
pr/sold by the editor (David Wilson, a 'teacher of vocal music') and John Sutherland, both in Edinburgh
remarks On p 29 is a hymn, SOUTH BRIDGE, whose music is adapted from AFCK's hymn printed on plate 20 no. 2 of *EMH* (where the text, beginning 'Praise the Lord Jehovah praise', is from the Rev. Richard Sandilands's versification of the 150th psalm).[16] The same tune with another text is found in the hymn ST JAMES published in 1816 and the hymn GOODNESS published in 1822?. Both are entered below.

St James 1815; >28/9/1815

vol title *Musica Sacra: A Collection of Psalm Tunes, Hymns and set Pieces. Compiled at the request, and published under the patronage of the Oneida Musical Society.*

---

[16] Richard Sandilands, *Psalms, Hymns, and Anthems, selected for the use of Ebury-Chapel, near Sloane-Square, Chelsea*, Chelsea, 1792, p 92. See *EMH*, p 87.

text 'Who shall the Lord's elect condemn?'

pr/pub Utica, New York, Seward & Williams

remarks On p 154–155 of this collection is a hymn, ST JAMES, whose music is adapted from AFCK's hymn printed on plate 20 no. 2 of *EMH.* The title of this book was deposited in the office of the clerk of the Northern District of New York on 28/9/1815; hence its publication date was after then. This hymn was reprinted on p 154–155 of the 'second edition, revised and corrected' of *Musica Sacra* that Seward & Williams printed and published in 1816. A different version of this hymn was printed and published by William Williams in Thomas Hastings and Solomon Warriner, *Musica Sacra: or Springfield and Utica Collections United...*, revised edition, Utica, 1818, p 14–15. The name 'St James' probably was taken from AFCK's address.

An Essay on Musical Harmony *(EMH^Am)* early 1817

title *An essay on musical harmony, according to the nature of that science and the principles of the greatest musical authors. First American edition, with notes. Published under the patronage of the Oneida Musical Society.*

ded Charles Burney, Mus. Doc.

pr/pub Utica, New York, Seward & Williams

copies **AUSTRALIA** K (two copies)

CANADA Moncton Université MT50.K811; Toronto University musi E-6 197 RBSC

UK CUL MR590.c.80.2

USA Azusa Pacific MT50.K6; Boston Athanæum TBMR TH.K83; Boston University MT50.E17; Buffalo & Erie County Central Library RBR MUSIC 1817.K7; Cincinnati University MT50.K65 E7; Colorado University MT50.K77 1817; Columbia MT50.A2K6 1817g; Florida State MT50.K811; Fordham SPEC AMER 1817 7; Georgia University MT50.K811; Harvard Houghton Acc. *65-1897 and Mus.310.4.5; Iowa MT50.K811 1817; Johns Hopkins MT50.K81; LC MT50.K811; New England Conservatory VAULT MT50.K63 E8 (two copies); New-York Historical Society MT50.K81 E5; NYPL Mus. Res. *MI and Drexel 3104 and Drexel 3105; Newberry V 54.468; New York State Historical Association Sp. Coll. 781.3 K81; New York State Library (Albany) 781.3 K81; Northwestern ML444.K65; Oberlin 781.3 K83; Philadelphia Free Library 781.3 K83; Philadelphia Library Company Rare Am 1817 Kol 60482.O; Phillips Academy Andover (Mass.) On 781.3 K83; St Charles Borromeo Seminary MT40.K81 1817; Sibley MT50.K81 (two copies); Southwestern Baptist Theological Seminary MT40.K74 E8 1817;

USA (continued) Trinity College (Hartford) MT40.K81; Tulane 781.3 K83; Utica Public Library R 781.3 K83; Utica College Library MT50.K811; Vassar MT50.K811; Virginia University MT50.K8 1817; Washington & Lee MT40.K811 1817; Washington University (St Louis) ML3815.K833 1817 and AER8517; Wayne State MT50.K811 1817; Yale MT50.K81 1817 (Lowell Mason's copy)

c/sig none

remarks A typographically reset edition of *EMH*, not authorised by AFCK, with the music examples integrated into the text and footnotes by an anonymous 'American editor' added. The book is dated 1817 and states that its title was deposited in the office of the clerk of the Northern District of New York on 19/11/1816.

review ['X.', i.e., Alexander Metcalf Fisher], *The American Monthly Magazine and Critical Review* v 2 no. 5 (3/1818) p 344–349

The Praise of God 6/1/1817

title *The Praise of God. A sacred oratorio, in two acts. Selected from the Holy Scriptures. / Das Lob Gottes. Ein geistliches Oratorium in zwey Acten. Aus der heiligen Schrift gezogen.*

instr solo voices, chorus and orchestra

mss
1. Bodleian ms Tenbury 852–853. 'First original manuscript' dated 'London, 1817' and inscribed by AFCK on ms 852 f 2 'To his son, George Augustus Kollmann, this score is presented by the Author. January 6th 1817'. This manuscript has no dedication.
2. BL R.M. 21.g.1. 'Original manuscript' dated 'London, 1817', wmk 'J Whatman 1817', with AFCK's autograph dedication to the Prince Regent. This is a presentation copy of ms 1.

ded The Prince Regent [ms 2 only]

remarks In both manuscripts the title-page and dedication page are in AFCK's handwriting but the music pages are not. The music pages in both mss have annotations by him. The text is in English and German throughout, allowing the work to be sung in either language. AFCK planned to have the English text printed, as an autograph copy of this text, included in Bodleian ms Tenbury 852, includes the phrase 'Printed for the Author, Friary St James's Palace' in his handwriting. No printed copies are known. The oratorio's finale 'The num'rous works of God proclaim' is set to the music of AFCK's 1803 *A Hymn with Various Harmonies.*

Op. 11 An Introduction to Extemporary Modulation — ESH 14/11/1820

title — *An introduction to extemporary modulation, in six general lessons for the piano forte, or harp, with directions how they may also be rendered useful for the violin and violoncello*

sold by — AFCK and 'the principal music shops'

copies — AUSTRALIA K
UK Bodleian Mus. Instr. I, 240(1); BL e.146; CUL MR588.a.80.3(3); GUL Cb3-x.2; St Andrews s M1.A4M6;260
USA Yale MT52.K81 (Lowell Mason's copy)

c/sig — AFCK monogram

reviews — [Anon.], *Monthly Magazine* v 50 part 2 no. 5 (1/12/1820) p 464
[Gottlieb Lewis Engelbach], *Repository of Arts, Literature, Fashions...* 2nd ser. v 11 no. 61 (1/1/1821) p 57–58
[Anon.], *New Monthly Magazine* v 3 (1/1/1821) p 30–31

Bemerkungen über Logiers System — 11/1821

title — *Bemerkungen über Hrn. J. B. Logier's sogenanntes 'Neues System des Musikunterrichts' (New System of Musical Education)*

pr — *Allgemeine musikalische Zeitung* (Leipzig) v 23 no. 46 (14/11/1821) col. 769-774; v 23 no. 47 (21/11/1821) col. 785–794; and v 23 no. 48 (28/11/1821) col. 801–814

remark — AFCK is incorrectly named 'A. F. B. Kollmann'.

Nachtrag zu den Bemerkungen — 20/3/1822

title — *Nachtrag zu den Bemerkungen über Hrn. J. B. Logier's sogenanntes Neues System des Musikunterrichts, im 46sten und folgenden Stücken der allgemeinen musikalischen Zeitung von 1821*

pr — *Intelligenz-Blatt zur allgemeinen musikalischen Zeitung* (Leipzig) no. 3 (3/1822) col. 9-13, issued with the 20/3/1822 number of that journal (v 24 no. 12)

remarks — AFCK's submission to the *Allgemeine musikalische Zeitung* is dated 1/2/1822. Its publication correctly names him 'A. F. C. Kollmann'.

Op. 10 Twelve Analyzed Fugues, 2nd ed. *(TAF²)* — late 1822

title — *Second edition. Twelve analyzed fugues with double counterpoints in all intervals, and introductory explanations. Composed for two performers on one piano forte or organ.*

sold by — AFCK and 'the principal music shops'

copies UK GUL Sp. Coll. Q.b.18
USA LC MT59.K71T9 1822
c/sig AFCK monogram
remarks Work has imprint date 1822. Advertised as 'just published' in *Journal of Music and the Drama* v 1 no. 2 (22/2/1823) p 31. Therefore presumably published late in 1822.

Goodness 1822?

vol. title *The Edinburgh Sacred Harmony, for the use of churches & families. ... Edited by R[obert] A[rchibald] Smith. Volume 1.*
text 'Lift your voice and thankful sing'
sold by Robert Purdie (Edinburgh); S[amuel] Chappell, Goulding & d'Almaine, and Paine & Hopkins (London)
remarks The work is no. 29 in this serially issued publication. The music is substantially the same as *South Bridge* entered at 1812? above. An advertisement in *The Harmonicon*, January 1824, announced that no. 7 of *The Edinburgh Sacred Harmony* was 'just published' and that no. 8 was to be published on 8/4/1824, a time-table that suggests that this work was published in 1822. The preface to the completed volume is dated 24/12/1829.

A New Theory, 2nd ed. *(NTh^2)* 2/1823

title *A new theory of musical harmony, according to a complete and natural system of that science. Second edition, with considerable improvements.*
ded 'the president [Sir Joseph Banks] and council of the Royal Society'
pr W[illiam] Nicol, successor to W[illiam] Bulmer and Co.
sold by AFCK and 'all the principal musicsellers and booksellers'
copies AUSTRALIA K
ITALY Florence Conservatorio Luigi Cherubini
UK Bodleian Tenbury c.7(1); Manchester Central Re f781.3Kt55; RCM E109
c/sig AFCK monogram (except Manchester Central copy)
remarks Work dated 1823 on title-page but its letterpress text and engraved music plates are printed on paper with wmk 1817. Presumably typeset before 15/1/1823, because sale catalogues (at BL S.-C. Evans) of the auctioneer R[obert] H[arding] Evans bear the imprint 'W. Nicol, successor to W. Bulmer and Co.' in all 1822 catalogues, of which the last (S.-C. Evans 17(8)) is dated 18/12/1822, but on all 1823 sale catalogues, of which the first (S.-C. Evans 18(1)) is dated

15/1/1823, the imprint reads 'W. Nicol' without naming Bulmer.[17] Advertised as published 'this day' in *The Times*, 7/2/1823 p 4, and as 'just published' in *Journal of Music and the Drama* v 1 no. 2 (22/2/1823) p 31.

Remarks on Logier 4/1824

title *Remarks on what Mr J. B. Logier calls his new system of musical education; with a sequel. Written, and translated from the German, by A. F. C. Kollmann.*

pr W[illiam] Nicol

sold by AFCK and 'all the principal musick-sellers and booksellers'

copies **UK** BL D-7895.b.39.(2.); GUL A.c.4 and A.c.5

c/sig none

remarks AFCK's translation of *Bemerkungen über Logiers System* and *Nachtrag zu den Bemerkungen*, with a new preface. Refers (p iv–v) to Logier's announced presence in London 'during the ensuing three months of April, May, and June'. Advertised as 'just published' in *John Bull* v 4 no. 17 (25/4/1824) p 137.

review [Anon.], *Monthly Critical Gazette* v 1 no. 1 (1/6/1824) p 47–48

Remarks on Logier, 2nd ed. 5/1824

title *Remarks on what Mr J. B. Logier calls his new system of musical education; with a sequel. Written, and translated from the German, by A. F. C. Kollmann. Second edition, with additions.*

pr W[illiam] Nicol

sold by AFCK and 'all the principal musick-sellers and booksellers'

copies USA LC MT24.L835 no. 8 Case;
Pennsylvania State MT24.K6513 1824

c/sig none

remarks Advertised as 'just published' in *John Bull* v 4 no. 21 (23/5/1824) p 169 and in *The Times*, 29/5/1824 p 4. Differs from the first edition by the addition of a new 'Preface to this second edition' on p v–viii.

review [Anon.], *Philomathic Journal and Literary Review* v 2 part 2 (4/1825) p 433–450

---

[17] See [Peter Isaac], 'Some sale catalogues printed by William Bulmer', *Bulmer Papers* v 1 no. 3 (August 1967) p 43–44.

Kollmann and Müller 8/1828

title — *Ueber Logier's Musikunterrichts-System von A. F. B.* [sic] *Kollmann, Clavierlehrer und Organisten an der Königlich-Großbritannischen Hof-Kapelle zu St. James in London und C. F. Müller, Clavierlehrer, Komponisten und Königl. Preuß. Gesanglehrer am Friedrich-Wilhelms-Gymnasium zu Berlin*

pub — Munich, Falter und Sohn

copies — **BELGIUM** Fétis 6326
GERMANY Bayerische Staatsbibliothek München Mus.th. 1792; Stadtbibliothek Leipzig I 8° 88; Universitätsbibliothek Rostock Dd-572(1).12
NETHERLANDS Openbare Bibliotheek Amsterdam, Toonkunst 212-G-40
UK BL 786.e.65.(2.)
USA Stanford ML423.L83K81

c/sig — none

remarks — Publication of this book noticed in *Intelligenz-Blatt zur allgemeinen musikalischen Zeitung* no. 13 (9/1828) col. 52, issued with the 3/9/1828 number of that journal (v 30 no. 36). It is not known whether AFCK was aware of this book. His chapter (p 5–37) is a slightly altered version of his *Bemerkungen über Logiers System*. Carl Friedrich Müller's chapter (p 38–56) is independent of AFCK's. The foreword by A. P. Schmidt (p 3–4) does not mention either author by name.

review — [Anon.], *Allgemeine musikalische Zeitung* (Leipzig) v 31 no. 39 (9/1929) col. 651–652

Antwerp 1830

vol. title — *Devotional Harmony ...*, 3rd edition, part 2

text — 'Yes since God himself has said it'

pr/sold by — L. B. Seeley and Sons

remarks — On p 124 of this volume is a hymn, ANTWERP, by AFCK. The music is from no. 2 of his *c*1784 *Sechs geistliches Lieder*.

later edition — Printed—without text, and dated 1790—as no. 119 in Henry Parr, *Church of England Psalmody*, 4th ed., London, 1864, p 65.

Kollmann's quintet, mentioned in *An Essay on Practical Musical Composition*, is presumed lost. In both editions of this *Essay* the opening section of its 'last presto' is printed on plate 1. In *EPMC*[1]

Kollmann described this work as 'written but not yet published' (p 3), and in *EPMC*[2] he referred to it 'a MS. quintet of mine' (p 2).

A hymn named CRETE, said to be composed by 'Kollmann', was published in Arthur Clifton's *An Original Collection of Psalm Tunes, extracted from the beautiful works, (chiefly sacred) of the most celebrated ancient and modern composers, to which are added several tunes composed expressly for this work*, Baltimore, 1819. Its text, beginning 'Thy name, Almighty Lord, shall sound through distant lands', is by Rev. Isaac Watts.[18] Clifton—who changed his name from Philip Antony Corri after he left London for Baltimore in 1817—was a director of the Philharmonic Society from 1813 to 1815, and may have met Kollmann, who subscribed to that Society, at that time.

Clifton's family had connections with Kollmann. Clifton's father, Domenico Corri, was a principal of Corri, Dussek & Co., the principal music sellers in 1796 of Kollmann's *The First Beginning on the Piano-Forte* and *The Shipwreck*. Clifton's uncle, Natale Corri, managed the Edinburgh affiliate of that firm and advertised in 1817 that he taught young ladies 'the principles of harmony and composition according to the institutes of the celebrated A. F. C. Kollmann and other eminent modern theorists'.[19] However, the attribution of CRETE to either A. F. C. or George Kollmann is doubtful, as its tune has not been located in any other source,[20] and evidence of direct contact between Clifton and the Kollmann family has not been found.

---

[18] I[saac] Watts, *The Psalms of David imitated in the Language of the New Testament, and apply'd to the Christian State and Worship*, London, 1719, p 306.

[19] *Caledonian Mercury*, 8 May 1817, p 3. Although Corri proposed to teach young ladies in classes, he noted that 'the plan which he intends to follow is essentially different from that lately adopted in Dublin and other places', i.e., by Logier and his followers, as described in section I.25 above.

[20] According to the *Hymn Tune Index*, http://hymntune.library.uiuc.edu/

3. Literary and Musical Works by George Kollmann

In this section George Kollmann's literary and musical works are listed in their estimated chronological order. The format of entries and the abbreviations used are the same as in the preceding section (see pages 224–225 above). Patents granted to or on behalf of George Kollmann are not listed here but are described in part I of this book.

Op. 1 Three grand sonatas 1808; <6/1808

title *Three grand sonatas for the piano forte. The second one with an obligato accompaniment for the violin.*
ded AFCK 'by his son and pupil'
pub GAK 'at Mr Kollmann's, Friary, St James's Palace'
copies UK BL h.726.f.(9); RCM LXII.D.25.(2) (J. W. Windsor's copy, presented to him by GAK)
facsimile of RCM copy of title-page and the third sonata, in Nicholas Temperley (ed.), *The London Pianoforte School 1766–1860* v 7, New York, 1985
c/sig G. A. K.
review [Thomas Busby], *Monthly Magazine* v 25 no. 5 (1/6/1808) p 447

Air from Handel's lessons ESH 7/12/1808

title *An air from Handel's lessons with nine variations for the piano forte*
ded 'Miss Wyndhams' [i.e., Misses Wyndham]
pub GAK 'at Mr Kollmann's[,] Friary, St James's Palace'
copies UK Bodleian Mus. Instr. I, 136(15); BL h.277.(19); RCM LXII.D.25.(1) (J. W. Windsor's copy, given to him by GAK)
facsimile of RCM copy, in Nicholas Temperley (ed.), *The London Pianoforte School 1766–1860* v 7, New York, 1985
c/sig G. A. K.
remark The air is Handel's 'Harmonious Blacksmith', HWV 430.
review [Thomas Busby], *Monthly Magazine* v 28 no. 3 (1/10/1809) p 317

Six waltzes ESH 19/8/1812

title *Six waltzes for the piano forte*
ded Miss Douglass
pub GAK

copies **AUSTRALIA K**
UK Bodleian Mus. Instr. I, 136(11); BL h.277.(18);
St Andrews s M1.A4M6;138

c/sig G.A.K.

Comparative Statement 1839; <2/1839?

title *Comparative statement of the imperfections of the present system of railways and locomotive and other carriages used thereon, and of the improvements offered in the new plan proposed by Mr G. Kollmann, for which he has obtained a patent*

pr W[illiam] Nicol

copies UK BL 1882.d.1.(136); National Archives in file MT 6/1/20
USA Illinois Urbana Q385.K833C

remarks Printed by Nicol at 60, Pall Mall, to where he removed (from 51, Pall Mall) in 1839.[21] Work printed on a single sheet, presumably distributed but not sold by GAK. Probably the 'statement of the qualities of my new railway and locomotive engine' that he enclosed in GAK→Henry Brougham, 2/2/1839. Presumably printed before 26/4/1839, when GAK presented the eleven 'improvements' listed in work to the House of Commons Select Committee on Turnpike Trusts, which reprinted that list on 6/6/1839.

A printed prospectus of George Kollmann's pianos, mentioned in his advertisements in *The Musical World* from 31 May 1838 to 27 December 1838, is not preserved. 'Grand symphonies and various other musical mss' noted in his obituary are presumed lost.[22] His manuscripts no longer extant included 'Canzonets' composed not later than 1824[23] and a quartet for piano, violin, horn and violoncello which was performed at his concert in the Hanover Square Rooms on 15 April 1839.[24]

---

[21] See Philip A. H. Brown, *London Publishers and Printers c.1800–1870*, London, 1982, p 138.

[22] 'The late George Augustus Kollmann', *Dramatic and Musical Review* v 4 no. 158 (5 April 1845) p 174–175.

[23] According to 'Kollman [sic], G. A.', *A Dictionary of Musicians*, London, Sainsbury & Co., 1824, v 2 p 23, George 'has composed many very beautiful canzonets'.

[24] 'Mr Kollmann's concert', *The Times*, 17 April 1839, p 5.

A hymn called QUEEN SQUARE CHAPEL in *Peck's Miscellaneous Collection of Sacred Music* (London, J[ames] Peck, 1810, v 3 p 87), is ascribed there to 'Mr G. Kollmann'. Its text, beginning 'Ere I sleep for ev'ry favour', is the first two verses of Hymn 20 in John Shepherd, *Selection of Psalms and Hymns ... designed for the use of the congregation at Queen's-Square Chapel*, 3rd edition, London, 1824, p 20–21.[25] These verses were written by Rev. John Cennick (1718–1755), a Moravian minister. The attribution of this music to George Kollmann in the *Hymn Tune Index*[26] is doubtful because he is not known to have composed hymns or to have had any connection with the Queen's Square Chapel, and it seems improbable that he would have set a text that was written by a Moravian minister.

[25] Prior editions of this book have not been located.

[26] See note 20 on page 251 above.

4. Calendar of Correspondence of the Kollmann Family

The extant correspondence of A. F. C. Kollmann and his children, and other correspondence that mentions them in a substantial way, is entered here in its estimated chronological order. The location of each original letter or copy thereof is given, followed by a reference to any prior printing of its text. A summary of the letter's content is then presented.

In the Introduction to *The Quarterly Musical Register* Kollmann cited his 'extensive correspondence' as one of the reasons for thinking that he could conduct this journal 'to the satisfaction of the public'.[27] Unfortunately, most of this correspondence has not survived.

Charles Burney→Mrs Chambers 19/1/1798

King's College, London, Archives, Burney;

printed in Robert Müller-Hartmann, 'Two unknown letters of Charles Burney', *Journal of the Warburg & Courtauld Institutes* v 3 (1939–1940) p 161–164[28]

Replying to a query from Mrs Chambers [perhaps Lady Frances Chambers], Burney regrets that he does not know 'any one elementary treatise on musical composition in our language that I can heartily recommend'. However, 'an excellent work on composition', *EMH*, was published 'last year' [in fact, two years ago]. AFCK, a German, 'did me the honour to address this work to me'. It can be had at [Joseph] Dale's Music Shop, Oxford Street. Although no one book is sufficient to solve 'all the difficulties which a young student in composition has to encounter', Burney can 'recollect no work, on the same subject, in our language, that contains so much useful instruction' as *EMH*.

AFCK→John Wall Callcott 20/5/1798

BL Add Ms 30022 f 1

AFCK thanks Callcott for sending [Elway] Bevin's treatise [*A Briefe and Short Instruction of the Art of Music* (London, 1631)]. In return AFCK sends a work by [Daniel Gottlob] Türk, who is 'a man of weight in Germany'.

---

[27] *QMR p 1.*

[28] Burney 'recycled' some of the content of this letter for the Correspondence page of *The Monthly Review* v 27 (September 1798) p 120, where he commented that there was 'no other' recent English-language 'book on Composition with which we were satisfied, except *Kollman*'s [sic] Essay on Musical Harmony'.

John Wall Callcott→AFCK 16/10/1798

BL Add Ms 27688 f 1–6

Callcott thanks AFCK for lending works by [Johann Philipp] Kirnberger and [Friedrich Wilhelm] Marpurg. Marpurg's works are easier to understand. As 'confirmed' in manuscripts by [William] Boyce [which Callcott owned; now Bodleian ms Don.c.136], Callcott thinks 'that a fundamental bass must have a perfect [and not a diminished] fifth'.[29] He accordingly questions a music example in AFCK's *EMH* in which a chord having notes {B,D,F} is given B as its fundamental bass.

AFCK→John Wall Callcott 24/10/1798

BL Add Ms 30022 f 2–3

AFCK is pleased to reply to Callcott's question [in the preceding letter] 'as it would be better if we could agree about it before we publish' our works [announced in AFCK's 1798 *EPMC Proposals* and Callcott's *Plan of a Practical Dictionary of Music ... to be published early in the year 1799* (London, 1798)] than to have public controversy afterwards. AFCK refers Callcott to passages in *EMH*. AFCK knows that Carl Philipp Emanuel Bach and 'some other modern authors' did not 'rank' as fundamental a bass that supported a diminished fifth. He sends a work by Kirnberger which he hopes will convince Callcott that Kirnberger's system 'is more natural and more applicable to all cases' than Boyce's. Dr [Johann Nicolaus] Forkel's comments about this work appear in his *Allgemeine Litteratur der Musik* [Leipzig, 1792].

Although Marpurg never 'revoked' his own system, he appears to have become 'convinced' that Kirnberger's system was preferable, as AFCK knows 'a gentleman [not identified] who assures me that he has instructed Marpurg's son [Johann Friedrich Marpurg] in harmony according to the system of Kirnberger'. Boyce probably did not adopt that system because 'it was not sufficiently well known to him'.

AFCK thanks Callcott for sending 'two pieces' and hopes that they can 'be an exception from those artists who are not friendly to each other'.

John Wall Callcott→AFCK 26/10/1798

BL Add Ms 27688 f 15–24

Callcott will be 'ever proud' to acknowledge his obligations to AFCK, even if he is 'forced to differ from the theory' that AFCK supports. Callcott conceives that the diminished triad has no 'quality to characterise it as a fundamental chord'. Kirnberger 'deserves the highest encomium for sweeping away the rubbish of the French system' [of Jean-Philippe Rameau], but ought to have gone further by 'neglecting the diminished triad entirely'. Callcott promises to send AFCK some extracts from Boyce's manuscripts.

---

[29] Boyce's manuscript is discussed and its history is given in *SOMIB*, v 1 p 110–111.

AFCK→John Wall Callcott 30/10/1798

BL Add Ms 30022 f 4–5

AFCK presents some 'leading points' of Kirnberger's system. Although a perfect triad is required to begin and end a piece, the 'imperfect [i.e., diminished] triad has all the other characteristics of a real fundamental chord'.

John Wall Callcott→AFCK 3/12/1798?

BL Add Ms 27688 f 30ʳ–54ʳ [verso sides used for other purposes; letter undated in this manuscript, but the next letter cites this date]

Callcott writes 'a very voluminous epistle'. He provides 'an historical sketch' of his 'musical opinions in point of theory'. Some time ago he printed a statement of his arguments and distributed it privately to friends in the music profession, including the late Drs [Thomas Sanders] Dupuis, [Benjamin] Cooke and [Philip] Hayes. Some of Callcott's tenets were disputed, and he set the matter aside, but was 'surprised and gratified' to find his old ideas justified by Boyce's manuscripts. He provides some 'general outlines' of Boyce's system.

AFCK→John Wall Callcott 6/12/1798

BL Add Ms 30022 f 8–9

AFCK has received Callcott's two letters of 3/12/1798 and read 'the musical one with particular attention'.[30] AFCK is unable to answer it without disappointing or offending Callcott and therefore declines to say anything on the subject until he has the pleasure of seeing him.

AFCK→John Wall Callcott 8/1/1799

BL Add Ms 30022 f 10–11

AFCK has read, and returns, Callcott's 'treatise and manuscript essay'. The more AFCK sees of the system Callcott proposes the less he approves it, 'because it departs from the three great fundamental principles of Kirnberger, simple, natural, unexceptionable'. As Callcott has 'already begun publishing' his system and seems 'determined to oppose' Kirnberger's system, AFCK proposes to suspend commenting upon Callcott's system until its publication is complete, when AFCK can convince Callcott and the public 'at once' of its deficiencies.

AFCK sends Türk's *Klavierschule* [Leipzig, 1789]. If Callcott has finished with [Christoph Gottlieb] Schröter's work AFCK would like it back because it belongs to someone else.[31]

---

[30] No 'non-musical' letter from Callcott to Kollmann dated 3/12/1798 is extant.

[31] According to a note by Callcott in BL Add Ms 27669 f 29ʳ, this work was Schröter's *Deutliche Anweisung zum General-Bass* (Halberstadt, 1772), which AFCK had borrowed from Charles Griesbach.

John Wall Callcott→AFCK 10/1/1799

BL Add Ms 27689 f 1-35

From AFCK's last two letters Callcott suspects that their difference of opinion is deeper than he had thought. He apologises for sending another long letter but wants (1) to explain his ideas 'on theory and practice', (2) to 'vindicate the simplicity' of Boyce's system, and (3) to send AFCK some further queries.

Callcott regards Kirnberger as the 'most useful author upon practical music'. His 'classification of suspended discords will obtain him immortal fame', and the English nation 'will be ever indebted' to AFCK for making Kirnberger's doctrines known. Callcott thinks Marpurg 'the greater man' in science, literature and arrangement but regards Kirnberger as 'the greater musician', although Callcott 'cannot yet overcome the difficulty of the diminished triad'. Boyce was one of the 'brightest ornaments' of the school established by [Johann Christoph] Pepusch, who brought to England some German musical doctrines.

Callcott is anxious to correct AFCK's comment that he has 'begun to publish' his system. The two pages Callcott sent were printed before he had heard of Kirnberger. Although Callcott had entertained publishing 'that little essay', he would not do this until AFCK had seen it and was satisfied that 'it could not be of any detriment' to AFCK. Callcott is 'pledged' to publish Boyce's manuscripts, but not for the purpose of opposing Kirnberger. Callcott's announced *Dictionary [of Music]* is progressing slowly and will not be completed for several years. As 'a young and unexperienced author', his opposition to Kirnberger would be useless were it not for the circumstance that Boyce's manuscripts 'confirmed' Callcott's ideas. He seeks AFCK's comments on Boyce's system.

AFCK→John Wall Callcott 17/1/1799

letter not extant; Callcott's copy at BL Add Ms 27689 f 36-39

Callcott's letter gets a brief response, as time is short for AFCK to finish *EPMC*[1]. AFCK concludes from Callcott's remarks that he is 'still unacquainted' with Kirnberger's system as explained in *EMH*; thus Callcott has not 'in the least opposed' it. When AFCK 'spake of Kirnberger's principles' he did not mean to say that Kirnberger 'formally professed them, but only that he clearly evinced them in every part of his system of harmony'. AFCK hopes that his 'sincerity' will not offend Callcott, as he wishes to remain his friend.

John Wall Callcott→AFCK between 17-30/1/1799

BL Add Ms 27689 f 40-48, undated, but clearly between the last and next letters

Callcott confesses that he is 'unacquainted with many parts of Kirnberger's work' and with 'some few' parts of *EMH*. However, Callcott presents 'mathematical' arguments related to tuning to assert (for instance) that an interval with ratio 40/27 could not 'form a fundamental bass when 3/2 was found in the harmony'. He is considering publishing an 'essay on the diminished triad' to express his opinions to the musical world. He thanks AFCK for his 'patience and attention in bearing with my tedious letters' and terminates their 'dispute', pledging not to publish 'any tract' without first showing it to AFCK and 'altering any passage which you may think would hurt your works'.

AFCK→John Wall Callcott 30/1/1799

BL Add Ms 30022 f 12–13

AFCK thanks Callcott for his letter [above] and for sending three pieces of music. AFCK believes that Kirnberger's system is 'so deeply founded in reason and nature, that it will bear the strictest mathematical as well as other investigation'. He is sorry that Callcott has termed their correspondence a 'dispute' but has no objection to their pursuing this discussion publicly.

John Wall Callcott→AFCK 1/2/1799

BL Add Ms 27689 f 52–57

It was only to oblige AFCK that Callcott had closed their correspondence. He again asks for a 'proof' that 'a fundamental bass can bear any ratio' not included in the numbers 1–6 'to compose its harmonic triad'. He did not mean to say that Kirnberger was not 'a very great man'.

AFCK→John Wall Callcott 4/2/1799

BL Add Ms 30022 f 14–15

Without invoking concepts relating to tuning, AFCK states that it is 'most natural' and 'reasonable' to consider that 'when a bass proceeds from the fourth to the fifth' of a diatonic scale, with an 'apparent triad' on both scale notes, the former chord should be considered to have an omitted fundamental bass a third below its scale note. Kirnberger's 'diminished triad' can be explained using a similar argument. AFCK requests that Callcott not show him anything contrary to *EMH* before Callcott publishes it.

John Wall Callcott→AFCK 9/2/1799

BL Add Ms 27689 f 61–66

AFCK's letter confirms that he and Callcott 'differ on principles'. AFCK, whose 'proofs' are 'by no means mathematical', regards the 'syntonic comma' [the difference between four justly tuned perfect fifths and two octaves plus a justly tuned major third] as 'destroyed by temperament'. Callcott readily allows AFCK's 'whole doctrine' if it is proposed 'only as a practical system', whereas Callcott has been concerned to reduce harmony 'to its true roots demonstrable by mathematics'.

John Wall Callcott→AFCK 28/2/1799

BL Add Ms 27689 f 66–68

From AFCK's silence Callcott thinks that 'we shall soon be favoured with' *EPMC*[1]. Callcott is now transcribing his essay, which AFCK can see if he likes, and is 'extremely anxious' to have AFCK's opinion whether Callcott's tenets are 'exactly consonant to the extracts which I sent you from Dr Boyce'. Callcott has no 'repugnance' to a public controversy on this subject.

AFCK→John Wall Callcott 3/3/1799

BL Add Ms 30022 f 16–17

AFCK apologises for his delayed reply to Callcott's letter of 9/2/1799. AFCK fears that Callcott misunderstands Boyce 'the same as' he misunderstands 'Kirnberger and me', because the examples Callcott supplied from Boyce 'were no proof of anything contrary to Kirnberger's system'. Callcott professes to be a 'friend to truth' but has paid no attention to any of the 'hints' AFCK has given to him, although he eventually must find 'the real truth' contained in them. AFCK wants not to see anything more respecting Callcott's 'favourite system' until he has published it.

John Wall Callcott→William Horsley *c*4/3/1799

BL Add Ms 30022 f 16–17

Forwarding the last letter, Callcott asks Horsley what he thinks of AFCK's claim that Callcott does not understand Boyce's manuscripts.

William Horsley→John Wall Callcott *c*5/3/1799

BL Add Ms 30022 f 16–17

Returning AFCK's letter of 3/3/1799, Horsley says that he has thought for some time that 'xxxx' [i.e., AFCK] 'knows very little about the question'. AFCK therefore cannot decide upon Callcott's judgement of the passages [by Boyce] that Callcott sent to AFCK.

AFCK→John Wall Callcott 23/3/1800

BL Add Ms 30022 f 18–19

AFCK apologises for the late return of a work by [Johann Friedrich] Daube. He is 'ashamed of accepting so many' of Callcott's 'pleasing compositions', as Callcott does not demand any of AFCK's works in return. AFCK hopes to be excused 'for having taken the money' for [Callcott's subscription copy of] *EPMC*[1], as this work has cost him a 'considerable sum' to produce. AFCK knows a gentleman who possesses a treatise by James Leman [*A New Method of Learning Psalm-Tunes* (London, 1729)].

AFCK hears that the [*Allgemeine*] *musikalische Zeitung* is now being published at Leipzig. He will get it 'from quarter to quarter' and will be pleased to 'communicate' it to Callcott.

A 'gigantic musical publication', amounting to 60 volumes folio and comprising music 'of all ages and nations', is now 'in agitation' in Germany. AFCK has told a friend who very much favours this work that 'there is no prospect of any considerable subscription' for it in England. AFCK suggests that 'a society of musical gentlemen' might subscribe for a copy, which could be deposited so that all of them could have access to it. The proponent is [Joseph] Sonnleithner of Vienna, who 'intended to come to England' but who, AFCK supposes, is now in Russia.

John Wall Callcott→AFCK 25/7/1800

BL Add Ms 27688 f 66v–65v

Callcott refers to a passage by [John Christopher] Pepusch [in *A Treatise on Harmony* (2nd ed., London, 1731)], and asks AFCK to show what fundamental bass Kirnberger would assign to that passage. Callcott asks if AFCK knows of Abbé [Jean Etienne] Feytou, who has sent Callcott 'some of his curiosities'. Callcott forwards 'the proof of some more of Dr Boyce's mss', together with some music [presumably by Callcott].

AFCK→John Wall Callcott 26/7/1800

BL Add Ms 30022 f 22

AFCK congratulates Callcott on his new degree [D.Mus., Oxford, awarded on 18/6/1800]. Regarding the 'printed abstracts' that Callcott has sent from Boyce and [*Padre* Giovanni Battista] Martini and the handwritten one from Pepusch, AFCK is sorry that Callcott still amuses himself with trying 'to controvert part of Kirnberger's system by that of' Boyce, and hopes that Callcott will understand AFCK's declining to discuss this further in private correspondence.

On 1 August AFCK intends to publish his *PGTB Prospectus* and will send Callcott a copy. Callcott 'lost a great pleasure by not hearing' Samuel Wesley and [Johann Anton] André play the organs at St Paul's Covent Garden, where AFCK had hoped to see Callcott, and at St Mary's [German Lutheran church] Savoy Square.

AFCK has been requested to collect biographies for [a new edition of Ernst Ludwig] Gerber's [*Historich-biographisches*] *Lexicon* [*der Tonkünstler*], and asks Callcott to send his biography including a complete list of his works to AFCK. He requests that Callcott ask [Samuel] Arnold, [William] Shield 'and those other of your celebrated friends whose memory you wish to see correct', to write accounts of themselves for this work, as autobiographical accounts are far better than those written by others. AFCK also seeks Callcott's help in obtaining biographies of Drs [Thomas Sanders] Dupuis, Boyce, [Benjamin] Cooke 'and others that are dead but not too long ago'. AFCK will mention 'to his friend abroad' his indebtedness to Callcott for any biographies that Callcott solicits or obtains.

John Wall Callcott→AFCK 23,25/8/1800

BL Add Ms 27688 f 60v-51v

From [Henry] Escher [a London importer and seller of German books], Callcott has just received no. 1 of volume 2 of the [Leipzig *Allgemeine*] *musikalische Zeitung*. He thanks AFCK for making him 'known to the literary characters of Germany'. From the initials Callcott guesses that the writer who mentioned him there was Forkel, whose article hinted that Callcott intends to oppose Kirnberger's system.[32] Callcott has 'not yet openly professed any such design'. As such an aim might prejudice AFCK's countrymen against Callcott's future attempts, he asks AFCK to state in his 'next letters to the continent' the principal points, which Callcott details, on which he and Kirnberger agree and disagree.

At his leisure Callcott will write a short account of himself for Gerber's *Lexicon* and will try to obtain information from others. A life of Boyce by Sir John Hawkins is prefixed to [John] Ashley's edition of Boyce's *Cathedral Music*. Callcott has been promised some more manuscripts of Pepusch that present the rules he gave to his scholars.

Escher 'has had an application from Germany about communicating musical news for the [*Allgemeine musikalische*] *Zeitung*' and spoke to Callcott about this. As Callcott 'can but barely read' German he took the liberty of recommending AFCK.

Callcott would be happy to send a complete collection of his music to Forkel. He has, and admires, the first volume of Forkel's *Allgemeine Geschichte der Musik* [Leipzig, 1788] and asks when the second volume will appear. He asks if AFCK knows whether Pepusch was acquainted with Hänfling [i.e., Conrad Henfling, who had calculated musical temperaments].

AFCK→John Wall Callcott 28/8/1800

BL Add Ms 30022 f 23

Although AFCK has not yet seen the *Allgemeine musikalische Zeitung*, he is glad that Callcott has got part of it and hopes that he will find 'anything coming from me or my friends' agreeable. AFCK would be happy to write to Forkel about Callcott's theoretical propositions if this would be doing Callcott a service. However, if AFCK sent them in the way expressed in Callcott's last letter, Forkel would see that Callcott 'will not understand' AFCK's *EMH* and 'consequently will not see' that Pepusch and Boyce 'agree with it in every respect, except perhaps in a few antiquities'.

A fair examination will show that AFCK and Kirnberger 'have offered nothing but proofs' and have 'never endeavoured to persuade the public by mere authorities', which is the 'only thing' that Callcott has offered up to now. Can Pepusch and Boyce be so infallible authorities as the Bible, and was not the Bible the authority upon which Tycho Brahe founded his astronomical system, long after Copernicus? Kirnberger's system is 'the system of nature itself, which requires not a single

[32] The article is signed 'F—l', a code for 'Forkel' (see Martha Bruckner-Bigenwald, *Die Anfänge der Leipziger Allgemeinen Musikalischen Zeitung*, Freiburg, 1938, facsimile reprint Hilversum, 1965, p 92).

exception'; it lies before Callcott, as the Copernican system lay before Tycho. Will Callcott oppose Boyce's system, which according to Callcott's account 'seems to want rules for exceptions', to Kirnberger's?

AFCK does not doubt that Forkel would be glad to have Callcott's works. In Germany 'men of learning have the custom to publish and send their friends the dissertation by which they obtained their degree'. Consequently, Forkel and 'the German public will be more glad to see the exercises of your promotion than your other works'. AFCK also would like to see these exercises. He thanks Callcott for sending two of his compositions.

AFCK does not know precisely when Forkel's second volume [of his *Allgemeine Geschichte der Musik*] will appear, but hopes to have this information soon. He thanks Callcott for offering to send Abbé Feytou's system but begs him not to send this until AFCK asks for it.

AFCK has not met Escher but thanks Callcott for having mentioned AFCK to him. When AFCK and Callcott next meet they can talk about Escher's request 'and other little professional affairs which I have lately thought of'. AFCK expects to send his parcel of biographies [for Gerber's *Lexicon*] in October and hopes to be able to include those of Callcott and his friends.

AFCK→John Wall Callcott 21/2/1801

BL Add Ms 30022 f24

AFCK is pleased to send Callcott a copy of *PGTB*. According to the last letter that AFCK received from Forkel [not preserved], his second volume [of his *Allgemeine Geschichte der Musik*] should be published about now. AFCK expects it 'about Easter or a month later' and will be pleased to lend it to Callcott. AFCK's dispatches for Gerber's *Lexicon* have been delayed, but he intends to send them soon. He asks what Callcott plans to submit for that work.

AFCK→John Wall Callcott 30/4/1801

BL Add Ms 30022 f20–21

AFCK has 'already written to Germany' [not preserved]. He does not know when he will have an opportunity 'to send more than a letter because the communications are interrupted' [because of the Prussian occupation of Hannover or other military conflicts in Germany]. If he finds an opportunity he will let Callcott know. Callcott's question about [Matthew Peter] King [presumably in a letter not preserved] will be answered 'another time'.

John Wall Callcott→AFCK 30/4/1801

BL Add Ms 30022 f20–21, written on the same sheet as the preceding letter

Callcott's 'communications for Gerber's *Lexicon*' are available 'at 24 hours notice'. His question concerning King is 'of some importance' to both AFCK and Callcott. At AFCK's request, Callcott has not shown his writings to AFCK prior to publication, but now advises that he wrote the review of *EMH* published in the August and October 1800 numbers of *The British Critic* and has written the review of *EPMC*[1] 'which will appear tomorrow' [in the April 1801 number of that journal]. Although the reviewer's name was not published, Callcott 'does not wish to be considered as anonymous'. He trusts that AFCK will find that his works and himself have been treated with 'liberality'.

Callcott has promised to review 'in the following month' [in the number dated May 1801] King's *A General Treatise on Music*.[33] In his review Callcott 'must notice' King's 'violent attack' upon AFCK, which 'deserves reprehension'. Callcott asks AFCK what his intentions are [regarding a reply to King's attack] and is 'concerned' that AFCK's comments did not distinguish Shield's system [his *An Introduction to Harmony*, published about June 1800] from King's.

Callcott intends to publish 'towards the end of the year' the essay that AFCK once saw, together with other essays on musical subjects.

AFCK→John Wall Callcott 2/5/1801

BL Add Ms 30022 f 25

AFCK will answer King's advertisement but does not now wish to say 'how soon and in what manner' he will do this, so Callcott can review King's treatise as he thinks proper, 'without the least hint from' AFCK.

AFCK is agreeably surprised to learn that Callcott wrote the review of *EMH* [in the *British Critic*], as AFCK had ascribed it 'to another gentleman'. Callcott's criticisms were 'expressed with that liberality which becomes a reviewer'. AFCK thanks Callcott for informing him of his 'intended theoretical publication' and assures Callcott that he would not 'carry on literary controversy with personal animosity'. AFCK hopes that 'when we shall once be theoretical friends' their joint endeavours will be more useful to the public and to themselves than their opposite ones.

AFCK asks for 'something for Gerber's *Lexicon*' as soon as convenient, which AFCK will endeavour to send when a good opportunity is available. He has not yet seen yesterday's *British Critic*.

---

[33] King's treatise was first published in 1800, but a 'new edition' appeared in 1801 with an 'advertisement' dated 8/4/1801 that attacked statements in AFCK's preface to *PGTB*. In that preface AFCK had accused King and William Shield, although not by name, of having 'revived the most confused and obsolete systems' without saying whether they were familiar with *EMH*. AFCK further claimed that King had taken 'great parts of his *General Treatise*' from *EMH* without acknowledging this, and without sufficient understanding to realise that he had 'transcribed a term, and a whole period' that 'ought to have been mentioned in a table of errata' to *EMH*. More details of this controversy are given on pages 68–71 above.

John Wall Callcott→AFCK 13/1/1803

BL Add Ms 27688 f 45^{v}–43^{v}

Callcott is 'concluding' his essays and he therefore renews his correspondence with AFCK. Some time ago AFCK suggested to him that if parts of [Carl Heinrich] Graun's cantata *Der Tod Jesu* were 'adapted to English words' this would please 'admirers of excellent music'. Callcott has received 'Hiller's copy' [the keyboard 'reduction' of the cantata prepared by Johann Adam Hiller (Breslau, 1785)] and has translated the first chorus into English. He asks AFCK what other parts of the work 'are most esteemed in Germany'. Callcott has 'some interest' with [Samuel] Harrison, [James] Bartleman and [Thomas] Greatorex, who are likely to perform the selections at their Vocal Concert. However, Callcott may have insufficient influence to have these selections performed before King George III at one of the Concerts of Antient Music.

Callcott asks for information about the dispute between [George Andreas] Sorge and Marpurg, and about the theoretical systems of [Justin Heinrich] Knecht and Abbé [Georg Joseph] Vogler.

AFCK→John Wall Callcott 14/1/1803

BL Add Ms 30022 f 26–27

AFCK thanks Callcott for his gift of music on 25/10/1802. All of Graun's *Der Tod Jesu* 'was much admired in Germany' and AFCK is happy to learn that Callcott is translating it. Another piece 'of the highest repute in Germany' is [Carl Philipp] Emanuel Bach's 'Heilig' [Hamburg, 1779] for two choirs. AFCK 'wrote for it long ago for a gentleman' [not identified] and will be happy to let Callcott see it. AFCK has not heard it himself and therefore cannot judge 'whether perhaps it is not too original and too intricate to please after Handel and the great authors here in vogue'.

AFCK has never troubled himself about the dispute between Sorge and Marpurg but, as AFCK's uncle [Carl Christoph] Hachmeister [Sr] was 'one of those called upon by Marpurg to decide the contest', AFCK will write to his brother [GCK] at Hamburg and let Callcott know the answer. Marpurg may have written about it in his *Historisch-kritische Beyträge* [Berlin, 1754–1778], which AFCK can lend to Callcott. As far as AFCK knows, Kirnberger never 'interfered in the dispute'.

AFCK has collected 'very little' for Gerber's *Lexicon* and has sent this off 'with only so much about myself as when and where I have been born'. He does not know whether there is still time to include Callcott's biography but will be pleased to forward it.

AFCK has perused, but does not own, Knecht's treatise [*Gemeinnützliches Elementarwerk der Harmonie...* (Augsburg and Stuttgart, 1792–1797)]. All he knows of Abbé Vogler's doctrines is from his *Data zur Akustik* [Leipzig and Offenbach, 1801]. AFCK owns a new [*Hymnus*] *Te Deum* [*Laudamus*] by Knecht [Offenbach, 1801] 'for two choirs and 16 instrumental parts', which he 'must send into the country', but can show to Callcott.

Callcott perhaps has not heard about GCK's organ performance, of which AFCK encloses some 'public accounts'. As far as he knows, GCK is the first organist to play a 'quintet' [i.e., five-part music] on four manuals and pedals, for which he seems to have received unanimous praise.[34] AFCK also encloses 'a plan of my announced Key' [his *Key Prospectus*].

John Wall Callcott→AFCK 17/1/1803

BL Add Ms 27688 f 35^{v}

Callcott has not had time to peruse AFCK's communications but has made a copy and returned the originals. Callcott has not seen the works of Knecht and Vogler that AFCK mentioned but will be happy to look at them. Callcott is defending [in his essays] Kirnberger's concept of suspensions against Marpurg's concept of chords by 'supposition'. Callcott asks what kind of [organ] swell was introduced at Hamburg [in the organ on which GCK performed]. Dr [Charles] Burney has just written to Callcott 'about that improvement in English organs'. Very soon AFCK will receive 'a specimen of my translation of Graun' [i.e., of Graun's *Der Tod Jesu*].

John Wall Callcott→AFCK 27/9/1806

BL Add Ms 27674 f 13^{v}

Callcott is preparing his essays for the press. He wants to know whether AFCK prefers [Charles, 3rd Earl] Stanhope's temperament to Kirnberger's.

John Wall Callcott→AFCK 30/9/1806

BL Add Ms 27674 f 14^{v}

Callcott [presumably replying to a letter from AFCK not preserved] rephrases his question. Since Stanhope's temperament contains seven 'perfect quints' [i.e., perfect fifths] and Kirnberger's has nine, which of these temperaments does AFCK think is 'nearest theoretical perfection'?

John Wall Callcott→AFCK 24/11/1806

BL Add Ms 27674 f 32^{v}

AFCK said in his last letter [not preserved] that 'Kirnberger's temperament produces stronger characteristics and more general satisfaction than other unequal temperaments'. Callcott does not understand 'how a system which opposes the tuning of the violin strings can be superior to a mss one of Mr [Marmaduke] Overend derived from Dr Boyce's theory'.[35]

---

[34] Callcott's copy of these accounts of Georg Christoph Kollmann's organ performance is at BL Add Ms 27688 f 42^{v}–36^{v}.

[35] Callcott owned Overend's manuscripts on music theory; they are now Bodleian mss Don.c.137–140. See *SOMIB*, v 2 p 806–807.

AFCK→John Wall Callcott 26/11/1806

BL Add Ms 30022 f 28

As he has told Callcott, AFCK's 'whole creed about temperament stands in' *NTh*[1], Chapter 2, to which he has nothing more to add. It is as indifferent to him 'which useful temperament one person or another likes best, as it is to know what sort of a tuning hammer Sebastian Bach used for his well tempered harpsichord'.

Samuel Wesley→Charles Burney 7/7/1808

Yale University, Beinecke Library, Osborn mss 3, box 16, folder 1192; printed in *LSW*, p 66–68

From a small drawing that AFCK lent to Wesley, an [unidentified] artist friend of Wesley's has almost completed a painting of J. S. Bach.[36]

Charles Burney→Samuel Wesley 17/10/1808

Yale University, Beinecke Library, Osborn mss 3, box 5, folder 319; summarised in *SWSB*, p 242–243

If the translation by [Edward] Stephenson of Forkel's biography of Bach is 'well done' it would be a pity to undertake a new translation. AFCK's 'geese, you know, are all swans' [i.e., his criticisms of Stephenson's translation are likely to be exaggerated].

AFCK→Charles John Smyth 20/2/1809

Cambridge University Library Add Ms 6247 letter 76

AFCK has perused Smyth's 'Questions and Answers' [an unpublished 'little work', not preserved] and will give his opinion of it faithfully. It is fair to abstract 'any little thing' from another author 'if it is acknowledged'. King was blameable for his plagiarism 'only because he denied the fact'.

Smyth's work follows *PGTB*, which is 'entirely superseded' by *NTh*[1] which Smyth has, and by *2nd PGTB* which Mr Vaughan [probably the singer Thomas Vaughan] has. If there was not 'a very great difference' in doctrine between *EMH* and *NTh*[1], or between *PGTB* and *2nd PGTB*, 'what would my new system be'? Why would Smyth 'revive an old confuted system' when he possesses 'the confutation of it'?

Smyth's work has clear diction but introduces unnecessary technical terms. It dwells most 'on what concerns beginners least, such as the contents of tones and semitones in an interval', and disregards the practical use of what is explained, though that concerns beginners the most. AFCK gives his 'humble opinion' that 'the

---

[36] The description 'small drawing' suggests that Kollmann may have lent to Wesley the title-page of the first volume of the *Allgemeine musikalische Zeitung*, which featured an engraved portrait of Bach. See Michael Kassler, 'Portraits of Bach in England before 1830', *EBA* p 403–415 at p 403–406.

little work' should not be published in its present state, and apologises if his sincerity displeases Smyth.

AFCK thanks Smyth for the approbation he has given to GAK's 'Variations' [his 'An air from Handel's lessons'] and is happy to report that this 'coincides with the general reception of them'. CCK, GAK and JSK join in returning best compliments to Smyth.

Johann Anton André→GCK 22/8/1809

André firm archive, Offenbach, Germany, in copy-book of letters written from 9/1807 to 12/1809; letter written in German

André is indebted to GCK for sending the talented and artistic compositions of his nephew [GAK, probably his 'Three grand sonatas' and his 'An air from Handel's lessons'] and asks GCK to thank AFCK and GAK on behalf of himself and [Georg Jacob] Vollweiler [who represented the André firm in London in 1806–1807]. Because the music trade is almost at a standstill, now is not the time advantageously to publish works by an author who has not yet become known through travels abroad. André therefore cannot print GAK's works now, but the situation may well change when GAK travels abroad and receives the approval that a person of his talents as performer and composer cannot miss.

Samuel Wesley→Benjamin Jacobs? 30/9/1809?

Royal College of Music, London, ms 2130 letter 18; printed in *LSW*, p 123–124

Wesley told Charles Burney that 'young Kollmann' [GAK] was 'quite capable of playing the [keyboard part of J. S. Bach's violin] sonatas', but Burney said that he preferred to have the recipient [Jacobs?] play with Wesley [who played the violin].

Samuel Wesley→Sarah Gwynne Wesley 13/1/1810

Emory University, Wesley Collection letter 54; summarised in *SWSB*, p 274

Wesley tells Sarah Gwynne Wesley [his mother] that he had mislaid a list of J. S. Bach's works and had got AFCK to write out a new list.

AFCK→Charles John Smyth 23/2/1810

Bibliothèque Nationale, Paris, Musique, L.a. Kollmann 1

In answer to Smyth's polite letter [not preserved], AFCK would be glad to provide 'the ratios of an equal temperament' if Smyth seemed inclined to attend to arguments that favour it. However, Smyth's critical and mistaken remarks about AFCK—for instance, that he 'never made the proper distinction between the piano forte and organ'—forbid him from offering this information in a private letter.

AFCK has taken 'long and great pains to rescue the science of music from the mysterious darkness in which it was wrapped'. Why should Smyth 'take such pains to counteract and dispute a similar simple and general rule in temperament as in harmony'? AFCK does not envy 'all the quarter tones, and pedals, and difficulties, which alone seem to satisfy' Smyth in regard to temperament, and asks to be allowed to say no more about it 'till I should find it a duty to the public'. AFCK will be happy to peruse, and to give his opinion about, the paper on fundamental bass that Smyth mentioned.

AFCK will send Smyth *TAF*[1] 5–8 and *2nd PGTB*, which Smyth has ordered, at the beginning of May. CCK, GAK and JSK join in sending best compliments to Smyth.

Frederick Griesbach & GAK→Governors and Court of Assistants of the Royal Society of Musicians 6/1/1811

Royal Society of Musicians, London, in file of papers concerning GAK

Griesbach recommends GAK for membership of the Royal Society of Musicians. GAK studied music under AFCK, 'teaches singing and the pianoforte' and 'plays the organ and violin'. He is 21 years old, unmarried and not likely to become 'chargeable' to the Society.

GAK declares that he has 'not served a musical apprenticeship' but has 'studied and practised music professionally under my father from my infancy'. He is not, and has not been proposed to become, a member of the New Musical Fund.

Charles Burney→AFCK 24/3/1811

Yale University, Beinecke Library, Osborn shelves c 30, p 169–170; printed in Frances Burney d'Arblay, *Memoirs of Doctor Burney*, London, 1832, v 3 p 393–395

Burney is sorry that, when AFCK called on Sunday [presumably 17/3/1811], Burney had not left his bedroom [in Chelsea College] since the beginning of the year [because of poor health]. On opening the 'valuable parcel' that AFCK left with Burney's servant Burney found its contents 'an agreeable employment ever since'. He has 'often admired' AFCK's 'science and ingenuity' and thinks that *TAF*[1] considerably surpasses 'in clearness, contrivance and pleasing melody' any of AFCK's 'elaborate and learned productions' that Burney has seen. The works AFCK left are a 'cheap purchase' at £1/1/–, which Burney has 'the pleasure to send, with thanks for my entertainment'. AFCK's 'Melody of the 100th psalm' is 'a work of great study and knowledge'.[37] Burney is seldom 'in health and spirits to read works of complication in music' and has 'totally quitted the modern world'.

---

[37] From this sum and the prices of the other works by AFCK mentioned it seems likely that AFCK's Concerto, op. 8, was the third item in the parcel.

Charles Burney→AFCK 8/4/1811

Yale University, Beinecke Library, Osborn shelves c 30, p 171

Although Burney has not yet been able to leave his bedroom to search for Padre [Giovanni Battista] Martini's *Saggio ... di Contrappunto* [Bologna, 1774–1775], he has instructed those about him to look for it in his apartment. If it can be found, Burney will inform AFCK so that he can borrow it.

Burney thanks AFCK, GAK and JSK for their kind wishes regarding his health. Alas! it is more than a year since Burney last 'quitted' his apartments. He does not intend to attempt this again. His 'much respected neighbour' Mr Graham [probably Richard Robert Graham, apothecary of Chelsea College] 'frequently mentions the extent' of GAK's 'inquiries and attainments in other parts of knowledge' besides his 'miraculous power' of execution on keyed instruments.

AFCK→Charles Burney 3/2/1812

Bibliothèque Royale de Belgique, Brussels, bound in Fétis 4680 (a copy of *QMR1*); reproduced as the frontispiece to this book; printed in 'Notes on an old musical journal: *The Quarterly Musical Register*', *The Musical Times* v 48 no. 776 (1 October 1907) p 645–648[38]

AFCK returns Burney's *The Present State of Music in France and Italy* [London, 1771, 2nd ed. 1773] and thanks him for lending it. He gives Burney a copy of *QMR1*, noting that Burney 'will recollect my having suggested to you many years ago' its 'idea'. AFCK hopes that the mild winter has benefited Burney's health.

Samuel Wesley→Robert Glenn 22/7/1814

BL Add Ms 35013 f 68; printed in *LSW*, p 233

Samuel Wesley has 'summoned some of the great guns', including the Cramers [John Baptist Cramer and François Cramer], 'Kollmann' [presumably GAK][39] and [Francis Tatton] Latour, to a concert 'of piano forte music' at [Muzio] Clementi's [piano] manufactory at 5 p.m. on 25/7/1814.

---

[38] The printed text was not transcribed accurately. For instance, Kollmann's address was printed as 'Priory St James's' instead of 'Friary St James's'.

[39] No evidence has been found that Kollmann and Wesley saw each other following Kollmann's criticisms in *The Quarterly Musical Register* of Wesley's changes to Callcott's *A Musical Grammar*. Wesley inscribed to Kollmann the first three books of his edition with Charles Frederick Horn of Bach's '48', published in 1810–1811, but apparently did not send Kollmann a copy of the fourth book published in 1813. See the note to *QMR p 30* on page 203 above and the note to *QMR p 129–130* on page 214 above.

AFCK document concerning German Chapel allowances 13/8/1816

Lambeth Palace Library, Fulham Papers, Howley v 9 f 256–257

AFCK lists the wine, manchets [bread] and candles that have been granted each year to the German Chapel since before 1784, when he became chapel-keeper. He has applied for these allowances from His Majesty's Board of Green Cloth.

Johann Hartmann Wilhelm Kuper→ William Howley, enclosing AFCK memorandum 11–12/12/1816

Lambeth Palace Library, Fulham Papers, Howley v 9 f 272–273

Kuper, in a letter dated 12/12/1816, sends Howley, the Bishop of London, a memorandum by AFCK dated 11/12/1816 [preserved with Kuper's letter] which specifies the 'former allowances' paid to German Chapel staff and the retrenchments that have been made to these. AFCK writes that 'the salary of the chapel keeper, who also does the duty of organist' [i.e., AFCK] is now £60 nominal or £47/16/– clear, to which £10 is added from the Lord Chamberlain's office 'out of which the Chapel cleaner gets £3'. AFCK's 'total present salary therefore is £54/12/–' [sic]. He has 'use of the apartments at the Chapel, with the coals granted for them', but must pay £12/12/– per annum to the clerk of the French Chapel [in St James's Palace], as fixed at the exchange of the two chapels in 1781.[40] He has had 'the perquisite of the candles not used in the Chapel, after delivering a fixed quantity to the ministers and the porter', and has got the old communion table linen 'when a new set was granted' every seven years. He also has had pitcher wine amounting to upwards of 40 bottles per annum.

From the above income AFCK's perquisites of candles, table linen, and wine have been retrenched. His actual loss from these deductions 'may be fairly computed' to be £25 to £30 per annum.

AFCK→William Howley 19/12/1816

Lambeth Palace Library, Fulham Papers, Howley v 9 f 274–275

In response to Howley's command, AFCK notes that the 'long established allowance' of candles for the German Chapel for the 'five winter months', including perquisites of the two ministers, is no more than is needed for lighting the chapel properly during 26 or 28 evening services which could be held in those months. Although evening services at the Chapel 'stand suspended at present' because of a 'want of congregation at them', the ministers have ordered AFCK to apply for these candles 'because they do not wish to lose the right of keeping service whenever they can, by the disallowance of the candles'. Tallow candles having a total weight of 60 pounds have been a perquisite of AFCK. He trusts that Howley's support of the cause of his subordinates [to retain their allowances] 'will be crowned with success'.

---

[40] See page 16 above.

AFCK→William Howley 24/1/1817

Lambeth Palace Library, Fulham Papers, Howley v 9 f 281–282

Since 5/1/1817 the delivery of madeira wine for the German Chapel has been suspended, pending the Bishop's granting 'a new order for the same'. The delivery of candles and manchets also is 'still suspended'. AFCK seeks Howley's 'protection in regard to the perquisites' that he loses by these retrenchments, amounting to about £25 per annum, 'a very grievous loss to me, considering my small salary, and the increasing disproportion of it to its original value'. The [German Chapel] porter's loss of perquisites of candles is estimated at £5 per annum.

AFCK→William Howley 28/1/1817

Lambeth Palace Library, Fulham Papers, Howley v 9 f 283–284

When Kuper spoke to Howley yesterday about 'the suspended allowances' for the German Chapel he spoke only of candles and did not mention the 73 bottles of madeira wine and 113 manchets *per annum*. The total value of these suspended allowances is estimated to be £62/13/–.

AFCK→William Howley 29/5/1817

Lambeth Palace Library, Fulham Papers, Howley v 9 f 291–292

By order of Rev. [Christian Hermann] Giese, as Kuper is 'on a tour to Germany', AFCK details requirements for candles, madeira wine and manchets for the German Chapel evening services and communion table.

Charles Wesley III→Sarah Wesley 5/6/1817

Emory University, John Wesley Collection in box 6;
summarised in *SWSB*, p 363–364

AFCK 'in the handsomest manner' has interested himself in the family of Charles Wesley III [Samuel Wesley's eldest son, whose family comprised Samuel Wesley's wife Charlotte (from whom he was separated) and their children]. Charles Wesley III tells his aunt Sarah Wesley [Samuel Wesley's sister] that AFCK proposed a benefit concert to raise money to provide better support for Samuel Wesley [who sustained serious injuries after jumping out of a window on 3/5/1817] and to relieve Charlotte Wesley's 'exigencies'. AFCK made several 'applications with success'.

AFCK→Robert Gray 25/1/1821

Royal Archives, Windsor Castle, ms RA GEO/30128

For 'many years past', as clerk of the German Chapel, AFCK received from His late Majesty [George III] a 'Christmas box' or gift of £2/2/– annually. AFCK hopes that

George IV has 'graciously granted the continuation' of this gift, and asks Gray [joint deputy-auditor of the Duchy of Cornwall] whether and where it will be paid.[41]

John Bernard Logier→AFCK 22/1/1822

Printed in *Remarks on Logier* p 41–42, and earlier, in AFCK's German translation, in *Nachtrag zu den Bemerkungen* col. 9–10. Date of letter stated by AFCK in *Remarks on Logier, 2nd ed.* p vii.

Logier has just seen AFCK's *Bemerkungen über Logiers System* and is surprised by it, as AFCK has never been present at an examination of Logier's pupils and therefore is 'ignorant of what progress they have made, or on what plan they proceed'. Logier asks AFCK to appoint 'an early day' when he can attend such an examination. If AFCK prefers, he can bring some of his pupils to Logier's house, and both sets of pupils then can be examined openly 'in the presence of gentlemen of rank and science'. AFCK can bring scholars whom he has taught for 'more than five years', which is longer than Logier has taught his pupils.

AFCK→John Bernard Logier 26/1/1822

Printed in *Remarks on Logier* p 42–44, and earlier, in AFCK's German translation, in *Nachtrag zu den Bemerkungen* col. 10–11

Logier's proposal [in the preceding letter] is an 'endeavour to draw the attention of the public away from' the comments that AFCK made in *Bemerkungen über Logiers System* and to direct it instead to an examination of Logier's pupils. Logier knows, having read *Bemerkungen*, that AFCK objects to such an examination being a test of Logier's system. AFCK therefore declines to attend one.

Logier's suggestion that AFCK bring some of his pupils to Logier's house 'to ascertain the comparative merit of our scholars' is extremely improper. Can Logier 'produce any instance' of an attempt 'to confute, or only to dispute' any part of AFCK's system of harmony or composition, or his instruction? By contrast, numerous objections have been made to Logier's system since its introduction, which Logier has 'never noticed, much less attempted to confute'.

If Logier can point out any errors in what AFCK wrote he will be willing to rectify them in the same journal [the *Allgemeine musikalische Zeitung*]. A translation of Logier's letter and this reply must be published in that journal [it was published there as AFCK's *Nachtrag zu den Bemerkungen*]. As Logier has 'taken up our correspondence in English, though you are a German, as well as myself', AFCK feels 'called upon' also to publish an English translation of his *Bemerkungen* 'together with your letter to me, and my present answer' [this was published as AFCK's *Remarks on Logier*].

---

[41] A receipt signed by AFCK, now filed together with this letter in the Royal Archives, acknowledges that he received 'of His Majesty' [George IV] the sum of 'two guineas for a New Year's Gift' on 26/1/1821.

AFCK→William Ayrton? 23/1/1827

BL Add Ms 52337 A, f 35 [addressed to 'Dear Sir', in a volume of letters of composers collected by William Ayrton; however, this letter is not obviously written to him]

AFCK returns, with thanks, J. S. Bach's *Musical Offering*, which he had borrowed. The 'small work' enclosed with it by [Georg Philipp] Telemann 'of course does not belong to it'. AFCK hopes that the recipient is recovering from his complaint.

AFCK→Editor of *The Harmonicon* [William Ayrton] 5/5/1828

Printed in *The Harmonicon* v 6 (June 1828) p 123

AFCK responds to the extract from Rev. William Lisle Bowles's book in the April 1828 *Harmonicon*, which endeavoured to prove that the Old Hundredth psalm tune was 'originally and intrinsically English'. Rev. [William Dechair] Tattersall, when preparing for the press his *Improved Psalmody* [of which editions were published in London in 1794, 1795 and 1802], 'communicated' to AFCK 'a collection of German psalms, with their tunes, printed for the use of the reformed church of [John] Calvin' in Switzerland 'as early as 1530'. In that collection the Old Hundredth psalm tune appears 'exactly in the form' generally used in England, for instance in AFCK's 'The melody of the 100th psalm'.

Tattersall asked AFCK whether there was proof that Martin Luther had composed this tune. AFCK advised him that he could find no ascription of the tune to Luther in authentic records, and that 'the tune itself contains internal evidence' of being 'only an alteration of an earlier composition', the German hymn 'Nun lob' mein' Seel' den Herren'. The words for this hymn were written by [Johannes Gramann, called] Poliander, who died about 1540, and conjecturally wrote these words about 1525.

AFCK→'Mr [Sylvanus] Urban' [editor of *The Gentleman's Magazine*] 27/10/1828

Printed in *The Gentleman's Magazine*, v 98 part 2 (November 1828) p 412

In the August 1828 *Gentleman's Magazine* AFCK saw extracts of a letter from John Herschel to the editor of *The Times* concerning Charles Babbage's calculating machine [his 'difference engine no. 1']. AFCK also owns Babbage's 1822 *A Letter to Sir Humphry Davy ... on the Application of Machinery to the Purpose of Calculating and Printing Mathematical Tables*. The 'high importance of such a machine' was felt by [Gottfried Wilhelm] Leibniz, who spent much of his leisure and 24,000 dollars [German thalers] attempting to make one, according to [Carl Günther] Ludovici's *Ausführlicher Entwurff einer vollständigen Historie der Leibnitzischen Philosophie* [Leipzig, 1737].

However, neither Babbage nor Herschel mentions that 'a complete and perfect machine of that kind' was shown by its inventor, Johann Helfrich Müller, 44 years ago, to the mathematical section of the Royal Society of Sciences at Göttingen, or that an account of this was published in the *Göttingische Anzeigen von gelehrten*

Sachen in 1784. The long war or other causes may have 'made it escape their notice or recollection'. AFCK possesses [Phillip Engel Klipstein's edition of] Müller's *Beschreibung seiner neu erfunden Rechenmaschine...*, Frankfurt and Mainz, 1786, which shows how Müller 'attained, in a short time, the great object which Leibniz had sought for in vain, so long, and with such great expences'.

Thomas Baucott Mash→GAK 6/12/1832

National Archives LC5/248 p 174, letter no. 1280

The king [William IV] has been pleased 'to present the old organ, lately taken down from the German Chapel, to the Royal Academy of Music'. Mash [comptroller of accounts in the Lord Chamberlain's department] authorises GAK to deliver it to the organ builder [James Chapman] Bishop, who has been 'employed by the Royal Academy of Music' to remove it.

Ignaz Moscheles→Editor of *The Musical World* 20/12/1836

Printed in *The Musical World* v 4 no. 41 (23/12/1836) p 5–6

Moscheles has become acquainted with Mr [Ferdinand Arnold] Wortmann, a 'professor of the pianoforte' [from Krefeld, Germany], who arrived in London recently 'to propagate [Johann Heinrich] Scheibler's new method of tuning by mathematical calculation'. Wortmann has tuned Moscheles's piano, and the result far surpassed Moscheles's expectations. He annexes testimony of GAK and letters by Moritz Hauptmann and Sigismund Neukomm, all praising Scheibler's system.

GAK's testimony, dated 15/12/1836, states that Wortmann's mode of tuning 'has been applied, with the completest success, to the open diapason of the organ' in the German Chapel. GAK and several other 'competent judges' were present this morning [15/12/1836] to hear the result. All agreed that the new mode of tuning 'combines more equality and purity in all keys than any [other] mode of tuning we have heard'.

William Watts→JSK 5/4/1838

BL RPS ms 328 f 88v

On behalf of the directors of the Philharmonic Society, Watts [the Society's secretary] expresses 'surprise' that JSK thought she had the right to sign for extra admission tickets to the Society's concerts. This privilege is confined to the Society's members and honorary subscribers. Mr [William] Dance [the Society's treasurer], who replaced JSK's name with his own, acted properly and 'with the sole intention' of securing the admission of her friends to the concert [presumably the Society's concert on 2/4/1838].

GAK→Henry Brougham 2/2/1839

University College London, Brougham Papers, letter no. 4279; misdated 2/2/1838

GAK submits his 'statement of the qualities of my new railway and locomotive engine' [presumably his *Comparative Statement*] to Lord Brougham and will be pleased to show him the models of it, which are now deposited at 6 Carlisle Street, Soho Square. Tomorrow GAK leaves London to see where a new railway line may be built near Pontypool [Wales]; he will return on this Thursday evening the 7th. GAK's 'piano forte model', which Brougham mentioned yesterday [when they met at GAK's hearing before the Judicial Committee of the Privy Council], 'will be ready to be presented in a few days'.

GAK→Henry Brougham 11/2/1839 (1)

University College London, Brougham Papers, letter no. 4277

GAK offers 'the models of my patent piano forte' to Brougham and would be 'much honoured' if he added them to his collection. The 'lesser model' represents, on a scale of 1½ inch to a foot, the case, framework, soundboard, mode of fixing the wires and the place of the piano forte mechanism. The 'larger model' represents the mechanism itself in 'real dimensions', including 'the mode of fixing and tuning the string'.

GAK has just returned from the Monmouthshire Ironworks [near Pontypool, see the preceding letter], whose managers gave him a 'verbal promise' to use his railway invention 'on a new short line they are about to make immediately'. He will be proud to show 'the model of it' [at 6 Carlisle Street] to Brougham at any time that he appoints.

GAK→Henry Brougham 11/2/1839 (2)

University College London, Brougham Papers, letter no. 4278

GAK is 'much honoured' by Brougham's note [not preserved, presumably replying to the previous letter]. GAK has no 'connection in Paris' concerning the manufacture of piano fortes. 'Very soon' after GAK obtained his 1825 patent, [Jean-Henri] Pape, who—GAK understands—had worked for the piano manufacturer [William] Stodart in Golden Square, left London for Paris, where a friend advanced him funds to establish a piano manufactory in the Rue Rivoli. Shortly after Pape arrived in Paris he commenced making pianos according to GAK's 'plan of striking downwards', but using an 'arrangement of mechanism' more complex than GAK's. GAK thinks that Pape has not imitated GAK's 'plan of tuning' and has left 'the structure of the case' largely unaltered by leaving the keys in the grand piano forte under the strings.

About the beginning of 1835 Pape 'formed a connection' with [John Charles] Schwieso, who previously had worked for GAK 'by contract'. Pape sent 'some piano fortes' from Paris to Schwieso, who 'took a house in Marlborough Street' and showed them 'to professors of music and others'. Within a few months 'Pape and Schwieso disagreed', and Pape returned to London, taking a house in Frith Street 'where he exhibited his piano fortes'. In the spring of 1836 'Pape gave some evening parties at Frith Street', and 'many professors of music' who 'would not come to look' at GAK's pianos went to Pape's parties and played on his instruments. GAK 'felt that a great opposition was against' him, but thought that this would not defeat him 'because Pape's piano fortes were a piracy' of GAK's and had been 'modified for the worse'. Events proved GAK right, and Pape 'gave up his house and quitted the field'. One or two of Pape's piano fortes then were left in care of a neighbourhood music dealer 'to be disposed of'.

The story of GAK's undertaking [as a piano maker], if he found time to write it, 'would show a continued and powerful opposition' in various shapes, and also 'some curious particulars' relating to piracy. GAK provides an 'explanation of the models' [of his piano] by listing 'specific points or the new qualities' that distinguish his pianos from the competition. [GAK's list is reproduced in *Figure* 7 facing page 143 above.]

JSK→Mr F. Crouch 29/5/1839

Royal College of Music, Centre for Performance History, in collection 88A1

JSK writes on behalf of GAK 'who has been most exceedingly engaged by the concert of Monday' [27/5/1839, his 'third grand concert' at the Hanover Square Rooms] and by a 'very pressing affair on account of the railway'. GAK will send 'a favourable reply' to Mr Crouch [of Plymouth; not further identified] by the post tomorrow, if possible.

JSK→Frances Braham [wife of John Braham] 23/1/1840

Somerset Archive and Record Service, in file DD\SH/49/68

JSK and GAK have considered Mrs Braham's proposition of yesterday concerning the piano forte owned by Lady Maryborough [Katherine Elizabeth Wellesley-Pole, Baroness Maryborough]. They will be happy to take it as part payment for 'one of our piano fortes', as long as they are not losers by this transaction. If allowed to see Lady Maryborough's piano, JSK can say 'in two minutes' what it is worth—it is worth very little 'if it will not stand in tune'. Wherever Mr and Mrs Braham may recommend GAK's pianos JSK is certain that they will bring satisfaction.

JSK has been 'very much engaged' today so 'could not view the theatre', but will do this early tomorrow morning.

GAK→C[harles] C[avendish] F[ulke] Greville 1/1/1842

National Archives, in file MT 6/1/20

GAK sends Greville [clerk-in-ordinary to the Privy Council] the 'Statement' of GAK's 'improved patent railway system' [presumably his *Comparative Statement*], in which 'complete safety is a chief object'. GAK urges that the Board of Trade [a committee of the Privy Council] investigate his plan. If they approve it the plan will be generally adopted, thereby increasing 'the profit of railway shareholders' and giving the travelling public 'cheaper fares, improved accommodation and complete safety'.

JSK→Henry Brougham 2/10/1843

University College London, Brougham Papers, letter no. 9729

JSK wrote [not preserved] to Brougham on this subject in spring 1843 but got no reply, and writes again. She urges that 'a patent remain the property of an inventor', much as a book's copyright protects its author or publisher from 'foreign impressions' of the work, which 'dare not be brought into this country'.

A man 'who has made an invention which is patented' labours under many difficulties. He must enter his drawings, specifying 'every minutia', at the Rolls Office, to which everyone has daily access for 1/–. Foreigners can make repeated visits there, memorise an invention and carry it abroad, where work is cheaper. A foreigner can reproduce and benefit from an invention and can 'even introduce it into England' before the patentee has received any return from it, unless he obtains a costly injunction to prevent this or had the financial means to take out foreign patents immediately. Thus an inventor to a certain extent is robbed of his patent by this system.

Further, by the time an invention has been proved to be superior and has got public acceptance, its patent is 'on the point of expiring' and the inventor must spend 'a large sum of money' and engage legal counsel to renew it, an opportunity for which the public are indebted to Brougham [who sponsored the 1835 *Act to Amend the Law Touching Letters Patent for Inventions*, which enabled the Judicial Committee of the Privy Council to determine whether a patent should be extended]. 'In all probability money has been borrowed' to manufacture the invention, and one dissatisfied creditor can make the inventor 'bankrupt, sell all the valuable property, destroy his factory' and sell his patent 'as they would a bundle of sticks'. Thus a man in a few months is deprived of 'all his prospects' and property, and 'sees his creditors defrauded' of what he would have done to benefit them. The invention 'is entirely lost to the inventor'.

JSK suggests that, through Brougham's effort, Parliament act to make a patent 'hereditary property'. In particular, a bankrupt patentee should retain his patent which would be placed in trust for the benefit of his creditors, and his manufactory should continue for their benefit until all debts are paid. If a bankrupt patentee dies and his creditors have received 15/– in the pound, his estate should be considered paid. Patent details should not be freely open to public inspection and should not be investigated without the inventor being present.

JSK was 'the largest creditor' to a bankruptcy estate [GAK's] 'which consisted in most valuable patented property' and is 'the most severe loser by this act of bankruptcy'. She was defrauded of her just claims by the petitionary creditor [the solicitors Martineau, Malton & Trollope] threatening to commence a suit in Chancery against her to prove that she was a partner [of GAK]. They threatened that if she ventured to prove her claims [of being a creditor], this would 'prevent all settlement of [GAK's] affairs'. As JSK had 'no more money to spend to defend a suit in Chancery', she gave up both her 'power as chief creditor' and her claims because of these threats. She still has to pay her 'responsibilities' on [GAK's bankruptcy] estate, which has inflicted 'grievous hardship' on her. On behalf of herself and others in similar positions, she hopes that Brougham will consider taking steps to have the patent laws amended in the ways she has proposed.

JSK→Henry Brougham 22/4/1845

University College London, Brougham Papers, letter no. 9730, written on black-border mourning paper because of GAK's death on 19/3/1845

JSK thinks that Brougham will remember the 1839 renewal of GAK's patent for piano forte inventions. In 1840 Martineau, Malton & Trollope made GAK a bankrupt 'in a most cruel and unjust manner'. They 'constituted themselves petitioning creditor, solicitors and assignee', finding JSK the 'great claimant'. They threatened that if she ventured to prove her claim they would bring a suit against her in Chancery, which would prevent GAK's affairs 'from ever being settled'. By these threats, and at their desire, they obtained a letter from JSK [not preserved] saying that she would not prove her claim provided that they would protect her where her name 'stood as security'. The solicitors replied that they understood she 'would not prove' but that she still 'remained liable'.

GAK's 'valuable property with his railway patents have been sold', defrauding JSK of her power and property, and GAK has just died 'from a dreadful accident'. She asks Brougham whether, having been defrauded, she cannot prove her just claim or 'revoke the fiat' [in bankruptcy]. Is it 'regular' for a firm to be petitioning creditor, solicitors and assignee?

Brougham perhaps will remember JSK's 'examination before the [Judicial Committee of the] Privy Council'. His 'philanthropy and desire to protect the unprotected' has encouraged JSK to present her case to him.

Charles James Blomfield→George Smith 6/6/1845

Lambeth Palace Library, Fulham Papers, Blomfield, v 43 f 264

Blomfield, the Bishop of London, acknowledges receipt of Smith's 8/12/1844 letter [not preserved; presumably from the George Smith who was solicitor to Kollmann's Railway and Locomotive Carriage Improvement Company] but regrets that he cannot assist Smith to recover what is due to him. 'Poor' JSK 'appears to have been involved, through no fault of her own, in great difficulties' by GAK's death. Although Blomfield has no doubt 'that she will pay her debts if ever it should be in her power', she has 'given up the little that remained to her' and has 'absolutely no means of satisfying' Smith's demand. Her 'present offfice' [organist and chapel-keeper of the German Chapel], to which she was 'recently appointed' [with effect from 25/3/1845], 'gives her a base maintenance'.

Charles James Blomfield→Mr Barker 19/1/1846

Lambeth Palace Library, Fulham Papers, Blomfield, v 43 f 281

Replying to Barker's letter [not preserved] concerning 'the debt incurred by' JSK, Blomfield regrets that he cannot help him recover it. Blomfield is informed that JSK 'lost everything by the death of her brother, to whom she had advanced all her property, in order to enable him to carry out some invention for which he had obtained a patent'. JSK's 'salary, as keeper of the German Chapel, is not sufficient for her maintenance'. Blomfield is unable to answer Barker's question whether JSK 'has any legal protection in that character'.

JSK →[Hugh] William Ruel 16/3/1846

in a private UK collection

JSK has tried several times without success to meet her cousin [Hugh] William Ruel [son of CCK's brother James Ruel]. She thinks that he holds an 'acceptance' of GAK, and asks him to send today 'the date, amount and name on the bill' to her dear brother's 'executor' F[rancis] M[arcus] Beresford, Pickleherring Wharf. She hopes that Ruel and his wife [Mary Ann] are well. JSK would like Ruel to leave out her book on [Martin] Luther for collection this evening.

Charles James Blomfield→Samuel Frederick Langham 18/6/1846

Lambeth Palace Library, Fulham Papers, Blomfield, v 44 f 125

Blomfield forwards a letter [not preserved] that he received from JSK in 1/1846. He asks Langham [a solicitor with a particular interest in bankruptcy matters] to return it. Langham will see from it that Blomfield 'has already interfered on behalf of one of her other creditors, but without effect'. Blomfield believes that JSK 'has no means of subsistence' other than the 'small salary she receives for her services' at the German Chapel 'and the little that she earns by teaching'. Her 'inability to pay seems to have been occasioned by unexpected calamity' and not by misconduct on her part. Blomfield believes that she 'is desirous of doing all in her power towards the liquidation of her debts'.

Charles Godfrey Ruel→'Dear Sir' 18/5/1849

in a private UK collection

Ruel informs his relation [not identified] that the funeral ceremony 'on the remains of' JSK will take place on 21/5/1849 at the Savoy Chapel, Strand. The recipient should come at 10.30 a.m. on that day to her late residence in the Royal German Chapel, St James's Palace, from where Ruel writes this letter.

INDEX OF PERSONS

The following index lists persons mentioned in *The Quarterly Musical Register* or elsewhere in this book who were alive or—in the case of bodies corporate such as societies, partnerships, companies, government agencies, schools and universities—were active before 1850. References to A. F. C. Kollmann are excluded.

Italic numerals refer to pages in *The Quarterly Musical Register*: *1–80* to pages in its January 1812 number, and *81–160* to pages in its April 1812 number. The four pages of the wrapper that enclosed the first number are indexed as *wr1–wr4*, and the four pages of the second number's wrapper as *wr5–wr8*. The four foldout sheets of engraved music issued with the first number are called *pl2–pl5* (a plate numbered 1 was never used), and the four music sheets that accompanied the second number are called *pl6–pl9*.

Composers named in the sun-shaped picture designed by Kollmann and reproduced in *Figure 3* facing page 15 are indexed by the word *sun*.